In the Land of Giants

MAX ADAMS studied archaeology at York University and has excavated widely in Britain and abroad, publishing more than thirty papers in academic and popular journals as well as several monographs. He has made a number of television programmes as the 'Landscape Detective' and co-convenes the Bernician Studies Group in Newcastle upon Tyne, where he teaches in the Explore Lifelong Learning programme. His active research interests include the monastic geography of County Donegal in Ireland and the Dark Age landscapes of the North of England. He is the author of *Admiral Collingwood* (2005); *The Prometheans* (2009), which was a *Guardian* Book of the Week; and *The King in the North* (2013).

IN THE LAND OF GIANTS

OF GIANTS

Journeys through the Dark Ages

MAX ADAMS

An Apollo Book

First published in the UK in 2015 by Head of Zeus Ltd

This Apollo paperback edition first published in the UK
in 2016 by Head of Zeus Ltd

5 7 9 10 8 6 4

A catalogue record for this book is available from the British Library.

ISBN (PB) 9781784080334
(E) 9781784080327

Printed in the UK by CPI Group (UK) Ltd,
Croydon CR0 4YY

Designed and typeset in Monotype Bell
by Ken Wilson | point918

Head of Zeus Ltd
5–8 Hardwick Street
London EC1R 4RG

www.headofzeus.com

FOR SARAH, WITH LOVE

Wondrous is this stone wall, wrecked by fate;
The city buildings crumble, the works of giants decay.
Roofs have caved in, towers collapsed,
Barren gates are broken, hoar frost clings to mortar,
Houses are gaping, tottering and fallen,
Undermined by age.[1]

KILMORY

Contents

Author's note

A FEW WORDS of explanation are required. The ten journeys took place over seventeen months between October 2013 and March 2015. With two exceptions they appear in chronological order. The sea voyage on *Eda Frandsen* and the motorbike trip, both for logistical reasons, took place out of kilter. I have put them where I intended they should be and hope that the reader doesn't find the result disconcerting. The interlude walks took place as and when I could fit them in.

At the end of the book is a record of the mileages for each walk: these include accidental diversions and getting lost; all have been measured with a map wheel apart from the sea voyage, for which the data were kindly supplied by James Mackenzie; and the two bike trips, which I measured on the bike's milometer.

All the photographs in the book were taken on the journeys as described. Inline photographs illustrate the text where appropriate; the gallery sections are divided into themes, and readers are invited to make of them what they will. The family of the young boy who accidentally jumped into the frame of a photograph taken at Din Lligwy will, I very much hope, forgive me for including the image in the gallery. He seemed to evoke perfectly the spirit of the place.

The maps are intended to give an idea of the routes taken and the distances covered each day. I have added some Early Medieval detail where appropriate. With one exception I have used as my base maps the very excellent *Reader's Digest Atlas of Great Britain*, long since out of print but a jewel of cartography and a treasure of information.

At the very end of the book is a short section of recommended reading. Explanations of potentially unfamiliar words have been incorporated into the Notes (pages 433–42) as appropriate.

Mallaig

Iona

Dumbarton

Inishowen

Rathlin Is

7

4

Nendrum

Whithorn

Isle
of Man

Irish Sea

Key

Standing stone	
Roman fort or settlement	
Native settlement	
Kingship site or royal estate	
Hillfort	
wic	
Battle site	
Holy well	
Christian stone cross or inscription	
Early church	
Non-Christian burial or memorial	
High cross	

Meigle

Inchtuthil

685

Stirling

Antonine Wall

Din Eidyn

St Abb's Head

Lindisfarne

8

Interludes

635

N

50 miles

588

9

633

York

617

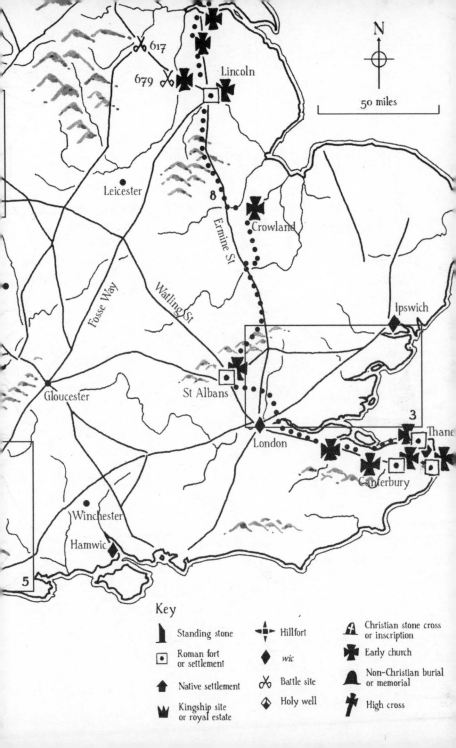

N

50 miles

617

679

Lincoln

Leicester

8

Crowland

Ermine St

Ipswich

Watling St

Fosse Way

St Albans

3

Thanet

Gloucester

London

Canterbury

Winchester

Hamwic

5

Key

Standing stone   Hillfort   Christian stone cross
                                            or inscription

Roman fort   wic   Early church
or settlement

Native settlement   Battle site   Non-Christian burial
                                            or memorial

Kingship site   Holy well   High cross
or royal estate

Prologue: *It is written*

Hadrian's Wall—Birdoswald fort—the Dark Ages begin—life after the end of the Roman Empire—natives and legions—granaries and mead halls—St Patrick and Arthur—Gildas and Bede—'the Ruin'—a series of journeys

THE WALL

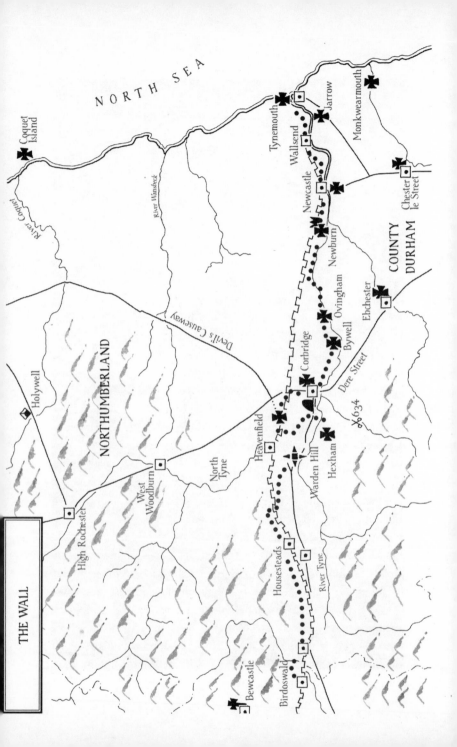

THE WALL

NORTH SEA

Coquet Island

River Coquet

River Wansbeck

NORTHUMBERLAND

Devil's Causeway

Holywell

High Rochester

West Woodburn

North Tyne

Heavenfield

Housesteads

Birdoswald

Bewcastle

River Tyne

Warden Hill

Hexham

Corbridge

Bywell

Ovingham

Newburn

Ebchester

Dere Street

COUNTY DURHAM

Chester le Street

Newcastle

Wallsend

Tynemouth

Jarrow

Monkwearmouth

634

Just after dawn on a late November day the North Pennines air is rigid with cold. A thick hoar of frost blankets pasture and hedge, reflecting white-blue light back at an empty sky. The last russet leaves clinging to a copse of beech trees set snug in the fold of a river valley filter lazy, hanging drifts of smoke from a wood fire. The sunlight is a dreamy veil of cream silk.

I am surprised when I come suddenly upon the Wall. I have not followed the neat, fenced, waymarked route from the little village of Gilsland which straddles the high border between Northumberland and Cumbria, but struck directly across country and, with the sun in my eyes, I do not see Hadrian's big idea until I am almost in its shadow. Sure, it stops you in your tracks. It is too big to climb over (that being the point), so I walk beside it for a couple of hundred yards. The imperfect regularity of the sandstone blocks is mesmerising, passing before one's eyes like the holes on a reel of celluloid. This film is an epic: eighty Roman miles, a strip cartoon story that tells of military might, squaddy boredom, quirky native gods, barbarian onslaught, farmers, archaeologists, ardent modern walkers and oblivious livestock. I am somewhere between Mile 49 and Mile 50, counting west from Wallsend near the mouth of the River Tyne. The gap in the Wall, when I find it, is made by the entrance to Birdoswald fort. Birdoswald: where the Dark Ages begin.

There is no one here but me on this shining day. The farm that has stood here in various guises for around fifteen hundred years is now a heritage centre. On a winter weekday I have Birdoswald to myself. Just me and the shimmering light and the odd chough cawing away in a skeletal tree. In places the stone walls of this once indomitable military outpost still stand five or six feet high. Visible, in its heyday, from all horizons, the Roman fort layout was built on a well-tested model: from above, it is the shape of a playing card, with the short sides facing north and south. Originally designed so that three of the six gates (two in each long side, one at either end in the centre) protruded beyond the line of the Wall, the fort was not so much part of a defensive frontier, more a launching pad for expeditions, patrols and forays in the lands to the north. Rome did not hide behind its walls; the legions did not cower. Any soldier from any part of the Empire would have known which way to turn on entering the gate; where the barrack rooms would be; where to find the latrines and bread ovens; how to avoid the scrutiny of the garrison commander after a late-night binge or an overnight stay in the house of one of the locals. Uniformity was part of the Roman project.

Any native on any frontier would get to know the layout too. The British warrior might, in those first years of the Wall's existence during the 120s, try to attack it; when that failed he would herd his livestock through its gates to his summer pastures and pay a tax on his sheep or cattle. British women would barter their homespun goods for ironwares or posh crockery; one day their sons might be recruited into its garrison. The *Brittunculi* or Little Britons, as a Vindolanda tablet suggests they were called by their imperial betters, might grow to like the idea of the Empire.

Outside Birdoswald fort, to the east, the frosted surface of a smooth, grassy field conceals the magnetic traces from geophysical mapping of a small village, or *vicus*, which grew up alongside. These *vici* were native British settlements, clinging like limpets to their military protectors, supplying them with goods and services and probably with children, wanted or unwanted. Much the same thing happens in frontier provinces today. You see it on documentaries filmed in the dodgier parts of Afghanistan—only there the Taliban regards such integration or fraternisation as a capital crime. When the Western troops leave, and they are leaving as I write, one fears for the safety of the inhabitants. When Rome came to this frontier, she came to stay.

To the south, the line of the Wall, and this fort, are protected by the deep, sinuous gorge of the River Irthing, the western of two rivers which between them create the Tyne–Solway gap linking east and west coasts. This gap has been a lowland route through the Pennines for many thousands of years. Two generations before Hadrian the Romans built a road along this line, known in later times as the Stanegate, so that they could rapidly deploy troops along its length. Much of that road is still in use, or at least passable. And long after Hadrian, General Wade had his redcoats build a road following much the same route and for much the same reason—in his case to keep Jacobites at bay. The gap between the headwaters of the Rivers Irthing and South Tyne is narrow: no more than four miles. Near Greenhead, just to the south-east of Gilsland, is the watershed boundary, the pass, a choke-point through which modern road and railway, ancient Wall and eighteenth-century military road must squeeze.

To the north, Birdoswald—*Banna* to the Romans—looks onto a landscape of boggy mires, dispersed sheep farms and conifer plantations, with another twenty odd miles before the modern border is reached. It is an odd thought: this land, so often fought over, has been at peace for two hundred and fifty years. The old border garrisons of Carlisle and Newcastle have almost lost their walls; standing on either coast halfway up the island of Britain, they are just like other modern cities. Had Scotland voted for independence in September 2014, that defunct border could have been revived; we might have had customs posts, and police on either side might have spent their time chasing smugglers once again. It may still happen. It would amuse the legionary builders of this place to think of their imperial customs booths being reopened after nearly two millennia; it would not surprise them. Sometimes borders are self-defining.

During the middle of the fourth century, long before the traditional date of AD 410, when Roman administration dissolved in the province of Britannia, the roof of one of the granaries (*horrea*) at Birdoswald collapsed. These things don't just happen. The Roman auxiliary cohorts who had been stationed here for two hundred years relied on periodic resupply from the coast ports and on storing the fruits of each year's harvest. Leaky roofs and military efficiency don't go together; so either slackness was creeping in or the fort had been abandoned. That's how it seems at first sight. But the subtle text of stratified deposits read by archaeologists tells a more complex story. The fort was not abandoned; and when, in the 360s, a huge barbarian onslaught threatened to overwhelm the province, Rome and her generals responded. After the north granary at Birdoswald lost its roof, its stones and tiles were used elsewhere. The floor of a second granary, immediately to the south, was reflagged, its under-floor heating flues blocked—to keep out draughts, or rats? The centurions' quarters were remodelled to allow for the construction of a building with a small apse—a by then fashionable Christian church, perhaps. The abandoned north granary was used as a rubbish dump, but part of the main street frontage was refaced with dressed stone and a new barrack block was built. Neither slackness nor abandonment explains the halving of the fort's storage facilities. More likely, the realities of the frontier zone changed.

Rome was not a static force any more than the British Empire was in its day. Three hundred years is a long time. As the empire stretched, then overstretched, as emperors' fortunes waxed and waned, as troops and political interests migrated from one distant land to another, local commanders became increasingly autonomous. Centrally organised lines of supply, overly bureaucratic and too bloated to adapt to local realities, were superseded or bypassed. Pay wagons turned up with hard cash less often. Commanders took an active role in supplying garrisons from their immediate hinterland; probably they got more involved in the administration of local politics. The relationship between occupying force and native elite became more intimate, the integration more complete. By the middle of the fourth century Wall garrisons consisted mostly of troops called *Limitanei*, that is, frontiersmen. Many of the men had probably been born within a few miles of Birdoswald; their fathers had been soldiers before them. They spoke the native language known as Brythonic—an early form of Welsh—and were embedded in the native communities of the Wall zone. They revered a suite of local divinities and the odd imperial god, especially Jupiter. After Constantine, who was declared emperor in York in 306, they may have felt inclined, or obliged, to rationalise their pantheon and worship the one true God Jehovah and his charismatic, earthbound son.

The garrison commanders were an elite cadre. They could afford to modify their official quarters with bespoke trappings like Christian chapels or bath houses. Their dress and social class set them apart culturally and politically. In many places they brought with them in their deployments personal retinues from far-flung provinces of the geriatric, obese empire, now disintegrating and under threat of being overrun. The rigid formal structure of the old imperial army, mirrored in the fixed, square-shaped identikit forts of the first and second centuries, became flexible, individualised. The emergence of a vernacular tradition, blending native and foreign with a distinct local cultural flavour, meant that each fort and town was recognisable by its own regional idiosyncrasies. Many of the late imperial commanders had been recruited from the northern boundaries of the Empire from whose ongoing conflicts and edginess fine warriors were raised. Many of them must have spoken Germanic tongues.

No one noticed the beginning of the Dark Age in Britain. It started in different ways and at different times in different places. Rome never lost interest in these islands; they bore valuable minerals, their soils were fertile and their conquest had been a prestigious triumph of the imperial project of the first century AD. But distance stretches and thins one's interest; as the Empire reformed in the East and as Western emperors focused their attentions on Gaul, Hispania and Germania, it became harder to keep up with what was happening in Britannia: the distant relative was slowly lost to the family. In the towns of Roman Britain decline may have begun as early as the third century, as local elites increasingly favoured the country life and became bored with Rome's urban experiment, its high-maintenance sewage and water supplies, tedious civic snobbery and the tendency of the urban proletariat to riot on almost any pretext. On the coasts, vulnerable to a Continental penchant for piratical raiding, life from the early fourth century onwards could be uncomfortable even with the presence of the imperial navy to watch Britain's shores facing Ireland and Saxony, Frisia and Pictland. In the cultured, decadent luxury of the Cotswolds, where superb country villas sat in an ordered, fertile and bucolic landscape, reality might not have dawned until the middle of the fifth century when effete toga-wearing Romano-British aristos woke up to find revolting peasants stealing their prize heifers and touting the heresy of a suspiciously liberal British-born cleric called Pelagius.

At Birdoswald the moment can, in its way, be quite precisely identified, with fifteen hundred years of hindsight to draw on. At the very end of the fourth century the south granary, renovated some decades before, had a succession of hearths built into its west end. When excavated, their ashes were found to contain some rather nobby personal items: a green glass ring, a gold and glass earring. More importantly for the excavator, Tony Wilmott, there was a worn coin of the Emperor Theodosius (reigned 388–95), which gives some idea of the date after which these fires were in use. Archaeologists, when finds and structures tell them they are excavating deposits of the fifth century, get a shiver down their spine: these moments are desperately rare.

Hearths seem odd things to have in a granary: fire and grain are a dangerous combination. Was the garrison now so compact, were the other buildings in such a state of disrepair, that the garrison commander had moved himself and his family into the grain store and fitted it out as domestic quarters because it was the only building left that would keep out the winter weather? Were these people cowering among ruins?

There is another way of looking at it. We are talking barn conversions. Not so much retreating to the corner of a barn because it's the only building with a roof; more likely, the commander liked to have the company of his men for good cheer and fireside stories in those long nights of winter when they talked of the old days, of battles and life on campaign. The barn still had a good solid roof, maintained because it was where all the local produce came in and had to be stored for the year ahead. This produce was no longer paid for in cash (these late coins of Theodosius were about the last to make it to Britain from the imperial mints); the natives were required to give a few days' labour and to donate a proportion of their harvest and other agricultural produce—say, a tenth. The commander still had his own quarters—nice bath suite, private chapel—wife from a local well-to-do family or perhaps an exotic Dacian bride who played a quasi-diplomatic role in the local community and kept a small but tasteful salon, as British army wives sometimes did in colonial India. Often, and especially

when there had been a good harvest or on the quarter days of the native festive calendar when communal gatherings were de rigueur, it seemed right to have a feast in the barn, to share the land's bounty, dispense a little justice and a few trinkets from the bazaars of Alexandria and reinforce old and prospective loyalties. The man who sat at the centre of the long feasting benches was more of a local worthy and judge than a garrison commander. One is tempted to use the word 'squire'. Gifts were exchanged; promises made; eligible young men and women affianced. Poems were composed and sung, wine and local mead consumed: drinking horns for the men, Rhineland glass beakers for the commander and his wife. Understanding the rules of patronage was becoming just as important as running a tight ship or ruthlessly enforcing the imperial law.

This cosy scenario takes us well into the fifth century, when there is virtually no narrative history for the British Isles, just rumours of civil war and raiding Saxons, plague and famine. Traders from the Continent came to these parts less frequently. We know that Gaulish bishops visited, retaining their solidarity with the British church long after secular links had been severed. But no emperor came after the departure of Constantine III in 407. Rarely does archaeology have anything meaningful to say about the two centuries after 400: there are no new coins to date the layers; almost no inscriptions, and those few that do exist are difficult to date. The pottery found in native settlements might just as well be that of the Iron Age. Even radiocarbon dating is unreliable for these centuries and, unless you are in the peaty bogs of Ireland, wood rarely survives to be dated by its tree rings. The fifth century existed all right—we just can't see it. It is like the Dark Matter which fills our universe but can't be seen or measured. The record falls silent, even if echoes and rumours of echoes are heard across the Channel and in the courts of Byzantium, Arles and Ravenna.

Almost the earliest indigenous written account of events in Britain after the end of Rome is a note in an Easter calendar called the *Annales Cambriae*, its only surviving copy belonging to hundreds of years after the event. Under *Anno I*, which historians believe equates to the year AD 447, is a simple, bleak Latin entry: *Dies tenebrosa sicut nox*: 'A day as dark as night'. That just about says it all, even if it is an obscure reference to some distant volcano or a really terrible winter.

At Birdoswald life went on, perhaps until the first years of the sixth century. On top of the defunct north granary a timber replacement was erected using the old stone foundations to give it solidity and a floor. Years passed. Finally, a similar structure was erected in more or less the same place, only it was designed to line up with a remodelled gate on the west side of the fort. The new building, imposing in its dimensions and constructed using great hewn crucks, looks for all the world like one of the timber halls of poetic legend: the Heorot of Beowulf. And if, at times, the walls were hung with spears and shields and the air rang to the sound of drunken song and poetry, with boasts of victories and laments for fallen comrades, it was, after all, still a barn. Were its carousing warriors and petty chiefs, its quartermasters and poets Romans, Britons or Anglo-Saxons? Who can say? Did they themselves know or care? And was the successor to the commander in whose name this grand design was built a rival, an imposed replacement or a son?

Even the casual visitor to Birdoswald can't fail to be impressed by the solidity of the foundations where the north granary has been excavated, its footings and buttresses consolidated. Where the post pads for the new timber hall of the fifth century were sited English Heritage has installed great round logs, like oversized telegraph poles, standing a few feet high to give an idea of the size and layout. It is a crude reconstruction, and yet viscerally effective in demonstrating the moment and mindset that changed

Roman into Early Medieval. What is particularly striking is that the new timber hall was much wider than the old granary. If the south-granary-cum-barn-cum-feasting-hall was mere adaptation, with a hearth at one end and perhaps a partition in the middle, then the new hall built over the ruins of the north granary was a more ambitious vision, designed for the commander of the fort (be he a *dux* of his cohort, a war-band leader or petty tribal chief) to sit in the centre of one of the long sides with his companions ranged on benches either side, a glowing fire before him in the centre and, perhaps, with doors at either end. This is truly a building in which the mythical Beowulf would have felt at home. And we must suspect that this was not an isolated structure: the Birdoswald of AD 450–500 was a busy place.

The fort at *Banna*, high in the Pennines, may just have an even more potent role to play in our history. St Patrick claimed, in his *Confessio*, that he had been born and brought up in a place called *Bannavem Taberniae*, son of a local landowner called Calpurnius whose father, Potitus, had been a priest. His *vita*[2] is difficult to date, but some time in the middle and later decades of the fifth century is plausible. Several modern scholars believe that this place name should read *Banna Venta Berniae*: the 'settlement at *Banna* in the land of the high passes'. Berniae shares its root with the name Bernicia, the Anglo-Saxon kingdom of north Northumbria. That Patrick, taken by slaves to Ireland, should have unwillingly launched his epic career as Irish patron saint at this remote, beautiful spot, is quite a thought.

And then there is Arthur. Historical references to the legendary Romano–British warlord are very few: a list of twelve battles; a great victory recorded at a place called Badon (perhaps Bath in Somerset); a death notice; a possible mention in a battle poem. Arthur may be, as many historians have argued, an irrelevance, a distraction. There are 'southern' Arthurs and 'northern' Arthurs, never mind the medieval romantic hero of Camelot. Those who favour the northern version argue that the notice of his death in 537 during the 'Strife of Camlann' places him on the Roman Wall; for Camlann seems to be derived from *Camboglanna*. It used to be thought, erroneously, that this Roman fort, mentioned in the very late Roman list of imperial postings called the *Notitia Dignitatum*, must be Birdoswald. Now it is accepted that it should be Castlesteads, some seven miles to the west. Either way, there are those who would place both Patrick and Arthur on this stretch of the Wall between the fifth and sixth centuries.

Narrative histories do not get us very far towards an understanding of these islands in the centuries after Roman rule. An early sixth-century British monk called Gildas wrote of civil wars, of invasion, fire, sword and famine (and mentioned a victory at Badon without naming the victor), but nothing of the everyday comings and goings which sustained life. The Kentish Chronicle, fascinating in its melodrama but of doubtful veracity, tells of the foolish British tyrant Vortigern who made a fatal drunken deal with two Saxon pirates (a pretty girl was involved) and sold Britain's soul and future.[3] Even Bede, the greatest of our early historians, writing nearly three centuries later, covers the nearly one hundred and fifty years after 450 with a single paragraph. The odd memorial stone offers us the name of a Christian priest living in a far-flung community; but no suggestion of when, or why. Occasionally a Continental source records or speculates on the visit of a Gaulish saint or bishop to these islands or on their encounters with pagans and heresies, but not of how people moved around their landscape, how they grew old, tended their sick or brought up their children. Archaeology sometimes tells us where people lived and what they ate, how they constructed their houses; but it says frustratingly little about their relations or their identity. We must piece together these fragmentary sources and animate them. But if we cannot construct a narrative history, what can we say about the journey of the peoples of Britain between the last days of Rome and those of Bede or the Vikings?

Birdoswald is the starting block for my own journey through an age when people believed that the material ruins of lost cultures—the walls and fountains, megalithic tombs and great earthworks, the aqueducts, henges and stone circles that populated their landscape and poetry and framed their psyches—had been built in a lost time by a race of giants. An Anglo-Saxon elegy called 'the Ruin', first written down, perhaps, in the eighth century, marvels at nature's conquest of these great works. After the opening lines, quoted at the front of this book, which describe fallen towers, wrecked gates and crumbling city walls, the poet writes:

> *The earth's embrace,*
> *Its fierce grip, holds the mighty craftsmen;*
> *They are perished and gone. A hundred generations have passed*
> *away since then. This wall, grey with lichen and red of hue, out-*
> *lives kingdom after kingdom,*
> *Withstands tempests; its tall gate succumbed.*
> *The city still moulders, gashed by storms...* [4]

These words could almost have been written somewhere along the Wall. Even if the story of these centuries is not written in words, it is surely written in the landscape. Christian or pagan, its denizens enjoyed an intimate psychological and mythical relationship with the mountains and vales, woods, fields, rivers and springs of these lands. They knew the winding routes of ancient trackways, the folds of the hills, the places where bright metals and precious clays might be dug from the ground, the ruins where they might yet scavenge materials and lost treasures. Their intimacy with a world at once wonderful and pragmatic tells the story of the British people in those enigmatic centuries which separate the ages of King Arthur and King Alfred.

It is tempting to visit the monuments of the Dark Ages, such as they are, and believe that we have understood them. Wandering among the Anglo-Saxon or Pictish displays in our national and regional museums and marvelling at the astounding workmanship of smiths and scribes appeals to a sense of awe; even more to an innate curiosity, the thirst to know more. I have been privileged to excavate at the sites of some of those monuments, and to have handled some of the art and craft of the peoples of the Early Medieval period. I have pored over texts and tried to insinuate myself into the mindsets of Gildas and Bede, Patrick and Arthur. Practising as an archaeologist fascinates and frustrates in equal measure: the more you think you know, the more you appreciate the severe limitations set on our understanding of the remote past. It feels as though one is a constant straggler, just keeping the tail of truth in sight on some over-ambitious journey into the unknown. In undertaking a series of journeys through the landscapes of the Dark Ages, mostly on foot but occasionally on the water and once or twice by motorbike, I hope to catch up a little.

My first journey, which I have presented as a sequence of eight interleaved fragments between accounts of nine longer itineraries, will end at Jarrow near the mouth of the River Tyne. It was here in the early eighth century that the monk Bede, in a career of astonishing productivity and erudition, began to lift a veil for his contemporaries (and for us) on these lost centuries by giving an account of the origins of the English peoples and their church from the arrival of Pope Gregory's emissary, Augustine, in 597, onwards. At Bede's World, close by the ruins of his monastery, are reconstructions of Early Medieval houses and a farm. And then, Jarrow has its own special place in the history of journeys and dark ages: there are still one or two left alive who remember stories of the Great Depression and of the Jarrow Crusade of 1936.

Sometimes I will follow the Wall; but I want to know how these landscapes fit together as a complete picture, so I may deviate from the path from time to time to follow other trails through the land. Since this is my own backyard, I can walk this walk in stages as the fancy and the weather suit. It is little more than a gentle sixty-mile stroll. I have other landscapes to explore: the Welsh Marches and Wessex, the lands of the Britons, and the west coast archipelago ruled by the Dálriadic Scots; the creeks and woods of Essex, and the Inishowen peninsula of County Donegal. I want to know if the map of the Dark Ages can be read from beneath our city streets. Some of the routes I follow are authentically those of the saints and warriors, kings and craftsmen whose lives I want to understand. And I want to get some idea of how the peoples of the Dark Ages used, and abused, the Roman road system which they inherited. Walking that, while interesting, might not be good for my health, much of the network now being subsumed by our own arterial routes. So that's an adventure to be undertaken on the bike. And I have a strong hankering to sail, in as old a craft as I can find, up the west coast of Britain from the Lizard to Iona in the wake of those intrepid, foolhardy or misdirected traders, pirates, princely exiles and pilgrims who made the same journey fifteen hundred years before me, carrying exotic pots, wine and oil from Byzantium and Gaul, tales of wonder from the Holy Land or merely hopes of a glorious future.

By Bede's day something quite new, breathtaking in its ambition, had emerged from the dark centuries (if, indeed, they were dark): the idea of a rational kingship embodied in a coherent model of statehood and a three-sided relationship between land, church and 'nation'. With King Alfred (r. 871–99) it achieved an unprecedented expression of maturity and intellectual subtlety which allowed him to fend off the most formidable enemy of the age and elevate the kingdom of Wessex towards something like a core of the nation of England. The same goes for Wales in the person of Hywel Dda (r. 942–50) and in Scotland with the dynasty of Cináed mac Ailpín (r.841/43–58/59): three distinct entities that survived the next twelve hundred years and played their parts on the global stage. If the Dark Ages began with nothing more sophisticated than a barn conversion, that takes some explaining.

I want to answer a few burning questions of my own: how can we explain the revolution in political thought and practice that takes the self-serving, augury-watching petty chief of fifth-century Birdoswald on the journey to becoming the rational head of state of the seventh century and beyond? What is the cultural engine that drives this new idea? Is it revolution or evolution? I want also to trace its inspiration: the inherited wisdom of the past, or a new idea imported from the other side of the known world?

It is eleven o'clock in the morning on a perfect day in late November. With Birdoswald fort at my back, I head east along the Wall, following its uncompromising, celluloid ribbon towards the distant crags of the Whin Sill and beyond, to the sea.

CHAPTER ONE

The kingdom of Dál Riata:
Rothesay to Kilmartin

*Argyll and Northumbria—walking insights—Bute—landscapes of
memorial—Dunagoil fort—wild camping—Dark Age entrepôts—
Kingarth and St Blane—St Ninian's Point—Inchmarnock—rescue
by boat—Tarbert—St Columba's cave—Cladh a Bhile—Kilmory
chapel—another rescue—Lochgilphead—Dunadd—Kilmartin Glen*

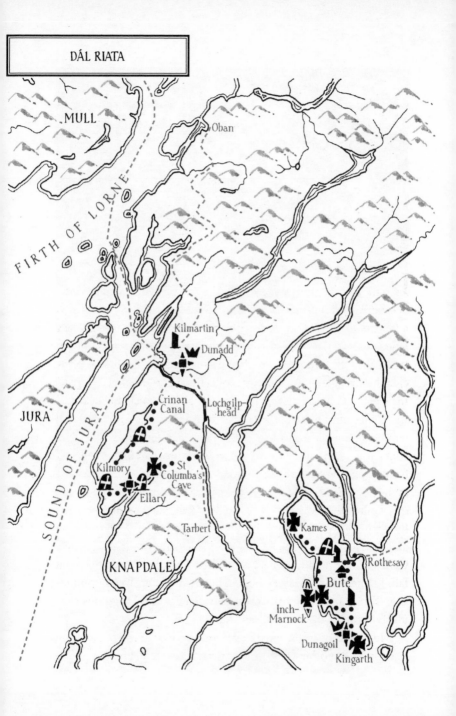

In the early medieval period the west coast of what is now Scotland, together with its islands from Arran to Skye, formed a Gaelic-speaking kingdom with very strong ties to the ancient lands of Ulster. As a historical entity it comes into focus only in the later sixth century: from then on the fortunes of its four principal kindreds, the Cenél Loairn of central and northern Argyll, the Cenél nGabrain of Kintyre, the Cenél Comgaill of Cowal and the Cenél nŒngusa of Islay are recorded in the annals of the famous monastery on Iona. Scholars cannot agree whether Dál Riata was originally carved out by Irish warbands or emerged from an immigrant community, but its kings laid claim to much of Ulster and its greatest holy man, St Columba (more properly Colmcille), was born in Donegal. Dál Riata came into conflict with its neighbours the Picts, the Britons of Dumbarton and the Northumbrians; but its most celebrated king, Áedán mac Gabrain, had a daughter who married into the Bernician royal family and the monastery on Lindisfarne was an Ionan foundation. Kings and clergy travelled between the two kingdoms regularly through the seventh century.

Much of that traffic must have come by way of the sea and the Stanegate. But other cross-country routes existed. I explored one of these in 2011 when I walked from my home on the north-west edge of County Durham to Glasgow, the city on the Clyde founded by the enigmatic sixth-century saint Kentigern, or Mungo as he is often called. That walk reminded me that a proper journey is more than a day trip; that the trail only makes sense when you live on it; that landscape can best be read at walking pace. In choosing a place to camp, you have to read the countryside with your senses far beyond merely checking for car parks or cafés.

A more profound insight is that when you are teasing a route through a landscape which has changed only superficially over the millennia—that is to say, the hills and rivers have not moved much, and many of the settlements are very ancient—you find yourself confronting and solving problems that would have been familiar to generations of travellers on foot or horseback. Sometimes the names of places give you clues: *fords* will naturally enough guide you towards crossing points on rivers; *welles* offer the chance to locate fresh spring water; a *tun* with the prefix *straet* suggests an establishment on a Roman road where goods and repairs might be sought. And some ancient settlements were named after local landmarks with prominent features like flat-topped hills so that you could navigate your way towards them. The landscape is full of signs and waymarks for the informed traveller. The name Peebles means both a place where tents are pitched (handy) and a *shieling*[5] where animals were pastured in the summer. If I didn't have a map or the internet, I would head for this place, hopeful of a night's stay and food. Peebles still has a very excellent campsite (hot showers, soft grassy slopes; a washing machine) and offers plenty of good food. Travellers, like columns of ants, tend eventually to find the best routes through the land, avoiding hazards like bogs and brigands, often keeping to high ground once it has been gained and trending towards the gaps between major river systems, although just because a ford or ferry exists doesn't mean to say that the traveller wishes either to pay the fare or attract what might prove to be unwanted attention.

These days, bridges have replaced ferries and fords for the most part. Even so, the traveller on foot aims to avoid main routes, by and large. Walking along the verges of a busy A-road is a form of sensory torture and a risk to life and limb. So it was that I found myself making for the gap between the headwaters of the Rivers Clyde and Tweed. This gap, in the glen where Biggar sits, is no more than seven miles across. A Roman road runs through it and in experiencing for myself this age-old reality, I came closer, I thought, to an insight into the ancient mind. The whole journey, ending in Paisley where St Mirren, the Ulster-born contemporary of Colmcille, founded his famous church, took eleven days and spanned a hundred and eighty miles; but it took me back fifteen hundred years and more to the days when saints, pilgrims and warriors trod the same paths.

For my venture into the Land of Giants I wanted to complete the journey between Northumbria and the ancestral seat of the kings of Dál Riata, so I persuaded my partner Sarah (an Ulster Scot) to join me on a small adventure through the hills, lochs and glens of Argyll to Dunadd in Kilmartin Glen, where a footprint carved in rock tells of kingly inaugurations and where excavation has revealed a treasure trove of exotic European luxuries. Even today this is not an entirely straightforward journey. By car it is a much longer route than it would be as the crow flies. Sea-lochs must be crossed where there is no ferry service. But the improvisational spirit in which we set out from Paisley in October 2013 (friends; a warm welcome and send-off) seemed entirely in keeping with the Dark Age task in hand. We knew there would be days when we might see no shop. No campsites existed on our route, so we took big packs, more than I have ever carried before on a long walk.

From Paisley a railway line runs west along the southern shore of the Clyde estuary, designed originally to bring workers into Glasgow and take day trippers to the seaside. From the windows of the train the hulking fist of Dumbarton Rock (*Alt Clut* in Brythonic: Rock of the Clyde), fortress of the British kings of these parts in Bede's day, appeared across the water.

I still feel a childlike sense of excitement at a ferry port and in climbing aboard a ship: the prow pointing towards the future and to adventure; the long wake of ruffled water aft a memory-cleansing refugee trail, like Ariadne's ball of string in the labyrinth of the minotaur. From Wemyss Bay to Rothesay on Bute is less than an hour across the Clyde, but the sun was setting, the light golden against dark clouds, and we had only the pure, uncluttered trail ahead to think of. I say uncluttered: by that I mean that the walker, unlike the driver or the traveller by train and plane, never has to wait; never has to rely on anything but his or her own wits. You start walking when it suits you. You stop for a pee when the need arises, for lunch when you find an agreeable spot or shelter. Your arrival at a day's destination is perfectly timed to coincide with you finding the right spot. You can't be late except on your own terms.

Even so, there's nothing like a good breakfast and a shower to set one up for the trials ahead; so we indulged in a room overlooking Rothesay harbour. Bute is a self-contained paradise, a short remove from the industry, bustle and energy of Glasgow; and yet, many Glaswegians have never been there. It is a comfortable island, sheltered, well watered and rarely suffering damaging frosts; twenty miles or so long, narrow in the waist and nestling between two long-flooded fjords at the southern end of the Cowal peninsula. Nowhere does the land rise above a thousand feet. It is famous, like Ireland, for its dairy and beef herds. The farms are prosperous; and yet, as we walked along Rothesay's seafront in an ultimately fruitful search for fish and chips, the town played us a pianola song, in a minor key, of lost Edwardian grandeur. We saw faded advertisements for bespoke headboards. The drab shop windows could have been used as a seventies film set; we struggled to find a postcard; the older buildings set back from the shore were falling into disrepair. In this sense Bute has more in common with Eastbourne or Filey than with Scotland's vibrant Silicon Glen. It has suffered a sort of genteel neglect; and that is part of its charm. Perhaps post-Roman Britain, far from the desolate, ruinous, plague-ridden chaos of Gildas's portrait, was a genteel, faded seaside town of a land. Perhaps.

Our first day's walk took us south towards Dunagoil and Kingarth. In spite of its well-behaved fields and pastoral somnolence, there is something ghostly about Bute's landscape. Prehistoric chambered cairns and tumuli, stone circles, cup-and-ring-marked rocks and *duns*—small prehistoric or Early Medieval forts—lie as if scattered by a giant's hand across field and wood. Labour invested in monuments and field boundaries is evidence of agricultural surplus and of social hierarchy. Bute's richness must therefore stretch back deep into a prehistory when the heavens were populated with hunters and bears and the rocks, trees and springs of the land by the ancestors. There are so many burial sites distributed across Bute—many, many more must have been lost—that one is tempted to think of it as a sort of island of the dead. The ancestors were everywhere, watching us. Even as we left the last houses of Rothesay behind, we came across a medieval chapel almost overwhelmed by the graveyard of its nineteenth-century replacement and dozens of rows of tombstones, their inscriptions etched sharp in bright early sun. A holly and a yew reminded us of ideas of the eternal; of the blood sacrifice of prophets; that symbols of death transcend religion.

From here to the southern tip of Bute was no more than an eight-mile walk, the first part along the banks of Loch Fad where we watched two fishermen casting from a white-painted rowing boat against the blue-black of the water and a rich late-summer green fringe of woodland behind them, so still that they might have been figures in a painting. An enterprising industrialist once fed this loch with aqueducts to power his cotton mill; but there are no mills on Bute these days. Beyond the loch was a more open land of whins and rough pasture; we realised we were following an old route, a droveway that kept to the modest ridge which is Bute's spine. Far to the south-west the mountains of Arran brooded beneath impenetrable grey clouds that we kept a sharp eye on all day. Above us the flying V of a flock of geese heading in the same direction told of the coming season. For the present, in early autumn, Bute was good country for the forager. We munched on Sunday-lunchtime water mint and handfuls of blackberries from passing hedgerows. We must have looked a slightly misplaced sight, tramps mingling with the dressed-up folk of Kingarth arriving at their village cemetery to lay flowers on the graves of loved ones. A little further on, following a mark on the map, we poked our heads into a conifer plantation where three giant monoliths, one of them held up by a jerry-rigged iron tie-bar, were all that remained of a once monumental stone circle. Memorial, it seemed, was the theme for the day.

Dunagoil is a whaleback massif of metamorphic rock that rises, not unlike Bamburgh in Northumberland or Dumbarton on the Clyde, almost out of the waves. A prehistoric fort once stood here. Somewhere on its east side are the remains of a small fortlet occupied from the Bronze Age to the Medieval period: our first bona fide Dark Age site. A small excavation in the late 1950s produced longhouse-type buildings and sherds of both Roman Samian pottery and exotic imports from later centuries. These are tell-tale signs of an Early Medieval kingly entrepôt, like Dunadd on a smaller scale. Such a site is irresistible to the archaeologist, so we had planned this as our first stop. Now, looking down from the farm track at the glowing orangey-green hill against the wine-dark sea and Arran's late afternoon battleship grey, and with grim weather looking like it might arrive from the Atlantic at any time, it seemed as if it might be a bleak place to spend the night. It was a treeless land.

The omens weren't good: I failed to spot the wires of a powerful electric fence, 'accidentally' earthing through the farm gate and I received a punch in the arm that stopped me in my tracks. Slightly disconcerted, we made our way down to the shore in the lee of the giant natural ramparts. Our luck was in: here was shelter. A small brook a couple of hundred yards away offered water for boiling up and we found plenty of flotsam and jetsam to gather for fuel. The rain held off. We pitched in a discreet spot in a little natural bowl of rough grass looking out magnificently onto the Sound of Bute. Neither the sheep nor the oyster-catchers paid us any attention. As we busied ourselves setting up stove and bedding, a curious seal, who was to follow our fortunes for three days, bobbed its grey head out of the water to see what we were about.

I am not one for fancy technology on a walk; too many gadgets can wear out or run out of fuel. So I cook on a Wild Woodgas stove. It is light and simple, cannot fail or break. It is fuelled with sticks that one finds lying about on almost any campsite, leaves no trace behind and cooks beautifully; and I always carry with me a bag of dry birch bark—the perfect waxy kindling, light as paper. There being two of us, we had indulged in the luxury of a storm kettle too, for nearly instant hot water. It's no more than a small aluminium chimney with a water sleeve around it and a fire tray at the bottom. It will light in just about any weather and for a quick, morale-boosting cuppa laced with whisky it is hard to beat. We ate well, and in the fading orange light I went off to explore the remains of the fort. In truth, humps and bumps in the landscape are not always much more revealing for the archaeologist than for the casual tripper. I had already read the site report, however, so I knew what to look for: rectangular stone foundations and the grassed-over remains of a timber-laced rampart which had enhanced the natural battlements of this rocky fortress.

What counts, on this sort of journey, is the sense of place, the passing of time. There is no better way to insinuate oneself into the Dark Age mind than to camp close to the ramparts of an ancient fort on the edge of the limitless sea and ponder the spiritual and secular worlds of those who built it. To properly understand these people, if that is possible, it helps to have read the literature, and there is more of that than one might think. But the key to Dunagoil was not just in the notes of the excavators, nor even in its striking setting and naturally defensive architecture. The secret lay just beyond the next hill.

The first night on a trail can be strange and disorienting. You are not quite sure where you are when dawn breaks and the only sounds are those of sheep munching the grass next to the tent and the odd bird calling overhead. At Dunagoil the night was so peaceful that even the rhythmic lapping of waves on the shore did not disturb us. One of the many pleasures of walking with Sarah is that, being a Scot, she will make porridge for breakfast come hell or high water. Oats are the best trail-setting food: full of slow-release carbohydrates; light to carry and easily flavoured with honey, hedgerow fruits or hazelnuts.

I was keen to get started: I wanted to see St Blane's church, which lay hidden behind a bluff immediately to the east of Dunagoil. None of the pictures or plans I had seen gave much idea of its setting. By nine o'clock in the morning we were tramping along the small path that led off a narrow road through a field of dairy cows. Our breath was cloudy but the sun was up and the air perfectly clear. The church was invisible until the last few yards, when the subtlety of its location became apparent. A key component of that location, inevitably, was its proximity to Dunagoil. Encircled by two walls which have created a sort of concentric terraced citadel, the monastery was set in a natural bowl sheltered by hills and trees but with a narrow view out to sea and easy access to the protective fort. There was, and is, open pasture near by, and the year-round fruits of the sea; and early monastic communities were nothing if not handy when it came to farming. The church, built in the sixth century like Iona Abbey, much altered and enlarged in a twelfth-century rebuild and now partly ruined, is nevertheless a jewel in the Early Medieval landscape of Scotland's west coast. Stone-built cells, a chapel, burial ground, the core functions of an early monastic foundation, were later complemented by guest house, bakery, workshops, a scriptorium, perhaps, and the lodgings of the abbot. The beach at Dunagoil gave access to the water; not just to the coast of Bute but to its Kyles with their fine fishing and to other monasteries and centres of power sited on the hundreds of miles of Argyll's shores. Ireland, *Erin*, lay three days' sailing away.

This is now an obscure landscape; few pilgrims or seekers of ecclesiastic and royal patronage come this way today. In Colmcille's day, such prestigious spiritual sites were often located close to contemporary seats of secular power. Lindisfarne's relationship to the ancestral fortress of the Northumbrian kings at Bamburgh is similar. It is that between a sun and its planet. The same goes for many fortress/monastery combinations across the British Isles, and one of the keys to understanding the Dark Ages is interrogating this relationship. The Early Medieval saints' lives, or hagiographies, tell us about elites, and especially how kings and holy men managed their expectations of each other. Other records, mostly genealogies, survive and tell of the so-called 'erenachs'—lay patrons of many of Ireland's churches, and tribal sponsors of holy men. It is easy to see how a fashion for having such intellectual lodgers might catch on. Monks prayed for their patrons, for their dynastic successors and their souls. They brought learning and kudos and provided convenient careers for those of the Irish elite who were either not disposed towards the alternative (fighting; an early if glorious death; life in the testosterone-fuelled mead hall) or who might otherwise present a

threat to the chosen line of succession. They healed the sick and sometimes saw into the future. In return, monasteries benefited from the protection of their lords and were provided with lands which could not, like those held by warriors, be taken back. Monasteries patronised by kings or lay patrons were freehold and each one, because of the stability conferred by its status, acted as a sort of seed corn for agricultural, artistic and artisanal investment. At Nendrum monastery in County Down (see page 321), a corn mill powered by the tides on Strangford Lough was constructed in the seventh century: hard evidence of the benefits of such capital investment, and by no means unique. The monastic movement which brought monks together in cenobitic communities—that is, communal life—beginning early in the sixth century, was a stabilising feature in an unstable world, like tough grass holding a sand dune together.

In key places along Argyll's coast, the same relationship between aristocratic or kingly *duns* and important early church foundations is repeated. As it happens, St Blane's and Dunagoil are exceptional: they are the twin foci of royal power. The Scottish historian of this period, James Fraser, believes that Dunagoil was the princely seat of Conad Cerr, warlord chief of the Cenél Comgaill in Cowal and very briefly king of all Dál Riata in the year 629. The abbots of St Blane's were *his* holy men. Dunadd, our destination, was the seat of the Cenél nGabrain, the dominant kin group during Colmcille's day and up until the mid-seventh century.

From Kingarth at the extreme southern end of Bute, we turned north-west along the coast. All the while Dunagoil was visible behind us, protruding into sea and sky, making as bold a statement as could be imagined of the power and status of its lords. On Loch Quien we saw the low, rush-covered mound of a *crannog*,[6] an artificial island that would have supported a pile-driven circular dwelling. Such places, summer retreats for a transhumant elite, are known to have existed from the Iron Age onwards, right into the high Medieval period. But we did not pause on the trail. Our destination today was another monastic establishment, much more modest than St Blane's but in an equally evocative setting. St Ninian's chapel lies on a rocky plinth at the end of a narrow spit of sand dunes halfway up Bute's west coast. The spit shelters a cove where boats can be drawn up onto the strand; in turn it is sheltered from westerly gales by Inchmarnock. St Marnock's[7] island is a special place, and I would have liked very much to go there; but perhaps seeing it from across the sound was enough. Most of what we know about Inchmarnock comes from a campaign of survey and excavation which revealed that it was once an important monastic school. It has yielded the largest number of inscribed slates from any site in the British Isles. One of these records the founding saint's name, Ernán; another appears to show a monk kneeling at the feet of a warrior, perhaps imploring a Viking for mercy or being carried off into slavery. Eight gaming boards were also found here: evidently the monks relieved the boredom of long winter evenings on the island by enjoying a game of Nine Men's Morris, or *merels*, whose origins can be traced at least as far back as imperial Rome. The relationship between St Blane's foundation and that on Inchmarnock is intriguing to contemplate: were they competitors for the patronage of the Cenél Comgaill, or twin aspects of a single entity with one a sort of feeder school for the other? We may never know. Archaeology can be very successful at revealing what happened; rarely can it say why.

You could be forgiven for missing Ninian's chapel on the spit: it looked more or less like an abandoned drystone hut, now grassed over and with walls only standing a couple of feet high, swaddled in the tough, wiry machair grass that clings to the sand and rocks and defies autumn and winter gales. Excavations in the 1950s revealed that it sat in a small circular cemetery containing inhumations on a north–south orientation, overlain by graves in an east–west, more obviously Christian alignment. At the east end of the chapel stood a stone altar with a box-like cavity for holding the bones of its founder (perhaps Ninian, but much more likely another local worthy whose name has been forgotten and absorbed into the geographical mythology of one of the Atlantic West's celebrity saints).

Next to the chapel, on the leeward side, stood a small single-storey holiday cottage, once presumably a fisherman's hut. On our way out there, with the evening drawing in and the sky once again looking menacing, we passed a herd of dairy cows trooping wearily back from a day's paltry grazing, and a man walking his dog who pointed at a small hollow beyond the cottage, suggesting it would make a good bivouac. Neither tide nor wind would reach us there, he said. Travellers gather intelligence where they may; and he was right. The pitch was soft, close to the water's edge and just out of the wind, so even if it blew a gale we should be all right. Our only mistake was not to have filled our water bladders (a neat twenty-first-century reinvention of ancient technology, with plastic substituting for sheepskin) at the last spring we'd passed: so it was rice boiled in salt water for supper; and since that night's protein was provided by a dried, cured chorizo sausage, it was a salty meal all round.

The sky cleared as it darkened. A three-quarter moon rose in the east, its tilted asymmetry perfectly imperfect. The moon is a traveller's friend: on these bright nights its light is sufficient for navigation—sometimes even to read by. The experienced sky-watcher knows that the full moon lies due south at midnight; that each day it rises forty-eight minutes later than the night before; that broadly speaking it follows the same east–west path as the sun: so here is a night-time compass, clock and calculator in one. Only when I am sailing or on the trail do I come to know instinctively the phases of the moon; and on such a journey as this, accompanied by the sea, the state of the tide also becomes part of a subliminal dialogue with the earth and stars which must have been so much more intimate and wondrous a part of the Early Medieval mind and soul than it is of today's amateur voyagers.

After a tranquil night of comfort that would have fooled a princess, the golden early light was enough to make one drunk: we gorged on it, and so did my new camera, acquired especially for the trip. We were treated to rich, saturated colours, a pulsating, dynamic range of tones and sharp lines: Arran in the distance, banks of pinky-grey and purple cloud capping it like a frown; Inchmarnock's low humpback bathed in cadmium yellow; each palette scattering its colours in brilliant shards off the shimmering surface of the sea. And, as if to endorse our choice of pitch, the morning saw our friend the seal bob his shiny head out of the water to see what we were up to. Trail days mean early starts: light penetrates the tent; the world around wakes up and starts its racket—squabbling geese and ducks, lamenting oyster catchers and curlews; the rumble of distant tractors across the bay. Breakfast was eaten on the go while we packed the tent and stowed our gear. That morning a brisk offshore wind blew; for two days the weather had been looking menacing to the west but a spell of easterlies had kept it at bay. Now a line of cloud overhead seemed to presage change; but by midday it had dissipated and once again we got away with a dry day.

North, then, along Bute's west coast. The map showed that at Ettrick Bay, more or less due west of Rothesay, there was a public loo where we could wash and replenish our water supplies. It looked like a good first stop, and nearby was the promise of standing stones and an early cross to look at. St Ninian must have been on our side that morning, for as we traversed the bay on an ebbing tide the loo morphed into a café. The Dark Age traveller takes comfort where he or she can. We ate their biggest breakfast and washed. I dashed off to the nearby hamlet of St Colmac (an otherwise obscure saint) to have a look at a cross; but could not find it in a huddle of farm buildings, slurry pits and byres. Sated by our unexpected feast, and clean-ish, we resumed the trail along the coast, past chambered cairns and small *duns*. Sarah noticed how many wooden benches we passed, set up to watch the sea with little plaques commemorating loved ones. Bute, it seems, if not truly an island of the dead, is certainly the island of memorial.

At Kilmichael, on the rugged and little visited north-west coast of Bute, the trail finally ran out. There is a small chapel here, perched on a grassy cliff overlooking the Kyles, with the small villages of Kames and Tighnabruaich (literally 'the house on the shore') sitting snugly a mile across the water. The Kyles of Bute is a flooded fjord separating the island from the western branch of the Cowal peninsula: remote, rugged terrain. There is no harbour anywhere on the west coast of Bute, nor fishing pier, nor ferry. The land rises and steepens, and those who venture here need to be lucky, well equipped, and—if they wish to make further progress to the north—have a plan for how to do so. After snacking with our backs to St Michael's little chapel, soaking in the views of Cowal's rocky, conifer-cloaked hills, we climbed down to a beach made up entirely of broken oyster and scallop shells (we spied a man in a small boat directing divers to live ones on the sea floor), whelks and clams. We set up the storm kettle for a cup of tea. Sarah stripped off and swam—endurance swimming is her thing; I prefer boats. I've no doubt that unencumbered by me or the rucksack she would have made it across easily enough, although I'm not sure what the natives would have thought; and for a moment I wondered how many Dark Age denizens took to the water for a dip. Bede tells of a monk, Dryhthelm, standing up to his waist in the icy River Tweed, close to freezing, so that he could be nearer to God in his transcendental semi-starved coma; but you don't hear much of swimming monks.[8]

At three o'clock we gathered our things and walked to a prominent rocky point that sticks out into the Kyle. All was quiet and still. And then, right on cue, the small fishing vessel *Morag* steamed into sight from behind a bluff to the north and chugged gently towards us until she was no more than a hundred yards offshore. From her waist, Donald Clark, her owner and skipper, dropped into his outboard dinghy and plucked us off the beach as cool as you like. Donald—anyone, indeed, who might give us passage off the west coast of Bute—had been hard to track down. Today, as it happened, was *Morag*'s last day in the water before she was to be hauled up into dry dock for the winter. We felt very lucky to have run him to earth (via online shenanigans, emails and phone calls over the previous month); but the traveller grasps serendipitous moments like these without dwelling too much on what-ifs and what-might-have-beens. With a quick backward glance, we made our escape. Bede, Adomnán and other Dark Age hagiographers would have made much of such a story; portrayed it as divine providence, a miracle.

After three days' walking and wild camping, we treated ourselves to a night at the Kames Hotel: showers, food, a beer in the bar, the closest we could get to Beowulf's feasting hall. A reluctant (on my part) taxi ride first thing the next morning got us, with a few minutes to spare, to Portavadie on the west side of the Cowal peninsula. The ferry was one of those small flat-bottomed vehicular drive-on affairs in which the ramp is lowered as the vessel revs up against the sloping concrete shelf of the harbour. A brisk wind blew from the south up Loch Fyne and the ferry bumped around a bit as she carved a bow-legged wake across to the fishing port of Tarbert. I stayed out on deck, smelling the kelpy breeze and watching other sea traffic pass by, like a maritime version of a trainspotter. Our fellow passengers included a woman travelling to her holiday cottage on the island of Gigha and a solicitor on his way to the Sheriff's court in Campbeltown. The woman who took our money carried small parcels for delivery on the other side.

Tarbert is one of those special place names. Several of them survive in Scotland and Ireland and they generally describe a narrow isthmus across which boats were once pulled or carried between parts of the open sea or great inland lochs. The portage here was about a mile, the narrowest point on the Kintyre peninsula; and if a mile still seems a fair way to drag a boat, think of the nearly one hundred sea miles it saved. In truth, if there was a system of runners or sleds and if one considers that only half the portage can have been uphill (and with a high point of forty feet above the sea not far uphill at that) it's not quite so daunting a prospect. A tough day, yes; a *Fitzcarraldo*-style jungle endurance epic? No.

There was no time to explore or to shop. From the ferry ramp at Tarbert we had little choice but to dash for the once-a-day bus that runs along the east coast of Kintyre, until we could find a walking route across to our next destination. It felt like cheating. At Inverneil we were disgorged, the only passengers. Now we set our heads towards the south-west along a tiny B-road with rain in the air and low, cold, wet cloud skimming across the tops of the hills directly into our faces. Up through conifer plantations where over-stocking and wind-throw had left brutal scars, to a gentle col six hundred feet above sea level. After that a more benign and nourishing land of broadleaved woods, of oak, hazel and alder, drew us on and downward. Six miles along this road we reached the hamlet of Achahoish (Gaelic: the 'field of the hollow'). Oak leaves turned golden brown fell in curtains across the road; a thin sun glinted off mirror-like lochans on the braes around us; rushing burns and limp bracken, stoical livestock and empty roads spoke for themselves of the coming season. We found no shop here in this sheltered hollow; and no prospect of another for a couple of days. The postmistress, who opened her front door to let a yapping spaniel out, was not available for consumer purchases; she only really posted letters for folk, she said.

We had almost walked our own unofficial tarbert here, north-east to south-west across Kintyre. Now we rounded the head of Loch Caolisport, whose waters lead on to the Sound of Jura and beyond that to the open sea, past a small chapel which proclaimed itself the parish church of South Knapdale (current population 2325). We sat for lunch on a damp sward next to a meandering river flooding under the moon's influence as the high tide backed it up. A mile further on, along the west side of the loch, we stopped again so I could visit St Columba's cave. My expectations were low: Columba, or Colmcille, is one of those celebrity saints, like Cuthbert and Ninian, whose name has become attached to holy places in Scotland and Ireland for all sorts of reasons, in much the same way that Arthur, Julius Caesar, the Devil or Robin Hood are attached to any mysterious landscape feature in England. Often this naming was an attempt to cement and expand the so-called *paruchia*, the zone of influence, of a great foundation like Iona; sometimes it reflects a fading memory of the true founding saint or hermit, too obscure to make it onto the A-list. The tiny medieval chapel here, whose walls stand almost to roof height, had been swallowed by trees, shrubs and tall bracken. Out here there is no Ministry of Tidy Monuments to cut grass, mend signs or point stonework. I wished, for a moment, that I had brought a machete. A small track wound up towards the escarpment behind the chapel and here was the real treasure: a tall, deep, dank cave with a mouth like a hungry fish, an odd little wicket gate before it and tentacles of ivy and honeysuckle draped across its dark entrance.

Inside, set on a rocky shelf some five yards from the entrance and built against the wall of the cave, stood a drystone rectangular altar. On its flat top lay the empty aluminium shells of tea lights, a little rustic cross made from withies, some pennies and a cheap plastic necklace. Above the altar, carved into the wall, were the remnants of two simple crosses; on the front of the altar the outline of a fish had been crudely painted in cheap emulsion. For some this is at best mawkish hokum, at worst mere vandalism; for others it is a touching revival of ancient faiths. I put on my anthropological hat and observed, trying to get the best photograph in terrible light. Above me, on the opposite wall, was a line of holes which may once have held beams for a ceiling of some sort or a shelf for a bed. The cave has been excavated, or interfered with, many times. There is evidence of Mesolithic hunter-gatherer occupation and of burials. A metre and more of material built up during long, ancient use of the cave included Roman Samian ware—the finest dinner service to be had in the Western Empire—and a Viking Age merchant's bronze balance. If this was once home to a hermit, it was also, at times, something more. The very fact that St Columba's cave is so far off the beaten track that no official pays it a visit more than once in a score of years, makes it special. Much more than at Kingarth, one feels the presence of the Early Medieval spirit, of solitude and retreat; of temporal remoteness and of peregrination: the great pilgrimage into the unknown for Christ.

A little further south-west along the shore we came to Ellary. A grandiose, rhododendron-infested Victorian estate, it did not welcome. Keep Out signs warned and gates were closed across what was left of the road, a barely metalled track. But Ellary boasted one of the most important Early Medieval cemeteries in the country, and we were not for turning back. It was late, though, and our feeling that the long-anticipated break in the weather was about to befall us suggested that the first priority was shelter, food and a good pitch: somewhere away from the eyes of any gillies who might be out on the hills patrolling for poachers. One feels the need to be discreet when camping wild; but we were dog-tired and footsore from so much tarmac-walking. Again we were lucky. Above Ellary, after a stiff climb we insinuated ourselves into the ramparts of Dun a' Bhealaich (the 'fort at the red pass'), another of those perched Dark Age fortresses, apparently never investigated, which watches over its saints. It occupies a rocky promontory looking across the loch and commands the route—surely an ancient droveway—across the peninsula. Its ramparts now seem feeble, colonised by birch trees and hidden beneath suitably reddish-brown bracken. But the site says something about prestige, privacy and privilege, which are the currency of elites. At any rate, when it comes to accommodation, location is everything: here was a pitch out of sight of the track, with sticks for the fire and the fresh, if peaty, water of a lochan just twenty yards or so below us; here too was a misty autumn evening closing in like a suffocating veil of net curtain. We pitched the tent in deepening murk, fired the stove and ate quickly—just in time. For the next fourteen hours the rain was unceasing. There was nothing for it but to retreat to the tent on our atmospheric ancient campsite.

A half-hearted dawn, tea and porridge and the stealthy drip of rainwater down the back of the neck; cold hands, frosted breath on the air and a horizon cropped on all sides to a measly hundred yards or so. I packed all my gear but the cameras and, leaving Sarah in possession of the castle for an hour, trudged off to find Cladh a Bhile, the 'earthwork of the sacred tree'. Back down the trail to Ellary; a plunge into a boggy field and through a long tunnel of rhododendrons and yew trees, mud and running water up to the ankles; a fruitless search for a signpost or a path; then tell-tale signs, I hoped: a half-hidden Victorian iron railing and a little clearing. No sign here of any earthwork, but above me the precipitous massif of the dun where we had camped. I'd walked a long way to see this place. Neglect had beaten me to it. This age-old cemetery, with its unique collection of grave slabs, was almost impenetrably obscure on a day which was, truly, as dark as night. I spied a couple of Victorian stone crosses, one of them broken into fragments. And then, as my eye began to discriminate between scrub, bracken and stone, I saw a slab, upright, a metre and a half or so tall, encrusted with lichen and green with moss. The other side was carved, magnificently, with a Maltese cross below a marigold, or flabellum. These are very special carvings: the flabellum was a ceremonial fan, Egyptian in origin and used in the most intimate early Christian liturgies to ward insects (and evil spirits, perhaps) away from the priest celebrating mass. As the iconography travelled west and north, it found new life as a motif separated from any physical utilitarian object, and became more a sort of stylised cross. I have seen examples at Fahan and Carndonagh in Donegal and they are occasionally to be found gracing the manuscripts of the illuminated Gospels. Stylistically they belong to the seventh or eighth centuries.

The Ellary stone was first brought to the notice of a wider academic community by two remarkable women, Marion Campbell and Mary Sandeman, who double-handedly surveyed and then published the archaeological monuments of Argyll in the late 1950s and early 1960s, when nobody seemed to know or care what an extraordinary rich heritage they represented. Campbell was a fervent nationalist, a novelist and author of more than eighty books, including many on Argyll, into whose monuments she was an indefatigable researcher. The historian and archaeologist Neal Ascherson, a friend of Campbell's, described her as a 'patriot antiquary', but also as a formidable intellect, kind but tough, an inveterate smoker with a sharp sense of humour which she applied equally to herself and others. She lived in Kilberry Castle as a farmer all her life, much of it with her friend Mary Sandeman, and died in 2000.

The current state of Cladh a Bhile would sadden Marion Campbell. Many of the thirty or so stones in this important place were impossible to locate; others just about poked their heads through the dingy vegetation. I managed to photograph half a dozen, but in that light I could do them no justice. I felt a grim sense of anti-climax, sploshing and splodging my way back up the hill.

Grim, to be sure; but as Sarah and I went on our way again I experienced a growing feeling, barely describable, of the exultation that only the nomad knows; that in packing my entire current existence into a bag and leaving nothing behind, looking forward only to the day ahead, I was complete—as complete, perhaps, as a human being can hope to be. Saturated colours of bracken and rough grass, and bare rocks and silky water on reed-ringed lochans formed a serene aesthetic backdrop to the steady pace of our early morning trudging.

Even so, by eleven o'clock, now as wet inside as out, we were cursing the drenching squalls that came barging in off Loch Sween, one after the other. The view, if one could have seen anything of it, should have taken in St Cormac's chapel on Eilean Mòr—a tiny medieval church used as an inn in later centuries and which still boasts part of a turf roof. Beyond that Jura, if only the cloud would lift.

At the tiny hamlet of Kilmory—a cluster of low drystone cottages wedged in against the wind-battered hillside, a telephone box and not much else—a sign pointed to a roofless chapel supposed to house some fine early carvings. Professional enthusiasm wavered. Sarah was all for going on despite the lashing rain, just to keep moving. We were footsore and stiff and after more than four days on the trail the heavy packs were taking their toll. But my conscience won. The chapel, of vivid orange drystone schist like the cottages, was set in a neat little churchyard with a view out onto the tousled waves of the loch. A small notice on the door invited the visitor to pluck the heavy iron key off its peg and enter (and to lock and replace it afterwards). Hardly worth the effort, surely. But there is something satisfying about opening an old church door with a great heavy key, and you never know what surprises might lie beyond. At Kilmory the saints (and the secular powers) smiled on us. Some enterprising bod from Historic Scotland had found the money to construct a glass ceiling to shelter the treasures within: here was dry land, a refuge, a sanctuary. Here, too, was an astonishing collection of stone memorial sculpture. I unburdened myself of dripping pack and waterproof, leaned out of the door and with a look, I dare say, of smug complacency, beckoned my drenched partner to share in the miracle.

Kilmory was more a museum than a chapel. Thirty-five crosses and grave slabs were arranged around and against the walls or standing upright on the gravelled floor. This was a homage to a grand cultural school of stone carving, the so-called West Highland tradition. It probably began on Iona in Colmcille's day towards the end of the sixth century, and continued into later medieval centuries under, some believe, the patronage of the Lords of the Isles. The earliest and simplest, stunning in their unaffected piety, were grouped in a corner. These were either way-markers for pilgrims or memorial stones to early holy men and women whose own peregrinations led them here. My favourite was a lozenge with a round head; carved on it in relief was a splayed cross with hatches between its arms, as if it had been copied from a more elaborate original. The texture of the grey sandstone from which it had been cut was irresistible; I had to touch it, to read from its surface not just the skill and faith of the mason but the passage of the years as its neatly incised lines weathered and shed their detail. These lozenge-shaped grave markers are known as '*leacht*' crosses. The shape allowed for the insertion of the slim cross base into the top of a *leacht*, an altar like the drystone affair at St Columba's cave or St Ninian's chapel. Beneath some of these the bones of holy men and women have been found: the crosses are symbols of their faith in life and their protective presence, their *virtu*, in death. Several of the simpler plain crosses here might date to the sixth or seventh century, although the church belongs to the eleventh or twelfth century.

Outside, the heavy squalls that dogged us all morning had blown away on the wind; now the day offered a panorama of blue sky and the vast, thrilling disc of the western sea spread out to our left as we walked northwards along the peninsula. Jura, now blasted by a great white squall, now shining orange and grey in the distance; Eilean Mòr, closer at hand, wind-torn but like a gem against the deep blue; jagged ridges of hard ancient rocks scattering towards the south-west, showing the line of the great geological fault that thrusts the Highlands against northern Britain; and opposite us the half-connected tidal Isle of Danna at the southern end of the Tayvallich peninsula. The tide races here are fearsome and spume trails betraying conflicting currents stretched away across the open sea. From our elevated path it was easy to see how interconnected the maritime archipelago of the Western Isles once was; how hermit, saint, warlord and farmer brought their own culture and traditions together and created a matrix of complex relations borne on the sea between them.

It was a long hike up the eastern side of Loch Sween; wear and tear were slowing us down. We stopped by the shore to look at the tree-graced slopes across Loch Sween. We snacked on dried fruit and cheese, nuts and oatcakes; and an otter charmed us with her exuberant fishing antics no more than thirty yards away. At Castle Sween, a lumping great medieval fortress, we passed an incongruous caravan and holiday park (NO CAMPERS). On again, sustained by chocolate and the odd swig from a flask of the water of life, we passed an unassuming stone cross in a field, divorced from the ruin or landscape that would have framed its story.

It was not easy to see where we might stay that night; there are no campsites at all in Knapdale and the comparative urbanity of Lochgilphead and Crinan were beyond our capabilities for that day. Everywhere was soaking wet. Sarah was feeling rough. More than once I consulted the map, hoping to identify the sort of spot where we might pitch early, not attract too much attention and get a good night's sleep. Kilmichael, no more than a group of houses, offered nothing. More miles. The track became a narrow road, busy with trippers' cars. The odd house passed by; fences and walls everywhere: this is an owned, proprietorial landscape. At Achnamara, according to the map, there was a school. Might there also be a bus? There might; but this being Scotland's half-term, it was not running. Only Tayvallich, tantalising across the bay, offered civil society and transport. Sarah saw a chance, in a woman bringing shopping in from her car, to gather intelligence. The thought crossed my mind, ridiculously, that in the Early Medieval period each woman would have immediately assessed the other by her hair, her clothes and above all by the design and quality of her brooch—a penannular iron or bronze ring with a pin which slots through the gap and which, with a twist, anchors brooch to cloak. A brief conversation ensued. Sarah walked over to where I was sitting by the packs, a resigned look on her face. No buses; no taxi will come out here.

A minute or so later the husband appeared with his car keys; would we like a lift up to Barnluasgan, where the four o'clock bus would take us all the way to Lochgilphead? We would. We did not get around to learning his name (too busy thanking him, Sarah's natural chutzpah and nameless saints). We were left at the bus stop, or at least outside the house where the bus was said to stop, and in a state of modest complacency ate the last of our choc-olate, congratulating ourselves provisionally on another huge slice of luck. The bus came. In fifteen minutes it brought us out onto the Crinan road. Here we had our first view of the extraor-dinary lowland bog landscape that is Mòine Mhòr and beyond it the encircling hills of Kilmartin Glen, sensuously bathed in warm but vibrant yellow evening light. Crossing the bog was a joy to be savoured for the next day. The bus, meanwhile, crept along the line of the Crinan Canal with its neatly numbered locks and equally neatly numbered lock-keepers' cottages. The canal was the late eighteenth-century product of the minds and energies of John Rennie, Thomas Telford and hundreds of Irish and Scots navvies, designed, like the former portage across Kintyre at Tarbert, to speed passage from the Atlantic and the Western Isles up the Clyde, avoiding a hazardous passage around the Mull of Kintyre. The line of the canal bypasses Lochgilphead, which ought to have been a strategic port but which sits wearily at the head of a muddy bay, thirty years behind the rest of the country. Here we were deposited by the bus in the hope of finding a bed for the night. Cut off from Scotland's infrastructure, it ought to be the gateway to Kintyre; but there's no money on the peninsula either. The damaged sign on the wall of the drab S-ag Hotel just about said it all. It is hard to get here from anywhere and we wondered, walking through its down-at-heel streets, if it might not be better to put Lochgilphead out of its misery. That is a little unfair; it does have a certain faded charm.

What Kintyre needs is a revival of the Dark Age superhighway that made it a centre of maritime and cultural activity. In these days when the sea is no longer the arterial hub that it once was, this place wants a railway. The roads are narrow and slow, clogged with heavy vehicles, caravans or tractors. It's an economic backwater and no amount of central government subsidy will drag it up by its bootstraps. Fishing is dead and so is any business from across the Atlantic. Only fresh-laid iron tracks and a visionary giant like Telford might pull it off; but who will pay? Just look at Argyll and Kintyre on a map: topography and history are against them: suppression, exploitation, clearances, clan rivalries, political and economic remoteness; mountains, lochs and rivers; and very little infrastructure for the traveller wanting to discover it. Kintyre seems to be having its own Dark Age. We are still only forty miles from Glasgow as the seaplane flies; we might as well be a thousand away. The irony of all this is that for several thousand years Kilmartin Glen was one of the busiest places on the island: it has the greatest density of surviving (and buried) archaeological monuments in Britain.

In the morning, only a little less sore but drier and cleaner, we recce'd the bus times on the town promenade (for want of a better word). They were all a year out of date. The driver of the bus that took us over the canal and onto the Oban road was no wiser than the timetable. When was the last bus to Oban (train station; civilisation)? No one knew. So we began our trek across Mòine Mhòr in informational, if not spiritual, darkness. But there was no mistaking the rocky rump of Dunadd, one of the most famous Dark Age fortresses and seat of the legendary kings of Dál Riata. I had seen so many pictures of this place and been to so many lectures about it, read of it in so many articles and books, that I feared the reality would disappoint. It did not. Mòine Mhòr was a great flat expanse of bog, now very much drained and tamed, but in the days of Colmcille a marshy, oft-flooded plain with an amphitheatre of rocky hills surrounding it. Out of this lowland morass rises the clenched fist of Dunadd like an underwater leviathan bursting to the surface through infinitely deep waters.

It is approached by a tarmac road which must once have been no more than a wooden causeway across the peat. From a distance the shelving plane of the rocks give the impression of a sort of spiral, rather like the castle rock on Lindisfarne, curling up and around (I was hungry: a Walnut Whip came to mind). A small cluster of cottages nestles at its base. They would not get planning permission now, one imagines. There is a car park. Up the twisting narrow path through its ramparts and the deliberately awe-inspiring rock-cut barbican, once topped by a stone curtain wall that leads to the first terrace: much larger than I had imagined, and evidently the principal defended enclosure. It is large enough to contain a significant domestic set-up. Now grassed over, the site was excavated in the early part of the twentieth century and then briefly in 1980 by Leslie Alcock, the great Early Medieval scholar. From this first terrace, artificially flattened and containing a rock-cut well, another steep, narrow spiral path leads around the twin-domed fastness that makes its outline unforgettable. Up here, visible for miles in any direction, once stood the great hall, the feasting barn conversion that was the hallmark of the Early Medieval fortress.

Three things make Dunadd unique. Its setting, evident from the highest point (a hundred and fifty feet above the plain) even on a wind-blasted grey day, is sublime: flatness on all sides as far as the sea, with which it may have been directly connected in its heyday; south to the canal and to Kintyre; east to the wooded hills of Argyll and north to Kilmartin Glen. The lazy meander of the River Add encircles and defends it.

The second remarkable feature of the fort is its famous footprint, supposedly carved into the bare rock to act as part of a ceremony of royal investiture. Colmcille was said to have been the first holy man in the west to perform anything recognisable as a Christian royal inauguration or anointing, although historians have their doubts and in any case Colmcille had the kings of Dál Riata come to him on Iona, not the other way around. But here was the footprint. Or rather, under here: what we saw was merely a facsimile, the original being too important for humans to touch and in recent years buried a foot deep beneath us. But there is more than just a footprint: laser scanning of the original stone before its interment showed faint traces of a carved bull, decidedly Pictish in style, and a line of ogham script. (More of ogham later—see page 266.) For the archaeologist, what is so striking about Dunadd is the amazing wealth of material culture which excavation has yielded (if not always using scientific techniques).

From Dunadd[9] the kings of Dál Riata were able, in the sixth and seventh centuries, to lay hands on *objets d'art* from across the lands of the former Roman Empire. They commissioned gold- and silversmiths to create jewellery and weapons of exquisite finery and technical brilliance. They knew how to acquire a super-valuable purple dye which could only be obtained from the mucus of the Atlantic dog whelk *Nucella lapillus*. They drank from glass vessels imported from a thousand miles away on the Continent.[10] And they ate from (or perhaps just coveted) the best tableware that Africa or Francia could produce. They were able to call Colmcille, the greatest of early saintly potentates, their royal priest, ambassador and chief legitimiser. Through his monastic successors on Iona and through their own canny dynastic fostering of princely exiles, these kings amassed sufficient political capital to send protégé athelings[11]—of whom the most celebrated and influential was Oswald Iding (see pages 179 and 231)—back to Northumbria to expand their influence over the islands of Britain. In turn, Áedán mac Gabrain (*c.*574–609) and his successors as kings protected Colmcille's earthly interests and fostered the expansion of his spiritual empire, the Ionan *paruchia*. In theory, at least, the kings of Dál Riata were able to summon fifteen hundred men in two hundred curraghs to go raiding among the islands of the Hebrides and to Ireland where they claimed lordship over the kings of Ulster. They were a formidable force; and more, because they had the vision to see in the rational, stabilising and everlasting model of kingship constructed by their saint a new sort of political reality that would survive the person of the king. These were the kings, borrowing from their priest's invocation of the Old Testament, from whom the medieval idea of divine right springs.

Descending from this rocky citadel, this one-time Tower of Babel, Sarah and I set out along the dead straight causeway roads of the bog towards Kilmartin Glen. During the Neolithic and Bronze Ages, before Mòine Mhòr became wet and peaty under the influence of the warm Atlantic Drift, the glen was a potent focus of ancestral memorial and power. A miles-long processional route led from the glen out onto the fertile plain at the sea's edge. Great standing stones, their broken-shoulder profiles a figurative nod to the giants of their own past, litter the now-drying tamed peat lands. Hundreds of cairns and tombs have been uncovered and excavated here.

But whatever ritual landscape came into being in this place, it was eventually consumed by peat accumulating over a thousand wet summers. Back home, pondering Dunadd's place in this vale of ancestral tears, I asked a colleague, the distinguished palynologist Richard Tipping, if the kings of Dál Riata would still have been able to see these monuments poking ghostly out of the peat; to sense or in some way tap into their potency for their own psychological ends. Yes, he told me, the monuments would still have been visible. And in that realisation of a self-doubting society tapping into a source of power at once visceral, mythical and untouchable, I suddenly thought of the stranded, emasculated Napoleon staring at the pyramids in Egypt in 1799, and the words of a sonnet came to me:

> I met a traveller from an antique land
> Who said: Two vast and trunkless legs of stone
> Stand in the desert. Near them on the sand,
> Half sunk, a shattered visage lies, whose frown
> And wrinkled lip and sneer of cold command
> Tell that its sculptor well those passions read
> Which yet survive, stamped on these lifeless things,
> The hand that mocked them and the heart that fed.
> And on the pedestal these words appear:
> 'My name is Ozymandias, King of Kings:
> Look on my works, ye mighty, and despair!'
> Nothing beside remains. Round the decay
> Of that colossal wreck, boundless and bare,
> The lone and level sands stretch far away.[12]

At the time, after a couple of hours' stiff walking along unforgiving back roads and wishing only that we could reach our destination at Kilmartin (a café, and the bus to Oban beckoned), Shelley was not in my thoughts. We had left art, mystery and pathos some miles back and only irony remained. We passed a road sign, pointing along another dead straight, featureless road towards some unpromising destination. It said 'Long walk'. No shit, I thought.

DUNADD

Interlude *Gilsland to Haltwhistle*

Early spring—surviving Dark Age winters—food renders—
population—Early Medieval environment—strangers in
the landscape—Wall and Stanegate

IT WAS MARCH of a new year before I got out to the Wall again.
We had seen barely a flake of snow all winter; already lambs were
gambolling in the fields and a few tentative spring flowers were
trying their luck in the hedgerows of western Northumberland.
A woodpecker drummed in an unseen copse. The light was dead
flat. It was as if the season's forward march was held on pause,
sensing the coming change but not daring to tell the land. At this
time of year cloud cover keeps new growth down but insulates
the land through the long, dark hours. Clear skies bring sunshine
and warmth during the day, encouraging leaves and blossom;
but at night they bring sharp frosts. These can be cruel months:
promises withheld or betrayed, the rewards for survival just out
of reach. There is tension in the air.

At Gilsland village spring tends to come late anyway, and
the sense of time lag is sharpened by its halfway-house location between the oceans, its jumble of houses, yards, paddocks,
garages and sheds, all slightly down-at-heel and endlessly interesting to the archaeologist. As if to reinforce the air of uncon-
ventionality a lugubrious horse, which had itself seen better days,
stood four-square on top of Britain's second most famous monument—hoping, perhaps, to be rescued from boredom by a tourist

passing with an apple or the butt-end of a carrot. In the background a stolid brick Victorian villa with part of its roof missing seemed to have spilled its contents onto the paddock through which the Wall ran: rubbish littered the matted grass and mud. Hens rooted around for scraps of grain among dilapidated coops. Upended plastic chairs, bits of fencing, tarpaulin, buckets, rolls of barbed wire, corrugated iron and an enamel bath completed an apocalyptic picture of neglect. The archaeologist in me tends to overread rubbish: one man's abject laziness is not evidence for social catastrophe.

As I walked east beneath the railway arch of the Newcastle to Carlisle line and out of the village into airier countryside (past Milecastle 48, clinging to the edge of a steeply falling burn), I contemplated what life must have been like up here, at this season, in the Early Medieval period. March was the lunar month *Hreðmonað*, which Bede says was named after an otherwise obscure goddess, *Hreð*. For farmers it was, and is, the month for digging and sowing, for optimistic lambing and watching the skies for signs of late, dangerous snows. What did the peasants and lords of the Dark Ages eat during this lean time when autumn's surplus was running low or, after a poor harvest or bad winter, had run out? There is little direct contemporary testimony. An obscure monastic tale tells of paupers huddling in the discarded hot ashes of the monks' fires. Many of the monks we hear of seem themselves to have been half-starved; there were winters of desperate cold. And a story, famous in its day as an example of kingly munificence, tells how King Oswald of Northumbria gave his Easter feast to be shared among poor supplicants at the door of his hall; and then gave them the silver dish on which it had been served. The Old English word for a lord is *hláford*, a provider or guardian of bread.

Archaeology supplies the infrastructure for storage: the excavated remains of hundreds of sunken-floored huts whose plank superstructures allowed grain to dry and stay mould-free through winter; the late seventh-century Laws of King Ine of Wessex, in listing the render demanded of an estate of ten hides (that is, nominally ten family farms), includes among the bounty of the land honey, cheeses and hay, supplies that could be stored right through winter. To those we can add dried, smoked or salted meat (slaughtered in the viscerally named *Blotmonað*: *November*) and fish, the bread and ale that came from stored barley and wheat; perhaps fresh-slaughtered small livestock such as hens or geese. Peas and beans, turnips, leeks, onions and apples would be available until partway through the winter, but must have been in a poor state by this time of year. These domestic products were supplemented by wild food: birds and fresh fish, berries and nuts. We know that in the later Medieval period a form of agricultural insurance was practised. The division of open fields ensured that farmers shared the best and poorest land in a community. The corduroy ridge-and-furrow ploughlands that still grace the rural landscape more or less guaranteed some sort of harvest: in a wet year the corn grew better on the ridges; and in a drought it grew better in the furrows. And a wide variety of grains was grown: oats, barley, rye and more than one strain of wheat. How far back we can project these strategies is not yet clear.

One of the hoariest questions of Early Medieval studies is the extent to which the population of these islands fell during the centuries after the demise of the Western Empire. It would help if we knew how many people lived here during the Roman period; opinions differ widely, although there has been a general trend in recent decades, prompted partly by ever-increasing evidence for rural settlements of this period, to allow a figure of perhaps two or three million. Many experts agree that whatever the figure was in, say 350, it was not reached again until perhaps a thousand years later, just before the Black Death of the mid-fourteenth century. So we suspect that the population in Bede's day was lower, perhaps very much lower. How can we find out? If we could map all the settlements and cemeteries of the Romano-British period and those of the eighth century, for example, we might come to a reasonable estimate. We can't, because most of those settlements are invisible beneath later farms, villages and towns. Valiant efforts have been made to estimate national populations from the archaeology that we can look at: especially those cemeteries which come up for excavation or detailed survey. The idea is to estimate, using what dating evidence we find, the number of people who died in a community over a period of, say, two hundred years and then project those numbers into calculations based on minimum and maximum ranges for numbers and densities of settlements. The method is fraught with difficulties, because small changes in estimates or starting points produce wildly different outcomes.

Place-name scholars have looked at the chronology of name formations and mapped the settlement or reoccupation of places whose names are a clue to their age, but the names which survive are not necessarily a good guide to when they were first settled. More smoke on the glass; but there has been some successful research conducted on names associated with the clearance of woodland, which shows a patchy record of areas where land cultivated during the Roman period reverted to forest; and there is room for more work here. We do, at least, have a pretty good idea of what woodland existed where in the eleventh century, thanks to the Domesday Survey. For those of us living in the north-east, one frustration is that Domesday did not cover Northumbria (William the Conqueror having wasted it in his 'Harrying of the North', there wasn't much left to record).

A more scientific approach has been to use the evidence of pollen diagrams retrieved from sediments with long records of formation: lakes and bogs, primarily. Palynology is also not without its problems, but if we could map the relative decline or spread of those pollen grains associated with farming, woodland, wasteland or abandonment, we might be getting somewhere. Again, the resulting evidence for population decline or even growth is patchy; that, at least, means that the Gildas/Bede invasion-apocalypse scenario of fire, sword and famine on which all narratives of the British Dark Ages are hung must be challenged at the most basic environmental level. People survived; some thrived; some left in the hope of a better life in Brittany. Others, like Patrick, were captured and enslaved. Some (though not many) died in battle. Some must have starved (but probably fewer than we think). Archaeology will, in the end, narrow the parameters of the discussion. One thing we can say, backed by evidence from tree rings, ice cores and annals, is that from the middle of the sixth century the climate cooled markedly, before recovering about fifty years later. Coinciding with the arrival in Britain of a serious plague, these may be the decades when we should look for a dramatic population decline; and it may or may not be a coincidence that many of the surviving genealogies of Early Medieval kings have their origins at this time.

The two hundred years between the end of Roman rule in Britain and the revival of written history may be obscure, but they cannot have been centuries of unvarying chaos, starvation and anarchy. Society survived and evolved; kings ruled, warriors fought, monks prayed and peasants farmed.

For a while after Gilsland the Wall has been systematically robbed; only the massive ditch which fronted it follows the inexorable line eastwards, through a farmyard where I exchanged a wave with a sturdy borderer up a ladder, mending a roof next to an old, immaculately maintained barn. For a long stretch the ditch was full of water and bog grass; far off I could hear the winter wail of a curlew, and a flock of lapwings cavorted in its fruitless search for good grazing. I asked myself if I could live off the land at this time of year and thought that, on the whole, I would struggle. In all probability I would become a thief, stealing eggs and hens. The odd pheasant and rabbit caught in my field of vision were no consolation—neither of these was present during the Dark Ages.[13] A story told by Bede in his life of St Cuthbert, when the saint happened upon a barn from whose thatched roof a loaf and a lump of meat fell providentially into his hands, comes to mind. At six feet four and in the exotic dress of the twenty-first-century rambler, I would, in any case, make a lousy thief for those times. Strangers would have stood out like sore thumbs in a countryside that was much more crowded than our own because everybody worked on the land: even if Britain's Dark Age population was no more than a million or so, its fields and woods were full of endeavour and of the sounds of ploughman and woodcutter. I recalled one of the Laws of King Wihtred of Kent, dating to the early eighth century, which says that:

> If a man from a distance or a foreigner goes off the
> track, and he neither shouts nor blows a horn, he is to be
> assumed to be a thief, to be either killed or redeemed.[14]

At Thirlwall the line of the Wall descends into the narrow valley of the Tipal Burn; on the other side the remains of a twelfth-century castle sit squatly and the path rises steeply past and around them. These borderlands were never more dangerous or unwelcoming for the traveller (horn or no horn) than during the Anglo-Scottish wars of the thirteenth to sixteenth centuries—in these years a state of perpetual war existed among the so-called 'surnames', old-time ranching clans forever poaching on each others' turf, stealing cattle, slitting throats on dark nights and wreaking blood-feud revenge on their enemies over the generations. Northumberland is still full of those names: Nixons and Grahams, Fenwicks, Campbells and Armstrongs.

From now on Wall and Stanegate went their separate ways,

the road running parallel to the south. The wall climbed onto the crest of the Whin Sill, a north-facing cliff of intrusive igneous rock which hardly needs any artificial enhancement. For the walker it is an aerobic challenge, as Wall and Sill rise and fall, switch-back and swerve to conform with millions of years of origami strata and erosion. The rewards are heart-raising views from the scarp, a sense of awe at natural and human engineering and the indomitable character of this almost untameable landscape, the Wall and its hinterland etching a narrative of endurance and determination from sea to sea. Past the fort of *Magnis* at Carvoran and over Greenhead Crags; the great green fog-bank of Wark Forest away to the north and the Tyne valley folded into invisibility to the south. At Great Chesters, the Roman fort of *Aesica*, I came off the Wall and followed Haltwhistle Burn down to the small town that bears its name and which makes the proud boast that it lies at the exact axial centre of Britain.

Haltwhistle's survival is as improbable as that of the Wall, its industry gone and the town bypassed by the modern A69. Survive it does, though, and after a day braced against the elements and two thousand years of hard tales it was a welcome sight.

§ CHAPTER TWO

Marches: *Telford to Wrexham*

Ironbridge—giants—River Severn—Wrekin and Cornovii—
*Wroxeter Roman town—an odd dedication—Shrewsbury—place
names and settlements—Welsh and English—St Winifred's Well—
Wat's Dyke—Oswestry and King Oswald—an engagement—Offa's
Dyke—boundaries—Llangollen—Pillar of Eliseg—Pont Cysllte
aqueduct—the River Dee—Bangor-is-y-coed—a long day—
serendipity*

IRONBRIDGE

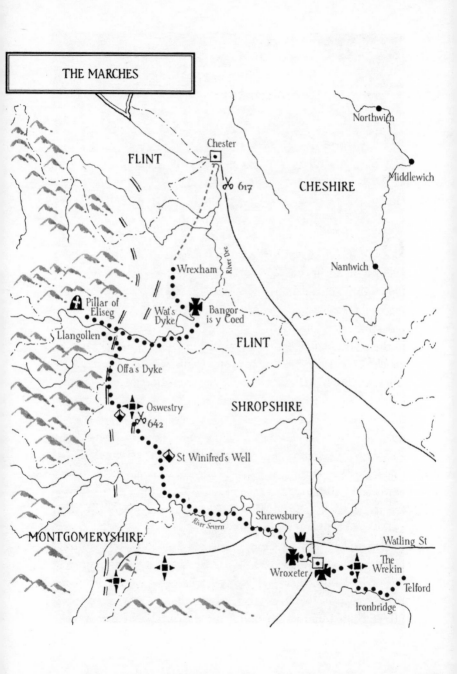

On a monday lunchtime in the middle of March 2014 I stepped off a train at Telford, a West Midlands new town of the 1960s whose bland shopping centre and suburban box-like housing could not have been less evocative of the Age of Arthur. Five miles later I walked across one of the most iconic monuments in the world, defining its own special moment in a dark, satanic epoch. The wrought-iron span at Ironbridge, built in 1779 by Abraham Darby III, marks for me the transition from an empirical, wooden world to one driven by science and metal. The Ironbridge Gorge, and Coalbrookdale, so vividly animated in the poetry and art of the Age of Enlightenment, are the lands of our ancestral spirits, the giants of the Industrial Revolution. Even at the dawn of a century of super-fast travel and communication, I am awed by the monumental honesty and grandeur of this henge erected as much to honour the Promethean masters of the forge as it was to bridge the River Severn.

Ironbridge, and the Severn, seemed a good place to start a journey through the Welsh Marches. My first destination was Shrewsbury, and there are two obvious ways for the wannabe Dark Age traveller to reach it: along the A5, Roman Watling Street, from Telford; or by following the river. In many ways the

A5 makes sense. The Romans were nothing if not logical, and in aiming to open up (or suppress, depending on your point of view) the mountainous lands of central and northern Wales and join both sides of Britain, the legionary road gangs were linking key strategic points in the landscape. Look at a map of the Marches and you'll see that, east of the mountains, it is delineated by the courses of the Severn running east, then south, and the Dee running north to Merseyside. At Shrewsbury the Severn emerges from the heart of the Welsh valleys. North of Shrewsbury is a gap running towards the Dee in the Vale of Llangollen; and through that gap runs the modern A5 towards Anglesey, the fastness of druids and rebels. Watling Street heads north to Chester; and so would I. But modern A-roads are no fun for the walker, so on a dank and drizzly morning I set off to walk along the Severn. Two months after devastating floods the debris of destruction and inundation lay strewn everywhere. Unlike much of the upland Tyne, there is no realistic crossing of the Severn for many miles without the aid of a bridge: it is deep, swift and powerful. It is its own borderland.

The floodplain west of Telford is narrow, enfolded on either side by gentle Shropshire hills dotted with small, red-brick mixed farms, woody copses and the odd village with a half-timbered cottage. Few, if any, houses are built from stone here. The river meanders, and so did I, keeping to the north-east bank beneath the mouth of Coalbrookdale where small industries still find a niche; past the massive orange cooling towers of the Ironbridge power station. At the small village of Buildwas I turned north, rising up from the plain and following a more direct path than the river: through farmyards and small coverts, across fields dotted with dairy cows and early lambs where I made the acquaintance of an enthusiastic border collie (what else?). Coming out onto a narrow deep-cut lane, an ancient cattle-worn thoroughfare that might have taken me east to Little Wenlock and a tempting pub,

I saw ahead beneath clouds gravid with rain the long, sloping humpback spine of the Wrekin, a thirteen hundred-foot monster of a hill that promises, in better weather, stupendous views of the north Shropshire plain. It was a long climb; the pack seemed heavy after a winter's slothful, self-imposed confinement. It began to rain: a squally, penetrating, sideways kind of rain, and cold with it. The Wrekin's slopes have been planted with conifers these many years, but the native oak and beech which must once have covered it are still to be seen here and there among the pines. There was not a spring leaf in sight yet, although I had already seen violets, primroses and celandine in the hedgerows. I could hear tits and chiff-chaffs even if I couldn't see them; and a woodpecker's randy, manic drum roll echoed from the hollow acoustic of the woods.

Before the long, long backbone of the Wrekin flattens out at over a thousand feet, a rocky crag, known as the Needle's Eye, makes a natural entrance through the ramparts of a great Iron Age hill fort that watches over, and is seen from, a grand swathe of country. This natural fortress, called by the Romans *Uriconium* (and hence Wrekin), was the headquarters of the tribe known to the second-century AD geographer Ptolemy as the *Cornovii.*

Here their chiefs accepted tribute in the form of cattle and perhaps slaves, dispensed justice, received petitions; judged the actions of their people and planned campaigns of war (rather like the commander at Birdoswald but on a vastly grander scale). It is some HQ: twenty acres in extent, a military and chiefly base sufficiently threatening to first-century imperial armies that they constructed Watling Street just a mile to the north of it. For the first Roman legion exploring these parts, the XIVth *Gemina*, it was a strategic key to western Britain. They disestablished the hill fort in about AD 58 and built a city in its shadow to pacify, subdue and civilise the natives after a campaign of resistance under Caratacus was overcome by their military might. A. E. Housman caught the spirit of the place in his poem 'On Wenlock Edge', with sentiments that the Anglo-Saxon author of 'The Ruin' might have appreciated.

> On Wenlock Edge the wood's in trouble
> His forest fleece the Wrekin heaves;
> The gale, it plies the saplings double,
> And thick on Severn snow the leaves.
>
> 'Twould blow like this through holt and hanger
> When Uricon the city stood:
> 'Tis the old wind in the old anger,
> But then it threshed another wood.
>
> Then, 'twas before my time, the Roman
> At yonder heaving hill would stare:
> The blood that warms an English yeoman,
> The thoughts that hurt him, they were there.
>
> There, like the wind through woods in riot,
> Through him the gale of life blew high;
> The tree of man was never quiet:
> Then 'twas the Roman, now 'tis I.
>
> The gale, it plies the saplings double,
> It blows so hard, 'twill soon be gone:
> To-day the Roman and his trouble
> Are ashes under Uricon.

I did not stay long enough to explore the former British tribal capital. Brief gaps in the relentless clouds that skimmed the hill-top were enough to show how physically dominating this place was. A glimmer of sun reflected off the spires and houses of Shrewsbury, eight miles or so to the west; beyond that loomed the Border hills. Laid out beneath me were the north Shropshire and South Cheshire plains and, looking back whence I had come, the mouth of Ironbridge Gorge and its own weather-producing cooling towers periodically appeared between sweeping showers. Enough, though; I headed back down the steep slope, stopping under the shelter of a Scots pine to munch on trail food and peer through steamy spectacles at a soggy map.

The Roman fortress and subsequent *civitas*[15] capital of the *Cornovii*, established just four miles west of the Wrekin in the first century at Wroxeter (*Viriconium Cornoviorum*), became the fourth largest city in Roman Britain. The walls of the second-century bath house and public exercise buildings still stand to a height of fifteen feet, surrounded by the exposed foundations of a typical imperial Roman town centre. From the road, and with the Wrekin framing it against the horizon, it is still an imposing ruin nestling on the right, east bank of the Severn. That was as close as I got: it was too early in the year for the Visitors' Centre to be open, even though the men from the Ministry of Tidy Monuments were hard at it mowing the grass, the rain having given way to cool spring sunshine and fluffy, busy clouds. I took my lunch to the nearby church of St Andrews, where Roman ashlar masonry was reused for the walls and where the churchyard gates are held up by Roman lathe-turned stone columns. Inside was a magnificent old red sandstone font, perfectly circular and pre-Conquest in date. Had that, too, been rescued from the Roman city?

The prelates and potentates of the Dark Ages were great imperial recyclers: they scavenged pottery and coins, gold and silver, stone and ideas, and if they did not often understand the symbolism or currency of the works of the giants, they were not averse to incorporating them into their own world of empirical magic, rough justice and dynastic patronage. But Wroxeter gives the lie to any idea that Early Medieval life was one of noble savagery, of skin-clad natives huddling among ruins praying for intervention from their thunderous gods. A brilliant campaign of excavation here by Philip Barker, whom I remember as a beady-eyed, white-haired magus looking like William Hartnell's original Doctor Who, showed that scientific excavation could unpick the ruins of Roman towns to reveal the subtle traces of occupation that lasted into the fifth, sixth and even seventh century, when English history begins. For archaeologists of my generation, Barker almost defined a new level of technical expertise: he was perhaps the first truly forensic excavator in Britain and a pioneer of digging large open areas, giving archaeology the confidence to believe that it could not just supplement the meagre history of the Dark Ages ('paper-cup' culture, as Roman archaeologists used to call it), but rewrite it. Just as at Birdoswald, the beginning of this enigmatic period is marked by the erection of timber halls among the footings of urban contraction and abandonment. Wroxeter had its own barn conversion. Twenty years before Barker began to excavate here in the late 1960s, such traces would barely have been sought, let alone found and made meaningful. It is technically exacting, expensive and time-consuming sculptural science.

Wroxeter survived Rome; the *Cornovii* survived Rome, too, to become the Early Medieval people known as the *Wreocansaetan*, more or less retaining the name by which Ptolemy knew their capital. Some time during the period of its post-Roman existence, perhaps around 500, Wroxeter became the burial place for a native man called Cunorix, son of the son of Coline (an Irish name)—his memorial inscription was recovered from the ruins in 1967. Cunorix means something like hound-king, which reminds one of Gildas's excoriating complaint against five contemporary tyrants. Cunorix may have been the successor potentate of the *Cornovii* or *Wreocansaetan*. The ninth-century compiler known as Nennius recorded Wroxeter by its contemporary British name, *Caer Guricon*, in his list of the twenty-eight 'cities' of Britain.[16]

Wroxeter lies halfway between the Wrekin and the county town of Shrewsbury; it also lies halfway between the Iron Age and the Medieval period, for Shrewsbury was its replacement. Deliberately founded, like Wroxeter, as a defended town, and situated in a strategically handy bend in the River Severn, medieval Shrewsbury was the eventual product of a system of defence envisioned by King Alfred of Wessex, expanded by his son Edward the Elder and daughter Æthelflaed, the so-called Lady of the Mercians. But if, as we believe, Shrewsbury was founded in the early part of the tenth century, there is a break in the trail that leads here. Between Roman city and medieval burgh there is a gap.

At Atcham, more or less halfway between Wroxeter and Shrewsbury at a point where an important bridge still spans the river, is a church whose origins lie during the century in which Wroxeter was finally abandoned. Oddly, it is dedicated to St Eata (hence the name of the village, whose name means 'homestead of Eata's people'). Quite why he was commemorated here is a mystery, for he was an abbot of the Anglo-British monastery at Melrose in the Anglo-Scottish border after the year 651; and not just any abbot: he was the mentor of St Cuthbert and one of the first generation of Lindisfarne-trained monks who came to preach the Irish form of Christianity to the Northern English. He died as Bishop of Hexham.

To add intrigue to this mystery, aerial photographs of a crop-mark site two miles due north of here, at Attingham Park, show that a substantial, perhaps palatial township site existed in these parts in the seventh century; it bears a striking resemblance to the Anglo-British complex at Yeavering in north Northumberland (another brilliant excavation, this time by pioneering archaeologist Brian Hope-Taylor in the late 1950s and early 1960s). Early Medieval texts relating to the Welsh kingdom of Powys (much larger than the modern county: the name seems to come from Latin *paganses*—country folk), which some historians suggest was the successor kingdom to the *Cornovii*, cite the existence of a palace called Pengwern, the site of which has never been located. Does Pengwern lie here?

From Atcham I followed the meander of the river (a king-fisher flashed by in a wink of lapis-lazuli blue; a drowned stoat lay across my path; there was flood damage along the banks where flotsam still lay piled against hedges, trees and fences: I sensed a washed-out, tired landscape desperate for spring) and entered Shrewsbury from the east. The local college had just disgorged its chattering pupils and a whole crowd of us crossed the deep, wind-ruffled waters of the river at the appropriately named English bridge. After a twenty-mile hike I felt road-rusty and weather-beaten, stopping at the first homely-looking café I could find for a cuppa and a large slice of chocolate cake. My prospective night's pitch lay on the other side of town, but when I got there it had been washed out—I should have guessed. I slunk back into town as darkness fell and took a room above a pub. No guilt: the shower was marvellous, I ate a steak pie and chips downed with a Guinness and luxuriated in a double bed.

Shrewsbury is unlikely to have enjoyed its later status as a great border town during the Early Medieval period. It was not made the centre of a diocese in the eighth century when Mercia was the rising power of central England and ancient tribal regions were busy acquiring bishops. Cathedrals at Worcester and Lichfield and royal centres at Repton and Tamworth suggest its marginality—or perhaps the instability of a marcher region in which British and Anglian dominance swayed back and forth too readily. Shropshire is named from Shrewsbury; but Shrewsbury is not named either from the former capital or the original tribe. Its Early English name is the rather unpromising *Scrobbesburh*, a shrubby or scrubby fort—a name that brings to mind the coconut whiff of yellow gorse or perhaps a phase of neglect. Its Welsh name sounds better: *Amwythig*, meaning simply 'fortified place'. By the early tenth century the town mattered sufficiently to have a charter drawn up, in which it was called a *civitas* in imperial style. Its emergence as a central, fortified place owes more, perhaps, to external threat than to antecedent history: during the Viking Wars between 865 and 927 Mercia and its ultimately more successful rival Wessex were under periodic but sustained attack from an army of enterprising, battle-hardened and well-led Scandinavians. The fortification of the Marcher towns was not an immediate response to this danger, but hard evidence of a strategic fight-back against the expansion of the Danelaw at the very beginning of the tenth century under the children of Alfred. Shrewsbury's key position on the river and east of the mountains made it worth fighting for, right up to the Wars of the Roses in the fifteenth century. Watling Street and the wool trade ensured its commercial success, reflected in the large number of grand medieval buildings which confer on the town its architectural virtues.

Leaving Shrewsbury the following morning, briefly following the old A5, Watling Street, and having passed a milepost promising Holyhead in only another one hundred and five miles, I wondered when I would start to see Welsh names popping up on signposts as I tracked west. I followed the river for a while, but this early in the year its bleached banks, meadows and trees, still in a forlorn state of winter undress, began to depress the imagination. At Montford Bridge I crossed the river again and took a small back road westwards. Here the plain of the Severn has a striking settlement pattern. Villages are very small, often little more than hamlets or clusters of half a dozen houses, and they are widely dispersed. This has perhaps to do with impermanence; it may also have to do with a large number of small settlements feeding a few larger central places—if so, is this a remnant of the burghal system which provided a central point of defence and trade within a day's march of every settlement in its hinterland? Sometimes I saw no more than a dozen or a score of houses spread over half a mile, and after the last house I would find I had left the 'village'. Once I paused in front of a simple, unaffected red-brick Primitive Methodist chapel with an inscription above the door, which provided me with some sort of an answer—one that could only, perhaps, have been inspired by a border region.

ERECTED A.D. 1865
THE LORD LOVETH THE GATES OF ZION MORE
THAN ALL THE DWELLINGS OF JACOB

The Primitive Methodist movement, born in Staffordshire in the early 1800s, was partly inspired by the American frontier pioneers' camp communions—open-air gatherings for prayer and communal meals in places where there was no church or priest— and a conscious revival of ideas about early Christian assembly. Here, where the secular geographical landscape has so often been disputed and where settlement is so dispersed, it seems quite natural to celebrate a mythical otherworldly place of permanence and security.

I sensed the swell of hills to the west; and although behind me the Wrekin still lurked like a slow-moving tanker against the horizon, the hill fortress of Breidden was now my compass mark, a few miles upstream. A closer look at the map showed something else: a large number of early names reflecting something of the landscape history of the region. There were Charltons (the houses of *ceorls*, or free farmers); Walcotts, hamlets of Britons[17] (presumably in an English area); and a Sascott—a *Saes*, or English, hamlet in a British/Welsh area. Then a first, truly authentic Welsh place name: Pentre (meaning little more than just 'place' or 'settlement'). If the river has often been a border over the millennia, it has been a very porous one: English and Welsh have always mixed here, and continue to do so. This is a patchwork land. That night, settling down to a pub dinner, having pitched my coffin-like trekking tent on a welcoming grassy sward on the north bank of the river, I got chatting to an Anglo-Welsh couple. She worked with horses; he was a gamekeeper. The thought of them choosing between nationalities was facile: their identity was defined by their lives and families and their landscape: a cultural and physical chequerboard. Welsh or English, they were Marcher folk; and I have heard much the same thing in the Anglo-Scottish borders and in the border counties of Ireland. Maybe we should get over the idea of nation, reserving it for the rugby pitch.

A third full day on the trail saw the back of the Severn. My destination that evening was Oswestry where I had an engagement at the town's annual Litfest. That meant a change of clothes, which I had been obliged to carry with me; but also a comfortable room at the Sebastian Hotel courtesy of the organisers. Oswestry was also a place of personal pilgrimage: I had never before been to the site of King Oswald's martyrdom—rather shameful to admit, having written a book about him. But before Oswestry came other pleasures and challenges. This part of Shropshire, it must be said, suffers from some poorly signed paths and a few that have been disestablished by farmers. Between Melverley Green and Argoed I became hopelessly disoriented in a metaphysical maze of existing, former and purely mythical paths. A field full of rather frisky-looking steers forced a diversion across a small ditch whose apparently firm banks dissolved into red clay as I landed on the other side. Knee-deep in filth was not the way I had intended to make my entrance in Oswestry.

At Woolston, around lunchtime, my travails were rewarded: one of those 'shall-I-take-the-quickest-path-or-follow-my-nose?' moments. Behind the last house in the village a narrow path led between hedges, showing hawthorn just coming into leaf, down to a pretty stream; and above the stream an equally lovely, if not enchanted, late medieval half-timbered cottage consisting of a single room, which straddled St Winifred's well. She is an interesting saint, one of those holy women who, for their faith, got their heads cut off. Her other, more elaborate and more celebrated shrine lies at Holywell in what used to be Flintshire. A broad contemporary of the Northumbrian King Oswald, who also lost his head in these parts, she was a Welsh noblewoman whose vow of chastity and desire to become a nun enraged her lover to the point of homicide. Where her severed head landed, a spring with miraculous healing powers appeared. The hagiography is conventional; but the frequency with which decapitated holy women became associated with local miracles evokes those head cults known to have existed long before Christianity co-opted such wise and virtuous souls.

Peering through the window of the cottage, I was surprised to see a man sitting in an armchair reading a newspaper; and thinking he must be some sort of warden, or even a work of installation-art, I knocked on the door. A dog barked; there was a long pause, movement at the window, a short conversation half-heard. The door opened a fraction to reveal half the face of a timid-looking chap who explained that he and his wife were renting the place from the owners, the Landmark Trust. He did not encourage discussion of the saint, and closed the door. I felt slightly miffed until I realised what an abject sight I must have been: dressed all in black, with a three-day beard, woolly hat and the lower half of my legs a very bright, crusty terracotta. I nevertheless sat on the edge of the pool where Winifred's holy waters emerged from beneath the cottage, and ate my oatcakes and cheese with as much sangfroid as I could muster. I am glad to say that Winifred's story turned out well. Her uncle, St Bueno, stuck her head back in its proper place and restored her to life. Turning his attention to the murderous suitor, one Cradoc, he cursed the man, who dropped dead on the spot. Winifred later became a nun and abbess.

Unlike those of island, coast and highland, the landscape of the Marches is not steeped in such tales. Early monuments and sacred places in the lowlands have been overwritten by the pragmatic plough and lore of farming and the claims and testimonies of secular and ecclesiastical estates. Song and legend, myth and folk culture are heard more faintly here, and the historian is not helped by a distressing lack of sources from the Early Medieval kingdom of Mercia. If there were historians in these parts of the stature of Bede, their works have been lost. But the sine wave of road and river, the tell-tale of place name and church, holy well and hilltop rampart are there to be read. And so it was that as the sun's arc declared its late afternoon passage towards the Welsh hills, I found myself walking, somewhat in a daze by now, along a suspiciously straight lane between Amesbury and the little hamlet of Ball, a few miles south of Oswestry. If I hadn't had a map I might have taken no notice. But then the road deviated from the straight to circumvent the site of a derelict, beautifully decrepit watermill; I stopped to take pictures and check my map. After this kink, the line of the lane cut back at right angles to cross its former course. A slight bump (only a car driving too quickly would have noticed it) in the tarmac betrayed the true nature of that straight line: Wat's Dyke, little brother of the grand rampart that bears the name of Mercia's greatest king, Offa.

Wat's Dyke rarely forms more than a ditch, sometimes filled with rainwater, accompanied by a modest bank; it was never conceived on remotely the same scale as its twin, four miles to the west. It belongs, archaeologists now think, to a period some little time after Offa but well within the period when Mercia and its neighbouring kingdom Powys competed for control of this frontier zone: that is to say, the eighth century. Its actual practical purpose is quite obscure—it is no Hadrian's Wall, no great defensive barrier to turn back an army; more an administrative line that says where one man's writ runs. For now it was sufficient for me to recognise that its line was taken up again by a small path through fields where farmers had, in their opportunistic way, used it as the line for a barbed-wire fence and a drainage ditch. No great monument to the Dark Ages, but it would lead me directly to Oswestry, a shower and my literary engagement.

Oswestry (originally Oswald's Tree)—*Croesoswald* in Welsh—is the grisly name that commemorates the battle in which King Oswald of Northumbria was defeated, decapitated and dismembered by his foe, Penda of Mercia, in the year 642. The head was placed on a stake as a token of prehistoric, pagan triumph. A year after the battle Oswald's brother, Oswiu, came with his warrior band to retrieve the head and arms of his brother in an equally pagan gesture of possessive defiance. Unsure which body parts he should claim, the young king was shown a sign, by a 'great bird of the crow family', who carried the martyr's arm to an ash tree (the bird in Reginald of Durham's tale is surely a raven; the ash tree a symbol of the Norse *Yggdrasil* or World Tree, from which Odin hanged himself in order to acquire the knowledge of magical runes).[18] For Bede, and in the medieval imagination, Oswald was a great English Christian king dying for the cause, his body parts and relics a famous source of miracles; but the manner of his death and retrieval carries the strongest pagan overtones.[19]

In a small, municipal, grassed and paved enclosure on the outskirts of town I came on St Oswald's well, traditionally the place where the bird dropped Oswald's arm and whence a healing spring spontaneously arose. I decided not to refill my water bag there, having a deep respect for the science of bacteriology. Above the well, curiously, is a modern bronze of an eagle grasping an arm complete with gauntlet. I wondered how the raven had become an eagle; does *nobody* read their Reginald of Durham these days?

I could not leave Oswestry without exploring its hill fort, an immense complex of earthworks just north of the town which I reached in the light of a low, golden sun so that on approach its massive ramparts, surely commissioned by a lost race of giants,

seemed to clatter like bursting Atlantic rollers onto the unsus-
pecting shores of the town. The proximity of battlefield and hill
fort has suggested to some historians that Penda, the most potent
of Mercian warlords before Offa, had a headquarters here and
that Oswald mounted a pre-emptive strike on his enemy's heartland. A recent archaeological watching brief on works near the
entrance yielded a bas-relief carving of a horse, much damaged—
a reminder, perhaps, of the value that Dark Age warlords placed
on this potent symbol of speed, power and princely virility.

Oswestry, the birthplace of Wilfred Owen, had a suitably humbling literary feel about it: slightly somnolent, easy-going, welcoming in a sort of stand-offish way. I did my thing (it was not the
potent virtue of Oswald who rescued the evening from a projec-
tor that would not communicate with a laptop, but a kind member of the audience, who fetched one from home). I slept well, in
comfort, and managed to wash some of the trail from my dirty
clothes, while outside it poured with rain all night. On the news
the story of a missing Malaysian airliner, lost incomprehensibly
in the vastness of the southern Indian Ocean, gave me a chilling
sense of fragility as I retired.

The next day, the spring equinox, when the sun rises due east
and sets due west, I made my acquaintance with Offa's Dyke, the
greatest single engineering achievement of the Early Medieval
period. Here, for once, was real walking terrain, room to stretch
the legs, enjoy the open sky and feel the undulating conveyor
belt of the land beneath my feet. From Oswestry I took lanes and
tracks west towards the hills, rising all the time through sheep
pasture and conifer plantation, all glistening after the heavy rain,
until I came onto a broad ridge which, in Offa's day, must have
given huge vistas of the mountains, valleys and kingdoms of Central Wales. At first I saw only trees; then the path opened out
and I found I was walking across what had once been Oswestry
racecourse; and for a mile or so after that path and dyke diverged

so that I was ready for a trailside snack by the time I came onto the dyke proper at Carreg-y-Big, a hill farm at a crossroads on the height of the ridge. The dyke is a grand design all right: massive 'look-at-me' bank along the east side, 'keep-out' ditch to the west; but it is the unflagging, uncompromising momentum of the beast that really impresses itself, like a boulder that will not be stopped or a crusade that marches under its own unfathomable dynamic. The dyke and I, we have the same thing in mind today, heading north across the grain of the land whose rivers drain the mountains eastwards towards the headwaters of Severn and Dee, nature's Anglo-Welsh border.

What we think of as the Welsh border is a much less coherent landscape than, say, the Whin Sill or the Tyne–Solway gap along which Hadrian's big project runs; or, for that matter, the Forth–Clyde isthmus that carries what is left of the Antonine Wall. The dyke has to cross rivers as often as it skirts mountains and surfs ridges. It does not even run from sea to sea, as King Alfred's biographer Asser claimed in the ninth century when Offa's memory was still fresh in Wales. In that sense it is more of a frontier than either of the Roman walls—an artificial line drawn in the sand between what the expansionist Mercians wanted to regard as the lands of the Angles, and the kingdom of Powys. But as the place names show, the cultural frontier is patchy and porous, even non-existent: the dyke is the legacy of a turf war, of political competition. Offa built his dyke because he could; it did not necessarily reflect historical realities, nor those of subsequent relations between England and Wales, even though, in later times, it came to be used as a convenient marker for legal jurisdiction.

Sometimes the dyke has been emasculated by the plough, or hijacked by a stream. Sometimes I was stalled by a stile or gate or the twist in a road; at these times I stopped to munch on a dried apricot or a handful of peanuts, relishing the trail's pleasures. Only once did I pass another human; and he was running, with his dog. Offa's Dyke does not have the same offensive capabilities as the Wall: it was not, I think, designed to launch punitive raids against the kings of Powys; more to remind them that Offa claimed descent from gods (or giants) whose potency legitimised his bid to dominate this landscape. He had probably not seen either of the great Roman walls unlike his predeccesor, Penda. But we do not know whose labour constructed his dyke. There is a world of difference between building a fence to keep out the neighbours and forcing the neighbours to construct a wall over which, once built, they cannot climb. Was the dyke built with tributary blood, sweat and tears? One thing is clear: no small population was co-opted as navvies. Near Chirk, whose impressive, fist-thumping castle belongs to the true Marcher lords of Edward I's late thirteenth-century campaign of oppression against Wales, I took lunchtime shelter in a plantation from a short but vicious squall which held the unpleasant promise of much colder weather. Looking at the map I saw that I had just unknowingly crossed the border, where the dyke meets the River Ceiriog. Now decidedly in Wales, I parted company from the dyke, turned north-west and came out onto the scarp which overlooks the Vale of Llangollen, all metamorphic schists and raw screes; but even in the teeth of a chilling wind the descent into the Vale, and my first sight of the Dee, was exhilarating. It was four o'clock in the afternoon. One last steep climb from the foot of Pengwern Vale up through Pen-y-coed made me realise how tired I was. With sore feet I stepped at last onto the back streets of Llangollen and crossed the river next to the railway station whence runs a small steam tourist line into the valleys. I was delighted to see the taxidermist's shop still there on the corner below the canal, where I had last seen it fifteen years earlier. In the window was a brilliant blue-flashed jay, which I mean to go back for some time. I followed the line of the canal for a mile or so out of town and came at last to the Tower campsite—a field next to red-brick Victorian farm buildings. I was the only camper, although two small caravans stood forlorn in the next field close to the showers. I pitched my small home from home, gathered the cameras and headed off up the valley to find the Pillar of Eliseg.

The Vale of Llangollen is lovely in any weather: a broad, sometimes braided river with the canal running along the contour above it, tracking its wild spoor like a hunter; the side closing in, steeply sloped and wooded, as the valley narrows to a gorge and then turns back on itself in a great loop. The way to the pillar took a detour from the gorge up the smaller valley of the River Eglwyseg, which takes the A-road through the Horseshoe Pass and which sounds suspiciously like the name for the site of an early church. Here, indeed, are the remains of the Cistercian Valle Crucis Abbey, named after the cross of which the pillar is a stunted, phallic remnant. It lies in a broad, sheltered plain, steep scarps on either side, with smooth green sheep pastures surrounding neat grey farms. I was delayed in my approach to the pillar by the sight of a poor young shepherd on a quad bike, losing control of his flock. As a dozen of them escaped onto the main road I ran to head off the traffic and eventually order was restored without damage to anything more than the lad's pride.

By now the sun was so low that the ancient Bronze Age barrow on which the pillar sits was beginning to be wreathed in shadow; so I took my shots quickly in the day's dying orange glow. I could feel the night's cold creeping up from my feet as the shadow of the ridges above sapped the last light and warmth from the air. There is, as every visitor to this famous monument knows, very little now to be read of its original inscription. Most historians accept, though, that the transcriptions made in the seventeenth century by Edward Lhuyd[20] are likely to be more or less accurate. Even then, the carving was sufficiently weathered that the full text could not be read. Essentially, it records the achievements and genealogy of kings of Powys from Cyngen, who died in Rome in

854, back into the fifth century and earlier. Cyngen's descendants traced his line not only from Gwrtheyrn (the Vortigern of the *Historia Brittonum*) but as far back as Maximus—that is to say, Magnus Maximus, the usurping Roman Emperor of the late fourth century known elsewhere in the genealogies of the Welsh kings as Maxim Gwledig. Outside the debateable value of the genealogies and the *Historia Brittonum*, the pillar is the only supporting material witness for either Vortigern or for the supposed familial links between this legendary tyrant and the imperial dynasties. Inferentially, the pillar attests to Cyngen's assertion of Powysian independence from Mercia and associates him with his famous great-grandfather Elise who, we gather, also threw off the yoke of Mercian hegemony at some time in the middle of the eighth century—just before, perhaps, the reign of King Offa.

Even the genealogies of early Welsh kings and their role as federate allies of Rome in the last days of the Empire could not keep me awake that night. I ate as large a plate of food as I could find in a pub on the north side of the river in Llangollen, watched for a few moments the roaring passage of the swollen Dee beneath the town's bridge and retreated to my sleeping bag. I woke early next morning thinking that dawn must just be breaking until I realised that the dimness of the light penetrating the canvas was due not to the hour but to a covering of snow.

Saturday 22 March was the longest day of any of my journeys, and the furthest I have ever walked in a single day. I had not planned it that way. My aim was to get to Bangor-on-Dee where I knew of campsites and a hotel, thence to Chester on the day after; and it started well enough. I scraped the now-frozen snow off the tent, dragged my gear to the shower block in freezing drizzle, packed it wet as well as I could and set off eastwards to follow the canal and river out of the mountains. I got into the groove of the trail in good time, and the towpath was as flat as a pancake. The odd barge slipped by. At Pontcysyllte I stopped to admire

Telford's and Jessop's magnificent 1805 aqueduct, hoping that at the busy canal basin which lies on its north side I would find something warming in the way of a hot drink and a pie or pastry. Nothing doing. I crossed the aqueduct on foot, feeling hungry and slightly queasy: the footway is very narrow, and on the other side of the waterway there is an unnerving unfenced drop to the river, pulsing through the gorge more than a hundred and twenty feet below.

A mile further along the canal towpath, on the south side of the Dee, I crossed the line of Offa's Dyke, invisibly, at right angles, and migrated back into Mercian territory at Pentre, a small village where road, rail, river, canal and trail meet and where the Dee swerves north on a lunatic hairpin. The names are still mostly Welsh here, another indication that the border, ethnically and culturally, does not even respect such an obvious barrier as the Dee. I negotiated the muddy, steep paths of a woodland valley, crossed the A483 on a footbridge and then took to whatever back lanes, paths and trails I could find that would keep me close to the Dee. A crossing would have been a fine thing, but the river here is unfordable and there are no bridges for many miles. Without a friendly boatman there was no crossing, especially with the river in spate. At Coed yr Allt I embarked on a muddy climb through conifer plantation and timber track, only to find a landslide blocking my way. I had to retrace my steps; and then backtrack again to find a way round. Climbing over farm walls and barbed wire fences and feeling guilty, I eventually managed to retrieve the route: by now fed up, sore from falling over a few times in slippery grime and decidedly filthy.

There was nowhere dry enough on this miserable day to sit for a bite of lunch and rest. I stopped on the slithery bank of the river opposite the Boat Inn at Erbistock (at this point I had, oddly, passed back into Wales) and wished as hard as I could that the ford marked on the map wasn't under several feet of fast-flowing water. But it was, and I walked on, noticing the first wood anemone of the year coming into its delicate, perfect white blooms. After another half hour I came out of the flood plain at Overton and walked north, smoothing out the curves of the river and heading now more or less directly for Bangor-is-y-coed, Bangor-on-Dee.

The racecourse aside—and I could see and hear from a couple of miles away that a meeting was in full swing—this Bangor's fame rests on its hosting of a profoundly important synod in the year 602 or 603. The monastery at *Bancornaburg* witnessed the convocation of British bishops and 'learned men' called to consider Augustine's call for their church to bring its practices into line with contemporary Roman orthodoxy.[21] Augustine had already met their representatives further south on the borders of the Hwicce and the West Saxons, right on the edge of the realms in which his sponsor, the Kentish King Æthelberht, might afford him authority and protection. He had pulled off a perfunctory miracle, restoring the sight of a blind man. Impressed but unconvinced, the British clergy called the synod at Bangor whose very large community—Bede told his readers that it was said to house more than two thousand monks—would make their decision and give Augustine an answer. The site cannot now be identified (I like to think it lies beneath the grandstand of the racecourse), but it must have been a substantial establishment, very likely the nearest thing to a town in all the kingdoms of the British. The bishops were reluctant to give up or change long-held traditions and must have found the admonishing words of a representative of the auld enemy, the *Saes*, offensive in the extreme. They may have thought his urbane Latin unclassical and vulgar. Even so, they agreed to consult and meet the Archbishop to debate the issues involved—effectively, to decide whether they should submit to his primacy, much as a secular lord submitted to an overking superior in arms and authority.

Before the meeting, held presumably in the same year, seven British bishops took counsel from a hermit, a very holy man much treasured for his sagacity. He told them that if Augustine came truly from God, they should obey him. But how should they know if he was God's appointed? Because he would be meek and humble, like a hermit, they were told. And how should they determine his humility? Contrive, answered the holy man, that he and his delegation should arrive first at the appointed place and time. If, when you enter, they rise to greet you, you will know he is meek and humble and truly God's messenger.

Dressed up as Bede's language is, and apocryphal as the story sounds, what this boils down to is diplomatic protocol, a matter of high sensitivity to the British. Augustine failed the test spectacularly, and in the heat of subsequent exchanges he threatened the British that if they did not accept peace from their brethren, they must expect war from their enemies. Bede tells the story with relish, for it sets the stage for the entry of the Bernician kings as righteous overlords of Britain and bringers of enlightened Roman orthodoxy even to those schismatic Britons too stupid or stubborn to accept it from the Pope's own appointed minister: as, in fact, God's army. Bede's retributive sword was not wielded until fourteen years later, by Æthelfrith—a pagan warlord. Æthelfrith, ruler of the combined Northumbrian kingdoms of Bernicia and Deira for a total of twenty-four years and the first great overking to emerge among the Northern English, slew an army of Britons at a battle some miles north of here, just outside Chester, in about 615. The story goes that he saw a large party of monks from *Bancornaburg* praying for the success of the British army, and had them put to the sword.

Bangor today is just a small village on the east bank of the Dee, site of a bridge carried by the modern A525 but surely much older in origin; but the huge sprawl of the racecourse and its temporary township were a reminder that at great gatherings Early

Medieval populations came together at central places to trade, gossip, transact social business and oil the wheels of patronage. Not much has changed. The first fairs took place at sites of cultural importance—the henges, perhaps. During the Iron Age and beyond many were held in hill forts and coincided with tribute ceremonies where renders were brought from farms in their hinterland and from further afield by subject lords. Much of that render was in the form of cattle, which are largely portable, and treasure, likewise. No doubt prize bulls and horses were shown off, admired, traded and envied, just as they were in the holding enclosures and paddocks of the race meeting that I passed on the way to Bangor.

It had been a long day. I checked my map, registering almost subliminally that the *cantref*[22] just north of Bangor was called Sesswick, which I took to mean the 'farm of the English'. I scouted the farm where I thought my campsite would be; no dice—just a small field with a caravan and a tap and no sign of life but for a barking dog. Searching the village yielded neither intelligence nor enlightenment. I went into one of the pubs and after a long, cool drink asked if they had room at the inn. No chance: not with the race meeting on. I tried the other hotel; same answer. I made my weary way back to the racecourse where a large temporary encampment of caravans and trailers offered a Dark Age solution. I found a nice sloping patch of grass, pitched my tent gratefully and was about to go in search of someone to pay when I was unceremoniously asked to leave. Not the right sort, I suppose. Dangerous to the racing classes, perhaps. I was not happy, and tempted to utter a curse against my antagonist's descendants; instead I packed the tent and left under threat of physical expulsion. I sat on the levée overlooking the liquid snake of the Dee and looked at the map. Tomorrow I wanted to be in Chester. Another twelve miles north. The day was closing in and that seemed like an awfully long way; I had already walked more than twenty-five miles. The nearest other campsite seemed to be in Eydon, two or three miles west. I trudged off along a dead straight road full of fast cars, their headlights blinding in the deepening light but barely noticing the pilgrim until they were almost on him. As I came into the village it started sleeting. The campsite, which on the map had seemed conveniently close to the village pub, had been disestablished along with the hostelry. If we were to measure civilisation by the rise or decline of inns, the present age would seem dark indeed.

Another three miles, directly north, would bring me to Wrexham and, I hoped, the surety of a bed. The wind and sleet in my face, I walked the distance on autopilot. The only hotel in the centre of town was full of drunken stag-nighters. I wandered vaguely in the direction of the station, the tourist information office being long closed, and eventually found a room at one of those mega-corporate chains whose name I refuse to remember. To their credit, they let me in, mud and all, and I was finally able to disengage the pack, shower, warm up and set to pricking the blisters that had been working at my feet most of the day. Looking at the soggy map laid out on the bed to dry, I saw that the hotel lay within yards of the line of Wat's dyke.

A night's good sleep has the most amazing restorative effect on a tired body and mind. The same goes for breakfast (all you can eat; and I did). I had given up on the idea of walking to Chester; a pity, since my route from Bangor would have taken me past the site of a great burial ground lying next to the Roman road at Heronbridge, where excavations have recovered the remains of what may have been the army defeated by Æthelfrith in the battle of 615. I decided to cut my losses and get a train; I had another professional speaking engagement to get to at Nantwich the next day, and had frankly had enough of this wet and unwelcoming trail.

I hobbled the couple of hundred yards to the station, only to find that there was no service. By now in quite sanguinary mood, I joined the queue for the replacement bus service. I dropped my pack on the ground. The gods succoured me with a small moment of serendipity. The woman in front of me in the queue, a rucksack on her back and holding the hand of a young girl, turned round. Rachel Pope, a very, very old digging pal, former student of mine and now distinguished Lecturer in European Prehistory at the University of Liverpool, was on her way to see a man about a car, with her daughter Bella. The bus trip to Chester went by in a flash of catch-up news, gossip, Dark Age shop talk and a scribbled list of sites that I simply must visit when I went to Anglesey and the Llŷn peninsula. And that is another story.

Interlude *Haltwhistle to Hotbank*

*Celia Fiennes—Highland cattle—*Aesica *fort—purpose of the Wall—*
Vindolanda writing tablets—dilation of historical time—engineers
and farmers—Beowulf's landscape

HALTWHISTLE'S HEYDAY was forged from a combination of
sheep, lead, coal and the railways. Lead, coal and water together
suggested a good place to make paint, and so the town exported
colour east and west. Now the railway carries mostly tourists
who come for the Wall and the Northumbrian landscape. An earlier intrepid traveller passed this way in the 1690s and recorded,
in her wonderfully chatty, waspish Restoration English, an
encounter with the natives of these parts:

> This Hartwhistle is a Little town, there was one Inn
> but they had noe hay nor would get none, and when my
> servants had got some Else where they were angry and
> would not Entertaine me, so I was forced to take up in a
> poor Cottage wch was open to ye Thatch and no partitions
> but hurdles plaistered. Indeed ye Loft as they Called it wch
> was over the other roomes was shelter'd but wth a hurdle;
> here I was fforced to take up my abode and ye Landlady
> brought me out her best sheetes wch serv'd to secure my
> own sheetes from her dirty blanckets, and Indeed I had her
> fine sheete to spread over ye top of the Clothes; but noe
> sleepe Could I get, they burning turff and their Chimneys

are sort of fflews or open tunnills, yt ye smoake does annoy the roomes.[23]

Sarah and I, setting out from the town one Sunday afternoon, could console ourselves with the idea that the natives look much more comfortable these days, plumes of smoke from wood and coal fires rising lazily from brick and stone chimneys as we passed by. Higher up the gorge of Haltwhistle burn (the name Haltwhistle means 'height above two streams'; and has nothing to do with steam trains), pausing to look back down on the Tyne, we encountered a herd of magnificent shaggy orange Highland cattle chomping on hay from a manger, their breath like panting locomotives. We reflected that these sympathetic creatures, peering curiously through their fringes at gawping passers-by, have no idea at all that they could savage us should they choose. They posed patiently to have their pictures taken before we moved on, crossed General Wade's military road and made a reacquaintance with *Aesica* fort on the Wall, forty-two Roman miles from the estuary of the Tyne.

Within half a mile of the fort to the south are the remains of no fewer than nine Roman camps, temporary accommodation for the legions who constructed it and the Wall sections either side. The Wall is not the product of a single build; it went through several incarnations and west of Birdoswald was originally constructed from turf. In places a wall-walk topped it; in others the thickness varies as a reflection of about-turns by military planners. Nothing new there: like Rome, the Wall adapted to reality. Over three centuries dozens of modifications and adaptations reflected local conditions and changing times. Parts of it were abandoned or overrun. For a time in the late second century the frontier stood nearly a hundred miles further north, along the Forth–Clyde isthmus. But the idea of the Wall endured, and as late as the 370s, after it had been comprehensively outflanked by Pict and Scot, it was still being reinforced and garrisoned. I suspect that one reason for its longevity, apart from its value in keeping troops busy, was that it lay just to the north of highly productive lead mines, the most northerly in the Empire. The Romans were great consumers of lead, being very fond of their plumbing, and if at times mines in Spain and elsewhere in Britannia provided the bulk of the Empire's needs, the Pennine mines never lost their value. Britain was a Roman mineral prospector's paradise. As for *Aesica*, or Great Chesters as it is called these days, its outline survives as part of a farm whose builders scavenged much of its stone; but an altar stands close to the south entrance and on it offerings of coins have been left (none of them worth nicking: they are all pennies or twopence pieces, with the odd five-pence piece glinting silver). I doubted if the gods of the Wall would bother listening to such paltry pleas for their favours.

We felt cheated by the day's weather. It had promised much when we left the house at 6.30. The sky might have been made of locally sourced lead sheets and even the magnificent view from the Whin Sill was more imagined than experienced as we trudged up and down, in and out, barely bothering to count off the milecastles and turrets. The film-strip of the Wall was beginning to look like a repeat. Looking south, the uncompromising slick grey eel of the military road rationalised our eastward trend. Sometimes the line of the *vallum* stood out even in this dismal light; beyond both, hidden by the next ridge, lay the Stanegate and the famous fort at Vindolanda where hundreds of writing tablets, dating to the first and second centuries AD, excavated in a decades-long campaign from the early 1970s, have cast a fascinating light on the lives of Roman squaddies of the decades before the Wall was conceived. Would that we had their equivalent for the centuries after Rome.

It set me thinking about the dilation of historical time. The tablets, written in ink in cursive script on folded wooden sheaves the size of postcards, record the mundane—party invitations, purchases, fort business. The mundane is, naturally, what we would most like to know about those distant epochs whose narrative is a fragmented, compressed, skewed and otherwise barely legible account of battles, royal succession and the march of ecclesiastical progress. The only equivalents of the Vindolanda tablets from the Dark Ages were retrieved from the preserving conditions of a bog in County Antrim early in the twentieth century: the Springmount tablets, texts cut with a metal stylus into wax set in yew wood sheaves bound together by a leather thong looped through holes. They are extraordinarily precious but, while they tell us something about monastic technology during the late sixth century, they do not offer any gossipy insight into monks' lives: the texts are from the Psalms.

When such detail emerges from the historical or archaeological record, it intensifies our gaze. Without Bede, who allows us to look at events from the seventh century decade by decade, sometimes year by year, we would know very little about the rise of the great kingdoms, of the conversion of their kings. His narrative spans more than a century; but try to map the events of a single year through the months and one comes unstuck: Bede's story is ruled by annual events: 'in this year'; 'at about the same time'; 'at the beginning of so-and-so's reign' are the phrases he uses to tell us when important events occurred. His own chronology was constructed from monastic annals which recorded interesting or important events in the margins of Easter calculations; and from lists of kings, so that he was able to draw events together under what are called regnal years. Such and such an event occurred in the seventh year of the reign of this or that king. When his evidence was contradictory, he became vague or fudged a compromise. We should be grateful, though: Bede was a master scholar of time: he wrote a book on it, adopted the AD form of dating and towers over his contemporaries as a true historian.[24]

Archaeologists are usually delighted if they can pin events down to within a half century. In this period pottery is found rarely and when it does turn up it is not diagnostic even of a century, let alone a decade. Roman coins stopped flowing to Britain at the end of the fourth century and it is not until the end of the seventh that they reappear; even then, not enough of them are found in the right contexts to help us with the major questions: how long was a site occupied? When did a settlement burn down? Which saint founded a church? As it happens, radiocarbon dating for the first millennium is also poorly refined: no fault of the scientists, it is just that the amount of atmospheric carbon absorbed by living things fluctuates, and in these centuries so much so that any sort of precision is difficult to achieve. In Ireland, whose bogs provide anaerobic conditions, dendrochronology occasionally comes to the rescue. The tide mill at Nendrum monastery in County Down, for example, was built in the year 619, dated precisely by the timber used in its construction. In some of our towns—London and York, for example—wood also survives in deeply stratified deposits, and can be dated. In most cases, however, while archaeology is very good at describing sequences of events—sometimes in stunning detail—those sequences often hang suspended, drifting between the generations. For the fifth and sixth centuries the problem is acute: the securely dated archaeological sites from these two hundred years barely fill the first term of an undergraduate degree; and these are precisely the years when historians are almost silent. We have the same trouble with individuals: there is a sequence to St Patrick's life—from his childhood somewhere along this Wall, perhaps, to his capture and slavery in Ireland; his wanderings and return; his Bishopric in Ireland; his confession and a letter to the soldiers of King Coroticus—but no one can agree whether these events happened in the earlier or later fifth century. Patrick floats above our timelines, in perpetual limbo.

One thinks of Roman Britain as a better recorded, chronologically tighter period; in fact, although we possess a lot of general information about emperors and governors, know much about the development of the Wall and have seen hundreds of villas and forts excavated, and although we have detailed insights into particular military campaigns, it is a striking feature of the Roman period in Britain that there was no native chronicler of those centuries: they are foggier in many respects than even the misty patches of Bede's history. Just like the Wall, which in places stands above head height and which elsewhere has disappeared, or must be located by excavation, our sense of Early Medieval time is disjointed and incomplete. The period between the end of Rome and King Alfred of Wessex is about the same as that between the accession of Henry VIII and the year of my birth.

We stopped for lunch with feet dangling over a steep drop above a small turret enjoying our cheese, oatcakes, hard-boiled eggs and coffee. At Shield on the Wall a minor road cuts through the line of the Hadrianic frontier, and to the north a cluster of very comfortable-looking houses shows that in good times sheep farming has provided a secure living, although the unseen labour of generations of farmer-engineers must have gone into draining and improving the pasture. Also unseen from here is the sinuous, contour-hugging line of a Roman aqueduct which brought water to the Wall forts in their heyday. For the next couple of miles the Wall line rises to the magnificent heights of Winshield Crags at more than a thousand feet above sea level. Here are the grand vistas of so many calendar and postcard views of the Wall in its prime, the high country of south Northumberland. The sky is big, the air limitless as the oceans. The swell of the land is like a country where Beowulf's foe, the monster Grendel, had his lair in 'wolf-fells, wind-picked moors and treacherous fen-paths'.[25]

The trail descends briefly to a gap where another small road cuts across; there is a car park where over-large vehicles disgorge wellied and gloved children and their clucking parents; the path rises steeply back to the ridge of the Whin Sill, dips down to the famous Sycamore Gap, then along a ridge that drops precipitously from a sheer cliff onto Crag Lough. Here Sarah and I stopped to watch two swans, perfectly white against the blue-black water, probing among the reeds that fringe its banks. At the evocatively named Hotbank Farm, we came down off the Wall and walked back to Haltwhistle along the Military Road.

CHAPTER THREE

Looking for Giants:
London to Sutton Hoo

GREENSTED

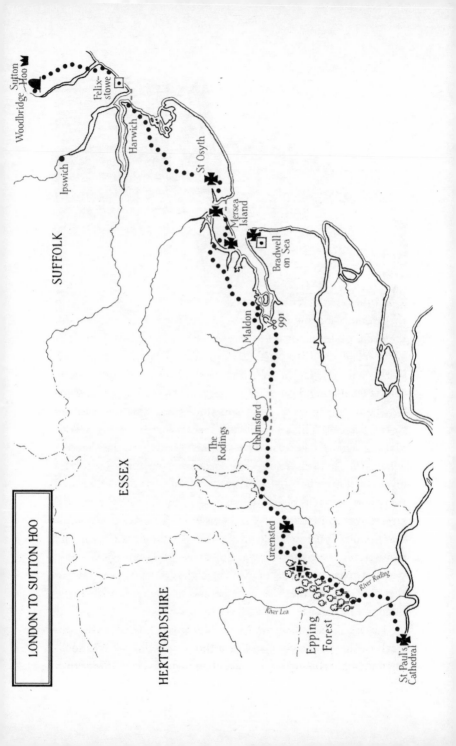

LONDON TO SUTTON HOO

Woodbridge • Sutton Hoo

Ipswich

Felix-
stowe

Harwich

St Osyth

SUFFOLK

Mersea Island

Bradwell
on Sea

Maldon
991

The
Rodings

Chelmsford

ESSEX

HERTFORDSHIRE

Greensted

Epping
Forest

River Roding

River Lea

St Paul's
Cathedral

A CIRCLE LINE TUBE from King's Cross to Cannon Street in the Monday-morning rush hour; an ascent from the bowels of the earth by escalator into a grey morning; the beating capitalist heart of the City of London: a million people dashing for work, coffee and fag in hand; taxi horns blaring. Sirens wailing, shouts emanating, high in the sky, from the scaffolding of some new henge being erected to venerate the god Sterling. Visitors to the Smoke, William Cobbett's Great Wen, Emerson's Babylon-on-Thames, have, for hundreds of years, been dazzled and appalled by the value that Londoners place on time. Turnstiles once stood at either end of Waterloo Bridge, and two hundred years ago the press of carriages along some of the city's narrow streets was as much a frustration as cars and buses are today. I don't doubt that in Roman *Londinium* pompous merchants and magistrates complained about the same things. In Bede's day, which is to say the first third of the eighth century, London was the 'chief city of the East Saxons and an emporium for many nations who came to it by land and by sea'.

I crossed the pulsing waters of the River Thames by Southwark Bridge in the company of a thousand others. I was looking for a giant somewhat younger than Bede but much older than

Adam Smith: King Alfred of Wessex, who 'restored' London in the 880s after the Viking wars. To be sure, the Dark Ages are not easy to detect on the surface of the capital. Even below ground it is a strangely obscure period in London's history. When archaeologists excavate here, 'decontaminating' the footings of future skyscraping, god-touching pillars of enterprise, they constantly encounter the marvels of the Roman city, but find much less evidence of Bede's great emporium. The layers above imperial *Londinium* lie feet deep in so-called 'dark earth', abundant evidence of the housebuilding and horticultural expertise of its East Saxon citizens; but there is little, even in the shadow of St Paul's Cathedral, that bears witness to the arrival of a bishop here in 604 or of thriving trade and public buildings. That is partly because the settlements of the post-Roman period, generally constructed of light, organic materials—wood and wattle, daub and thatch—are almost impossible to detect unless they are seen in plan, and large-scale plan at that (a lesson learned from Philip Barker's work at Wroxeter). Modern open-area excavation in rural landscapes has proved that extensive settlements existed and thrived in the post-Roman centuries. In London archaeologists rarely get the chance to open sufficiently large holes: much is seen (or not seen) in section. Even so, two hundred years after the end of the Roman empire there was probably no single functioning town in Britain; not in the sense that we understand towns, with their commercial, judicial and civic functions, their crowds and public spaces. No, not even in the Square Mile. On the Strand, one suspects, there was a *wic*[26]—*Lundenwic*—where traders from all the nations of the North Sea and Channel coast came to show their wares and barter information. There may have been royal halls here, built, like their counterparts at Wroxeter and Birdoswald, on the half-buried stone footings of a forum or bath house. But London, the medieval town, was a project of Alfred and his successors. And he did not build north of the river, but south, establishing a burgh at Southwark on the riverbank where Shake-speare's Globe would one day rise. He leased the other side to the ealdormen of the Mercians so that they might share the burden of reconstruction. There is a plaque to commemorate his vision, somewhere between Southwark Cathedral and the bridge. But in searching for it, one June morning, I had to admit defeat. Even so, it's an appropriate place to start a walk: a couple of streets away, on the other side of Borough High Street, lies the site of the old Tabard Inn, the tavern whence Chaucer's Canterbury pilgrims set out on their storytelling venture to the shrine of Thomas Becket.

I could not indulge in more than half an hour's pleasant nosing through the alleyways surrounding the cathedral or among the vaulted railway arches beneath which Borough Market, smelly and brash, survives in its unlikely urban niche. It is no coincidence that market place and cathedral precinct are so close that they might as well embrace: church and market, even before Alfred, were twin motors of the Early Medieval economy. Churches, especially those with a notable saint or a set of quality relics, attracted pilgrims and seekers of miracles; and where folk flock there is sure to be an entrepreneur ready to relieve them of their cash (or pigs, chickens, daughters or magic beans). At Southwark that relationship somehow endures with the boot, perhaps, on the other foot.

Time was short (maybe I am still a Londoner at heart) and I had miles to tread: I was bound for a more tangible monument to the Dark Ages, a ritual landscape of the dead at Sutton Hoo in Suffolk. In the City the past lies deeply buried, ephemeral and unreachable below the pavement. Somewhere along the way I hoped it would emerge into the light of day, like the Central Line. Somewhere in Essex, perhaps, land of the East Saxons, of cheap blonde jokes and petit-bourgeois bling.

Over London Bridge, then, site of the original river crossing in the Roman period, which offers a view down towards the Tower, marking the south-east corner of *Londinium*, and the Pool of London. I walked up Gracechurch Street and past the Monument, along Fenchurch Street to Aldgate. Like Southwark (meaning 'southern work or construction'), the name Aldgate is Old English in origin. The 'Old Gate' through the City wall defines a legal and cultural boundary between urban and rural, rich and poor, insider and outsider. The gate is long gone, but the sense of transition from interior to exterior is palpable. This was familiar territory for me: Whitechapel, Shoreditch, Spitalfields, where I excavated for three years in the crypt of Hawksmoor's epic baroque church disinterring wealthy parishioners from their lead coffins. I passed my driving test here too, on a miserable, snowy winter's day in 1987. At one time I used to frequent Rosa's café whose regulars included the East End artists Gilbert and George. Church, synagogue, mosque, temple and chapel claim the attentions and hopes of the faithful. There is a public library, the closing of which, surely, would be the mark of a society suffering terminal apathy. A cluster of markets clings limpet-like to the edge of the city: Petticoat Lane, Brick Lane, Whitechapel itself; and all life is here, for better or worse, richer or poorer, sick or healthy. Britain's hub is still an emporium for all the nations and, as I walked along Whitechapel Road, a millennia-old thoroughfare, I wondered if the noise and smells, the bustle, the racial and social tensions that hold this extraordinary urban orrery in perpetual, confounding, vibrant equipoise, were not as authentic a Dark Age experience as holding a handful of Anglo-Saxon earth.

The road is dead straight, pointing towards Roman Colchester like a lodestone: down the Mile End Road and past Queen Mary University; through Bow and past the church with its eponymous bells whose territory marks the birthright of the true Cockney. The church is in a sad way, marooned on a traffic island, the haunt of winos and pigeons, unnoticed by the traffic flowing on either side. Here too is a boundary: between the old, semi-real East End of Pearly kings and queens, pie-and-mash, cor-blimey honky-tonk pianos and the brash, concrete and steel of New Stratford, the Olympic Park, of the latest government attempt to rewrite the apparent inevitables of social and geographic inequality. Not much sign of the Early Medieval here; not, that is, until I negotiated my way off some megalithic tentacled roundabout—evidently erected by gods of a malign disposition—and came out on the towpath of the River Lea Navigation, the canalised, buddleia-and-graffiti fringed orphan of a once-vital waterway. The River Lea used to mark the beginning and end of the Danelaw, that area of Eastern England subdued and rendered tribute to the Viking armies of Alfred's day and whose limits were sealed by treaty between Alfred and Guthrum. Viking ships sailed all the way up the Lea to Hertford in 894 but were left stranded when the enterprising king of Wessex dammed and drained the river not far from here at Old Ford, the lowest ancient crossing point on the river. Happy to get away from the traffic, I crossed a small bridge where canal and river join at Three Mills. Here, unexpected and little known, is an authentic legacy of Dark Age history. The House Mill is the largest tide mill in the world. The current building is no more than three hundred years old; but the technology belongs to the sixth or seventh century and is distinctly monkish.

Tide mills employ sluices and a pond to trap incoming tidal water inside a dam. At high tide the sluices are shut; when the ebb reaches the level of the base of the mill wheel, another sluice is opened which directs a jet of trapped water at the wheel, which spins like a turbine. The power available to the miller is variable with the phases of moon and sun, but predictable, and the mill can be employed fours hours at a time twice a day in every month of the year regardless of drought or ice, unless the sea freezes. The technology is sophisticated—it's a delicate engineering balance between structural solidity, hydraulic refinement and the vagaries of nature. A mill overwhelmed by a fifty-year tide or a storm surge is vulnerable to sudden destruction. Over-engineered, it risks losing significant milling power. It amazes me that the medieval River Lea and its tides produced sufficient power for eight or nine mills. But the discovery that such mills were constructed and maintained in Bede's day, and that they were successfully operated for centuries, is enough to force a mental readjustment in our respect for a culture that had lost (or discarded) the knowledge to make wheel-thrown pottery and forgotten, for a while, the function of coinage. Since tide mills are unknown in the Baltic or Mediterranean, those seas not having much in the way of tides, archaeologists are forced to conclude that the presence of these turbine installations along the Atlantic fringes of Early Medieval Europe is an indigenous innovation. In Ireland, more than thirty early monasteries boasted such wonders. In England, there was a seventh-century tide mill at Ebbsfleet in Kent. Others have been found scattered through France, the Netherlands, Atlantic Spain and Portugal. They are striking evidence of the ability of religious communities to invest in the sort of capital infrastructure and engineering expertise that seeded the regrowth of commercial activity fractured, in the West at least, by the collapse of the centralised Roman command economy. The mill being shut for the day, I stopped for a few minutes and watched the grey river flow through the open sluice gates, playing to a long-established rhythm as old as the hills, and wondered, as I went on my way, how many of London's natives or visitors know what treasures lie on their doorstep.

Stratford: I stopped for a coffee and a bun in the terminal of the international high- speed railway hub that has, at least superficially, transformed this traditionally liminal, once marshy land into a European nexus. I sat next to some inter-continental commuter, they with their sleek, shiny luggage and 4G phone, oblivious of their identikit surroundings; me with my rucksack, tent and sleeping bag, writing notes in my journal and checking the map to see how I far I had yet to walk that day.

From Stratford town centre I followed the old road to Leytonstone, that uninspiring north-east London villagey township that looks like so many others: a mixture of stable and transient pavement-fronting stores and fast-food shops, council offices, banks, housing association flats, nursery schools and the odd architectural caprice. Plane trees dotted the pavements at intervals, one for every beauty parlour by my reckoning; For Sale signs and removal vans, satellite dishes and ribbons of parked cars are so familiar that their intrusiveness on life is easy to miss. Everyone was speaking on the phone or texting. London is always changing, always staying the same. It could have been Stamford Hill, Neasden, Acton or Kilburn, they are all one—and most of them have Early Medieval names, the hamlets and farms of people trying to get by, just like their modern counterparts.

Leytonstone, and my urban odyssey, ended with a large roundabout (Woden's hoopla, perhaps? The Devil's doughnut?) pierced with underpasses. Here was the A12, the modern route to Romford, Colchester and Southend; on the far side Leyton Flats, a large semi-open tract of heath and grassland, woods and ponds (the result of historical gravel extraction), the beginning of the great royal forest of Epping; behind me, the never-ending sprawl of London. For the next day and a half I walked beneath trees.

Epping Forest is owned and managed by the Corporation of London following a Parliamentary Act of 1878 which protected the rights of its verderers to collect wood for fuel, graze their cattle and set their pigs to pannage in the autumn, and which ensures continued public enjoyment of a landscape already ancient when the Norman kings decided to co-opt it for their hunting pleasure.[27] The woodsman in me felt like a child in a sweetshop: here were ancient pollarded oaks and hornbeams by the hundred and thousand: trees which had been cut at head height on a regular cycle over centuries to protect their regrowing shoots from browsing cattle and deer. Pollarded trees tend to live longer than their unmanaged counterparts. They produced straight, knot-free poles every fifteen or twenty years for monastic estates and manors across the medieval landscape of south-west Essex and, no doubt, supplied much of the capital's voracious need for charcoal. I was sorry to see that only very rarely have these traditional management practices been maintained into the present. A managed forest left to its own devices may be picturesque, but its biodiversity declines year on year; and Britain imports tens of thousands of tonnes of poor-quality charcoal annually, when it need not. Chirruping birds can be heard here, to be sure; and butterflies dangle on invisible strings in sunny glades; but there is much dense canopy and little understorey (its presence being a sign of a healthy wood); and the wildlife I saw was largely of the rat and grey squirrel variety.

In the Early Medieval centuries in autumn, winter and spring-time, the woods would have been alive not just with furry mammals, birds and insects but with woodwards and sawyers, barkers, turners, colliers and swineherds: the Dark Age agricultural economy, the construction and functioning of settlement, was dependent on the technology and labour of woodsmanship. Although I was thoroughly enjoying my woodland walk, the greenness and the botanical evidence of former management, my senses missed those tangibles that would tap me directly into a Wood Age that lasted from deep prehistory right into the nineteenth century: the sounds of axe, billhook and snuffling pig and the rasp of the turner's chisel on his pole lathe; the chocolately whiff of a charcoal kiln tended by its collier; the sappy scent of fresh cut greenwood. Nevertheless, I allowed myself to daydream for a while. Today's residents of Epping Forest still have the right to collect a faggot of dead wood every day; even if there is not much sign of them exercising their privilege. Nor did I see any trace of the cattle whose rights to graze here are enshrined in the Act of 1878.

The forest may have been here for a very long time, but it is just as dynamic a landscape as any other. It has migrated over the centuries. It used to be closer, much closer, to the City. As demand for high value land close to London grew in the Medieval period, so bites were taken out of Epping's southern and western edges. In return, more land further out, to the north and east, was brought into forest stewardship: like Tolkien's Ents, the woods are on the march, the slowest of armies.

My reverie was dramatically interrupted by the North Circular: the notorious A406 Inner London ring road that many a commuter curses daily. A concrete and steel bridge spanned the dual carriageway in a lazy parabolic arc, the dash of traffic below seen through the grill of the parapet as through prison-cell bars. The forest narrowed here—traffic droned in both ears—as the path followed the slender course of the River Ching squeezed between Chingford (of Norman Tebbit fame) and the appositely named township of Woodford to the east. Another couple of miles brought me to a small café at Queen Elizabeth's Hunting Lodge: a cool drink and a snack. Here the heath was sandy and open, picnickers and dog-walkers briefly more common than pigeons and squirrels. After that came Epping Forest proper: nearly two miles across at its widest point and rising eventually to 320 feet above sea level—not exactly Highland, but respectably undulating— the valley of the River Lea, still northbound, sloped away to the west; to the east, running parallel, the more modest River Roding which joins the Thames under the *nom de flume* Barking Creek and whose acquaintance I would make more closely over the next two days.

Walking under trees for so long induces a sort of dopey contentment in the traveller. Time and distance are distended; trees merge into a green-brown kaleidoscopic backdrop; only the very occasional dog-walker or super-keen runner offers a reminder that the twenty-first century lies within striking distance. Otherwise, I might be unwittingly trapped in a seductive sensory treadmill loop, walking but not moving, victim of my own ambulant fantasy; if I slowed down sufficiently the forest might catch up and overtake me. So much ancient European mythology is predicated on the defenceless becoming lost in the spirit- and baddie-infested woods that one expects at any time to come upon a gingerbread cottage inhabited by cast-off children or lounging, porridge-slurping bears; or the sight of a wolf devouring a poor innocent red-cloaked maiden. In the real world of the forest, nothing is quite so sinister or quite so innocent.

Hidden somewhere in Epping Forest are two Iron Age hill forts whose position along this broad ridge must have been designed to dominate the terrain on both sides and control a key route south towards the Thames—although, oddly, neither lies on the highest point of the ridge. After a certain amount of jungle-bashing I found Loughton camp, a concentric, if not circular set of double ramparts almost completely subsumed by the woods. It seems unlikely that when Loughton and its north-easterly counterpart, Ambresbury Banks, were built, they did not command views on either side—so I suspect that in the Iron Age the woodland was more open than it is today. In the eighteenth century this part of the forest was the hangout of one Dick Turpin, highwayman.

The afternoon was murky, the light poor; and one Iron Age rampart, I find, is much like another. Besides, I was tired. I had crossed London Bridge at eleven in the morning and it was now past five. Epping Forest's many paths run like braids of a river and it is easy to lose one's sense of direction; but in the end I managed to find my way out of the trees and into the small village of Debden Green, where I found my camping pitch for the first night on the trail. In keeping with the corporate spirit of the place, the site was owned and run, and very efficiently too, by Newnham Borough Council.

On a mizzly morning I went back into the gloom of the forest, picking a path that seemed to go my way—to the north-east. Hornbeam woodland was still a novelty for me: I am more used to seeing those leaves in hedges. Nor was it the original native species of the forest, for this country naturally belongs to the small-leaved lime or pry, *Tilia cordata*. It is, or was, a tree much valued by woodsmen for coppicing, since it produces good turning wood and fine charcoal and its fibres were utilised for rope-making and matting. Its flowers make for a very good honey. But there is something splendidly primeval in the muscularity of the hornbeam's trunks which, with their grey pimpled bark, reminds me of the skin of a gherkin. It is a native only of south-east England, tolerant of the shade of greater trees. The name is pure Old English, *beam* being a derivation of the Germanic *baum*, and *horn* referring to the hardness of the wood—it was traditionally used to make yokes for oxen. The leaves are like a cross between those of the beech and elm, although it is more closely related to alder and hazel. I have a suspicion that the leaves would have been used for winter fodder, as those of elm were.

Trees and woods loomed large in the minds of Early Medieval men and women. Not only did their daily lives revolve around their arboreal seasons and products; their imaginations were filled with sacred groves, ideas of the tree as gallows or cross, thoughts of ancestral spirits reincarnated, of wisdom, judgement and the World tree, *Ygdrassil*. Part, at least, of the deliberate transition from wood to stone in church architecture and monumental cross of the seventh and eighth centuries may have been propelled by the Christian church's deep mistrust of pagan veneration for trees—not just individual species like hazel, yew and rowan; but for trees associated with springs where divination was sought; for sacred groves where unnamed sacrificial rituals might be carried out. Carved wooden images, of which regrettably few survive, carried effigies of spirits or gods. The eighth-century missionary St Boniface felled one such tree, a giant oak, before the appalled gaze of German pagans and proceeded to build a timber oratory with its wood. In the first years of the Augustinian mission to England, attempts were made to burn or destroy pagan shrines, but Pope Gregory performed a spectacular U-turn in his strategic advice to the mission.

> I have decided after long deliberation about the English people, namely that the idol temples of that people should be no means be destroyed, but only the idols in them. Take holy water and sprinkle it in these shrines, build altars and place relics in them… On the day of the dedication or the festivals of the holy martyrs… let them make huts from the branches of trees around the churches which have been converted out of shrines, and let them celebrate the solemnity with religious feasts.[28]

It was not an entirely successful strategy. Well into the Medieval period churchmen still admonished each other and their congregations for indulging in suspiciously pagan practices, such as holding open-air services in the woods. Yule logs, burials with hazel or yew sprigs, Christmas trees and Maypoles all attest a stubborn attachment to our animist past. Trees and woods are deeply rooted in the European psyche.

Even Epping Forest must end (it does so with a tunnel carrying the M25 motorway beneath its roots). Around coffee time on my second morning abroad in Essex I came upon the long, straight High Street of Epping itself. Here, finally, the London Underground (now in fact an overground railway) runs out. Yes, I could have got here in less than an hour with my Oyster Card. The name Epping is early, as most names ending in *-ing* are.

Ing is Old English for 'the people of' or 'the descendants of'. In Epping's case the 'Epp' refers to the high ground of the wooded ridge; but often the *–ing* suffix was added to a personal name to indicate a clan or tribal affinity. In the year 600 my children would have been Maxings; and if I was regarded as the progenitor of a successful ruling dynasty (I fantasise), all my offspring's offspring would claim their descent as Maxings. It's a nice thought. So were coffee and a bacon roll, especially since the mizzle, now that I had emerged from the greenwood, had turned to rain—wet rain at that. I did not hurry over breakfast.

I was not quite done with trees and woods. Heading east now, I quickly found myself back under leafy boughs; and to my delight I passed through a thriving and actively managed coppice-wood of sweet chestnut, its sawtooth leaves shining brilliant grass-green in the rain. The chestnut was an introduction to Britain courtesy of Roman legions who couldn't live without their polenta or chestnut stuffing. Good for them. The nut is highly nutritious—good marching food—and the wood, which splits easily, is still used for fencing. Looking at my map in the sort of detail that comes from having no other reading material, and being intensely curious about the origins of landscapes, I already had hopes for Essex in the matter of coppicing. I saw how many 'spring' names there are scattered across the open farm-and-field countryside of this maligned county. It is true that Essex has many streams, natural springs and ponds; and hundreds of medieval farmsteads were once protected by moats, some of which survive. But 'spring' around here often means a coppice-wood—perhaps because of the habit of broadleaved trees to spring back into life once they are cut to stump level. Here are Dolman's Spring and Round Spring, Long Spring and Kettlebury Spring—each name attached to a small patch of woodland which must in the Medieval period, and probably long before, have been coppiced to produce poles, charcoal, tool handles, barrel staves, fencing and billets for

SWEET CHESTNUT

turning. With my fluorescent pen I was able to highlight dozens of them on a single sheet of the Ordnance Survey. Even in such a rich farming land as this, the rural economy spun round the axle of wood and woodsmanship.

Out into the open countryside, then: through the little village of Toot Hill, whose vernacular architecture sets the pattern for the county: white or black clapperboard walls and red ceramic-tiled roofs offset with climbing roses and hollyhocks— charming if the brashness of the in-your-face over-powered four-by-four people wagons didn't spoil the effect. The rain was becoming more assiduous; leaving the village I picked the wrong path, taking an unwelcome diversion before coming at last upon Greensted-juxta-Ongar and its famous church. Famous, because some time before the Norman Conquest (how much time is debated) a church was built here whose walls were constructed of half-round oak logs set in a horizontal sill-beam, a technique rooted in the Early Medieval period. The beam has been replaced over the centuries—it is a knowing sacrificial damp-course which can be removed and replaced without compromising the wall above—but the logs are still present along the south-west and north-west walls of the nave. Greensted, an example of what is called a 'palisade church', is a most impressive and symbolic survival of the Anglo-Saxon period, when the first churches of Columban missionaries were constructed of hewn oak 'in the Irish manner', according to Bede, before stone became the material of choice. This place is as much a shrine and site of pilgrimage for the archaeologist or woodsman as it is for Christians seeking the unaffected simplicity of an English village evensong. In the manner of many Essex churches, the tower is clinker-built, clad in wooden boards painted white, with a steeple roofed in wooden shingles; the nave and chancel roofs in orange tiles. The vernacular effect is carried up to three dormer windows. Camera out, I was able to shelter from the rain under a suitably iconic English churchyard tree: a yew, that symbol of death and everlasting life, of sacrifice and longevity.[29]

At Chipping Ongar, soaked from walking through damp undergrowth and heartily wishing that the rain would give over, I stopped for supplies and more refreshment—tea and cake, fruit, oatcakes and cheese—and paused long enough to be enraptured by a barney between two aggressive men over a parking space, oblivious to onlookers as if they were performing some sort of street theatre. The church in Ongar is flint-walled; inside (out of the rain) is a sublime hammer-beam roof. I circled the small town centre looking for its motte-and-bailey castle and just managed to catch a glimpse through dense undergrowth of a ditch and bank, much neglected.

From the back end of Ongar I dodged around the edges of a couple of fields and a sports ground, cutting downslope across the natural grain of the land until I reached the banks of a small stream. Meadow and arable fields sloped up gently on either side. The waters were fringed with hawthorn, whose creamy blush had passed, and elder, whose champagne blossoms were just beginning to scent the air seductively. Both banks were lined with pollard osier willows, the withies of which were once such an important source of material for baskets, fish-traps, fencing and shelter. The stream was sinuous, slow-moving—sluggish almost, despite the rain. Flag irises abounded. This was the River Roding which, rising at Dunmow twenty miles to the north, emerges into the Thames as Barking Creek. Many, if not most, British rivers have pre-English, Brythonic names. The native predecessor of the Roding is lost; it was renamed for the numerous settlements in this modest valley which carry the moniker of the East Saxon progenitor Hrotha, whose descendants called themselves *Hrothingas*, or Rodings. There are still eight Roding parishes, very rare survivors of a single contiguous Dark Age landholding, later variously carved up between monasteries, kings and local magnates but still somehow retaining their historical identity through fifteen centuries or so. With no trace of irony, the path that runs along the west bank of the Roding is called the Essex Way.

It is tempting to imagine the entrepreneurial Saxon, sailing across the Frisian Sea from his homeland at the base of the Jutland peninsula, navigating with a small band of warriors up the Thames and along a promising creek until the dwindling draught of the stream brought him and his two or three keels to this small patch of paradise. Tempting, yes; but what we don't know is whether these early Germanic settlers were invitees or invaders; whether they recolonised a land emptied by plague and civil war (as the British monk Gildas would have us believe); or if they came as a protection squad hired by the local British squire with his eligible daughter—and took it over by marriage rather than by force (or both), as the legends of the Kentish Chronicles suggest. Whatever the means and motives, it turned out to be a good gig. Such petty fiefdoms which historians suppose were forged in the chaos or lassitude of the fifth century merged with, or were subsumed by, larger polities during the sixth century. Many Roding equivalents made up the kingdom of the East Saxons which emerges in the pages of Bede. In Early Medieval Britain kingdoms came in all sizes, from the giants of the so-called heptarchy[30]—Northumbria, Wessex, Mercia, Sussex, East Anglia, Kent and Essex—down to much more Roding-like entities clinging to independence just long enough to be recorded in a list called the Tribal Hidage: the *Arosaetna* of the valley of the River Arrow in what is now Worcestershire; the East and West *Wixna* of the Fens; the unidentified *Færpingas* (a mere three hundred 'hides' or farms) and the *Lindisfaran*, the people of Lindsey.[31]

At Fyfield, a couple of miles upstream, drenched in that resigned, slightly warm, can't-get-any-wetter kind of way that somehow comforts, I saw the river grow wider and deeper, as if its lower reaches were a disguise, a topographical sleight of hand. I found my way to the Black Bull Inn, there being no campsite within reach, and was glad to be able to dry some of my gear, eat a hot meal (like the vehicles hereabouts, the meal was super-sized; I wondered what all the other punters had done that day to deserve theirs) and enjoy a pint of beer. The sun came out. I lanced a blistered toe and studied the map for my onward trail. Less than a month later, Fyfield and the Rodings were the object of a latter-day European invasion, the outrageous travelling circus that calls itself the Tour de France. The Tour passed through, wowed the twenty-first-century descendants of Hrotha, and rode on, in all likelihood never to return.

Wednesday was a long, hard slog, mostly on tarmac roads and then through chest-high fields of damp, sticky, stinky rape. Over-grown and unused public footpaths, ill-marked and clogged with bramble and nettle, slowed me down. More back lanes; more rain. Huge houses set in green acres, cars the size of sheds—all priv-ilege and privacy—and no one to meet by chance or talk to; no walkers of any kind. I took a guilty bus ride through the sprawl of Chelmsford (at the slightly shabby bus station, bedraggled and tending to my sore feet, I did not feel out of place) and so gained a few necessary miles as I headed east towards estuarine Essex. Yet more back lanes, a moated manor, then a busy A-road with a diamond-tipped squall dead in my face; lines of suburban semis, the southern outskirts of Maldon and endless flat square fields. I found my path between two houses (abandoned children's plastic buggies and bikes in scrappy front gardens; garage doors open to reveal more junk; cars half-parked on the pavement). More or less beyond caring, I zig-zagged through a farmyard and followed a track past a field of amiable bullocks. Ahead of me the horizon was truncated by the grey-green line of a levée, and beyond that, with a thrill that never diminishes, I caught sight of the masts of what turned out to be two Thames barges lying-to in the estuary

of the River Blackwater. I breasted the levée—this was land inundated in the terrible storm of 1953—and came out onto Southey
creek, with Northey Island before me connected to the mainland
shore by a slim, crescent causeway. On either side, milky water
mirrored a still-angry sky, although the rain seemed finally to be
easing. Wading birds browsed at the water's edge. Mudflat and
saltmarsh oozed. Behind me a cuckoo called; the nosey bullocks
in the field below nudged each other to get a better look at the
stranger. Otherwise, it was as if the day, making terms with itself,
had come to rest: all was silent and peaceful. The creeks and low
islands, the expanse of the sky and the estuary, gave the scene a
limitless quality; it was a tone-poem in grey-blue and sea green,
from the palette of Turner.

Three weeks before Whitsun, in the year 991, this was the site
of a great battle between the armies of King Æthelred II[32] and a
Norwegian warlord. A cursory note in the *Anglo-Saxon Chronicle*
recounts that in this year Ipswich was harried, that Ealdorman
Byrhtnoth was slain at Maldon and that it was decided, for the
first time, to pay the Danes off with a fabulous treasure amount-
ing to ten thousand pounds. The bulk of an epic poem describing
the engagement on this spot has come down to us. A Viking fleet,
it seems, had sailed up the Blackwater, then called the River Pant,
some ten miles inland from the open waters of the North Sea. The
king's levies tracked its progress and came to meet it two miles
south-east of Maldon—then, as now, a settlement of fishers, traders and salters. The Norwegians, under their chief Olaf Trygvasson (King of Norway 995–1000), landed on Northey Island,
directly opposite the point where I now sat mesmerised by the
timeless and ethereal magic common to those places where land,
sea and sky meet in stratified perfection.

With the causeway evidently covered at high tide, Olaf called
across the narrow strait—no more than a hundred and fifty paces
wide—challenging the English, arrayed on the bank in their

battle finery and bristling with spears in the close-press of a shield wall, to 'send treasure quickly in return for peace'. The ealdorman's reply was such as to stir the blood of his warriors.

> Byrhtnoth lifted up his voice, grasped his shield and shook his supple spear, gave forth words, angry and resolute, and made him answer: 'Hear you, sea-rover, what this folk say? For tribute they will give you spears, poisoned point and ancient sword…'[33]

The two armies faced each other, then, with slack water between them just as it seemed now: silent, perhaps, apart from the clank and chink of war-gear—straps, buckles, mail shirts and helmets; or hurling insults at each other, jeering, nerves at breaking strain and eager for battle, the smell of sweat and fear in the air. A warrior called Wulfstan was given the honour of going out to hold the passage single-handed; he it was who felled the first enemy to step onto the causeway as the tide fell, hurling his javelin and raising a cheer on the English side. Olaf then asked Byrhtnoth if he would not let his foes across, to fight in straight and fair battle. The ealdorman's pride was pricked; he assented as the line of the causeway began to emerge from the ebbing tide clad in seaweed. The enemy did not wait to cross dry shod…

> The wolves of slaughter pressed forward, they recked not for the water, that Viking host; west over Pante, over the gleaming water they came with their bucklers, the seamen came to land with their linden shields. There, ready to meet the foe, stood Byrhtnoth and his men. He bade them form the war-hedge with their shields, and hold their ranks stoutly against the foe. The battle was now at hand, and the glory that comes in strife. Now was the time when those who were doomed should fall. Clamour arose; ravens

went circling, the eagle greedy for carrion. There was a
cry upon earth.

No other Early Medieval battle site has been identified with
such precision; and apart from the levée and the draining of the
fens the landscape cannot have changed much in the intervening
eleven hundred years. It is still a place of small sailing boats, suck-
ing mud, of lapping tides and the snake-rattle of breeze through
sedge and reed, the indignant squawk of the oystercatcher and the
sham pleading 'peevit' of the lapwing. This is an Essex where the
East Saxon is still present in spirit. With not a single other living
soul in sight, I contemplated the poetic thuggery of Anglo-Saxon
warfare against this most unwarlike backdrop, picked up my pack
and walked out onto the causeway. Northey Island belongs to
the National Trust and you need permission to step on it; but
I thought I might at least take to the causeway and cross far
enough to look back at the battle site, imagining the slaughter as
Byrhtnoth's ranks began to fail, their leader cut down. The ram-
paging Vikings took the field and the glory that day.

To the north I could see the spire of a church on the skyline,
and Maldon's nestled houses looking down on its Hythe, a bris-
tle of masts along the upper reaches of the River Chelmer. From
behind me, on the island, came the diesel roar of a tractor tow-
ing a trailer loaded with hay bales for the bullocks. I stepped off
the neck of the causeway to let the farmer pass, we exchanged a
wave and he rumbled over the narrow road. I bent to scrutinise
my map. Halfway across his tyres splashed through water and I
suddenly realised that I had come here not at slack water or at the
beginning of the ebb, as I had thought, but a little before spring
high tide: the causeway was flooding as I watched. It was time to
leg it before, like Olaf's warband, I became trapped on the island,
a desert castaway in a land of tides, mud and lowering sky.

Maldon was a delight. I enjoyed a coffee and a large slice of

MALDON MARSHES

cake and eavesdropped on a fascinating conversation about someone's son home from the wars in 'the Afghan'. The quayside bustle, the jumble of traditional craft and the sheer three-dimension-
ality of the town, rising up from the water's edge in an irresistible
organic, muddled palimpsest of ages, restored the spirits, and I
went looking for my campsite tired but satisfied.

On the following day I walked along the back lanes of another
Essex; the genteel hedgerowed farmland of Margery Allingham's fictional detective Albert Campion, a mid-twentieth-cen-
tury parody of Lord Peter Wimsey. At Tolleshunt Major I passed
her house, a splendid Georgian street-fronting townhouse. In
the perfect, rustic hamlet of Salcott-cum-Virley—a reference to
early salt production—I imagined myself in a 1930s mystery set
in a vicarage. Missing my path and, perhaps, guilty of dreaming, I stopped in the churchyard for an oatcake and to consult the
map. I had come too far: to a dead end, in fact. A small sign said
'church wharf'; inadvertently I had reached another end of Essex,
where the fingers of the small Salcott Channel reach deep inland.
I rather liked the idea of a vicar having his own wharf, perhaps
supplying complicit villagers with cross-Channel contraband or
smuggling detectives out from the clutches of their pursuers.

At any rate, I had to turn back and make a large loop to achieve
that day's target. The Island of Mersea, with the sites of pre-Conquest churches at either end of its five-mile length, can only be
reached by another Dark Age causeway still called, as it probably was when built, the Strood. This causeway was constructed
in the late seventh century during the reign of King Sæbbi—a
saintly monarch—using thousands of oak piles sunk into the
mud of the Pyefleet channel. It is now hidden beneath a modern,
busy concrete roadway with a narrow footpath alongside. Mersea
might, like Maldon, have evoked the spirit of the Saxon seafarer.
Instead, it was all blue-rinse teashops and static caravans—but
it gave me a chance to get off tarmac roads and walk along its

sand-and-shingle beach accompanied by mile after mile of bright-painted beach huts. The rain of the last two days had given way to sunshine and the sea sparkled. Shading my eyes and looking south I could see the monstrous form of Bradwell nuclear power station standing megalithic on the horizon. Bradwell makes no more electricity, having outlived the Magnox reactor that powered its turbines; but they say another will rise in its place. Given the way the world is going, nuclear power doesn't seem quite so sinister these days as it did in my 1970s youth; not by comparison with environmental meltdown and rumbling Middle-East tribal conflict. Still, it's hard to like the idea.

In the second half of the third century Bradwell was part of a great late-Roman project: here was built one of the forts of the Saxon Shore—known as *Othona*—constructed to deter Germanic pirates from harrying the east and south-east coasts of Britain and upsetting its solid citizens. St Cedd, one of four remarkable evangelising Northumbrian brothers and Lindisfarne-trained, founded a church within the walls in 654; it still stands, a reminder not only of the relationship between Roman fort and early church (the fabric contains reused Roman brick and stone), but also of my inevitable inability to get to all the places I would have liked to visit. Some other time, perhaps.

The only way off the east end of Mersea island, as my camp-site-manager friend Jane informed me, was to call the ferryman at Brightlingsea on the far side of the River Colne, this being outside of the school holidays when he runs a regular service. So the next morning, at a leisurely ten o'clock, I sat on a shingle beach gulping in sunshine and fresh sea air, with dry clothes and feet, watching the boats go by and waiting for my ferryman to see me back to the mainland. I fell into conversation with two women who, having escaped their husbands by the simple expedient of stealing their campervan, were having a jolly time exploring the coastal villages of the county. Very Margery Allingham. They caught me scribbling in my diary and, thinking I might be an artist (if only), came to see what I was about. That I was a writer actually writing a book seemed to console them, and we spent a very lovely half-hour in chit-chat before I was whisked off the beach and carried over to Brightlingsea to continue my trek.

Inland again, following the south bank of St Osyth creek as far as the village of the same name. St Osyth is said to have been a granddaughter of Penda of Mercia, King Oswald's slayer. She was forced into a political marriage with King Sighere of the East Saxons but chose, like many royal women of the era, to abdicate, found a monastery and take the veil before being killed during a pirate raid at the end of the seventh century. The priory, refounded in her name after the Conquest, still boasts a gatehouse whose magnificence testifies to the one-time wealth of its canons. More interesting for me was the boatyard that lay below the bridge across the creek. A jumble of mastless barges lay high and almost dry in the mud as if their owners had no intention of them sailing again. All sorts of improvised and bespoke structures adorned these half-earthbound dwellings: small pot-plant gardens; children's swings on foredecks; miniature corrugated-iron extensions. There were ancient steam-driven cranes and winches; what looked like a conservatory clad in the vernacular style of the local houses with creosoted clapperboard, its windows shimmering in the hot sun; the chimneys of pot-bellied stoves poking through painted decks: all jumble, chaos and individuality, an antidote to the prevailing cult of exclusivity and conformity followed by much of the rest of Essex. A community of perhaps thirty or forty people lives here in attractive, slightly eccentric denial of the over-wealthy, complacent county to whose salty margins they cling.

Leaving the village I had to compete with a main road and roadworks for a few hundred yards. The traffic spat freshly laid gravel at me. A man in a low-slung Corsa didn't much like sharing the road and shouted abuse at me from his window. It was too hot for such irritations. I found my trail and crossed a prairie expanse of hedgeless fields; for once the paths were well marked, or at least visible, and some of them had been recently trodden. Out of a sea of cabbages three white monsters rose, soaring high into the deep blue sky. Built by a race of giants to tame the heavenly breath of the wind, their blades swished and thrummed through the air in an unstoppable, relentless rhythm and I wondered if some future ambulist, long after their blades had stopped turning, would attribute to them the spirits of ancient ancestors, frozen and trapped for ever like trolls turned to stone with the break of day. I felt a fleeting Don Quixote desire to tilt at these giants, but in the end we tolerated each other's presence. They got on with the business of making electricity; I headed north-east for Harwich.

Most travellers passing this way know only Parkeston Quay, the unremarkable terminal whence ferries leave for Esbjerg in Denmark or the Hook of Holland. I needed to catch a much more modest ferry that crosses the mouths of the Rivers Stour and Orwell to Felixstowe. The ancient town of Harwich—its Old English name *Herewic* means 'army camp', probably in reference to an Alfredan campaign against the Vikings—is a lively huddle of Georgian houses and pubs on a narrowing peninsula bearing traces of a formerly grander presence in Britain's naval history with its wharfs, lighthouses, Trinity House and castle. Back at the beginning of the eighteenth century, even before its heyday as an Admiralty dockyard during the Napoleonic wars, Daniel Defoe had much the same reaction to it as I did in the twenty-first. A night's stay at the Stingray Inn on Church Street convinced me of the natives' enthusiasm for beer and laughs.

On the morning of Saturday 7 June I took the passenger ferry from Harwich across the harbour and passed from the kingdom of the East Saxons into the kingdom of the East Angles. There was a strong breeze and showers periodically swept across the harbour mouth. As I sailed into Suffolk the spray in my face was part salty, part fresh, part bilgewater.

Felixstowe, whose inward-facing, unpopulated peninsula lies a mile or so across the estuary, ought to have been named after Felix, the Frankish bishop who came to help King Sigeberht underpin the Christianisation of the East Angles in the 630s. In fact the two are unconnected, the name deriving from the burgh of a thane called Filica by misassociation. The town begins as one rounds the peninsula and faces the North Sea proper: a miles-long sprawl of beaches, promenades, amusement arcades and B&Bs. The old part of Felixstowe, a down-at-heel Edwardian sea-side resort now dominated by a vast container port on the banks of the Orwell, has been partly lost to the sea. There is an even older settlement here: the village of Walton, whose church stands on the hill behind the later town. The name denotes 'farmstead of the native Britons' in Old English. Off what is now the shore, in the late third century AD, a stone fortress stood, another defence against seaborne raiders[34] and mirrored, in the late eighteenth century, by a system of Martello towers. Remnants of the fort at Walton were still visible in the seventeenth century before they were swallowed by the waves. Others survive along the Norfolk coast, in Essex (as at Bradwell), in Kent and Sussex. Several of them fostered early monasteries or churches.

You have to feel sorry for King Sigeberht. His Frankish-sounding name is a reminder that the East Anglian kings looked as much across the water for political support and inspiration as they did to the other kingdoms of the heptarchy. Sigeberht spent time across the Channel as an exile during the reign of King Rædwald (of Sutton Hoo fame), returning to claim the throne in the late 620s. His court, perhaps based at Rendlesham some miles north of here, welcomed not only the scholarly Bishop Felix but also a famous Irish holy man, St Fursa, who established a

GIANTS

△ DUNAGOIL
'glowing orangey-green
hill against the wine-dark
sea and Arran's late afternoon battleship grey'
(page 28).

▽ THE WALL
AND WHIN SILL
'it looked to us like some
immense humpbacked
prehistoric monster'
(page 141).

▷ SNOWDONIA
'The giants were there too'
(page 253).

▽ DINAS EMRYS
*'Three times his masons
and carpenters built their
ramparts, and three times
they fell down in the night'*
(page 260).

GIANTS

△ Here Lyeth...
'people came by sea from many parts to be buried at Cooley'
(page 313).

▷ All Hallows, Goodmanham
'Christian missionaries, at least the savvy ones, came bearing the promise of an upgrade, not a revolution'
(page 357).

▷▷ St Andrew's, Wroxeter
'...like the wind through woods in riot, through him the gale of life blew high' (page 68).

▽ St Martin's, Wareham
'I stopped before the creamy-white marble effigy of a great warrior'
(page 196).

ANCESTORS

ANCESTORS

△ DIN LLIGWY
'We found Din Lligwy
hidden in a copse of trees,
like some sacred grove'
(page 240).

◁ DIN LLIGWY
'Din Lligwy must have
been the settlement of an
elite family, the massive
neatness of the stone
foundations... tell of
wealth and architectural
pretension' (page 240).

RUINS

△ ROTHESAY
*'Perhaps post-Roman
Britain was a genteel,
faded seaside town of
a land'* (page 27).

▽ LYSTYN GWYN
*'It was as if the inhabitants
had vanished minutes
before, never to return'*
(page 266).

△ St German's
Cathedral
'...its dedication may be
original and pre-date
the island's ascription to
Patrick' (page 168).

▽ St Cybi's well
'...it was a rather lovely
spot, green and quiet and
perfect for a mid-morning
break; and I drank the
water' (page 268).

RUINS

ARGONAUTS

△ THE NORTH
CHANNEL
'…the sea-kingdom of
the British of Rheged'
(page 169).

▷ A DISTANT GLIMPSE
OF JURA
'It was exhilarating
sailing, utterly absorbing
of mind and body and
lived entirely in the
moment' (page 172).

△ THE RIVER FROME
AT WAREHAM
*The Great Heathen Army
made their headquarters
here in 876'* (page 195).

▽ ST PATRICK'S ISLE
*'Monks and traders, raiders
and royal fleets found the
same places convenient'*
(page 162).

ARGONAUTS

monastery in the kingdom at *Dommoc* (possibly Dunwich). The king was so taken with the idea of monastic retreat that, perhaps around 632 (while Mohammed was dying at Mecca) he gave up the kingship and entered a monastery which he had founded. Taking the tonsure became a popular way for reluctant or knack-ered kings to retire during the later seventh century. The monk's tonsure is a form of emasculation, a premature alopecia and a sign that one's testosterone-fuelled warrior inclinations have passed. In Sigeberht's case it did him little good. Under his successor, King Ecgric, East Anglia was invaded by the armies of Penda, the expansionist Mercian warlord. Bede tells us that the East Angli-ans were no match for the rapacious Penda. Poor Sigeberht, once a noted warrior, was dragged out of retirement protesting as, perhaps, time-expired sporting champions do when called on one more time by their country, and took to the battlefield under pro-test, wielding only a staff. Bede recorded grimly that he and King Ecgric were both cut down, their armies 'slain or scattered by the heathen attacks'.

Today, Felixstowe's shore is protected by great linear dumps of stone blocks which keep the town's precious sand from wash-ing away. Unlike the wooden groynes of old on which children used to climb and slip on seaweed and barnacles to peer at crus-taceans, their scale is superhuman: they do the beach and the children no favours. Nor does the sad pier, at whose entrance I passed two young women attempting to keep a plastic inflatable ice-cream stand from blowing over in the wind. Even Suffolk's hardy folk, inured to British seaside weather, had abandoned the Edwardian yellow-and-cream painted wooden promenade shel-ters in favour of inland tearooms, although I spied a group of indefatigable wet-suited swimmers plying up and down the surf for their daily endorphin fix. Felixstowe ran out, eventually, at the mouth of the River Deben, marked by the tidy bunkers and fair-ways of a links golf course, and by two Martello towers.

Here the scale was more human. The estuary is only two hundred yards wide—on the other side a red-brick mansion could be half seen, blanketed by oak woodland. In the foreground wooden groynes dipped their toes in the sheltered tideway behind a sand spit; and the blue-green sparkling water was crowded with the small sailing dinghies of a yacht club. A few hundred yards along the riverbank I came to one of those water-margin settlements that was beginning to define, for me, a Saxon coast that is the human equivalent of the foreshore rockpool: a community clinging to its marginal niche, fascinating in its detail and easily neglected in favour of open sea and rich land. Precious, therefore. Here were huddles of clinker-built sheds and workshops, shacks and jetties, beached sea- and rivercraft, populated by transient visitors and the occasional wealthy punter, but above all by a community comfortable in its diversity and shared rejection of societal norms. The crevices between building, boat, slipway, mooring and path were jammed with still lifes: coils of faded rope and rusty cable, crab and lobster creels, fish boxes, crumpled tarpaulins, tins of bright paint, trailers, discarded rigging and fluorescent plastic buoys. I found the visual mosaic irresistible.

It seems that there has always been a ferry here: how else could east-coast communities connect with each other except by water? To the modern traveller, this might seem an inconvenience, a divide; but to a seafaring and riverine people like the native British and their Anglo-Saxon antagonists, water was a thoroughfare uniting and facilitating, an artery of storytelling and trade, kin affiliation and opportunistic exploitation. I sat in the ferry café and enjoyed a coffee and a cherry scone, listening to the conversations of a dozen other diners. I had seen a sloping wooden ramp that looked sufficiently formal to be the ferry jetty, but no sign of a boat or timetable. I asked the woman behind the counter what time the ferry would leave (and if I'd have time for another scone). She smiled and told me it would leave whenever I was ready: all I had to do was go down the ferry ramp to the flag pole, pick from its slot the table-tennis-like bat taped to the end of a stick, and wave it at the other side. If he wasn't busy, the ferryman would see it and pop over. As indeed he did. Meantime I ate another scone.

An almost exactly similar arrangement must have operated here, and on a thousand other rivers and creeks, over the last two or three millennia. And on the other side? Somewhere among the sandy lowlands of Suffolk, along the north bank of the River Deben, I would find the place where the East Angles buried their mighty kings in ships. I saw no more weatherboard houses on the north side; it was all red-brick, often painted white, blue or pink with orange pantiled roofs; and now that the sun had come out decisively they made a very pretty picture against field, hedgerow and sky. This has not always been a rural idyll; not even in living memory. Seventy-eight years ago, in 1937, the first operational RADAR station was built here, close to the RAF research base at Bawdsey—the manor house I had seen from across the river. The mysterious 360-feet-high tower transmitters, as enigmatic in their day as any megalithic stone circle, were the key to intercepting Luftwaffe bombers during the Battle of Britain and became, in their turn, bombers' targets. The towers have gone; the tallest creatures in this landscape today are a more familiar sight: Scots pines, long-lived natives perfectly adapted to the sandy heathlands of south-east Suffolk and magnificent on the skyline in their deep green early-summer plumage.

I spent my last night on the trail at a campsite in the cute village of Shottisham (brick cottages, roses, white picket fences and flowery verges; an unfussy inn), kept awake by the noise of children playing and the wailing of the vicar's peacock from the nearby church. I woke at six-thirty with sunlight streaming through trees and filtering down into the tent. On a glorious blue-skied morning I had the broad, sandy heathland trail to myself. Stands of Scots pines formed the backdrop, scenting the warm air with resin. A cuckoo called. A few miles further north, taking a path off the main road to Woodbridge, I came across the National Trust sign that told me I had found my destination: Sutton Hoo, the burial place of East Anglia's kings. It is a disappointment, to be sure. Fields full of rank cabbages and pigs gave onto a flattish, grassy field that could not be less evocative of the Dark Ages. Ploughing, drainage and Second World War anti-glider trenches have taken their toll. The River Deben, and Woodbridge across the water, were invisible beyond a line of trees. The only really impressive mound to survive the depredations of time and the archaeologist's spade is a reconstruction, looking like a giant upturned bucket smoothed over with turf. Otherwise, this unique mortuary landscape of ship burials looks like so many mere tumuli. The signage was poor and the museum would not open for another ninety minutes. As so often on these journeys, I had the place to myself.

To understand the significance of Sutton Hoo, you first have to know the background. In 1938, with war looming and not long after the erection of those first giant RADAR towers, an archaeologist called Basil Brown was invited by Sutton Hoo's owner, Mrs Edith May Pretty, to investigate her intriguing-looking mounds. Three of them yielded a mix of cremations and an inhumation that seemed to have been contained in a small boat. They had been disturbed, ransacked by treasure hunters, perhaps. In 1939 Mrs Pretty commissioned Brown to open the largest and most elongated of the mounds, then supposedly standing to a height of nine feet. Oddly, despite its size, it had not been disturbed. Mound 1 yielded the most significant Anglo-Saxon treasury that Britain had, or has produced: a kingly burial complete with trappings of immense wealth and power contained in a great ship, ninety feet long, whose planks and rigging had decayed in the acid sandy soil, but whose surviving rivets perfectly mapped the grace and scale of its hull. Those treasures reside at the British Museum, much studied and admired over the decades since. In recent years the identity of the mound's inmate (no physical human remains were ever retrieved) has been pinned, by general consensus and using the dating evidence from its contents, on King Rædwald (circa 599–624) of the line of *Wuffingas*. He was not just the greatest of the kings of East Anglia, cited as a Bretwalda in later annals, but also played a significant part in the conversion story told by Bede.[35] To his court, probably at Rendlesham a few miles to the north-east, Edwin of Deira fled as a refugee in about 616. Emissaries of Edwin's rival—and brother-in-law—King Æthelfrith of Northumbria first tried to persuade, then bribe, then threaten Rædwald with destruction if he did not give up his hostage. Rædwald initially refused; then agreed but then, under pressure from his queen, decided to fight Æthelfrith instead, on a point of honour. At a great battle on the River Idle, south-east of the Roman town of *Danum* (Doncaster), he and Edwin destroyed the Northumbrian overlord and his armies. The rest is history.

Rædwald's equivocation towards Edwin was matched by his attitude towards Christianity. He was born a pagan; underwent a conversion sponsored by King Æthelberht of Kent, but was said to have kept both Christian and pagan objects in his shrine and, perhaps, to have apostatised on his deathbed. The ship burial is distinctly heathen, a real-life expression of the sentiment so movingly evoked in Beowulf's funerary rites.

> Then the lords of the wind-loving people upon a seaward slope a tomb wrought that was high and broad, to voyagers on the waves clear seen afar; and in ten days they builded the memorial of the brave in war, encompassed with a wall that the fires had left, in such most splendid wise as men of chief wisdom could contrive. In that mound they laid armlets and jewels and all such ornament as erewhile daring-hearted men had taken from the hoard...[36]

As if to reinforce that tension, among the artefacts retrieved from the burial were a pair of silver spoons, carrying monograms of Sts Peter and Paul, an enamelled bronze cauldron, perhaps of Northumbrian workmanship, in whose base is a remarkable rotating fish; a whetstone sceptre with a stag motif; and the possible remains of animals sacrificed to accompany the dead king on his journey into whatever afterlife he believed in. The iconography on the purse, the famous helmet and the great gold brooch are distinctly pagan.

That Sutton Hoo was the burial ground of the Dark Age East Anglian kings is widely accepted. Even so, I left with a sense not, perhaps, of deflation or anti-climax, but of emptiness. My expectations had been too high, the road too long. I had not been able to read it in its landscape context; it seemed, like a museum exhibit, divorced from its original environment. To bring it to life I had to imagine away a thousand years of change; I must picture those mounds in costume: bristling shields and spears clustered around a totem decked with battle standard, perhaps the skulls of dead enemies hanging there. I had to visualise a funerary feast: warrior companions, a pall of smoke, the smell of cooking meat; the sound of drunken lament.

I came back onto the main road and, crossing the bridge over the River Deben, took to the footpath that ran along its south bank. My thoughts went back to rivers and creeks and their denizens, and to the sea. The English had come by sea; Rædwald's ship had been dragged from the river up to that place on the hill; these were boat people just as the East Saxons were. Water and land, earth and sky, Christianity and paganism fed the tensions that had brought their kings here. Huge swathes of fenland separated, protected them from their Midland enemies in the north and west. They looked across the water for inspiration and support: to Scandinavia, to Kent and to Francia. They lived at the edge literally and figuratively. As I approached Woodbridge, another of those edgy communities of houseboats, small yachts, barges and assorted shore-bound clutter distracted me. This jumble of cultural treasures speaks louder to me than bare mounds in a field. It is absolutely uncontrived, artless and authentic. But, not for the first time, I had underestimated the potential for the Dark Ages to intrude on the present.

The sparkling, eddying waters of the Deben drew my eye across the river. On a rise, through a gap between trees on the far bank, the flat horizon was pimpled with the distinct shape of a mound, grass-covered, beneath which, in my mind's eye, lay the soul of Beowulf and his dragon's treasure.

Interlude   *Once Brewed to Warden Hill*

Companions—monomaniac Wall—long-distance walking—
peregrinatio—Dark Age travellers—Housesteads fort—
transhumance—Cold Comfort Farm—Warden Hill

WHEN I RESUMED my Wall journey, it had been snowing. I asked my old friend Malcolm Pallister to join me for a day's walk. Malcolm is a fellow veteran of the West Highland Way and has travelled the whole eighty-four-mile length of the Wall on foot and solo. He is a clever, thoughtful systems engineer; a Buddhist, blacksmith and musician. He fixes things: he would do rather well in the Dark Ages.

The hills, farms, loughs and lanes of the Tyne–Solway gap wore their winter coats like old bears. There is nothing new in ice and snow, storm or flood; the small death of winter is just one more rotation of the unchanging, ever-turning wheel of renewal. Spring will come. Today the light, a monochrome palette of white, grey and black, erased all but the essentials of form and line, pattern and texture. There was hardly anyone else out: we had the Wall and the hills more or less to ourselves.

We parked next to the visitors' centre at Once Brewed (there is an old inn close by called Twice Brewed, but there is no agreement on the origins of the names), clad ourselves in lurid winter gear, and struck out eastwards. I had already walked the first part of this section, the cliff above Crag Lough, with Sarah. Malcolm had, on his long march, come the other way, from the east. Neither of us had seen this landscape stripped bare to the white bone as it was now. Now I began to see Hadrian's project for what it was. The line of the Wall was visible for miles in either direction, geological in scale, timeless in extent; but minuscule against sky, hill and moor, as intangible almost as a pure mathematical line. Up here on the crags it could have no defensive function: it was superfluous. What had it all been for? Fort after milecastle after turret: ditch in front, vallum behind, the theme repeated end over end like the cycle of the year, only stopping at the wet, salty sea. To the north and on our left, we are supposed to believe, the unwashed, uncivilised Britons who, having not bought into the idea of Empire, were outside it: legally and psychologically labelled barbarian. To our right, the south, like it or not, everyone was a citizen of the Empire.

The sheer stubbornness of the enterprise struck us: a monomaniacal idea pursued beyond reasonableness, a psychosis of a project. Where Offa's Dyke spoke of real political might, of public power arrayed against a foe, of subjugation and tribute, of one people abutting another, the Wall—as opposed to the frontier, which already existed in the line of the Stanegate and its forts—now seemed like fantasy realised: a folly, a hamster wheel of engineering endurance and squaddie fatigues, designed not to keep anything out, but to show what the legions could do when they put their minds to it. It seemed to monumentalise, also, a Rome that outgrew the bold Republican ideals of its early centuries to become a bloated oligarchy. Thus the Wall was maintained, rebuilt, re-envisioned and reinvented over three hundred years for no better reason than that *it already existed*. It became the whitest of elephants; it was never, had never, been useful. At no time has it ever formed the border between races or nations. It just *was*.

These were walkers' thoughts. An earlier wanderer, an Anglo-Saxon poet, full of melancholy, weary of spirit and looking back on his lonely life, had this to say:

> The ancient works of the giants stood idle,
> Hushed without the hubbub of inhabitants.
> Then he who has brooded over these noble ruins
> And who deeply ponders this dark life,
> Wise in his mind, often remembers
> The many slaughters of the past and speaks these words:
> Where has the horse gone? Where the man? Where the
>   giver of gold?
> Where is the feasting place? And where the pleasures of
>   the hall?[37]

Long-distance walking can induce melancholy, for sure; but it is also therapeutic. Rousseau, Nietzsche, Thoreau, Rimbaud, Laurie Lee embarked on journeys of self-discovery: what Nietzsche called outdoor thinking. For pious Dark Age argonauts setting out across the wolf-prowled hills on the long straight road to Rome or dipping their oar into the icy waters of the northern seas, the models for walking heroes were to be found in the New Testament and in the lives of the Desert Fathers. The ideal was *peregrinatio:* the journey abroad in imitation of the Temptation of Christ in the desert, as a voluntary exile and perpetual stranger in a foreign land. Christ had wandered in the baking wastes of Jordan, starving and alone, for forty days. For some churchmen, those who believed in the communal endeavour of the cenobitic monastery, such wanderings were an indulgence, a distraction tending towards fanaticism. For others, the voyage into the dangerous, uncharted, un-Latinate unknown was a trial of faith beyond the edge of knowledge—and therefore of high virtue. Pilgrims, on the other hand, knew where they were going, even if they had a very imperfect idea of what the journey or the destination—Rome, Jerusalem, Tours—would be like. Some made the journey to Rome more than once: the seventh-century bishop St Wilfrid thrice; Benedict Biscop (founder of the priory of Monkwearmouth-Jarrow) no fewer than five times. Alfred of Wessex was taken to Rome twice as a mere child; many kings made pilgrimage their retirement; there were those who set out and never reached the promised land.

There were also those who journeyed for more earthbound reasons: to flee persecution or escape justice; to conduct their lord's business; to visit friends or to carry messages and gifts; to trade and to fight. Pragmatism and superstition governed the time of departure, the route, the method of travel. Bishop Aidan, the first abbot of Lindisfarne from 635 to 651, astonished and offended King Oswine of Deira, his patron, when he gave away to a pauper the king's gift of a horse. The king understood bishops most easily in the context of a warrior elite, to whose caste they belonged; the horse reflected their dignity, rank, honour. Aidan eschewed these and walked. The journey of Abbot Uttar of Gateshead to retrieve a princess and bride-to-be from Kent was so risky a venture (physically and probably politically) that he sought approbation and blessing from Aidan, and was comforted by the gift of a phial of holy oil which he used to quell a storm in the North Sea. Travellers, especially pagans, had superstitions about crossroads and, in particular, places where three roads met. Auguries and omens were physical manifestations of the pre-Christian imagination; rituals were performed before setting out and after arriving safely. Journeys, by their very nature extraordinary and ambitious enterprises, were attended by miracles and portents. Age was no barrier to travel. The monk Theodore, a native of Tarsus in Asia Minor, was sixty-six when he was chosen by Pope Vitalian to travel to England to become Archbishop of Canterbury in 668. His likely route was overland, via a string of monasteries across northern Italy and Francia. The journey did him no harm: he held the metropolitan see for more than twenty years until his death in 690.

The most-travelled men and women of the Early Medieval

period were kings and queens. Kings must visit their royal estates in turn to receive tribute and be fed; to dispense justice, gifts and land; to consult their wise men. And every year it was their duty to gather a host and go to war against their enemies for glory, treasure and the pride of their folk. After the later seventh century it became fashionable, as an alternative to death in battle, to abdicate and set out for Rome to retire there, as did Cædwalla of Wessex in about 688, his successor, Ine, in 728 and Cyngen of Powys in 855.

Malcolm and I lunched at the edge of a copse of Scots pines that straddles the Wall south of Greenlee Lough. Malcolm's Wall walk had been something of a personal struggle: walking alone can take you to places you didn't know existed or perhaps did not want to visit. In company the trail is all about camaraderie, companionable silence, satisfaction at day's end; anecdotes. A walk with each different sort of companion is an adventure in adaptability, in shared pace and perspective; two people notice more than one.

We passed through the fort at Housesteads, all neat, square buildings and ordered space; one of the best-preserved forts along the Wall and, like Vindolanda and Birdoswald, the site of a late-fourth-century structure identified from its apsidal ground plan as a church. We crossed the line of the Pennine Way. It occurred to me to wonder how many transhumant paths and droveways must have been severed or diverted, no doubt at the cost of a toll, during the Wall's construction and lifetime. We cannot know whether, as with today's motorway projects, accommodation was made for those aboriginal farmers whose traditional lands and routes were cut in half by the onward march of the Wall, or whether the natives had to like it or lump it. No doubt local deals were cut for backhanders; no doubt grudges were borne. Injustice has a long memory.

At Sewingshields the high line of the crags ends; looking back at the rollercoaster track of Wall and Whin Sill in low, creamy sunlight, it looked to us like some immense humpbacked prehistoric monster, a kelpie, diving and surfacing, broaching the unfathomable waters of the ages. The country east of here is increasingly benign, less confrontational: now Wall, military road and vallum join together in a strip several hundred yards wide, three plough furrows racing eastwards across the Northumbrian uplands. It struck both of us how useful a plume of smoke might have been for earlier travellers: in the stiller air of the Tyne Valley a monstrous exhalation of steam is constantly emitted by a locally notorious chipboard factory; it had been our unspoken marker all day.

A little after the fort of *Broccolita*, where the winter-flooded remains of a Mithraic temple looked like nothing so much as a Christian holy well and shrine, we left the Wall and stepped out across country, heading south-east on the 'Roman' side. The path became a lane. We passed a very odd little establishment, a Cold

BROCCOLITA

Comfort Farm, shabby and slightly sinister with lines of abandoned rusting vehicles, filthy net curtains in the windows hiding goodness knows what domestic history. These are the backwoods, the neglected corners of the landscape that you don't come across in a car; they are the secret discoveries of the trail, sometimes to be investigated; sometimes to be passed swiftly by.

We rounded the fence of a defunct quarry that for centuries chewed at the hill overlooking the village of Fourstones but which now bristles with conifers. We turned east to join a back road that would take us south towards the Tyne Valley and that plume of steam. The weather had been kind to us all day: piercingly cold but bright and more or less dry; now fine snow drifted in veils across the hills and hurried us on. The light was failing and an indistinct twilight gave notice of the day's end. We crossed, at right angles, the line of the Stanegate, no more than a mile west of the River North Tyne whose dramatic confluence with its parent valley was our destination. On a path running along the lower contours of Warden Hill I left Malcolm with his pack and flask and trotted up to the summit, at something like six hundred feet: Warden Hill, a domed expanse of pasture that gives views right along the Tyne Valley both ways, and which, as its name suggests, guards the confluence of the two rivers, commands the passage of people and animals heading east, west or north. The Iron Age hill fort whose grassy ramparts survive, truncated, for the sheep to graze on, has periodically been investigated by archaeologists. There is evidence that it was occupied during the Roman period; like the Wrekin, it must have been slighted[38] by the legions, a much too dangerous strategic objective to be allowed to function as a tribal headquarters. But I could still see chunks of masonry poking out from sheep scrapes, and the distinct outlines of roundhouses visible even in this failing light. I rather like to think that it was reoccupied after the legions left; and a new airborne laser (known as LiDAR)[39] survey shows some tantalising shapes lying just beneath the turf. As the last of the light drained away, I paused in the centre of the hill fort long enough to see lights from the villages and roads of the Tyne Valley pinprick my eyeline, evoking a strong sense of time's inexorable passage and the unchanging realities of power, chiselled on our land in the straight line and the circle.

CHAPTER FOUR

Eda Frandsen:
Falmouth to Mallaig

John the Almsgiver—Tin Isles—Falmouth—Eda Frandsen—
fellow crew members—Scilly Isles—night sailing—Dark Age
argonauts—Isle of Man—heaving-to—pilots and anchorages—
Peel and St Patrick's Isle—navigation—wics—Atlantic lands—
Irish Sea and Solway Firth—North Channel—Vikings—
a blast—Crinan and Dunadd—Corryvreckan—trade and intellect—
Tobermory—Inverie and Old Forge Inn—parting

THERE IS AN unlikely story, preserved in an Eastern Mediterranean hagiography from the time of King Rædwald, that tells of a sea voyage from those parts to the Atlantic west coast. John the Almsgiver, patriarch of Alexandria, took pity on a sea captain who, through ill luck and the 'sinful acquisition of money', had fallen on hard times. John gave him five pounds of gold with which he bought a cargo; but his ship was wrecked off the great lighthouse, Pharos. The captain again applied to the patriarch and, admonishing the man to be more careful with his and God's money, John gave him ten pounds to purchase another cargo. Again, his ship was wrecked. You would have thought that each man would have learned his lesson; but the patriarch, trusting in God, now gave the captain a swift-sailing vessel belonging to the Holy Church and carrying twenty thousand bushels of corn. After many days' sailing, during which violent winds beset the ship, the captain lost his way and landed in the 'Islands' [sic] of Britain at the edge of the world. Here, it seems, the people were in the grip of a terrible famine. The captain, with enlightened self-interest, took a shipment of tin from them in return for his corn and then, returning to the Mediterranean and stopping off at an African port, found that his cargo now consisted of the finest silver. This tale of the power of the Christian god in protecting his chosen sons from the perils of fate and ensuring that the patriarch's precious assets and trust had been wisely invested, almost prefigures Calvinism in its depiction of the salvation of the elect.

Whatever one thinks of such stories its credibility, or at least the non-miraculous part of it, rests on a supposition that the famine-afflicted land must have been the south-west peninsula of West Wealas—Cornwall—which was rich in deposits of tin ore; and that Alexandrians knew of it. Britain and Ireland were famed prehistorically for their deposits of gold, silver, copper and tin, the latter two metals highly valued as the constituents of the alloy bronze. That reputation evidently survived into the Early Medieval period and provided one incentive for entrepreneurial, or lucky, merchants to come to these parts even after the collapse of the Western Empire. Other texts show that the Atlantic lands were also famous for furs and hunting dogs, for salt deposits and for the slaves produced by decades of conflict between warring tribes. Adomnán, Colmcille's hagiographer, told a story of Gaulish[40] sea captains arriving at the *caput regionis*, probably Dunadd, as if it was the sort of thing that was expected to happen now and then; and Bede recounts the famous arrival on Iona of a bishop, Arculf, who had been to the Holy Land. His Ionan host (no less than Abbot Adomnán himself) wrote an account drawn from his interviews with Arculf, called *de locis sanctis*—'On the holy places'. In the 690s he took a copy as a gift to the scholarly King Aldfrith of Northumbria; it was much copied and adapted (by Bede among others) and the work survives in several manuscripts.

Many an Irish or English monk travelled to and from the Continent in the seventh and eighth centuries when the universal language and culture of the Christian Church fomented an intellectual network across Western Europe in the face of barbarian invasion and economic collapse just as, to the east, Islam was building the first caliphate. In recent decades archaeologists have been busy retrieving the material evidence for these contacts in the ephemera of pottery sherds, metalwork and glass fragments and in the material transmission of ideas—of art and inscription, technology and literature.

In April 2014, in Falmouth harbour, Sarah and I stepped aboard *Eda Frandsen*, a fifty-five-foot 1930s Danish gaff cutter, for a voyage across the same waters that Arculf and many other Dark Age argonauts had sailed a millennium and a half ago. Our destination was Mallaig, on the north-west coast of Scotland, where *Eda* is based for the summer season cruising the Hebrides. Our route lay in the hands of the wind and tides and of skipper James Mackenzie.

The gaff cutter is one of the most beautiful sailing boats, adapted to the rigours of offshore fishing but sufficiently light-footed for the demands of coastal waters. *Eda* has a single mast stepped amidships bearing a gaff mainsail: that is, its upper edge is held stiff by a boom, the gaff, which juts out behind the mast at an angle of about forty-five degrees. Forward, she carries jib, foresail and staysail, while the gaff can be extended with its own distinctive triangular topsail. *Eda*'s gaff was an earthy, deep orangey-brown weather-bleached and patched canvas; the other sails a rich clotted cream. When we boarded her she was in harbour trim, the gaff lashed to the main boom, the other sails in their seagoing bags. The sky was a crisp blue flecked with white cloud, the waters of the harbour ruffled only by a light wind. *Eda* rocked very easily on her mooring with a seductive creaking of ropes and the even more reassuring sound of a kettle boiling. The welcome provided by the standing crew—James, mate Melissa Williams and cook Chlöe Gillat—was all good cheer, tea and scones with fresh cream and jam. We introduced ourselves to the rest of the crew: Paul Rowan, a local who sails whenever he can (and oddly enough an old shipmate of Tony Wilmott, the excavator of Bird-oswald); Georgia Witchell, who skippers her own boat in these parts; Rolf Winzeler, a Swiss border guard and square-rigger enthusiast; Frank Herrity, a retired psychiatric nurse; and Alexandra (Alex) Goodman, another local sailor who runs a small inshore boat.

We stowed our gear forward in a space on the port side just large enough for two tight bunks and a double locker where the bluff curve of the bows sweeps in from amidships. My space on the top bunk was about the same size as my one-man tent: sufficiently snug that I banged my knees on the deck planks overhead whenever I turned over. It had a small electric light for reading,

EDA FRANDSEN

although I don't suppose I ever read more than about half a page before falling asleep in the entire nine-day voyage.

Opposite us to starboard, on the other side of the forward gangway and hatch and the anchor locker set tight in the bows, lay another two bunks. Beneath the gangway and aft of our bunks were the two heads with loos and shower combined so that the effect was something like astronauts must experience on space-station duties. After a day or so I found that, even in a moderate swell, I was able to wedge my head against the ceiling, rotate about a point and shut myself in, conducting the necessaries without crashing against the walls. There was no great privacy about toilet operations: the pump that flushed them into a tank was electric, and noisy; in the middle of the night you won no friends at all.

Aft of the heads lay the saloon: just large enough for the ten of us to sit lined up five on either side with our backs against padded benches and our knees pressed against the table—all hidden lockers, fridges and fold-out extensions, so that once we were all seated there was no escape, no musical chairs. Everything was varnished wooden perfection. The table was mounted around the mainmast and glass-and-cup holders circumnavigated it in a nautically efficient way—nothing could fall out of its place except in a really big blow. Plates and cutlery were similarly confined behind bungee cords and retaining battens. At night the saloon was lit by an electric lantern, slung from the ceiling alongside an ocean-going stuffed toy parrot. Forward of the saloon to starboard, the matching space to the heads, was the galley: a small miracle of efficiency—Chlöe's preserve except during washing-up duties. I have lived in some small spaces, but I couldn't even stand upright in the galley, let alone turn around. At the rear of the saloon was the foot of the main gangway and hatch; either side and aft of that were more bunks for the guest crew.

We made a short crossing of the harbour on Saturday evening, anchoring off St Just in Carrick Roads as the sun dipped low and set a little north of west. Falmouth harbour and the Roads are whiskered with green woods below lush pastures—dairy country. But not far away are the remains of the mines that drew merchants here from across Europe when Britain was known as the Tin Islands. We had our safety briefing (don't fall off the boat or get clouted by the main boom) and James talked us through some of our route options, asking if we had any thoughts on places we would like to see. I had a list: a gazetteer of Dark Age emporia, royal and monastic sites whose archaeology I knew; some of which, like Dunadd, we had recently visited. But I knew, as the realistic pilgrims and merchants of those centuries knew, that such voyages are essentially opportunistic and in experiencing for myself the vagaries, happy chances and capricious fates that rule the lives of voyagers at sea, I surrendered my fortunes to the joint enterprise. I gave the skipper the list anyway.

On Easter Sunday we sailed for the Scillies: due south until we weathered the rocks known as the Manacles (*Carn du* in Cornish)—the site of many a wreck—at a healthy distance; then south-west to round Black Head before the loom of the Lizard's green cliffs appeared to starboard. In good weather the Scillies are a day's sail from Falmouth. By good weather I mean good sailing weather; not so good, perhaps, for those who need a little time to find their sea legs. We lost a few below deck on a very lumpy Channel that bore traces of contrary Atlantic winds and the opposing northerly that set in behind us. It was a blast. I had last seen Falmouth in 2005 when, during the bicentenary commemoration of the Battle of Trafalgar, I crewed on the square-rigged barque *Lord Nelson* from Cadiz, carrying a copy of Admiral Collingwood's immortal dispatch with its dramatically poignant account of Nelson's death and the defeat of the combined French and Spanish fleet. From square-rigger to gaff cutter is a huge drop in scale—*Eda*'s freeboard at the taffrail is not much more than eighteen inches—but being so close to the water, and on such a weatherly and beautiful boat, was perfectly exhilarating; like swapping a Land Rover for a toboggan.

I was given the helm for the two-hour passage around the Lizard and Wolf Rock and the dimly viewed Land's End, grey skies pressing down overhead and white horses galloping along the Channel before and behind us. With the wind at a steady force six, we knocked along at a very respectable eight knots and made landfall late in the afternoon—a twelve-hour, sixty-mile passage. We anchored in the tight, rocky bay of Porth Cressan off St Mary's, the perfect shelter in a northerly wind. It was raining and the process of stripping off layers of waterproof clothing in the confines below decks farcical. It had been a tiring first day; we were cold. But the craic was good and a beef stew with mashed potatoes restored us. Some miraculous chocolate confection followed and we shared a bottle of wine and a dram. Only Sarah had not sailed much before; the others were all sea-dogs. Melissa crewed on the Clipper Round the World race and survived a dismasting in the Pacific, so she has seen a thing or two. James is a veteran of Atlantic crossings; he is also a boat builder and a thoroughgoing seaman, who loves getting the most out of his boat and whose veins run with salt. That first night we slept right through, barely noticing a considerate but not very discreet operation when skipper and mate weighed anchor and motored *Eda* round to Hugh Town as the wind veered easterly. We woke with a view of the Scillies' main harbour and of the archipelago of small islands to north and west that bring thousands of tourists here in the summer for an easy-going, nostalgic holiday. Small boats filled the grey bay, pricked with fluorescent orange buoys and alive with the sound of clanking halyards and cries of seabirds out on the scrounge.

In the early Roman period the islands were still a single land mass; rising sea levels created the islet landscape we see now. A sense of detachment from the real world is palpable. The Scillies have, charmingly, not caught up with the twenty-first century. Their natives ride bicycles. We saw a woman driving a 2CV with an article of furniture poking through the roof. The pace is slow, the scale intimate. Red telephone boxes look as though they might be used occasionally. Cornish, a dialect of Brythonic, seems to have died out here late in the Medieval period.

I would have liked to make it to St Helen's, almost the most northerly of the islands and right on the fringes of this semi-submerged Atlantis. An Early Christian oratory stood there, with a seventh- or eighth-century chapel and a cluster of monks' cells associated with St Elidius. It is the very ideal of the desert island, the perfect location for a contemplative life on the edge of the world. Intriguingly, the chapel is reported to have contained an altar similar in construction to that at St Ninian's Point on Bute, where we had camped the previous autumn. After Rome's withdrawal the islands were busy with maritime traffic, from the Mediterranean and especially from Francia. Tin ingots have been found here and although several of the islands have saintly connections (not least St Samson, which we could see across the harbour from Hugh Town), many of the material remains are distinctly secular, even domestic: E-ware[41] cooking vessels, for example, of the sort found at Dunadd and many other sites along the Irish seaboard. The most recent review of evidence for Continental trade with the Atlantic West, by Ewan Campbell, suggests that the Scillies were an important stopping-off point for European merchants on their way up the Bristol Channel and the Irish Sea; that the natives actively encouraged them by providing shelter and accommodation. Merchants may have stationed themselves here during the summer months. Looking at the charts of these waters it is easy to see how central the Scillies were to the shipping lanes, especially in an era when passages were made by short hops rather than long ocean-going routes out of sight of land. But even if the Scillies were busy in the Dark Ages, those monks seeking solitude and the contemplative life had fifty or so of the now-uninhabited islands set in the shallow, sandy jade waters of the Atlantic's eastern edge to choose from.

The tides were against both a visit to St Helen's and my plan of exploring St Mary's for its prehistoric field systems, cairns and Dark Age settlements. It was as much as we could manage to visit the small, crammed museum, stroll among the four-square granite houses, taking in the succulent and semi-tropical plants flourishing in the mild Oceanic climate (in Northumberland spring buds were only just appearing) and join a couple of our fellow crew members for a coffee, before Melissa whisked us away in *Eda*'s dinghy to her anchorage. After that first full day's passage since her winter makeover, skipper and mate had shaken a few things down on board: tightened lashings, checked blocks and bitts and generally given *Eda* a pit stop before the next leg. Even shorn of her sails she made a striking silhouette against a sky that had begun to brighten after the rain and murk. Her prow is high, in common with fishing boats all over the world; her bowsprit long to give maximum sail area for the single mast. Tourist ferries came and went past us as we readied for sea, with envious looks from those dreaming vicarious dreams of blue-water sailing ahead.

The skipper had plans for a two-day passage to the Isle of Man that meant sailing watch-on-watch overnight. We caught the afternoon tide on Monday and cruised north on a desultory breeze coming over the starboard beam. We were formed into two watches: me, Sarah and Rolf in Melissa's watch; Paul, Frank and Alex under Georgia's supervisory eye. From the helm, an idiosyncratic arrangement like a cowboy saddle with the wheel before it, you could see the skipper below with his charts and AIS system—satnav for sailors—tracking tides and other shipping and calculating our speed through the water and over the ground.

Unless there was an emergency or a need to heave-to to gain or lose canvas, the watch on deck sat four-hour shifts on and off around the clock. In line with the traditional double-watch system, two watches of two hours each (the so-called 'dog-watches') began at noon, so that every twenty-four hours the shift pattern alternated. It meant that nobody got the midnight or four a.m. shift two days running. Even so, with only four hours off, the body had to get to grips with the rhythms of the shift pattern pretty quickly.

Sarah was not wholly gracious the first time she was tumbled out of her bunk at midnight; but at least, that first night, the sea was calm. It was not so easy in anything like a rough sea, piling onto a deck sloping at thirty degrees with waves washing through the gunwhales. Getting clothed took a good fifteen minutes in the dark and longer in poor weather: thermals, lined trousers, warm fleece; then oilskins and wellies, lifejacket and harness, all clips and trailing belts, clumsy cold fingers and heads banging against bulkheads. Then a very hurried cup of hot tea gulped down; and maybe a biscuit or a bun. You stumbled up on deck in the pitch black, disoriented and grumpy, grabbed something solid to stabilise yourself against the boat's corkscrew pitch and yaw, clipped the safety harness onto one of the jack stays that ran aft along the deck, and went to relieve the knackered watch huddled around the wheel or sitting backs to the taffrail with senses overwhelmed. Anyone going overboard in these conditions was unlikely to be found very quickly. But it is surprising how soon one gets used to it; how quickly the routine assumes an ever-present reality that has no future and no past. You exist entirely in the moment. Minutes at the wheel become hours; the odd conversation breaks out now and then, or the skipper pokes his head up to see how the wind has changed; a reef might be taken in at three in the morning; an adjustment to the bearing for a fishing fleet to be avoided; then a change to our course of 010 degrees as we

BITTS

headed into the black expanse of the Atlantic, Cornwall now far to the south-east, the coast of County Cork eighty miles off to the north-west. The sea is a giant; we were mere nothings in a horizon of endless night and limitless, lightless depths.

I don't know any other Swiss border guards, but I imagine them to be quite a straight-laced lot. Not so Rolf, a man with a face like a bearded teddy bear who relished every single moment at sea in the companionship of others. I hardly ever caught him without a smile. He was handy on a rope, so that he and I often formed the sweating partnership on sheet or halyard, hauling while others tailed the rope tight against its belaying pin. Not that there was any gender division on the boat: Melissa was an extremely handy and powerful girl, tough and strong, endlessly patient and unconsciously witty. Sarah, a nurse, is not shy when it comes to shifting heavy weights. We made a good team.

In the dead of night, in those moments after going below from such a watch, shedding all the wet gear and climbing into the bunk in an adrenalin daze, the gurgle of water against the hull, inches from my head, the occasional slamming of the bows into the surf and the clanking of block or anchor chain: these were lullabies, seductive, pulling mind and body down into the arms of sleep.

During that first full night at sea we passed through the ranks of north Cornwall's fishing fleet, their navigation lights a shifting constellation. Tuesday 23 April dawned with *Eda* motoring, appropriately, through St George's Channel in a milky flat calm. We were on watch from eight a.m., our breakfast eaten on deck. The sea was for the most part as empty as the sky. Puffins, guillemots and shearwaters, an adventurous warbler far from land and a curious seal were our only companions. A few promising gusts of wind died without a whimper; the jib hung limp and the skipper, bored, had us sewing whips onto a new set of reefs for the mainsail. Chlöe brought tea and biscuits on deck, looked around at the blank canvas (she is an artist, among other things) and disappeared below. The galley skylight opened and interesting smells wafted aft, torturing us. The skipper, still bored, went below and cleaned the heads—not many skippers take that unenviable chore on. Then he bled the radiators; he was really bored. At twelve our watch passed seamlessly into the hands of the starboard crew as we drew level with the Smalls lighthouse on its isolated rock twenty miles or so off St David's in Pembrokeshire. Wales's patron saint, unlike England's (St George was a Palestinian), was born in the country that venerates him, around the year 500. An opponent of the prevailing Pelagian heresy (see note 42), he founded monasteries, became archbishop by popular acclaim and established a hard-line ascetic rule. He is an exemplar of the pure virtues of the Desert Fathers, coming from quite a different tradition to George, a martyred Roman soldier of the late third century in the decades of persecution before Christianity was officially tolerated.

Some time during the second dog-watch, an east-south-east breeze first teased and then caressed the mainsail, which rippled with pleasure like a cat being stroked. James, still bored, had us hoist a staysail and rigged it with the boat's spare boom to starboard while the mainsail was braced to port, like a goose wing, and in this unlikely rig we pootled along at three knots, with a knot of tide helping us along. By the time we came back on watch at eight it was about dark; the wind had got up and the sky was a duvet of cloud.

Those next two watches, separated by fitful dozing, fully clothed, on the bunk, were so intense—black sea all around, waves piling up under the stern propelling us north at a crazy speed; anxious looks at the sails in case we carried too much canvas; porpoises zipping beside and beneath the bows and cutting the surface like tracer fire; no stars visible so that steering was by the seat of the pants, responding only to the swinging compass needle and the feel of wheel against current—that later, pooling the watch's collective memory, we could remember practically nothing except the blur and buzz. The only other time that has happened to me was during the first week on Corsica's alpine GR20 trail, whose narrative is fragmented, discontinuous, images lying curled and chaotic on the cutting-room floor of memory.

We gybed across Cardigan Bay all night, taking short turns on the wheel and watching and feeling the boat's excitement as the wind rose again: a rocky night, cold, wet and sensationally alive. James came on deck at some unremembered time and we took the topsail in to ease *Eda*'s frantic capers. The odd celestial sparkle appeared, tantalising us, and I remember staring manically at the Pole Star for an hour or so while I was at the helm, trying to keep it in an eyeline triangle between the tip of the mainmast and the starboard shrouds, ignoring the compass's lurching and letting the wheel pass through my hands almost without conscious thought. Steering is a pure art, subliminal. And the relationship between helmsman or walker and Polaris is as old as the ages of man. The empirical cycles of day, month, season and year are rocks to which we moor ourselves gratefully; and at times it seems as though we can still hold the hands of those who have gone before in an unbroken chain of cultural adventure. At midnight we slunk below with Bardsey Island, off the tip of the Llŷn peninsula, twenty or thirty miles away to the north-east.

At four, with no sign of dawn yet, we were back on deck, all clumsy from the motion: *Eda* still heading more or less dead north with the lights of Holyhead to starboard and a succession of dazzling firework-display light shows from car ferries crossing to and fro before us. Dublin lay thirty miles or so to the west—a purple glow on the horizon. Now the tide was with us we cruised over the ground, some three hundred feet beneath, at almost nine knots, ten miles every hour. A short orange burst of low sun at dawn to the west, then the cloud closed in again and we careered on. With first light it became a little easier to steer and to move about on deck; just before we were due to go below, the off-watch emerged (we had hardly seen them in two days) and for forty minutes nine of us cluttered the decks hauling on ropes: we hove-to and swapped the large jib for a smaller sail so that *Eda* would not plunge her forefoot down so much, wasting the wind and making her helm sluggish. James was the all-seeing, all-thinking conductor, barking orders when someone was about to come a cropper but always patient and always wanting us to understand why we were doing what we were doing.

Heaving-to is one of those counter-intuitive seagoing manoeuvres that landlubbers (among whom I count myself) find it hard to credit, even when they see it for themselves. The vessel is steered dead into the eye of the wind: there is a tremendous cracking and flapping of sails, sheets, stays and halyards and it feels as if something must tear loose, or snap—the racket is terrific. The rudder is turned fully to one side and lashed in that position; the boat bounces up and down on the spot, giving the crew time to get sails in, haul the boom amidships (four of us on the mainsheet, wellies slipping on the tilted deck and water washing around us as we braced ourselves against the port gunwale) and take a reef in the mainsail. Apart from sail-changing, this is the standard procedure if somebody goes overboard: it's the marine equivalent of pulling onto the hard shoulder. The decks were slippery and we suffered a few comedy falls; no one was hurt, though, and no one got whacked on the head by the boom swinging across the deck as *Eda* resumed her course. At half-past eight we went below for a sausage-and-bacon butty and mugs of hot, sweet, reviving tea. At midday, just as we came on deck again, the skipper spotted the faint murky outline of the Calf of Man, dead ahead: we had made our landfall.

The mole at Peel harbour, halfway up the west coast of Man and our mooring for the night, juts out from the north end of

St Patrick's isle—almost an island, it is connected to Man by a narrow, sandy isthmus and a modern promenade and road. Patrick may never have visited the place, but a monastery once stood beneath the site of the medieval castle and St German's cathedral which stands inside it. Germanus is well known in the literature—he was sent from Gaul to rid Britain of the Pelagian heresy[42] in the fifth century. Man's patron saint, Maughold, is said to have been converted by Patrick. The church that bears his name, on the north-east coast near Ramsey, was probably the core of the island's principal monastery. It is no coincidence that harbour and monastic site are so closely associated. Monks and traders, raiders and royal fleets found the same places convenient and congenial; and where economics and patronage meet in the world, power follows.

Early Medieval sailors suffered the disadvantages of their technologies: the square-rigged vessel with a shallow keel cannot very well sail up-wind—much of any windward advantage gained is negated by leeway; but it can be drawn up on beaches or sailed up shallow creeks when larger seagoing craft with greater draught cannot. And oars give the shallow-draughted coaster the ability to make progress up rivers or lochs, or when there is no wind. In those opportunistic centuries before trade was once more regularised and controlled, coastal trading seems to have been an ad-hoc affair; but not without its own unwritten rules. Navigational and geographical realities constrained the number of good landing sites. Often kings gave special privileges to locations close to their centres of power in return for first pick of the goodies. Sometimes, foreigners were kept at a distance so that their bona fides could be checked before they were allowed entry to royal township or stronghold. On the Continent, famous trading sites, merchant towns in effect, grew up at places such as Quentovic on the River Canche in Picardy; at Dorestadt on the Rhine; at Dalkey Island off Dublin.

PEEL HARBOUR

I have, over the years, compiled a map of sites where *wics*—coastal beaches with Early Medieval names that denote trading sites, markets or fairs—were sited around Britain's coasts (the Gaelic equivalent may be *porth* or *strand*). North from the Scillies the north coast of Cornwall is not particularly friendly, but at Tintagel there was a royal and perhaps monastic site with a small harbour from as early as the fifth century which has yielded significant amounts of imported Mediterranean pottery. With a westerly wind it might just be made in a long single day's passage from the Scillies. Directly north from Tintagel, Lundy Island has a beach, but is otherwise an unpromising port of call; on the other side of the Bristol Channel, though, on the south-west tip of Pembrokeshire, lie Milford Haven and several other appealing beach sites, including Watwick Bay, Musselwick Sands, Gateholm and Caldey Island (whence St Samson left on his travels after falling out with a drunken abbot). A few other islands off that coast offer good landing sites, too. Cardigan Bay has no *wic* names to tell of beach markets, but there are many early church sites, and plenty of sandy strands to land on. They may not have been popular with traders, though: the great inlet, easy to enter on a westerly, is difficult to leave on anything but an easterly. So from Pembroke onward northern travel must often have meant a long haul across to Dublin Bay or Dalkey Island just outside it; or to Holyhead, which had a famous early monastery and was a centre for British resistance against first Romans and then the Anglian warlords of North Britain.

One other Dark Age site might have provided a slightly shorter leg: Bardsey Island, off the tip of the Llŷn peninsula, was originally Ynys Enlli (the 'Island in the currents'), otherwise known as the Island of twenty thousand saints. Vicious currents and tidal races will defeat the unwary, but there is a good harbour sheltered from westerlies on the east side (as I found out later in the year), with relatively easy access both to the mainland and back out to sea. St Cadfan built a monastery here early in the sixth century, and the island was a pilgrimage destination until recent times. In legend it is one of many places where 'King' Arthur was buried. East of Anglesey, in an otherwise unpromisingly embayed location, there seems to have been an important trading beach at Meols on the tip of the Wirral. Although the site itself has either been buried by sand or washed away, many thousands of finds have been retrieved from here over the centuries, including a very rare and important pilgrim's flask that came from St Menas's shrine (Menas was another martyred Roman soldier) near Alexandria. Whether it was bought as a trinket, an important relic carrying holy water or oil, or whether it was brought back by a pilgrim to the Holy Land, we cannot say. Meols is perhaps an unlikely site: the key might be its location at the mouth of the River Dee, which gave access deep inland to Chester, the brine spring *wics* of its hinterland and the famous British monastery at Bangor-is-y-Coed (of painful memory).

From Bardsey it is a relatively straightforward passage to Man where, depending on wind and tide, there are ports either to the west or east, although Peel is one of only a few landing sites on the rugged west coast. So the early sailor or pilot of a curragh was able to hop from one harbour to another, each one more or less accessible in a good day's sailing or rowing, unless the fates intervened. Generally, such voyages as were made by saints and traders were confined to the summer months, April to October, perhaps; but the Irish Sea is notoriously fickle, subject to extreme tidal currents and to the short, choppy cross-seas that can undo all types of craft.

Man was a valuable and much fought-over kingdom from at least the seventh century, when Edwin of Northumbria conquered it by a naval assault. At other times it was subject to the kings of Gwynedd, its cultural heritage largely that of the Britons. It was conquered by Vikings around 900; still, there was sufficient Irish influence here for the Manx language to be a variety of Gaelic. Rivers aside, there are few Brythonic place names. Manx language declined to the point, in 1974, where the last native speaker, 'Ned' Mandrell died. It is now being revived, but English is the lingua franca. The accent is like a soft Cumbrian.

Peel was a cosy huddle of coloured houses, narrow streets rising up the hill from the broad sweep of pretty bay and harbour and river mouth crowded with boats and smokeries, only spoiled by the ill-sited power station that glowers down on it. The hills behind were emerald with dewy pasture, etched by drystone walls and the slick grey tarmac of narrow sine-wave lanes. Harbour facilities included a shower block, and the chance of a much-needed change into fresh clothes. *Eda* berthed too late for us to get a key; but Sarah, earning many Brownie points from her shipmates, slithered through a small high window in the ladies' facilities and opened the door for us all to get in.

After a sensational supper of roast lamb, and feeling clean and fragrant enough to join polite society, we left *Eda* riding at her mooring and went for a beer in a small pub that might have served as the set for a 1970s TV show. It was our first drink since the Scillies. We met a friend of Georgia's, a member of the RNLI crew here (I remember thinking that she was a little rash in accepting an offer of a ride round the TT course on his bike in the morning). Apart from two-wheeled latter-day invaders and tax exiles, Man keeps to itself and life's pace is slower than on the mainland. A long, hearty session would have been an excellent way to end this leg of the journey; but after a single pint we were all so tired that we drifted back to the boat and crashed, now surrounded by a bristling fleet of small trawlers. The day's brooding clouds were gone. The sky, as Rolf put it, had been polished: spring constellations shone bright and the harbour lights, fragmented by the water's rippling surface, seemed to bounce them back.

The next morning, after a long, deep sleep with no watch on

deck to interrupt it, I woke at seven-thirty and was out on deck soon after. The fishing fleet departing before first light had been ghostly quiet; now the morning was brilliant, and sitting on deck with a cuppa, taking pictures of the bay, I got chatting to a couple of local men perched on the harbour wall who had admired *Eda* and wanted a closer look. Slowly the boat came to life while the irresistible whiff of Chlöe's Scotch pancakes wafted up through the galley skylight. The skipper briefed us on options for the next leg: a possible all-night transit through the North Channel to carry us clear of the Mull of Kintyre and Rathlin Island on a north-running tide; the winds persisting in unusual easterlies; possible anchorages along the Sound of Jura and beyond.

Sarah, Rolf and I walked up Corrin Hill behind the castle: immense, invigorating panoramas along the rocky coast and out to sea, although Ireland was invisible behind a low bank of cloud that may just have been sea fret. The view down on the town and St Patrick's Isle was breathtaking, with the green sea beyond in late April's brilliant light and *Eda*'s slim, nut-brown hull and mast tiny and fragile-looking against the harbour wall. Late morning begged for a coffee in the sunshine at a café on the promenade. Then Sarah headed for the beach, Rolf for the lifeboat museum and I for an exploration of the castle, with its ruined medieval cathedral and St Patrick's church. It seems that wherever a sailing boat finds a comfortable anchorage or mooring, there will be the site of an Early Christian shrine, a hermit's cell, perhaps a burial ground and church or a fully developed monastery.

The walls of the castle, probably belonging to the fifteenth century but owing their origins to the Anglo-Scottish wars of Edward I, enclose the whole of St Patrick's Isle within its rocky natural defences. Inside, the stone remains of St Patrick's church and its ninth- or tenth-century watchtower occupy a central, elevated platform, surrounded by a bank which may have defined a monastic vallum. It probably replaced an earlier wooden

structure on the same spot. St German's cathedral was first constructed in the twelfth century when it became the seat for a
bishop, although its dedication may be original and pre-date the
island's ascription to Patrick.

The Dark Age world and mindset were not nearly so small as
we might suppose. Links with Rome, Jerusalem and Byzantium
were never entirely severed; the sea was the means and memory
of transmission. Royal, secular powers liked to control the flow of
trade even if they did not initiate it; ecclesiastical establishments
first enjoyed the liturgical fruits of exotica—oil and wine, perhaps; then trinkets and relics; glass, pottery, books and letters.
Sometimes a precious bundle of papyrus might make it all the way
to these maritime lands from Egypt. In return, tin, slaves, furs,
hounds, precious purple dye and other regional produce would
turn up in the markets of Marseille, Alexandria or Ostia.

Until about 650 the Atlantic lands of Britain and Ireland were
the absorbers of energy from the fissile politics and trade of the
post-imperial Mediterranean world; after that, their intellectual
energy and literary brilliance fanned Europe's cultural embers
and left a legacy not just of enchanting monuments but also of
a culture of learning and craft—the culture of the Lindisfarne
Gospels, the Books of Durrow and Kells and the enormous, abiding political influence of Iona and Northumbria in fashioning a
new sort of rational state from the raw material of tribal petty
kingship. For all the pottery, glasswork and trade in objects and
goods implied by the archaeology, the main freight in these centuries may have been people, information, learning and cultural
energy—a cargo of thought.

Lunch was a hot, juicy, distinctly indigenous kipper bap from
the stall on the harbour wall—followed by a wander into town
where we browsed a second-hand bookshop and bumped into
clusters of shipmates enjoying their time off. We slipped our
moorings at half-past three in the afternoon of a glorious clear,

sunny day and cruised north-west with the descending slingshot arc of the sun ahead to port. The sea was milky flat, gelatinous almost, with not a breath of the promised easterly wind, so we chugged along on the engines as the sun, bursting into an egg-yolk orange disc of pure energy, brazed the rim of the horizon with its brilliance and slowly set, leaving a purple-orange glow to savour for the first hours of the evening watch. The silhouette of the Rhinns of Galloway framed the view ahead to starboard. On the Rhinns themselves, and along the coast of the Solway Firth, the remains of Early Medieval settlements abound: famous Latin-inscribed stones at Kirkmadrine; the British and Anglo-Saxon monastery at Whithorn, where large quantities of Frankish and Mediterranean imports have been found; Mote of Mark—a small coastal fort where once a craftsman in fine metals plied his trade; Ruthwell, where one of the great high Northumbrian crosses still stands. These were the lands and the sea-kingdom of the British of Rheged.

Where Galloway comes closest to the Irish coast—and the North Channel is a mere twenty miles wide (narrower still where Kintyre opposes Rathlin), the villages and small towns are para-doxically among the more remote of Scottish communities. And yet, for the Early Medieval period and beyond, the Irish Sea basin is best looked at from the water, as a cultural and trading core united, not divided by the sea. Contacts, political and religious links, economic ties were lasting, sustained and penetrating. On the west side, the monasteries and royal centres of Strangford Lough, Down and Antrim looked not just to the competing king-doms of ancient Ulster for allies and rivals, but also to the Gaelic Scots of Argyll and the Britons of Clyde and Solway Firth. By the beginning of the seventh century their fortunes were also entwined with those of the kings of Northumbria, whose Idings and Yffings were Britain's most powerful and stable ruling dynas-ties for a hundred years before Bede.

We sneaked through the North Channel at dead of night, the pulsing beacons of Rathlin and Sanda marking the reassuring bounds of deep water on either side. Later, Rolf and I couldn't remember how much of that passage was under sail or powered: at one point we were dashing along on the tide at six knots with a steady wind on the starboard beam; at other times it seemed that the wind dropped off and *Eda* ran on her diesel engine. It was a night of intense watches, looking out for super-lit ferries crossing between Cairnryan and Larne; for smaller fishing vessels with their distinctive patterns of navigation lights drifting in and out of visibility ahead and to either side; then the immense loom of the Mull of Kintyre with its thousand-foot cliffs, absolutely dark and featureless and with seemingly not a soul living there, defined like a black hole by the absence of all light.

The evolution of the sailing boat to something near perfection in the last days of the age of sail is the record of a deep, deep past of human travel, knowledge and engineering apprenticeship in these waters, going back four thousand and more years. Sometimes one feels the embrace of all those sailors as comrades, tied by a unity of relationship to the sea. At other times there is loneliness in the knowledge that it can take you at any time; that fate can intervene in any passage in spite of all our modern navigational aids, the familiarity of the waters and reliable weather forecasts. It is possible to be intimidated by the sea, especially when it grows very big; but there is something humbling and comforting in the idea that humans are only ever indulged by the earth's oceans; the sea is never our servant.

Rathlin Island, to port: three lights of its own, such are its dangers. Anciently, it had a monastery and it bears the unhappy history of being the first Irish church to be raided and plundered by Viking pirates in 795, just two years after Lindisfarne suffered the same fate. Contemporaries saw these visitations by heathen seafarers, during which their churches were burned, their shrines violated, their crosses overthrown, as acts of divine retribution for sins unconfessed or unaddressed. The Viking sailors who braved the northern seas were looking for cash and portable wealth so that they might go back to their homelands and afford brides in a polygamous society in which access to marriageable women had become increasingly an exclusive of the elite. The monks and nuns of the coastal foundations were easy prey, their divine protection withdrawn or simply inadequate. The raids precipitated a quarter of a millennium of conflict between the Atlantic peoples and the militarily brilliant Scandinavian raiders; depending on your point of view, the Viking legacy was either disastrous or a rich addition to the cultural exuberance of medieval Europe.

Here is my diary entry for Friday 25 April:

> None of our watch can believe we have had four hours'
> sleep when we're dragged out of our bunks at 7.45. The
> winds have been variable all night; as we go on watch they
> are light and easterly but the engine is off. We see the
> cliffs of Antrim to SW; Rathlin Island on the beam; Islay
> forward to port; the Paps of Jura faintly ahead & Kintyre to
> starboard. We work our way up the coast making as much
> N and E as possible.
>
> Within ten mins of us going on watch the wind has risen
> to a stiff 4/5; we are steering stiff & with a heavy forefoot
> & it's time to drop topsail, jib and reef the mainsail. So the
> off-watch is dragged back up; we heave-to in rocky waves,
> having been on a fast reach with the lee rail well under
> water... she's happier & quicker with less canvas... And
> then 20 mins later, as we watch windfarms spinning on
> Kintyre, the wind drops dead, there's no steerage, and we
> have to run the motor.

And so it went all day. By the second dog-watch I was steering us through the narrowing Sound of Jura past the Point of Knap, and Kilmory, where Sarah and I had stumbled upon that blissfully sheltered chapel full of early sculpture during an autumn squall; *Eda* was just the right side of luffing and made her north-easting towards Crinan without getting too close to either shore, rails under water, riding the edge of a perfect wind along the ancient reptilian metamorphic scenery of the Tayvallich peninsula and the east coast of Jura. The skipper pointed out the cottage at Barnhill where Orwell wrote *Nineteen Eighty-Four* after the end of the war. It was exhilarating sailing, utterly absorbing of mind and body and lived entirely in the moment.

So to Crinan: a quiet overnight anchorage off the mouth of the canal that connects our Sound with Loch Fyne and the Sound of Bute. I took the chance of a restful evening off-watch to try my hand at some fishing, while the skipper deployed a couple of creels. Neither of us had any luck; but a chicken casserole, the setting—knobbly rocks, a quiet cove, gentle fading light, a few time-expired vessels at their moorings; a hotel clinging to the shore below dense woodland; mountains beyond and a sturdy fortified tower-house, Duntrune Castle, standing on the point—all those, and a late dram on deck after sunset, compensated. Dunadd, oddly, lay invisible beyond the bog of Mòine Mhòr, hidden by a one-hundred-and-fifty-foot-high spit on the north side of the bay through which the River Add drains. It was a pity not to be able to see the fortress from the sea; and I wondered how the sailor was welcomed to the ancestral seat of the Dál Riatan kings in the days of the curragh.

We found out next morning as we motored off our anchorage past Ardnoe point, back across the mouth of Loch Craignish and out into the Sound of Jura. One of the great tidal races in the world was running at full tilt: to port it looked as though we must be approaching the foot of a weir: a wall of water, a standing wave, seemed to tumble over some invisible subaqueous dam, boiling the sea around us. Dashing from the Atlantic into the Sound, the tides have to squeeze into a narrow gap, less than a mile wide, between the northern tip of Jura and the island of Scarba. Through the Gulf of Corryvreckan, the 'cauldron of the freckled seas', these waters ebb and flow twice a day, forming a great natural wonder—a whirlpool notorious among sailors and marvellous to visitors watching from the safety of the shore or the deck of a powerful boat. We kept a discreet distance. Sarah promises to swim it some time (at slack water).

Now I understood how complete was Dunadd's location in Kilmartin Glen, protected by an expanse of bog, the ancestral legacy of megalithic burial monuments and its own impressive ramparts, and by the potent magic of a great swirling circle of mysterious currents,[43] guarded in legendary days by the hag goddess Cailleach Bheur, who washed her plaid there. Any unwitting approach through the gulf by attackers or inexperienced sailors would lead to death; its safe passage must have been a sign of the indulgence of the king in his seat in the great mead hall at Dunadd. It is said that the roar of the whirlpool can be heard ten miles away.

This revelation got me thinking, in conversation with James McKenzie, about Dark Age navigation. We agreed that smaller vessels must have hopped along the coasts of the Irish Sea and Scottish archipelago in series of day-sails. I speculated that pilot knowledge must have been critical to a safe passage, and James showed me his pilotage notes for these waters, where the inexperienced or unwary sailor is as like as not going to come a cropper. We looked out the charts for our passage from Falmouth and pointed at likely places where boats negotiating these waters from Francia or the Mediterranean might land and pick up pilots to take them onward. Unsurprisingly, perhaps, it came to us that the Scillies were a key setting-off point—a cluster of safe anchorages and trading settlements where information and expertise might be sought in exchange for small, interesting or high-value goods. Many of the other places where such voyages might call were those that were, historically, the sites of early churches and monasteries, royal palaces or places where markets took place regularly or intermittently over the centuries of the Early Medieval period: Tintagel, Whithorn, Meols, Caldey Island, Peel and so on. In some cases these were neutral locations; in others, royal prerogative ruled and, given the large amount of human traffic evidenced by the travels of the early saints, no doubt the churches fostered their own nautical expertise. From the sixty or so accounts of sea journeys recorded in the life of St Colmcille, it's clear that the monks of Iona were their own pilots; might they have offered their services to traders and to ecclesiastical travellers like Arculf?

Adomnán called the Corryvreckan *Charybdis Brecani*, referring to the whirlpool which forms in the Strait of Messina between Sicily and Calabria. In a small tale of prophecy, he tells how Colmcille had a vision of a monk, Colmán mac Beogni who, on his way to Iona from Rathlin, was in danger of being sunk by the whirlpool and who raised his hands in prayer to quell the terrible and turbulent seas. In an animist world, albeit a Christianised one, the forces of nature loomed large in the physical and spiritual lives of generations of intrepid travellers. The most adventurous of them all, St Brendan, sailed far beyond landmark and pilotage to explore even more exotic worlds and wonders in his search for the ultimate in *peregrinatio*—the journey abroad for Christ.

If the Western seaways of the Dark Ages were busy with boats, traders, raiders and travellers, the effects of their networking on economy, religion and culture went beyond a coastal periphery. In Ireland goods were carried deep inland along the lines of major river systems; where kings' influence spread, so did their lines of patronage and the gifts and perquisites with which they maintained their networks of kin affiliations. But it is difficult to

directly comprehend the effects of this traffic, even in the arte-
factual record. The missionary wanderings of early monks are
often described with approbation; even so, the missions of the
nineteenth and twentieth centuries and the fanaticism of our
own times are a warning of the social and cultural devastation
that zeal carries in its baggage. It seems to me that the explosion
of monastic enthusiasm, particularly in the Ireland of the sixth
and seventh centuries, cemented existing tribal structures rather
than overthrew them; that it gave new opportunities and impetus
for elites to explore and exploit cultural niches as an alternative
to economically and socially unproductive warfare. Pre-Christian
belief in a suite of gods and mediating ancestors was probably
not replaced by a solid, universal belief in a single, all-powerful
God; rather, I think, a new version of animism was socially negotiated. The church understood that integrating existing sentiments with its tidings of Good News (the Gospels) worked. The
message of simplicity, generosity and asceticism might even have
benefited a population of rural poor (although I am sceptical).
But there is little doubting the intellectual revolution which took
place in ideas of kingship and statehood during the sixth and seventh centuries. It fostered a rational, self-aware theory of a state
that might survive the death of the person of the king; a sustaina-
ble and hugely influential model.

A more inadvertent effect of international seafaring and commerce, repeated with equally regrettable consequences by the
mercantile empires of the great European states from about 1600
onwards, was the introduction of diseases to societies with no
immunity. There is a broad consensus that the end of the trade
in goods from the East Mediterranean, which can be dated to the
middle of the sixth century, resulted from the arrival of a great
plague, mentioned in contemporary sources and originating in
the port cities of Constantinople and the Levant in the reign of
the Emperor Justinian. That plague had devastating effects on

Atlantic Britain too: among its suspected casualties was Mael-gwyn of Gwynedd, the greatest of the five tyrants of Gildas's 'complaint' epistle. When trade resumed towards the end of that century, its horizons were more limited: Western Gaul became the principal Atlantic source of trade in ideas and objects.

On the evening of the day in which we sailed out of Crinan,

we ghosted into Tobermory Bay, all brightly coloured houses, crowded jetties (we had to appropriate, with all due permissions, the lifeboat mooring) and drunks—it being the weekend of the Mull Music Festival. Bemused, we strolled along the prome-nade and front street and up steep, narrow lanes for a view back down onto the harbour, picking our way past clumps of revellers spilling into the road. The creamy light of evening, the reds, blues and yellows of the buildings with a backdrop of dark grey cloud, was an acrylic palette to set against the green waters of the Sound of Mull. No wonder artists and photographers flock to this place. We managed to get a shower despite the competition, sank pints of beer from plastic glasses sitting on the pavement outside a pub (there was no room inside) and tried a dram of whisky from the Tobermory Distillery stall on the front. Then, like outback recluses, we retreated to the safety and cosy fug of *Eda*'s saloon for a relaxing evening; and for the first time, I remember, we felt the painful contemplation of journey's end: goodbyes and partings.

Our last full day's sailing, in pearlescent sunshine and light breezes, took us past Ardnamurchan Point and the seductive island jewels of Rhum, Eigg and Muck, drawing us on towards the Cuillin ridge on Skye—awesome and compelling, a noble scar and haunt of legendary heroes. Our final anchorage was Inverie where we landed from the dinghy, after a farewell supper, for a beer in the Old Forge, mainland Britain's remotest pub (it is not connected by road: drinkers must walk or sail and earn their dram the hard way). A long, long sunset on deck, bathing in golds and greens among the glistening tumble-burn mountains of Knoydart. We cruised into the port of Mallaig the next morning: Mallaig, where Britain's railway system runs out.

Unable, really, to articulate our feelings, those of us who were leaving, abandoning *Eda* to her summer sailing, watched silently as the Highlands passed us by on either side, the rush of the swift-falling glens silent beyond the clatter of the train and our own internal peregrinations.

Interlude *A Corbridge circular*

Corstopitum—*Dere Street and Devil's Causeway—Stanegate—
royal estates—end of Roman Britain—General Wade's road—
Heavenfield—finding a farmer—caravanserai*

MY COLLEAGUE Colm O'Brien and I needed to track down
a farmer whose land we wanted to survey; on an overcast and
muggy Thursday early in summer we decided to make a day of it.
We set off from Corbridge on the north bank of the River Tyne
to walk to Heavenfield, which lies on the Wall some few miles to
the north. Heavenfield, where Oswald Iding, fresh from a youthful exile in the kingdom of Dál Riata, returned with a small army
in the year 633 or 634 to fight for the Northumbrian kingdom;
where he raised a cross the night before battle and had a vision of
Colmcille; the place where the northern English Christian state
was born.

A Roman town (*Corstopitum*, or more locally just *Coria*) constructed in the middle of the second century on the site of earlier forts, Corbridge is a key strategic location in the Roman and
Early Medieval landscape. At least three battles have been fought
close by. Its bridge has always been one of the most important
crossings of this sometimes untameable river. The siting of a garrison on the north, offensive side of a river is absolutely typical
of unapologetic, proactive Roman military thinking. The same
applies at York, at London and elsewhere. But Corbridge has
been bothering us.

Dere Street, the ancient road from York to Edinburgh and the Antonine Wall, crosses the river here and a lateral branch, known as the Devil's Causeway, links it with the mouth of the Tweed and the harbour at Berwick. The Stanegate runs west from here to the Solway Firth; to the east, twenty-five miles downriver, is the mouth of the Tyne. A major Roman supply fort, *Arbeia*, stood on the south side of the Tyne near its mouth; another (*Segedunum*) on the north bank, coincided with the end of the Wall, five miles inland. Corbridge was effectively the garrison supply town for the eastern half of the Wall and all forts to the north; its counterpart, at the other end of the Stanegate, Carlisle (*Luguvalium*; Brythonic *Caer Luel*) may already have been a thriving settlement before the Romans came, perhaps the *civitas* capital of the *Carvetii*. But, since there is no known Roman road linking Corbridge with its supply forts on the east coast, the question arises whether, in the Roman period and after, the river was navigable this far up. There is much debate. For that matter, the line of the Stanegate, and the point where it must have crossed the North Tyne, have not been satisfactorily traced—yet. And we would like to know for how long the Roman bridge—a mile upstream from the present construction—continued in use after the end of the Empire. These questions are important not just for understanding the geography of the Roman north, but for reconstructing the circumstances in which Oswald's small army, having perhaps sailed down the west coast to Carlisle and then marched along the old road from Carlisle, was able to surprise and defeat the most formidable force of the day: the battle-hardened veterans of King Cadwallon of Gwynedd.

Several scholars have floated the idea that Corbridge lay at the core of a royal estate in the sixth century, that it formed the heartland of the original kingdom of Bernicia as the principal administrative and strategic centre for the Tyne corridor and its fertile soils. The name *Coria* probably means something like a tribal

assembly or hosting place. Cadwallon of Gwynedd may have chosen the old town as his winter quarters before his fateful encounter with Oswald. So why, in later centuries, did it lose out to Hexham, just across the river, as the principal town in the valley? By
the third quarter of the seventh century a major church had been
established on a promontory at Hexham, a little upstream on the
opposite, south bank. It became one of England's earliest bishop-
rics while Corbridge, despite its location, has never been much
more than a large village since the end of the Roman period. History will give up no more clues to its Dark Age: only archaeology,
and the landscape, can shed light.

From the bridge, the seventeenth-century survivor of a great
flood in 1771 which destroyed every other bridge on the river,
Colm and I took the riverside path west, below the flood-proof
terrace on which the Roman settlement stood. Much of the town
was excavated early in the twentieth century under a regime,
typical of the period, when archaeologists removed any overbur-
den to get down to Roman strata and in the process destroyed
what evidence might have existed for Cadwallon's presence or
the existence of a Dark Age royal township. It is, to say the least,
a pity.

Colm and I were deep in conversation when we found ourselves crossing the Cor burn, turning north past a magnificent
mill house and emerging from the path onto Corchester lane. We
doubled back along the lane to the entrance of the Roman town
and paid our dues to English Heritage for a look at the ruins.
They are impressive, more civic than military: the granaries still
have their floors; the drains look as if they might still be in good
working order; there is a forum and all the urban trappings of
civilisation in Britain's most northerly Roman town. Its location
has obvious benefits: it looks down on the broad, fast-flowing
river and the site of the ancient bridge, across to the moors above
Hexham with their valuable lead deposits; and both ways up and

down the valley. Most striking is the metalled road on which we walked to view the ruins: the beginning of the Stanegate before it heads westwards through the North Pennine pass near Gilsland. Apart from its obvious functions in terms of shifting troops and goods at speed through a potentially hostile, then pacified land, it makes one hell of a statement of intent—more so even than the Wall, which it pre-dates. It sent out what modern governments like to call 'a clear message'. It said, 'We are here to stay, we know what we're doing, we've subdued every barbarian kingdom on the Continent and this is how we do it. We show you what Rome is like and then you become part of us. Everybody got that?'

Everybody, almost everybody, did get it; they bought into it with enthusiasm, especially the native elite who subsequently became the magistrates and civil servants, burgesses and masters of Roman Britain, doing rather well, thank you, under the overlordship of distant masters. The more or less permanent garrisoning of the frontier zone by troops ensured a lively economy (probably the odd riot and local scandal too). But Corbridge must have found itself on the front line when the Wall was overrun by revolting Northern Britons in the later fourth century, and those with material wealth were tempted to bury it in a safe place. We find those hoards from time to time and it goes almost without saying that their owners never came back for them. How long it took for the native warrior elite to become effete toga-wearers petty-politicking in the town's forum is hard to say. Human communities are nothing if not adaptable.

At the fifth-century end of the imperial project, we would very much like to know if, when and how those town-dwellers cast off their togas, picked up their ancestral swords, took to the hills and became warlords once more in the face of civil strife, invasion and piracy. An obvious answer is that they did not, having forgotten over the previous three centuries how to fight. They might, then, have either devolved responsibility for security onto the existing

commanders along the Wall, as at Birdoswald, or hired merce-
naries. Either way, the best fighters were those from Saxony and
Jutland, the tribes beyond the Rhine frontier that had never been
tamed; everyone knew that. But in the west and south-west of
Britain, and north of the Wall—so-called Outer Brigantia—those
native tribes still handy with spear and shield might well have
taken matters into their own hands. As late as the early seventh
century, the British of Gwynedd could realistically hope to wrest
this region from its Germanic kings.

We popped into the town's well-furnished museum to say hello
to Frances McIntosh, its curator, and assistant curator Graeme
Stobbs, a veteran excavator of the Tyne's archaeology; we were
treated to tea and biscuits and a question. They took us back into
the museum and showed us a sculpture—a gravestone, perhaps,
or an altar, not much more than a foot high. The relief carving
depicted a (now headless) woman stirring something in a barrel.
What did we make of it? Roundels had been carved either side
of where her face had been before being chiselled away. To the
right was a repeated motif of what looked like eagles—it was hard
to tell in the low light. The roundels, we speculated, might have
been flabella, like the decorative cross on the slab at Ellary—and,
therefore, possibly Christian. Who was this woman? A native
or Roman God, otherwise unknown? Or the depiction of a real
woman, erected by loved ones? What was in the pot? The closest
parallels depict the goddess of medicine, Meditrina, surrounded
by barrels of potions. We know that in the long history of the
Wall and in Roman towns across the Empire, native and Roman
deities often became associated with each other by virtue of their
common attributes. That Corbridge had a shrine to a medical
deity, or a sign outside a pharmacy, would not surprise. By the
time those with medicinal skills resurfaced in the literature of the
Dark Ages, they had either become something more arcane, even
sinister, or they were being called hermits and saints.

After this tantalising glimpse afforded by archaeology of the Roman town and its road, there is no sign of the ancient highway for a few miles. But it's always worth having a good nose around on foot, to get the lie of the land and look for subtle clues that might be preserved in the line of a hedge or wall, a low ridge through a meadow, a curious hump in a field. The Stanegate must have crossed the North Tyne somewhere between its confluence with the main river at Warden, just below the hill fort, and the nearest Wall fort at Chesters, nearly three miles to the north. So we followed the small road that keeps to the base of the valley side before climbing the hill up to the hamlet of Anick, peering over hedges and musing on those ancient routes through the land that might survive as footpaths, droveways and twisting deep-sunk lanes. We were detained for a minute by the curious sight of a flock of unmoving crows in a field. As we looked closely at them to confirm that in fact they were models—quite good models, convincingly disposed—a man with a shotgun wearing camouflage emerged from the hedge behind us, amused that his decoys had fooled us as he hoped they would fool other crows; it was slightly unnerving.

A tiny, straight lane led out of Anick, heading due west, along the line of the three-hundred-foot contour; with its commanding views of river and approaches, it seemed to us that this would make a very good line for the Stanegate. After a mile, where the lane swung north aping the line of the North Tyne beyond, we stopped at St John Lee, a little parish church perched on the hillside without a community, apart from a small cluster of farmhouses. It may be the site of a very ancient foundation, mentioned by Bede as a retreat used by John of Beverley, a Bishop of Hexham, and originally dedicated to the Archangel Michael. Michael was a frequent and popular dedicatee for early churches, especially those founded on high ground.[++] Our convenient road may be the ancient route to this church and yet have nothing to do with the line of the Stanegate; or, we might speculate that the church was sited on the old Roman road deliberately. A Roman altar was found near by and sits in a corner of the church. If nothing else, St John Lee boasts a very decent stained-glass window depicting St Oswald raising his cross at Heavenfield, along with images of Edwin and Oswald's brother Oswiu.

The contour-hugging lane became a path which brought us, via a small stream where there was once a mill, into the pretty stone-built village of Acomb (a 'valley of oak trees'), one of Tynedale's most desirable residential addresses. From here the path reverted to a road and rose steadily for a mile, still heading north, with majestic, open views towards Warden Hill and beyond. It topped out at something like six hundred and fifty feet above sea level. Below and before us the line of General Wade's road and the vallum underscored the hills beyond, the Wall itself having been scavenged here to send the general's own Clear Message to the local Jacobites. From here, road and vallum, heading west, descend into the North Tyne valley and to the site of a Roman bridge which carried the Wall across, just as it had near Birdoswald. We came out onto the Military Road at Heavenfield, the site of Oswald's famous vision of Colmcille and his last camp before doing battle with Cadwallon.

There is a wooden cross (less than a hundred years old) at the roadside and a path leads across pasture to the small church of St Oswald in Lee which is supposed to lie on the site of a much earlier building, erected, according to Bede, in 'recent times'— that is, in the late seventh or early eighth century. If the current church is modest, plain and uninspiring, its setting is not, for it looks north onto a vast sweep of open Northumbrian countryside towards the Cheviot Hills and the border. What made Oswald choose this precise spot for his pre-battle camp is not absolutely clear. One of the objects of our prospective geophysical survey was to get some idea of what happened here both before and after his army's overnight stay in 633 or 634. Oswald had been exiled in his thirteenth year on the death of his father, King Æthelfrith, in battle against his (Oswald's) Uncle Edwin. He cannot have recognised the geography; one must suppose that he had both native guides to assist him and older companions, survivors of his father's warband, to advise. But Heavenfield has advantages: it cannot be seen from the south or east, where the enemy may have lain at Corbridge.

A mile to the east along the line of the Wall, Colm and I took afternoon refreshment at St Oswald's Farm café. We were looking for the farmer in whose fields the church sits. We were in luck. John Reay was not there, but we met his mother, were able to explain to her what we were about (we did not disturb the rhythm of her knitting, I am glad to say) and to get his phone number.

Mission accomplished, we followed the Wall path eastwards towards its junction with Dere Street. The Wall is invisible here, not because it was removed by the thrifty general to build his road (now the B6318), but because Wade had his redcoats build the road directly on top of it: nothing like a firm foundation.

Before the Wall's and road's junction with Dere Street we struck out across country, with half a mind to reconstruct Oswald's putative dawn march to Corbridge on the morning after his vision. There is no obvious path; more likely they rode direct, avoiding routes where scouts might have been waiting and watching (the Wall; Dere Street; Warden Hill, perhaps). The surprise was complete, Oswald's rout of Cadwallon's British army astonishing and epoch-changing. The green lane we took was wide enough to have been an old droveway, leading to the site of one of the great cattle fairs. Stagshaw Bank, a flattish expanse looking steeply down onto Corbridge from the angle formed by Wall and Dere Street, would see a hundred thousand cattle pass through during these summer months. They came from all over the borders and beyond, on their way to London's Smithfield or other southern markets. Here they were shod for the hard roads ahead (eight shoes per cow: imagine the sheer weight of iron being forged, shaped and fitted). The droving industry died almost overnight with the arrival of the railways; but how far back this particular gathering might be projected is a moot point. Portgate, where Dere Street pierced the Wall on its northern track, is such an obviously key point in the ancient landscape that it is easy to imagine a very old tradition of gateway communities. There is an unexplained fort-like earthwork here, just on the edge of the road. The distinguished geographer Brian Roberts, noting the presence of large numbers of Roman coins recovered from Great Whittington, just to the north-east of Portgate, suggested to us in a brilliant insight that this may have been a place where merchants and traders from all points north were required to halt before entering the Empire, like caravanserai bivouacs outside the desert towns of North Africa. Here their bona fides were checked; dues were paid; deals and bargains made or broken; selected persons were given privileged access; the riff-raff—slaves, drovers, chancers—were kept out. Think Casablanca; think the Scillies, Peel or Crinan. Think Aldgate and Whitechapel. Was the fair at Stagshaw the successor to such a caravanserai?

Colm and I shadowed Dere Street back to Corbridge, these days a bustling and very attractive village, still trading on its ancient crossing of the river. Corbridge continuing to bother us, we wondered if our modern remote-sensing equipment would soon cast a faint light on a dimly seen past.

CHAPTER FIVE

Heroes: *Wareham to Yatton*

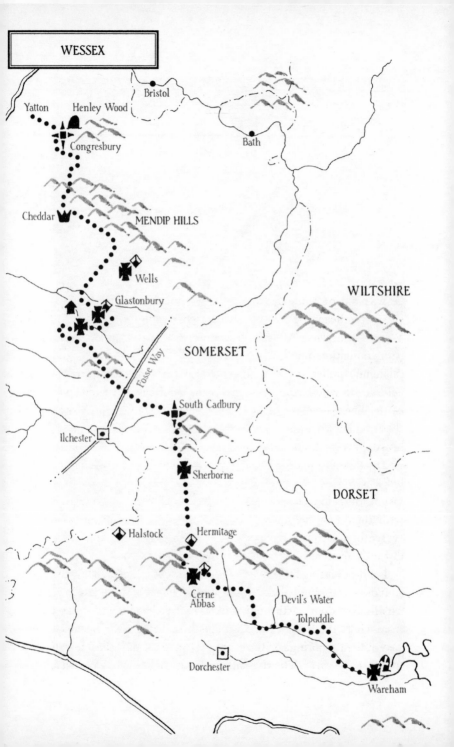

I WALKED OUT, one midsummer's morning, from a farm campsite at the head of Poole harbour in Dorset, to walk across the
Wessex peninsula. My fellow campers formed ranks of white,
shiny miniature mobile houses, either motorised or towed behind
glistening polished cars. This is the sort of conspicuous, portable wealth whose equivalent, in the ancient lands of Britain, was
cattle. There is an essentially petit-bourgeois competitiveness to
these vehicles that one catches fragments of evidence for in half-
heard conversations between temporary neighbours. Desocial-
ised by the self-imposed isolation constructed from garden fences,
block-paved driveways, security lights, CCTV and paranoiac television, they don't leap out of their doors to make conversation
with their new neighbours, or passing pilgrims; net curtains
twitch in a cultural semaphore that might have been inherited,
distantly, from nesting birds spotting raptors overhead.

Land-bound again, I was nevertheless accompanied by the
sounds of clanking halyards, squeaking fenders and the rustle of
a half-hearted breeze through willow and reed bed. A mile inland
from where the River Frome empties into the harbour, boats sat
easy at their moorings on the ebbing tide and the day's heat began
to infuse the earth. The riverside path into Wareham was dusty;

the forecast promised thirty degrees. July's brilliant light seemed to energise the air into a new level of clarity: saw-edged sedge leaves sharply pencil-drawn against china-blue sky; dark green hedges chiselling lines between oat-yellow fields fat with grain and ripe for harvest. To the south the protective line of the Purbeck hills, the ramparts of Wessex, crisply profiled the horizon. Ahead, and across the river, above tall waving banks of reeds, the square crenellated tower of Lady St Mary church marked the south-east corner of Wareham town. Following the lazy meander of the river, I came to the modern bridge that carries the road from Corfe Castle into the town centre along a route more than a thousand years old.

I went to Wessex to walk with the heroes of the Dark Ages: not to praise them, but to understand how a mythic past has infiltrated the fabric of the landscape. My route took me from the fortified town of King Alfred, via the martyrs of Tolpuddle and the virile chalk giant at Cerne Abbas, to the hilltop Camelot of Arthur, then to his supposed resting place at Glastonbury where Joseph of Arimathea planted his thorny staff. It took me to a site associated with the legendary St Congar and through the landscapes of Thomas Hardy's tragic heroine Tess of the d'Urbervilles. It also drew me back to associations of more obscure heroes from my own past. Along the way the idea of the hero morphed into something complex and ironic, while the apparently homely, very English counties of Dorset and Somerset took on, in my traveller's mind, a secretive and ambivalent cloak of obscurity.

Wareham, then, and a beginning rooted in geographical and historical certainty. The town is a neat square, planned, laid out and constructed under the orders of King Alfred of Wessex in the last decade of the ninth century. Wareham was a burgh, a fortified settlement whose purpose was to protect its hinterland against Viking raids, to provide a focus for civic functions and trade and to act as a fixed point in a comprehensive system of military co-ordination and cultural revival. Alfred was taking advantage of a strategic site at the head of Poole harbour and of the near-confluence of two rivers: the Frome, which marks the town's southern, unwalled edge, and the Piddle, which flows parallel to and just outside the northern ramparts. Within Wareham's earthen banks a regular grid of plots was established along north–south and east–west axes with a crossroads at the centre. The roads were lined with wooden houses, with craft workshops, with wharves and warehouses by the river; these days the buildings are of brick, but the layout is not much altered. Inhabitants enjoyed rights that went with the responsibility to man its walls. Despite the depredations of time and later military alterations over the centuries, the ramparts survive to a substantial and impressive height. Each side of the enclosure, which contains something like ninety acres, is more than five hundred paces long. As I made my tour of the perimeter, I realised it made a perfect dog-walking circuit. A woman, I guess somewhat past retirement age, passed me in the company of her dog and, noticing that I had my camera poised, stopped for a brief chat about photography, evidently her passion. I am ashamed to say that I was a bit terse, if not exactly impolite, and carried on my way, anxious to complete the circuit.

Where the northern rampart is pierced deeply by the main road there was once a gate; even now the entrance to the town is imposing, high walls rising sheer on either side of the cutting, and the sense of entering a canyon is enhanced by the tall west wall of the church of St Martin which looms above it. The church door was locked, but a notice promised that a key was available by application to A. F. Joy (outfitters) at 35 North Street. I had not been in a shop like this since the 1970s, supposing that they no longer existed. It smelled of old clothes for slow people. A woman there, looking slightly sceptical at the sight of me, as if my rucksack might be designed for looting precious church relics, took the satisfyingly solid, heavy iron key from the drawer that held gentlemen's ties, and made me sign for it. I was not, thankfully, required to purchase a tie.

St Martin's-on-the-walls was built in about 1030; but its dedication, to the fourth-century St Martin of Tours, may reflect an earlier foundation on the same spot. The interior was all elegant, catholic delicacy, with the splendid tall proportions of a tower-house. The Romanesque chancel arch was more refined than the squat dog-tooth of many Norman churches and pierced on either side by smaller arches which brought more light into the nave and gave it the air of a basilica—the sensibility was distinctly Carolingian. Above the chancel arch, and in the chancel itself, faded paintings almost floated on the lime-plastered walls: a twelfth-century depiction of St Martin on horseback; the lion and unicorn crest of Queen Anne; the Ten Commandments, and an extract from *Exodus*. It was a beautiful, peaceful place, cool and gracefully welcoming. It would have been a fine thing to have a companion to talk to, for sound diffused through its patient, dust-moted air like the faint echo of its own history.

In the north aisle I stopped before the creamy-white marble effigy of a great warrior, a flesh-and-blood templar returned to his homeland, honoured by art and family. Recumbent, dressed in the robes of a Bedouin prince, hand on ceremonial dagger at his waist, his feet were crossed, braced against a block of stone carved with a representation of Hittite fighting bulls. The body does not lie here, but in a small cemetery in the village of Moreton, not many miles to the west, wrapped in a union flag. This warrior hero was no medieval crusader but a latter-day adventurer, scholar and champion of Arab rights.

I spent some time in quiet contemplation of Thomas Edward Lawrence. The face betrays nothing of the emotions, but even in its apparent blank passivity an extraordinary, restless intellect can be read: the marble is cool, much polished from visitors touching it. His friend and sculptor, the war artist Eric Kennington, had intended the effigy for St Paul's Cathedral; but Lawrence, who died in 1935 on the back lanes of Dorset in a motorcycling accident (the official version),[45] was as divisive a figure in death as he had been in life. Like the incorrupt body of St Cuthbert or the relics of King Oswald, his remains were a matter of more than academic interest to contemporaries. Lawrence was too controversial a figure to lie alongside the remains of Nelson, that other troubled secular saint, in St Paul's. Neither man's heroism was by any means straightforward. Lawrence's Arab sympathies and discomfort with British policy in Arabia (the fruits of which are splashed across the newspapers as I write), his self-advertising memoirs, distinctly equivocal attitude towards Hitler's Germany and his refusal to play the part of gracious (and tight-lipped) English war hero, have corrupted the comforting narrative of perfection that we like our heroes to conform to. Dark Age heroes such as Alfred and Arthur are also less reassuring, less readily graspable than the simple certainties their mythic portrayals would suggest: for the archaeologist or historian, reality is always more complex, always more interesting.

Wareham has more secrets, and they subvert its Alfredan narrative. The parish church of Lady St Mary, which overlooks the river crossing and which seems such a fitting building to mark the south-east corner of the town, must in fact pre-date it. A king of Wessex, Brihtric, was buried here in 802, having apparently been poisoned by his wife, a daughter of King Offa of Mercia, long before Alfred left his mark. The Great Heathen Army, or *mycel heathen here* as they were called by the Anglo-Saxon chroniclers, made their headquarters here in 876 and had to be paid off by the embattled King of Wessex. His biographer, Asser, mentions the existence of a monastery here; and five stone memorials, inscribed with Latin names—the largest collection of such stones in one place in Britain—suggest that as late as the eighth century there was a British Christian community still active in Wareham.

That sort of evidence forces a radical rethink of the relations between Briton and Saxon in Wessex, whose conquest by the Germanic *Gewisse* is supposed (by their later chroniclers, the West Saxons) to have been absolute, and complete long before. Do we suppose a cultural tolerance? A cult ghetto?

King Ine, an active and enterprising warlord contemporary with this community, made provision in his law code for the wergild or blood-price of his Welsh horsemen, perhaps a cadre of native couriers; and it is clear that in his time, around the end of the seventh century, Britons could own property in the territories of the West Saxons, even if their wergild was less than that of a freeborn Saxon. Lady St Mary Church may have been a minster in the seventh and eighth centuries—sited at the heart of a royal estate to preach to a wide populace—that would explain a king's burial there. Was it also the court of an ancient community of Latin-speaking British clerics? If so, were they a conservative rump in denial of the new world order—or did they serve an active British community in these parts? There is an unspoken risk, for historians intimately versed in the loaded, anti-British narratives of Bede, of assuming a greater degree of cultural and religious homogeneity in his era than was in fact the case. There is a growing feeling among scholars in this field that Early Medieval England may have been much more a patchwork of identities and affiliations than the monumental record generally suggests, just as the Welsh Marches are. After all, Wessex had some distinctly British-sounding kings in its early centuries— the kingdom's alleged founder, Cerdic (r. *c.*519–34) and the later Cædwalla, who waged genocidal warfare on the Isle of Wight in the seventh century, among them.

Wareham's museum, sited next to the ancient crossroads at the heart of the town, was due to open at ten. I returned the key to its relieved keeper and walked the two hundred yards south along North Street, wondering why so many cars and vans choked the

street and thinking idiotically how appropriate gridlock was for
a grid-iron town. There had, it seemed, been a serious accident
on the A352 which links the major towns of south Dorset: Poole
with Dorchester. Everyone was trying to get around the blockage
by driving through Wareham. The museum was a ground-floor
room in the offices of the town council. At five minutes past ten
the metal grill was opened by the woman I had met on the walls:
my chance to purge guilt, and we chatted for a while about this
and that, cameras, Saxons, Lawrence and motorbikes. Pam Bowyer-Davis is a volunteer curator. She turned out to be a keen student of the town's past, having at one time run an Anglo-Saxon
festival here—but Saxons are not very interesting to people now-
adays, she admitted. Her prize exhibit, on loan from Dorchester
Museum, was a tenth-century sword, or at least the copper- and
silver-plated guard, hilt and pommel and the upper part of the
blade, found in the River Frome during the construction of the
modern bridge in 1927. Very few such weapons survive: this one
is particularly significant because, incised into the antler-bound
hand-grip is the first part of a name, Æthel…, meaning 'noble',
the sword of a great aristocrat or king; one of Alfred's brothers,
perhaps.

Much of the museum is, perhaps unsurprisingly, dedicated
to T. E. Lawrence whose cottage at Clouds Hill lies just a few
miles west—a place of pilgrimage for historians and followers of
his modest cult. Pam told me that there is a settle in one of the
local pubs which was a favourite perch of the warrior hero; that
she once had the privilege of sitting astride a Brough Superior
SS100 motorcycle (the model Lawrence rode when he was killed),
and would have kick-started it and taken it for a spin had she not
been prevented by a spoilsport at the Bovington tank museum.
It is a salutary thought that this motorcycle, whose top speed
was about the same as my modern Japanese hi-tech slickster
(roughly 125mph), was being ridden about the lanes of Dorset by

a semi-crazed adventurer with no helmet eighty years ago. The one that killed him is a priceless treasure in the Imperial War Museum in London.

I had rather hoped to walk along that iconic stretch of road towards the cottage; but the pedestrian takes his life in his hands negotiating these roads in high summer so, leaving Wareham behind, I followed instead the shallow valley of the Piddle. I was kept from the riverbank by a scout camp, a Highways Agency maintenance depot, a grassy meadow defended resolutely by two jet-black African oxen who looked as though they had liberated themselves from the philosophy of vegetarianism and might eat me; by a quarry and a golf club; by private roads and dense woodland of chestnut and hazel. I was afforded brief excerpts of Dorset's heathland, all bracken and spiky gorse. Not until I came out onto the Bere Regis road did I cross the Piddle, no more than a foot deep and running perfectly clear over a bed of gravel and chalk.

My second campsite of the trip was a mile short of Bere Regis (it has nothing to do with bears; the name means something like 'the king's pig-grazing wood'). I found a friendly welcome, a discreet field and a soft pitch; made my camp, showered and read a few pages of my old, thumb-worn copy of Leslie Alcock's classic archaeological survey of the Dark Ages, *Arthur's Britain*. I read it as an undergraduate at York in the early 1980s; I have reread it since: soon, for the first time, I would be visiting the site of Alcock's famous excavations at South Cadbury, a view of whose ramparts provides the cover image for the book. Hunger soon distracted me from this professional comfort food. From the back of the campsite a suitably time-worn hollow way, cut through the chalk and lined with coppiced hazels bearing their acid-green fruit, led to Bere Regis. It's a small, neat village with a couple of pubs, a Post Office and shop. The church has a remarkable decorated hammer-beam roof adorned with distinctly earthy figures;

otherwise, the village is famous as the ancestral home of the Turberville family, immortalised in Thomas Hardy's *Tess*. She is no less a heroic figure than Arthur, or Lawrence: wronged, raped, shunned and two-timed, her death by suicide is Shakespearean tragedy confined in Dorset's dark lanes and torpid, poverty-ridden hamlets.

Dorset emerges into history as a shire during the ninth century; its name derives ultimately from that which the Romans recorded for its Iron Age tribe, the Durotriges, whose lands also embraced the southern parts of Somerset and Wiltshire. Its physical and cultural landscape evolves slowly, not impervious to change but cautious, conservative. To find out what its native peoples were doing and where they lived over the last two millennia, you need to look beneath the farms and hamlets that survive in the present landscape and excavate there. Mostly, what you would find would be farms and hamlets much as we see them today, minus the veneer of technology and with many, many more people thrown in. For clues to its Early Medieval character you might as well look in the pages of Thomas Hardy as try to peer through the eyes of Bede or the Chroniclers.

For some reason I did not feel like eating in a pub that night. I bought a couple of pork pies, some tomatoes and a wedge of cheese, and took them back to my den via Bere Regis's near neighbour, the tiny but picturesque hamlet of Shitterton. People used to come and steal its village sign until, in 2010, the villagers had a new one carved into a ton-and-a-half block of creamy grey Purbeck stone. Shitterton is one of the very few properly attested scatological place names in England: it means, in Anglo-Saxon, the settlement of the open sewer—*scite* being the Old English word for, well, shit.

My second full day on the trail was hot enough without getting lost, first thing, in a maze of green lanes and sunken paths as I tried to effect a shortcut back to the Piddle. Dorset's myriad

footpaths tend to keep to the valleys and combs instead of breaking out onto the breezy, open spaces of the downs. So many trails
criss-cross each other that it's hard to navigate: landmarks are
invisible from these green tunnels, and it's as if I have stumbled
on a Wessex version of the Ho Chi Minh trail, thoroughly invisible from above during the summer months. In truth the paths are
so old that they have been worn into hollows by time, water and
the hooves and feet of drovers and their charges. The effect, after
a while, is slightly sinister, as if Dorset has something to hide. I
began to harbour *Rogue Male* fantasies.

I more or less stumbled out into the open at the tiny hamlet
of Turner's Puddle: a more Hardy-esque, ramshackle, dozy Victorian estate farm it is hard to imagine. The orange-tiled brick
barns and courtyards could easily be old Melbury's place in *The
Woodlanders*. I was all wide-eyed at this rural shabby-chic and had
my cameras out, until a woman, passing me at little more than
walking pace in a Volvo estate, gave me a look that suggested I
was off-piste and intruding on her privacy. I have been getting
used to the idea that a tall, middle-aged man walking on his own
with a rucksack and cameras might seem threatening. It wouldn't
be like that if I was young (impoverished gap-year student: harmless) or in company. I am not sure if they think I will steal their
daughters, or their televisions; rather, I think they are threatened
by my apparent poverty: for a middle-aged man, alone (and therefore single), must be a misfit, unable to hold down a job (he is evidently NOT at work) or purchase an automobile. In another age
I might be a refugee from some great conflict, or from Dust Bowl
America. The only thing I can do to assuage their fears, should I
choose to, is smile, wave, chat and tell them what I am about. Or
act the fool. It always worked for Lord Peter Wimsey. It is a pity
that I don't look quite so harmless.

When opportunity arises, in cafés and campsite receptions,
the response is universally kind and interested. But when I walk

along lines of white caravans and motorhomes I can feel the fear
behind the twitching of polyester curtains. Some people don't
give one a chance. Cars depersonalise in a way that not even brick
walls and closed doors do. There is also the sad fact that on all
these journeys so far I had not yet met a single other walker,
except those being towed by their dogs. Ambulists have become
an unusual sight, almost as rare as hitchhikers. The English are
forgetting their walking rights and privileges, neglecting to
keep their paths open. Like muscles, they atrophy through lack of
use: choked with brambles and nettles and eventually reclaimed
by nature, rights of way will become artefacts to be studied, not
defended and enjoyed. Like the Post Office and the rural bus service, the public footpath, and the chance encounter on the trail, is
in danger of becoming a casualty of the age of transport.

I came to Tolpuddle in the middle of a very warm morning.
It was the most impeccably kept village I have ever seen: every
house in its Sunday best with perfectly pointed brickwork and
neat thatch or tile, fresh paint on woodwork, windows clean,
lawns manicured and pavements swept, hanging baskets in their
mating plumage, the full glory of high-summer blossom—as if,
perhaps, royalty were expected. As it happened, I came here the
day before the Tolpuddle Festival, which annually celebrates its
nineteenth-century trades-union martyrs; and so a degree of
polish was not surprising. Even so, I got the impression that it's
always like this in Tolpuddle. It gave me a slightly uneasy feeling,
like Switzerland does.

I stopped, sweaty and thirsty, before the Methodist chapel
where memorials to the six men imprisoned and transported in
1834 are mounted either side of the entrance. It is still salutary
and depressing to think that, at the time of the Great Reform
Bill debate, when Combination Acts banning trades unions had
been repealed and when liberty and representation for the people
were matters of supreme public interest, small groups of rural

workers, their jobs threatened by low wages and the infiltration of agricultural machinery, were still being oppressed by government in a case which belongs more to the world of the 1790s, of Jacobin paranoia, treason trials and French regicide than to the dawn of the modern age. On the marble gateway to the church is an inscription which records the defence of George Loveless, their leader.

> We have injured no man's reputation, character, person or property, we were uniting together to preserve ourselves, our wives and our children from utter degradation and starvation.

After the first great public campaign of its kind in England galvanised opinion against the transportation of the six men, all but one were released in 1836. I was sorry to miss the festival: there is something compelling about watching large crowds of people drawn to a place—a village becomes a temporary town; old friends meet; new friendships are forged. Tolpuddle might have been an important meeting place long before the martyrs— a Roman road crossed the river here and it is a natural focal point in the landscape for farmers and travellers; another site for a caravanserai, perhaps.

A mile further west, my horizon now confined by a maize crop whose plants dwarfed me at well over six foot tall, I walked along the south bank of the river, sorely tempted to strip off and jump in, except that I would only have got my calves wet. Here I passed the confluence of the Piddle with the Devil's Brook which runs directly north into the chalk downlands through the old villages of Dewlish and Hilton.

The Devil's Brook bears an intriguing name—there are several like it in England, and they all seem to derive from an early form *Divelis* (as does Dewlish). This is an English corruption of a Brythonic river name, *Dhuglas*, or Douglas, meaning 'blue-black'.

In the *Historia Brittonum* the name occurs (Latin *Dubglas*) as the site of four battles fought by the British general Arthur in the region of *Linnuis* (unknown, but sometimes identified with Lindsey or Lincolnshire). Across the Tyne from Corbridge is a river called Devil's Water, also probably derived from a *Dhuglas* original, where Oswald slew Cadwallon in 634 to reconquer Bernicia.

As it happens, no river bearing the name Douglas or its several derivatives is to be found in Lincolnshire. Another candidate for the place-name root of *Linnuis* is Lindum on the north side of the Clyde estuary; a third, slightly corrupted, is *Lininuis* which, Leslie Alcock argued in his survey of the evidence, can be identified with a section of the Durotriges tribe of British Wessex around Ilchester (Roman *Lindinis*). And there are four rivers in West Wessex which bear the name Douglas in one form or another. So the would-be Arthurian geographer might justifiably be excited by the possibility of identifying a battle zone between Briton and Saxon in just the area and at the time—that is to say, late fifth-century western Britain—when we suppose tensions to have been at their greatest, and Arthur to have been militarily active.

By the time I reached Puddletown in the middle of a sweltering day, I was sorely in need of refreshment. I bought lunch from the village grocery store, downed a can of ginger beer in one and paused to sit on a wall to consult the map. It was time to leave the low ground and its limited-visibility frustrations. Dorset was acting like a teenager, monosyllabic, distant and impenetrable. I wanted to head for the hills. My first long-distance walk, in 2001, was the West Highland Way, from Milngavie on the edge of Glasgow to Fort William, all camaraderie, laughs, beer and mountain vistas. At the time it seemed epic. In 2007, with my friend Paul McGowan whom I had met on the West Highland Way, I tackled Corsica's notorious GR20 route along the island's alpine spine. It was hard: seriously hard. Three walkers had died on it the previous week in a freak blizzard; we passed the remains of their belongings on the trail. To spend two weeks in the mountains is to redefine walking—and life. These lowland trails are fascinating in the palimpsest detail of the topography, its intimacy, its crammed-in richness: a filo pastry landscape. But the experiences seemed to pile up, as if I was being buried under a sensory and cultural tumulus. I began to resent having to write so much, take so many pictures, read so many books. I longed for the open downs, their big air, their sightlines and an opportunity to think less. Thinking can be hard work; and walking is for hard physical effort, not for brain-ache.

The afternoon, leaving Puddletown, did not start well: the path that circumvented a crossing of the busy A35 was choked with briar and nettle; one needs a machete for this sort of jungle. After what seemed like a couple of miles (actually, just over half a mile), I emerged, cut, scratched and sweaty, onto a back lane, took a right, and at Druce Farm left the Piddle to follow the line of a small stream that would take me up onto the downs. The heat was like a lead weight slipped into the pack while I wasn't looking. The smell was a composite musk of straw dust and baked earth. The dead rasp of stubble against trail shoes, and ahead of me the growl of a tractor ploughing it into the crisp, dark reddy-brown earth, were welcome noises in that still air. I was reminded, for reasons I can't quite pin down, of Sholokhov's *And Quiet Flows the Don*, with its evocation of the dry intensity of the Cossack landscape and the crushing, infinite labour of the Russian peasant. The contemporary British landscape is largely devoid of peasants or labourers: it is a modern, industrial space. But its past is written in the lines of its boundaries and lanes, paths and monuments, and to be able to read them is the privilege of speaking a native language. The peasant experience was, I suspect, universally similar.

On either side now, on the rounded crests of these convex hills, pimples of tumuli perched on the horizon reminded me that

Dorset is primarily a prehistoric landscape of Bronze Age pastoralists, who cleared the wolds of their forests and buried granny on their summer pastures under a pile of stones and a mound to remind their children and their neighbours that this was their grazing land; that it had always been their grazing land. Thousands of barrows on the downs of Dorset echo a time before the construction of the great Iron Age hill forts—Maiden Castle, Hambledon Hill, Badbury Rings—that mark a feverish tribalisation of these rich lands in the three or four centuries before Caesar planted his untimely hobnail sandals on the shores of Kent.

Higher, then; and higher still, as the trail, surely an ancient route between sheltered winter quarters and summer grazing lands, followed the lazy incline of the valley sides. And then out, out onto Whitcombe Hill at over four hundred feet (not exactly Buachaille Etive Mor in Glen Coe; nor Monte Cinto in Corsica; but still). At last a vista, an uncoiled horizon. Grasshoppers chirped in the long grass; flies buzzed, the faint wind a gentle caressing murmur. Wiping the sweat from my eyes and dropping the pack for a few moments, I enjoyed what little breeze there was, stood beneath the boughs of a lone sycamore for its shade, and looked around. Puddletown lay to the south, now hidden in its valley; the Purbeck hills lost in blue haze beyond; the line of the downs sprawling east, back towards Bere Regis. Higher land spread to the north, land parcelled out three thousand years ago by cross dykes and join-the-dots barrows and interconnected by the even older Ridgeway, so ancient a route that it qualifies as a geological certainty almost as much as an artefact of long-distance prehistoric travel; or a Wall.

I had to point myself west; so I must descend once more into the valley and to the village of Piddletrenthide, where I found a pint glass of lemonade in a pub (shades of Lawrence again, after Aqaba and the Sinai crossing; that marvellous Officer's Mess scene in David Lean's film. 'We. Want. Two. Large. Glasses.

Of lemonade.' And later, General Allenby to orderly: 'What do you think of what Major Lawrence has done, Perkins?' Perkins: 'Bloody marvellous, Sir!').

Up the other side, then, and I found a very welcome camp-site perched at six hundred feet on the hills above Cerne Abbas. After pitching the tent, showering and enjoying a snack, I made a late-afternoon excursion to visit the celebrated phallic Giant. What to make of him—seventeenth-century folly or prehistoric message to the ancestors? He is Hercules or a native British totem, not Woden, but whether a Romano-British fertility plea to the gods or a Civil War parody of Oliver Cromwell none can say unless definitive archaeological evidence emerges one day to prove his antiquity. Cerne Abbas, reached by a steep descent off the chalk ridge, through a field of rape (that sweet, rancid smell again), a track carpeted with pineapple weed (the abiding odour of the day) and down sheep-worn paths has other pleasures— half-timbered houses, a tranquil spring and shady burial ground inside the high walls of the former abbey; good food and beer. The abbey was not founded until the reform movement of the tenth century; but the sweet water of St Augustine's well might conceivably link it with a visit by the first Archbishop of Canterbury on his way, perhaps, to that fateful meeting with the British bishops in 602/3.

That evening, heavy clouds gathered; the air became very close and dusk coincided with rumbles of thunder—Thor making his presence felt. During the night a terrific gusty wind came dashing across the ridge and with it a fistful of short, sharp rain showers, but they passed; and at first light there was nothing to see or hear but a grey, enveloping veil of swirling hill fog. Dorset was invisible again, and silent; sulking. More green lanes funnelled me through field and wood, across small streams. As I came down onto farmland, through the hamlet of Hermitage with its Lady's Well and small neat flint church, the fog lifted. I crossed a meadow whose hedges hosted great, ancient oaks and I saw, as my feet swiped the damp grass, thousands of tiny oak saplings, all delicate green, the fruits of the labours of dopey, forgetful jays and a bumper mast year. I reflected that, should this meadow lie neglected, uncut or ungrazed for just a few years, it would revert to oakwood. This mannered human landscape of field and hedge, wall and fence, is a very temporary borrowing from nature, whose colonising forces sit poised, leashed in like hounds and ready for deployment. Just a decade away from woodland regeneration that might look, to my future self, like the onset of a Dark Age of abandonment. Sure, it's a comforting thought.

Further on, emerging from a very minor road, I passed a row of down-at-heel bungalows with chickens and geese in the gardens; heaps of scrap metal and assorted piles of reclaimed wood everywhere; a wheel-less Nissan Shogun, mounted high and dry on axle stands, being used as an outdoor storage cupboard; suspicious looks when I took a snap. Here were Dorset's dark equivalent of the denizens of the liminal creeks of Essex: its rural poor.

When I planned this walk my intention was to explore a parallel track six or seven miles west of here to visit regions of my own past. In the long, hot summer of 1975 my mother sent me away for two weeks of the summer holidays to an archaeological excavation in the village of Halstock. It was the only dig we could find that accepted children as young as I was—that is to say, fourteen. The campaign to excavate a Roman Villa just south-west of the village was directed by an ex-Royal Navy, former child-probation officer, by that time some years retired, called Ron Lucas. Ron, his assistant Ted Flatters, his wife Joan and a small army of genteel but very sharp folk assembled every August to dissect the villa. I arrived on a rainy day from the station at Yeovil Junction wearing, I remember, a quite unsuitable pair of white flared jeans, wanting very much to be back home. It was about the last rain to fall that summer, or indeed the next. Ron wore a too-small khaki scout hat, bleached almost white by the sun. His trousers were tucked into battered desert boots. He spoke with a Brummie accent and knew everything about teenagers. His party trick, when anyone complained that they were wearing their fingers to the bone, was to hold up his forefinger, truncated to the knuckle by some naval accident years before. His digging technique was old-fashioned, meticulous, thoughtful and confident. With him I served my apprenticeship.

I was an unhappy young man. Ron and his clutch of retired schoolteachers, spinsters and various eccentrics from Dorset's cadre of part-time excavators took me under their collective wing, demanded nothing more of me than companionship and camaraderie, and gave me back my childhood. They taught me how to use a trowel, a dumpy level, a scythe (I still have the scars), a spade, shovel and wheelbarrow. They could not have been kinder; and I served my time with them almost every year for a decade, right through my own university career. They are the modest heroes of my archaeological beginnings. And Halstock retains a fascination: partly because it *is* my childhood; partly because it is one of those late Roman sites that can boast a mysterious saint: Juthware. The name Halstock comes from 'Holy enclosure' and near to the church, which lies a little outside the centre of the village, were once a spring and a shrine. Here Juthware was supposed to have led pilgrims until a jealous step-brother decapitated her. At the site of the murder a spring burst from the earth. Juthware picked her severed head up and walked to the church before expiring. The fondly remembered village pub of my youth, sadly no longer extant, was called the Quiet Woman in ironic veneration. In the British-speaking parts of the island, the site of a holy martyrdom was sometimes preserved in the place name *merthyr*.

Juthware, like St Winifred on the Welsh Marches whose shrine I had passed a few months before, seems to echo the memory of conflict in the early church between proprietorial rights and local cults—a tension in late Roman or Early English culture—perhaps between Briton and Saxon; perhaps between conservatism and radicalism, Christian and heathen. We cannot say; but sufficient numbers of these stories survive from around Britain for us to believe that they reflect a common set of tensions woven into the stuff of the landscape's fabric. Juthware is an example of what is called, marvellously, a cephalophore—a head-carrying saint, following in the tradition of the original martyrdom of St Paul and going back at least to Homeric poetry. St Denis of Paris was another; so was St Osyth in Essex; and Cuthbert, England's greatest saint of the Early Middle Ages, is depicted carrying the head of the decapitated Oswald. Oswald ties the motif into a very ancient, arcane head cult as, perhaps, does the first British martyr, St Alban, who lost his head to a Roman executioner before a well sprang up where it came to rest.

There is another side to the story. Richard Morris,[46] in his majestic and insightful book *Churches in the Landscape*, asks whether the earliest monastic establishments in Western Britain, during the fifth and sixth centuries, might not have evolved from the luxurious villas of a late Roman Christian elite. Villas have produced evidence for the new faith—the Christ and chi-rho mosaic at Hinton St Mary is not far away—and experts in early monasticism, notably Dame Rosemary Cramp, have noted the evident similarity between the classic monastic layout and the villa complex. Was Juthware the inheritor of the villa estate, and did she attempt to found a monastic community there in the face of family opposition?

It seemed a pity to miss out on Halstock; on the other hand, part of me was relieved not to revisit a place with such intense memories. It could not but be painful, especially since the villa now lies beneath a golf course, my old friends are long gone and the Quiet Woman is silent for good. I was afraid of what I might find there; or not find there.

Sherborne is a small, very pretty and venerable town grown up around its minster, supposedly founded by Aldhelm, the first Bishop of West Wessex, under King Ine (r. 688–726) at the beginning of the eighth century. Aldhelm was one of the great Anglo-Saxon scholars, a correspondent of Northumbria's King Aldfrith, a poet and former abbot of Malmesbury much admired by Bede. Crossing the River Yeo over the bridge by the railway station, I walked up the main street and found a community café where I consumed coffee and cake with the appetite of the refugee and chatted to a couple of customers and the waitress. I indulged in a room for the night, at the charming and cosily eccentric Old Bakehouse on Acreman Street. Arriving early in the afternoon I had, for once, ample time to explore the town; but not the abbey— there was a founder's day service or some such, for the famous school which shares the town centre, and I could not get in. It was a shame; not only does the church offer architectural splendours, but it is reputedly the site of St Juthware's translation in the eleventh century. Walks are strewn with lost opportunities; there is no space for the dead weight of regret in my rucksack.

The room was a mixed blessing; the bed too soft and hot after nights in a tent. The streets were full of school-leavers hell-bent on erasing the night with drink; traffic was noisy; the humidity oppressive. I had a poor night of it and woke to torrential rain that the weather forecast threatened would last all day. The early news was full of lightning strikes, flash floods and a generally apocalyptic prognosis. As it happened, this was to be my longest day's walk of this trip. I resigned myself to getting wet, so I stripped down to shorts and a vest—no point getting more clothes soaked than necessary—and set out early with Camelot my first destination. The sky was like a pillow, or a low corridor underground. The streets were wet with standing water, the back lanes and paths steamy with vapour. The atmosphere seethed moisture. I got lost, musing on Dorset's impenetrable personality; by the time I realigned myself and came out onto the north-running Corton Ridge I found I had crossed into Somerset. A creamy-white barn owl emerged ghostly from a hedge in front of me, not two yards away, and silently flew off in search of peace and quiet.

At last a view: west, to the flood plain of the River Yeo, the Roman town of Ilchester (*Lindinis*—perhaps the focus of four of Arthur's battles according to the poetic list in the *Historia Brittonum*) and the beginning of the Somerset lowlands so recently inundated by the floods of winter 2013/14. Laid out like a three-dimensional model, the counterpane drama of woodland and village, ribbon roads and church tower, farm and field, harvest interrupted by the rain, seemed held on pause. Low cloud scraped the top of the ridge and the morning's humidity was palpable. The clouds wore yellow. More arresting still was the sight ahead of me of the cover photograph of Alcock's *Arthur's Britain*: South Cadbury hill fort. I stopped as near as dammit at the place where the photographer had stood in about 1970, on the brow of Parrock Hill which overlooks the fort. Its strategic location was blindingly obvious—an outrider of the Dorset hills which dominates the plains north and west to Glastonbury. Even in today's murk the massive triple ramparts looked like a serious disincentive to anyone wanting to take it. The flat, kidney-shaped crest, grazed by brown and white cows, was open pasture; below the ramparts a fringe of dark green woodland made the whole look like a tonsured monk's head. It needed no *Time Team* reconstruction of its palisades and halls, bristling with spear and shield, to evoke an age of power, prestige and elite warfare: of glory and extreme violence.

I descended to the foot of the hill and walked widdershins around the base of the fort to South Cadbury, the hamlet that nestles below its eastern entrance. The path to the top is steep and, like every other track in this part of the world, deeply incised through each successive rampart. I came out onto the top, breath-less, and took a circuit of the formidable defences. This, then, is the place claimed by some desperate romantics to have been the Camelot of King Arthur. I have owned a copy of Leslie Alcock's account of his excavations here, *Cadbury/Camelot*, since I was a teenager. It's a riveting story of a campaign of excavation and a marvellous evocation of the appeal of archaeology in the late 1960s even if, as a technical publication, it leaves much to be desired. It was the campaign which set Alcock on the way to write his definitive account of the archaeology of the Dark Age Brit-ish Isles in *Arthur's Britain*. The project to uncover South Cad-bury, identified spuriously by the early antiquary John Leland as Arthur's Camelot in the sixteenth century, was an overt attempt to uncover the archaeology of Arthur. The results of five years' digging more than justified the time, expense and heartache that all archaeologists are familiar with. At the time, Alcock con-cluded that if one wanted to put a historical Arthur anywhere, it might as well be here, at South Cadbury. Over subsequent dec-ades, however, he took up a position of hard-line scepticism, treat-ing evidence with a much more rigorous, forensic scrutiny. But standing on this superbly atmospheric site, looking down on the plains and watching a raven perched jet-black in the clouded can-opy of a Scots pine tree, one could easily forgive him for allowing Arthur to infuse his earlier thinking.

So, let's get the Arthurian record straight. As Alcock himself pointed out, there are just three enigmatic references to a histor-ical Arthur in all the surviving literature which may lay claim to authenticity. In the *Annales Cambriae*, not compiled before the ninth century but based on a set of British Easter annals origi-nally dating from much earlier, two entries stand out:

> Ann. LXXII [equating to the year 518] The battle of
> Badon [*Bellum Badonis*] in which Arthur carried the cross

of our Lord Jesus Christ for three days and three nights on
his shoulders [or, more likely, shield] and the Britons were
victorious.

Then...

> Ann. LXXXXIII [equating to the year 539] The battle
> [or 'strife'] of Camlann, in which Arthur and Medraut
> fell.[47]

And, in the chronicle known as the *Historia Brittonum*, likewise a
British compilation no earlier than the ninth century, there is the
most famous entry of all, a list of twelve battles probably originating in a poem of praise for a great warrior.

> Then Arthur fought against them in those days, together
> with the kings of the British; but he was their leader in
> battle [*dux bellorum*].
>   The first battle was at the mouth of the river called
> Glein. The second, the third, the fourth and the fifth
> were on another river, called the Douglas, which is in the
> country of ?Lindsey [*in regione linnuis*]. The sixth battle
> was on the river called Bassas. The seventh battle was
> in Celyddon Forest, that is, the Battle of Celyddon Coed.
> The eighth battle was in Guinnion fort, and in it Arthur
> carried the image of the holy Mary, the everlasting Virgin,
> on his ?shield/shoulder and the heathen were put to flight
> on that day, and there was a great slaughter upon them,
> through the power of Our Lord Jesus Christ and the power
> of the Holy Virgin Mary, his mother. The ninth battle
> was fought in the City of the Legion. The tenth battle
> was fought on the bank of the river called Tryfrwyd. The
> eleventh battle was on the hill called Agned. The twelfth
> battle was on Badon Hill and in it nine hundred and sixty

SOUTH CADBURY

men fell in one day, from a single charge of Arthur's, and
no-one laid them low save he alone; and he was victorious
in all his campaigns.[48]

None of the battle locations have been identified with any confidence, despite the spilling of a positive lake of ink, the wearing
out of many a map and much tramping over hill and dale. Nor is
there any sense of the length of time over which that campaign
was fought. If we are to believe the *Annales*, Arthur survived
another twenty or so years after Badon.

The list seems, to begin with, straightforward, if rather thin
and with no sense of political or narrative context. The geography ranges from an apparent conflict in southern Scotland (*Cat
Coit Celidon*) to Badon, traditionally associated with a hill near
the Roman spa resort that later became Bath. In reality, it's not so
simple. The only other source—belonging genuinely to the sixth
century—that mentions the battle of Badon (but not Arthur) is
the epistle of the British monk Gildas to his fellow countrymen
on the history and woes of the Britons in the face of impious kings
and rapacious Saxons: *De excidio et conquestu Britanniae*, 'On the
Ruin and conquest of Britain'.[49] Gildas's broadly accepted dates
(a putative death in the 540s) and his account of Badon (he says he
is writing forty years after that event) mean that the *Annales Cambriae* date of 518 for this great siege is probably twenty years too
late. Who to believe?

I do not think that we need worry much about the modern
debate between a 'northern' and 'southern' Arthur. A sub-Roman
British commander of what amounts to a cohort or warband of
auxiliary mounted troops might perfectly well have fought campaigns along the length of Western Britain over two or three
decades. The appendant fluff of round tables, holy grails, excali-
burs and courtly chivalry belongs to a time when those tales were
composed, more than half a millennium later. Only archaeology

can offer more penetrating questions and answers to what Britain was like between about 430, when it seems Roman Britain was in a state of partial administrative meltdown, and a hundred and fifty years later when the Anglo-Saxon, Welsh and Caledonian kingdoms emerged into the pages of literate recorders of history. Archaeology tells us that South Cadbury was fortified in the sixth century or thereabouts—a rebuilding of Iron Age defences; that a great hall stood on the summit; and that there was, perhaps, a church here. Pottery from the Mediterranean found its way to the site (via Scillies and Bristol Channel?); there is speculation that Cadbury became a royal estate centre, replacing (or restoring) the function of the Roman town at Ilchester—perhaps a relationship like Wroxeter and the Wrekin and then back again. But we don't need to place the semi-mythical Arthur here; if we want to give its lord an identity, why not that of Cadda, the otherwise unknown Saxon who gave the place its name?

Some centuries later, in the aftermath of the Battle of Maldon (see page 119) and the resurgence of Viking power in Eastern England, King Æthelred's men reoccupied the fort, reinforced the defences one more time and set up a burgh here, church, mint and all. The place names and archaeology of the South-west which emerge from decades of scholarship and coal-face fieldwork suggest that for all the great deeds of kings, bishops and saints, most people, most of the time, stayed where they were. There was never a great immigration or colonisation of these parts by Germanic warriors or peasants (see Postscript: Who are the British?—pages 423–6). Control was concentrated in the hands of an aristocratic tribal elite, an exclusive warrior caste whose names, whether British or Germanic, reflect politics more than genetics. Most people were ethnically indigenous Britons, speaking first Brythonic, then a mixture of Latin and Early Welsh, and then, if they wanted access to lines of patronage flowing from Germanic-speaking lords, the language of Beowulf. I suspect that for several centuries bilingualism was common; that English became the lingua franca of trade and power and then the tongue of an English state and culture, even if the language of the literate remained Latin well into the Medieval period.

South Cadbury's most dramatic imprint on the history of the Britons came not, I think, in the Dark Ages, but in the first century AD when it was the site of a battle that seems to have resulted in the massacre of large numbers of the indigenous people by the armies of Rome, after which its defences were slighted and the site abandoned until Rome herself found the game not worth the candle, four hundred years later. There is something to be said for the idea that the Roman period was no more than an interlude in the late Iron Age.

Down into the plain of Somerset, then, with the sky threatening; through Sparkford and across the busy A303; down a muddy, thorny green lane, through rolling fields past Babcary and across the Roman Fosse Way (now the A37, it was built as a Roman grand design, to link the South-west with the Midlands and the East Coast in Lincolnshire) towards a group of villages, the Charltons, whose names reflect that caste of English farmer, the ceorl, who forms the backbone of any discussion about free warrior peasants in pre-Conquest England. Charlton is by no means an uncommon village name. It is often found in association, as it is here and in the Welsh Marches, with 'cott' names (Ashcott, Buscott, Hurcott)—small outlying farms, probably dependent on larger settlements or royal estates, probably poor, perhaps also liminal like those bungalows I had passed a day before. The small town of Somerton, immediately to the south-west, is the place from which this shire was named, a one-time capital of Wessex. It means 'summer settlement', a seasonal centre for the rich grazing lands of the high ground between the Rivers Cary and Yeo. In this layer cake of generations of farmers, drovers, artisans and cottagers, Arthur assumes his rightful place as a footnote to reality. Somerton sits on an island of high ground, never much more than 300 feet above sea level, surrounded by dead flat peatlands. On a much smaller, much lower rise a few miles to the west, lies Athelney. I had tried and failed to plan a route that would take me there. The fastness in the marshes on which King Alfred hid from the Great Heathen Army in 878 before his brilliant counter-attack at Edington is a place to evoke heroism like no other.

As I turned off the Fosse Way onto the lane that leads to Charlton Adam, the heavens opened: a great crashing bombardment of thunderclap artillery, lightning and torrents of rain that had me soaked to the skin in less than half a minute. Within four hundred yards I could not have been wetter had I jumped into a river. I came to a pub and dashed inside; thankfully they had stone floors so the extravagant pool I made at the bar didn't much bother them. I ordered a pint of Guinness, took the pack off and wrung out my vest; and at that moment a tremendous explosion overhead took out the pub's electricity supply, while a few customers who had been standing in the porch, watching the rain and smoking, scuttled back inside in a state almost of stupefaction. I had escaped the eye of the storm in the nick of time. One of the locals asked me if I would like a lift somewhere; or an umbrella, as if I were an object of pity, an inadvertent civilian trespasser onto a battlefield.

The storm passed. I trudged squelching onward, up and along the wooded ridge of the Polden hills between two levels and above the town of Street, from where I got my first view of Glastonbury's looming Tor; then on to the small village of Walton where I found my campsite, and a glimpse of sunshine, after a twenty-three-mile hike. Walton: not, as it appears, '*wealh tun*', an enclave of Britons in an Anglo-Saxon landscape, but '*weald tun*', the settlement in the woods. I hung damp clothes from the bowing branches of a walnut tree, and retired early to my tent. The next morning, confounding my prejudice against the white-goods campers of England, an elderly chap emerged from the small caravan on the next pitch and brought me a large mug of sweet, hot tea.

The small town of Street is famous as the home of Millfield School and as the birthplace of Clarks, the shoemakers, who began making their trademark sheepskin slippers here in 1825 and who still employ twelve hundred people at the company's headquarters on the original factory site, even if they do not make any actual shoes there these days. I made my passage along the high street too early in the morning to see the workers thronging to their desks. After yesterday's storm and Saturday-night drinking, it had a ghostly, quiet charm. A pub called the Lantokay reminded me that Street, whose English name (from the Latin *strata*) reflects both the proximity of a Roman road along the south edge of the levels and a medieval stone causeway that ran across the marshes here, is lucky enough to retain in documentary form the memory of its Brythonic name. Lantokay was the church of St Cai (Lan- deriving from Early Welsh *Llan*—a church enclosure). The present church is a Victorian restoration of a fourteenth-century building; but the churchyard is large and seems once to have been circular, typical of the Early Medieval *Llan* layout.

Avoiding the main road that links the high ground on which Street stands to Glastonbury and its Tor across the narrowest point of the levels, I tracked east along the edge of the peatlands for about a mile so that the Tor was in my sights all the time with the early sun silhouetting it against a sky of fluffy white cloud on a blue ceramic background. The Tor is such a striking and unmistakeable feature of the English landscape that to approach it on foot is to feel like a pilgrim reaching the base of a holy mountain. As if to reinforce that otherworldly sense, a young gentleman dressed in the guise of a Civil War cavalier pedalled past me on a bicycle, waving; and I was accosted by a man with a dog, who insisted that I share his packet of chocolate digestives. I wondered if I was beginning to look like a tramp, in need of alms.

Looked at on a photograph from directly overhead the Tor is an ossified prehistoric cetacean stranded on a green beach, its flanks ribbed like a humpback whale, its blowhole the crenellated church tower that seems to poke out of the top of the hill; the sheep on its grassy slopes are barnacles; the snaking age-worn path the uncoiled rope from a hunter's harpoon. The view from the top is quite stunning, especially on a day when cloud scurries before a brisk shepherding wind and the light is piercingly sharp. I found myself in the company of cross-legged yoga aficionados and t'ai chi practitioners, a couple of dog-walkers and a generic hippy or two in tie-dye baggies. We were tolerant of one another. I could pick out much of yesterday's route, at least as far as South Cadbury whence the sun shone; and this morning's walk across the orchards and meadows of the reclaimed peatlands, protected by levees that suffice to hold back its rivers in all but exceptional years. The ruinous outline of Glastonbury Abbey stood proud of its surrounding cluster of roofs; I could hear church bells faintly tolling. To the north, across another green expanse of wetlands lay the Mendip Hills, rich in minerals and history: my destination.

Between them, the abbey and Tor offer the Dark Age fantasist an irresistible potpourri of myth, conspiracy, forgery, mysticism and magic. I was lucky enough to be taught by Glastonbury's pre-eminent archaeological investigator: from the first days of my undergraduate career as an archaeology student at York University I was steeped in both the Glastonbury myths and in archaeology's achievement in testing them. Philip Rahtz was by no means a hardliner so far as fringe archaeology went. He was a polymath, a man of great intellectual appetite, an astoundingly prolific excavator and, with his second wife Lorna Watts, publisher of excavations. His is a unique legacy to our heritage. He was also an open-minded, hugely gifted and entertaining, if sometimes infuriating, teacher.

No amount of academic scrutiny or scepticism will dull the bright Excalibur blade of those who believe that Glastonbury was the fabled Isle of Avalon or that Christ himself founded a church here (despite the fact that there was no such thing as a Christian church during the lifetime of Jesus). There is no evidence at all that Joseph of Arimathea came to Glastonbury (or ever left his native Judaea) in the first century. It is a story invented a thousand years later to enhance the fame (and profitability) of the abbey. The Glastonbury thorn which, according to legend, sprang into life where Joseph placed his stick, is a natural hybrid of the native hawthorn; it sometimes flowers in winter. I know of another example not far from where I live, at Houghton le Spring, said to have been taken as a cutting from the Glastonbury thorn. There is, as yet, no direct evidence of any Christian activity in Glastonbury before the fifth or sixth century, when a hermitage of sorts (excavated by Rahtz) was built on the Tor. An early church, perhaps seventh-century, was constructed on the site of the abbey but destroyed and built over after a disastrous fire in the twelfth century. There seem to have been two decorated stone high crosses here, later described in masonic fashion as 'pyramids'. A well, sited close to the south-east corner of the earliest church, may belong to the Roman period. The supposed exhumation of the remains of 'King' Arthur and Queen Guinevere is almost certainly a deliberate forgery concocted by medieval monks in a bid to recover their prestige and economic fortunes after the fire. The Tor excavations aside, much of the archaeological or antiquarian work carried out in the grounds of the abbey was conducted before modern methods had been adopted; the sort of forensic detail that we might now obtain to resolve some of these questions is lost. It is a great shame.

I am not one of those who give any credence at all to the idea of ley lines or zodiacal marks in the fields surrounding the Tor. More exciting, I think, is the knowledge that tracks of thoughtful design and engineering cunning, dating to the Neolithic period (from nearly 4000 BC), were demonstrably built to afford early settlers access to the abundant resources of the levels. The ingenuity of the early monks of Glastonbury in controlling and channelling water courses, in manufacturing metalwork and glass; in managing to import all manner of exotic items from the far end of the known world, including Byzantium, is remarkable enough to keep any sane and inquiring mind happy. Even so, one has to admire the ability of the religious community at Glastonbury, and elsewhere, to generate the sort of theme-park fantasy of relic and superstition that kept pilgrims coming here for over a thousand years and creating the wealth that the abbey relied on for its splendours. I wandered dizzily through the town and marvelled at the proliferation of businesses offering 'psychic cartomancy readings', 'Wheel of light' bed-and-breakfast accommodation, 'Moon mirrors' and any amount of crystal-stroking, dragon-charming, homeopathic vial sniffing and transformation-inducing tat, designed to relieve the credulous latter-day tourist of a great deal of money and to provide a comforting affirmation of the supposedly harmless mass psychosis which spawns it.

Marvellous too, though invisible, is the site of the famous Lake Village which I passed on a back road lined with drainage ditches and pollard willows heading north-west out of town. It was excavated by two particularly brilliant and progressive archaeologists, Arthur Bulleid and Harold St George Gray, around the turn of the nineteenth and twentieth centuries and shows just how sophisticated were the settlements of the late Iron Age on the edge of the marshes. Here, preserved anaerobically in the peat, was the settlement of a complex, hierarchical society whose dwellings consisted of roundhouses and barns, threshing floors, weaving huts and 'special places' for women, and whose social structure was evolved and perpetuated through each phase of rebuilding. Their repertoire of domestic artefacts finds modern

equivalents in every household. The whole was enclosed in a large village compound whose foundations lay on stakes driven into the mud of the shoreline, consolidated by hazel hurdles laid flat to create a stable platform. These villagers were sophisticated managers of their environment and in their animistic kin-based, highly practical culture lie the roots of Early Medieval society.

That afternoon I walked along the lower slopes of the Mendip Hills from where the Romans extracted lead on an imperial scale to satisfy their voracious plumbing needs. On a more relaxed schedule I might have stopped at Wells, another important centre of pre-Conquest religiosity. But time pressed. As afternoon turned to evening, I came down from a delightful green lane that hugged the two-hundred-foot contour, through fields which had once been orchards and where I browsed on small, sweet plums, and into the village of Cheddar. Cheese and gorge notwithstanding, Cheddar's archaeological fame rests on the Anglo-Saxon palace excavated close to the church by none other than Philip Rahtz. There is nothing to see of the great timber hall and minster, built probably in the reign of King Alfred; the site is marked by concrete plinths in the grounds of a school. Such is the way with the fragile remains of the distant past: the monument is the published report, often written in very technical language that fellow professionals understand and can interrogate. In Philip's case, there has rarely been an archaeologist who did more to write accessible, unpatronising accounts for general consumption.

I woke in a quiet corner of a campsite close to Cheddar's medieval church on another perfectly clear morning to the sound of its bells tolling the sixth hour, struck camp early and, finding nowhere open for breakfast or supplies, climbed the south-west scarp of the Mendips through narrow green lanes and dense woodland. I broke cover on the crest at over six hundred feet, a quarry on my right a reminder of the precious treasures of the hills. A small tribe of hairy bearded goats with wicked-looking long horns accompanying me on the narrow road offered a sense of more ancient exploitation of the Somerset uplands. It was very fine to be high up and in the open and I motored along at a good pace, munching on the last of my oatcakes. From Black Down, at over a thousand feet, the view towards the Severn Estuary and the coast of South Wales was breathtaking and seductive and took my mind back to the sea. On either side of me squatted the mammiform burial mounds of Bronze Age pastoralists whose summer steadings can just be seen here and there as grassy humps in sheltered spots. A sharp descent on the north side brought me out through a shallow gorge and past the site of Avelina's hole, a limestone cave where a very early cemetery, dating to 8000 BC, testifies to the enduring appeal of these rich coastal lands.

At the small village of Burrington I attempted to make my passage along a green lane so choked with brambles and nettles that I finally gave in and had to backtrack, once again scratched and pricked and in militant pedestrian mood to berate the locals for allowing a right of way to fall into disuse. But there was nobody to berate; the twenty-first-century English live in their cars. I diverted via a winding lane that crossed the juvenile stream of another River Yeo and eventually brought me to Wrington: here my mood was lifted by the charming sweep of a Georgian terrace and an equally charming shop on the corner, where I was able to buy a packet of Eccles cakes, a beef sandwich, two hot sausage rolls and a can of ginger beer. The shopkeeper asked me if I would like a bag. No need, thanks, I said. Outside, I sat on the nearest bench and consumed the lot in a sort of last-day-on-the-trail demob happy ecstasy of guiltless gluttony.

Refreshed and refuelled, I climbed the last hill, up through mixed broadleaf and conifer woods. A maze of paths, timber roads and trackways linking old mine workings soon had me lost. I reverted to navigational glimpses of the sun and the lie of the land to bring me out at last onto a promontory at the end of the ridge before it descended to the plain and thence to the Bristol Channel. Here is another Cadbury Hill. This Iron Age hill fort overlooks the village of Congresbury, where the holy man Congar is said to have built a monastery. The site of his foundation was still known, and identified by, no less a bishop than Asser, the Welshman who became King Alfred's enthusiastic biographer at the end of the ninth century. Congar, a native of Pembrokeshire, lived during the late fifth century during the very earliest period of Western British monasticism; he may even have been a marginal contemporary of St Patrick, and of Halstock's Juthware. Did he inherit or acquire the nearby Roman villa which lay on the banks of the River Yeo just downstream?

There is no spectacular approach to the fort as there is at South Cadbury: one emerges from the woodland on the ridge, catches a glimpse of the village below and ascends through a hollow way beneath more trees onto a scrubby hilltop from which there is no view. It felt more like enclosed and secretive Dorset than open Somerset. Part of the summit interior of the hill fort was excavated in the late 1960s and early 1970s by a distinguished team of archaeologists, not least of whom was the indefatigable Philip Rahtz. The rock-cut features made excavation and recording complex and challenging; the reward for their endeavours was evidence for major circular buildings occupied during and after the Roman period; and a large quantity of imported Mediterranean pottery (amphorae for carrying olive oil and wine; late Roman fine tableware), type G penannular brooches (a decidedly unsexy name for a distinctly Early Medieval British decorative artefact) and a longhouse of barn-conversion form. One of the more modest but significant finds was a circular ceramic sherd, which archaeologists recognise as the stopper from an amphora—the implication being that Congresbury's masters were no second-hand receivers of dodgy goods or empty containers, but capable of purchasing unopened, full casks of wine or olive oil from the Graeco-Byzantine world of the Emperor Justinian. This was the Dark Age equivalent of a Fortnum & Mason hamper sent to an Indian rajah. Congresbury was not merely visited, but inhabited, and pretentiously so. It was a busy place, with much rebuilding and restructuring over two or three centuries, even if the complete picture of settlement and ritual activity here was not available to the excavators. The site also has to be seen in the context of a pagan Roman temple complex which lay very close to the north at Henley Wood; was Congresbury its ostentatious Christian successor?

The broader significance of the site is obvious when one looks at the geography. This River Yeo is tidal as far up as Congresbury village, which means that there is and was access to the sea; a former *wic* site lay down on Woodspring Bay where coastal craft could have pulled up onto the beach and traded elite, valuable goods in return for perhaps slaves, furs, hunting dogs and silver or lead. I might almost imagine this as the place where the Alexandrian ship's captain had his lucky landfall in the days of

John, the almsgiving patriarch. And on the other side of the Bristol Channel lies Dinas Powys, a more or less contemporary kingship site and hill fort which has also yielded significant amounts of exotic, imported material.

The native Christian elite of the South-west, immersed perhaps in a folk memory of their status under the Romans as town-dwelling traders and magistrates and even, conceivably, harbouring mythological fantasies of their tribal Iron Age ancestors, were attempting to live in a sort of imperial manner, even if they did not have a very clear idea of what Imperial Rome had been like, or had meant to the Romano-Britons. They refortified some of the great former hill forts, fitted them with grandiose houses and collected trinkets from distant lands. Occasionally they were able to drink wine from cracked glass goblets; their smiths made them beautiful brooches from recycled Roman metalwork, and they indulged in the sort of ostentatious tribal warfare, on a rather reduced scale, that allowed them to sing songs and tell tales of heroism; to dress up in battle finery once in a while; to celebrate minor war leaders like Arthur and praise both the gods of the animistic universe and the crucified one of the far distant Holy Land.

From the summit of Cadbury Hill down to the village of Yatton, its coffee shops and railway station, was a mere eye-blink on an epic journey in search of heroes. If those heroes are in most cases long departed, their spoor can still be followed in the folds of the hills, the river crossings and the names and stories that they left in their wake.

Interlude *Walking on the Wall on the spot*

Prince Oswald's vision—fluxgate gradiometer—Heavenfield—Ionan mission to Northumbria—Whin Sill—crossroads—leaving the Wall behind

PRINCE OSWALD IDING's brief sojourn at Heavenfield, some time in the early summer of 634, matches for impact the arrival of St Augustine in Kent thirty-seven years before. His victory against Cadwallon of Gwynedd ensured his immediate recognition as king of Bernicia and overlord of nearly all the Anglo-Saxon kingdoms. He restored Northumbria's lapsed Christian kingship, founded the Irish missionary church at Lindisfarne and instituted the beginnings of an English Christian monarchy that survives today.[50] Two accounts exist of that fateful night before battle. Adomnán, Colmcille's hagiographer, recorded that Oswald saw a vision of the great Irish saint and that it inspired him and his small army to victory. Bede told a story, remembered by his own generation, of how Oswald raised a wooden cross that same night and how, in years afterwards, sick people were healed by virtue of its miraculous properties. Oswald's rich tradition as a saint and martyr, whose relics possessed great potency, begins at this spot where Roman Wall, Dark Age myth and the origins of the English state come together.

Our peculiar means of getting at this enigmatic landscape is to walk up and down in narrow, marked rows carrying a device which measures the magnetic response of the soil beneath our feet. Where soil has been disturbed by digging, by construction or by fire, its magnetic response varies, subtly.[51] For every twenty-metre square that we walk with our gradiometer, its data-logger records 3200 points, which we plot in the form of a map of grey scales—a ghostly, grainy but telling sub-surface landscape, a human and natural palimpsest—doing so without disturbing the archaeology. For the surveyor, with two assistants moving guide ropes between fixed points, every grid square is a walk of eight hundred metres. Walking on the spot can be tiring.

During the last months of 2014, as the days were becoming uncomfortably cold and short, hardier members of the Bernician Studies Group[52] convened in the fields between the Roman Wall and St Oswald's church. Jack Pennie was our principal geophysicist: a retired Royal Engineer and bus driver, he has mastered the technicalities and logistics of the machine with admirable persistence—it is not very user-friendly kit. The other members of the team were Geoff Taylor, a retired solicitor, Ray Shepherd, a former engineer, John McNulty, a GP, and Deb Haycock, property manager and sailor—an interesting and rewarding group of fellow Dark Age enthusiasts. The prize for this unglamorous, chilly and repetitive work was the chance to see if Oswald's brief bivouac here left any archaeological trace that we could detect.

The Ordnance Survey map still records Heavenfield as the site of the battle in which Oswald slew his British rival Cadwallon; but since the nineteenth century it has been known that the battle took place elsewhere. Bede tells us that Cadwallon was destroyed at a place called Denisesburn. A medieval document uncovered by Canon William Greenwell, an indefatigable if sometimes unsubtle Victorian antiquarian, identified it as the Rowley Burn. That stream flows into the Devil's Water (that *Divelis/Dhubglas* name again) near Whitley Chapel, three miles or so south of the River Tyne. If the denouement of the battle was a rout that ended in this hilly, remote part of Hexhamshire, the main battle is likely to have taken place at or near Corbridge, where I believe Cadwallon based his army. In the surprise of a dawn attack his forces fled, fatally, south across the bridge and into the high country with no hope of escape.

There is also a curious tale told by Bede which suggests that Oswald's cross may not have been the only mark left here before the construction of the church. Bede admits in his otherwise smoothly persuasive account of Oswald's triumphant return to Bernicia and the founding of Lindisfarne by Bishop Aidan a year later, that in the intervening months an Ionan priest 'of harsher disposition' tried to preach to the Anglians of these parts. 'Seeing that the people were unwilling to listen to him, he returned to his own land.'[53] Aidan, it seems, was his more wisely chosen successor. If Bede's tale is true, it begs the question where the first priest set up his church. Intriguingly, when Heavenfield is viewed from the air, a suspiciously shaped enclosure can be discerned: it has a size and shape broadly similar to the monastic enclosures at Iona and Lindisfarne, even if its walls appear to be no earlier than the eighteenth century.

Over a half dozen days we plodded up and down, then huddled around the computer screen beneath the shelter of an immense, ancient and venerable oak tree to see the results appear, pixel by pixel, grid by grid. The Wall appeared as a ghostly, thin, dead straight line thirty yards or so north of, and parallel to General Wade's Military Road. The faint outline of the Roman turret 25b could be seen. Excavated in the 1950s, it yielded no significant artefacts, but a hole dug into its centre in antiquity offered the tantalising possibility that this was where Oswald raised his cross. In a corner of the field in which the Wall lies submerged, a pronounced, straight-edged black strip, which looked like some enormous military ditch, had us going for a while until, one evening, we traced it on a geological map—and found it to be nothing more or less than an outcrop of the Great Whin Sill:

extremely magnetic but entirely natural. This intrusive dyke proved to be a small nightmare: like the glare of a floodlight, its presence masked everything else near by. Even so, some careful filtering of the data and a switch to a less sensitive setting on the machine for another pass showed that there is indeed some archaeology here, across the Roman ditch beyond the Wall. We saw what looked like parts of circular ditches—buildings perhaps; but maybe just agricultural disturbance; that pesky Whin Sill hides all in its glare. It's hard to say exactly what these features are and the only way to positively identify their nature and origins would be to excavate. Nevertheless, they were enough to have us applying to renew our detection licence; and so we would be back again in the New Year. We had not given up on Heavenfield. The jury is out on the idea of some sort of early Irish establishment here; but there is a large subterranean landscape for us to explore and map; all it takes is a little walking on the spot.

Some weeks later, in February 2015, we gave a presentation on the results to the rest of the group. We also invited members of the local history society at Acomb, and with them Nick Hodgson, a Roman specialist who has been helping them to trace the line of the Stanegate. He drew our attention to a LiDAR survey of Warden Hill and to the curious spread of Roman coins at Great Whittington which Brian Roberts interpreted as a sort of caravanserai. Hogdson and his colleagues have, it seems, nailed one part of the Stanegate question by identifying two construction camps close to the confluence of Tyne and North Tyne, which strongly suggests that the Stanegate crossed at this point. So now we know two ends of the section of the road west of Corbridge. Geophysics will, soon perhaps, complete the line.

Hodgson was particularly interested in our geological anomaly, the intrusive dyke, because he believes that the Devil's Causeway, which runs from Dere Street about a mile north of the Wall, to Berwick and the Northumbrian coast, might once have extended to join the Wall line further to the south-west. If one projects its line (he showed us a convincing slide), it would come out at Heavenfield; and it would come out in pretty much the same place and on the same angle as our geological fault. Ray Shepherd soon spotted the significance: if Oswald, travelling east from the Solway Firth, hoped to rendezvous with sympathetic forces from his heartlands around Bamburgh, the junction of Wall and Devil's Causeway would be a perfect location, and invisible from Cadwallon's forces at Corbridge. If nothing else, it would be well worth our while to see if the gradiometer can confirm, or otherwise, that extension.

Mulling on these matters in a later meeting, we began to see that a rectangle formed by the Tyne and its northern branch, the Wall and Dere Street (about twelve square miles) was a landscape of considerable dynamic importance to the Romans and those who came after. Domination of that rectangle held the strategic key to the middle Tyne valley; to the crossing of the river at Corbridge; to military penetration north, north-west, west and south. Bede's suggestion that a small church and the remnants of Oswald's cross drew Christians here in the seventh century may be an understatement. Just across the river the great abbey of Hexham, founded by Wilfrid in about 674 to exploit his significant landholdings here and to tap into the powerful cult of Oswald's relics, shows the continuing value of the militarised Wall zone. This may appear, at first sight, to be a border, a frontier, but, on closer inspection, it looks very like a core of Bernician territory.

My time with the Wall was up; on my way to Jarrow I had to cross the river and visit Hexham Abbey with its famous crypt, then follow the wild River Tyne until it is tamed, somewhere between here and Newcastle.

CWM LLAN

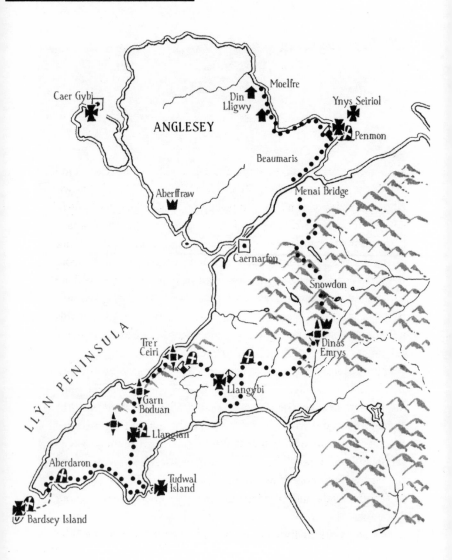

ANGLESEY AND LLYN

Caer Gybi

ANGLESEY

Moelfre

Din
Lligwy

Ynys Seiriol

Penmon

Beaumaris

Aberffraw

Menai Bridge

Caernarfon

Snowdon

Tre'r
Ceiri

Dinas
Emrys

LLYN PENINSULA

Llangybi

Garn
Boduan

Llangian

Aberdaron

Tudwal
Island

Bardsey Island

Aside from the fact that my great-grandfather Alf Richmond died in a boating accident off Cemaes Bay in 1895, my knowledge of Anglesey's history is limited to a line in Bede, a couple of entries in the *Annales Cambriae* and a vague idea that the Romans believed it to be an Island of Druids. It inhabits an exotic corner of the imagination, fortified by the Menai Strait and cut off from the rest of the world, as Sicily is from Italy or as Britain is from Europe. Its reputation as a bastion of Welsh identity gives one, perhaps, the sense that Anglo-Saxons are not welcome; that this ancient and magical land of mists and wizards, defended by fierce tidal races, wishes to keep itself to itself.

The gossipy Roman historian Tacitus, whose father-in-law Agricola commanded a campaign of conquest in Britain during the late first century, records that when confronted with the Menai Strait and with no fleet at hand, the general hand-picked troops trained in specialist assault and had them swim across to the island of Môn.[54] The enemy, he says, were so awestruck by the sight of swarms of amphibious semi-clad soldiers that they lost their heads and surrendered their island fortress without resistance.

We had seen the lights of Holyhead, one night, from the helm of *Eda Frandsen*, the Dublin ferries coming and going ahead of us in a blaze of lights. Now, in the second half of August 2014, Sarah and I crossed Thomas Telford's stupendous Menai Bridge on a small local bus—the twin arches that pierce the bridge's super-structure so narrow that there was barely more than a couple of inches' clearance on either side—and found ourselves deposited at a crossroads near the village of Moelfre on the island's north-east coast. I wanted to start my journey among the Britons at a suitably evocative spot: the ruins of a stone-built native village called Din Lligwy. In August the back lanes of Anglesey's roll-ing hills are choked with holiday traffic: refugees from the bustle of Manchester and Liverpool who succeed annually in bringing city-centre traffic chaos with them. The campsites are more like car and caravan rallies, with armies of marshals, electronic gates and myriad notices forbidding this and that. We poor pilgrims on foot were as invisible as sewer rats.

We found Din Lligwy hidden in a copse of trees, like some sacred grove, on a small limestone rise not far from the site of a medieval chapel now inhabited only by cows and crows. Din Lligwy must have been the settlement of an elite family: the massive neatness of the stone foundations which survive tell of wealth and architectural pretension; the trapezoidal curtain wall, of privacy; the setting, of a deep sense of belonging in the land-scape. The site, covering perhaps an acre internally, may have been inhabited since the Iron Age: two houses are perfectly cir-cular in the pure native tradition of the British West, but the long rectangular buildings which nestle against the inside walls are of a strikingly different tradition: more like miniature Roman gra-naries than anything you would find in a mainland British village. One wonders if the inhabitants had heard of, or seen, a Roman provincial villa and remodelled their farmstead on a suitably grandiose scale. The early twentieth-century excavators recov-ered pottery of the third and fourth centuries; and in the building close to the entrance they found evidence of ironworking. Curiously, and sufficient to get the Early Medieval archaeologist's nose twitching, many of the pottery sherds showed signs of having been repaired with iron wire. Those who could afford Roman kitchen pots and tableware could generally afford to replace them with new; either this rich family had fallen on hard times in the fourth century or the settlement survived beyond the end of the Empire, when the pottery industries of Roman Britain collapsed and even the wealthy were forced to make do and mend; shades of wartime Britain in the Blitz.

Strolling among the ruins of this lost race, I was struck forcibly by the sight of the door pillars flanking the entrances to the houses. If I had seen them standing alone in a field I would have had no hesitation in identifying them as memorials to the prehistoric dead or remnants of stone circles: here was the familiar asymmetrical, broken-shouldered, figurative form that captures the spirit of the ancestor, turned to stone like some troll at sunrise. Wooden round houses may have boasted carved icons or totems on either side of the porch to protect those inside, to make the broken circle whole and venerate family ancestors, but we never find them because they would long since have rotted. Did these people, perhaps in response to changing times, reinforce their ties to the old native religion, of shaman and ancestral patron, by creating a living monument in stone, the material of permanence and memory? It is a process, identified across the Early Medieval world and described by the archaeologist Sophie Hueglin as 'petrification', the physical expression of a profound need and desire for solidity, certainty, intransience in a transient world. Materially this is reflected in the transition from wood to stone in memorial and elite buildings; it is paralleled by developments in recording time, history and identity from oral to written forms. At Ironbridge a similar transition, from wood and stone to iron, is equally evocative.

DIN LLIGWY

Close to Din Lligwy lies a Neolithic chambered tomb whose importance to earlier settlers might still have resonated with these Romanised Britons. Another thought occurred: was this seeming hybrid of native and Roman architecture a sign, frozen in time, of the tensions between indigenous and Roman cultures being played out, consciously or subconsciously, in the geography and space of a wealthy farmstead—profoundly sensible to its past but with an eye on modern trends?

I experienced a powerful sense of this same cultural tension when I once stayed for a couple of days in Window Rock, the tribal capital of the Navajo nation high up on the Mogollon plateau of north-eastern Arizona. The beautiful and impressive Nation Council building is circular, echoing the form of the native *hogan*[55] but on a massive scale, built with giant pine beams radiating from the roof peak and semi-dressed stone walls whose plastered interior is painted with a cyclical mural history of its people. The space is both sacred and secular. The architecture carries echoes of a lost race, the Anasazi, who built marvellous drystone-walled towns with exquisite precision and delicacy among the mesas and canyons of that high country during Europe's Middle Ages. My hosts, Skip and Elaine Baker—oddly enough neither of them was Navajo; they were respectively Crow and Blackfoot—lived in a very ordinary house; their kids watched *Sesame Street* and attended grade school; they ate burgers and drank *Coors Lite* when they could smuggle it onto the reservation, and drove a pickup. Their census names were English (they had other, native names not to be shared) and when I spoke with them about their identity they reacted as if the convenient paraphernalia of modern capitalist America might easily be cast off like snakeskin: 'when you Anglos go away we won't miss you'. I remember Skip grinning when he said that. Out there they call it the Apache smile.

They may be deluding themselves. It's hard to shake off an

empire when it builds you nice roads and delivers water and beer on tap. The difference, I suspect, is that when the Romans conquered a people and gave them citizenship of their empire, they meant it: a barbarian might become emperor. Roman Britain was not a reservation. I cannot imagine a Navajo sitting behind the desk in the Oval Office of the White House. If it ever happened, one suspects the presidential face would be wearing an Apache smile.

If Din Lligwy is now deserted and long abandoned, Moelfre was in party mode when we strolled down to the village for an evening meal. They had just commissioned a new lifeboat which sat out in the bay, bright orange and blue, riding complacently at anchor on a light swell; ashore the beer flowed, music blared out and, in the warm evening light, locals and visitors spilled onto road, beach and quayside in a cheery assembly of colour and laughter with RNLI ensigns and bunting adorning the seafront houses. It might have been Cornwall; or Bute, except that here the native language is spoken universally. Blackberries ripening in the hedges, and a blanket of low cloud carried in on a sea breeze, were signals of autumn's approach; but it was still warm. We retired to our tent surrounded by the invisible inhabitants of motorhome and caravan, all busy watching television in case they missed anything.

Our first full day's walking followed the coastal path towards the south-east corner of Anglesey. At one point, we made our way inland along generously hedged winding lanes in the vain hope of finding a Dark Age settlement at Pant y Saer—consumed by rabid thorny undergrowth and completely invisible—which is supposed to be another enclosed settlement like Din Lligwy but with the additional Dark Age wow factor of a sixth-century penannular brooch retrieved during excavations. The diversion was not entirely pointless, for at one point we encountered a young red squirrel on the road, as curious as he was scared. Past the village of Benllech, we stopped for refreshment at a pub on the edge of Red Wharf Bay, a great sandy inlet facing the distant Cumbrian mountains. The tide was so far out that a thin line of white surf made our horizon. Despite the temptation to cut a mile or so off the day's journey, we decided to skirt the bay rather than risk impassable mud or uncrossable channels. Besides, it was a fine afternoon. South of the bay we climbed a steep wooded slope and found ourselves in the middle of a disorienting plantation whose rides and trails did not seem to match the map. I wanted to look at a patch of relict fields whose shape from the air suggested they were ancient; but we couldn't find them and had to take our chances at several forks in the timber road. Not for the first time I mused on the navigator's reliance on an open landscape. Still, we came out more or less where we wanted, on the moors above the village of Llandonna at about 550 feet, so that we got a lovely view back across the bay: orange sand against green sea and blue sky, a Mark Rothko abstract, a landscape without apparent narrative, only form, colour and texture. The open moors were rocky, not much good for grazing anything except sheep and the odd shabby-looking pony fenced in by thin, woolly strands of wire.

Llandonna was our first bona-fide Early Medieval Christian site—not that there was much to see in this dowdy cluster of houses, apart from a radio mast sticking out of the hilltop like a leafless Christmas tree. It's the name that gives the game away. *Llan* is that early Welsh word for a church enclosure, often circular. A cursory look at such names on the map of the island showed that there had once been at least thirty, probably more, sites with early churches. This was a well-settled, fertile and productive land right through the Iron Age and Roman periods and into the Early Medieval. The north-eastern part of Anglesey is open, broken country, of small valleys, exposed coast and blustery moors, tamed by farmers over the last millennium. South and west there is lower, more domesticated land and a fertile zone, easily cultivated and with rich pastures.

Churches need land to support them; but historians suspect that they were not often given the best land for their foundations; that perhaps they tended to be offered more marginal sites, more easily lost from the royal or lordly fisc, as if to say: sure, have some land—make of this rough patch what you will. In that way, the sweated labour of monk and nun, lay brother and sister, may have been deployed in a more or less conscious way either to colonise the wastes and what little wildwood may have survived, or to bring back into cultivation lands that had been neglected through the death of a lord, through famine and climatic deterioration or conflict. On Anglesey, early church names dominate the less productive land, fringing, as they seem to do elsewhere, the fertile corelands of their kingdoms.

The main Roman presence on the island, courtesy of Agricola, was the fort at Caer Gybi on Holy Island, close to Holyhead. St Cybi was the name of a Cornish holy man and prolific monastic entrepreneur to whom the fort was given in the sixth century to found a royal monastery. His patron, Maelgwyn or Maglocunos, was the nominally Christian king of Gwynedd at the time when Gildas vented his ire against five British tyrants. Maelgwyn was his 'Dragon of the Isle', last in the list but first in evil, strong in arms but stronger in what destroys the soul, killer and usurper of his uncle before apparently retiring to the monastic life, only to re-emerge more powerful than before. A formidable king, then; and well qualified as a Dark Age warlord and patron. Gildas must have been gratified that Maelgwyn is said to have died in the great plague of the 540s, the European pandemic that seems finally to have ended the trade in Eastern Mediterranean goods to the Atlantic west. From Gildas's point of view it would have seemed a divine punishment.

If St Cybi became the royal holy man of West Mon, he had a contemporary counterpart in the east. That evening, after we pitched wearily at a campsite close to another *Llan*-named village,

Llangoed, I walked out towards the easterly extreme of the island at Penmon Point where magnificent views reach south across the strait to the Snowdonia massif and east to the peninsula on which Llandudno sits. That popular tourist destination, once served by daily summer steamers from Liverpool, was the foundation of St Tudno; but long before and after him it was known for its proximity to the limestone headland known as the Great Orme, Wales's copper mountain. Snowdon sat sulking beneath heavy grey cloud; the verdigris waters of the strait were choppy but the lighting was sublime.

Just inland from Penmon Point is Penmon Priory, a medieval Augustinian abbey, largely intact, which houses some fine pre-Conquest crosses. To my amazement the priory church was still open, just. Anxious not to miss anything, I hurried round it, camera in hand; not the quietly contemplative visit I had hoped for. One should never rush an ancient church; they are places of stillness and silence where time ought by rights to run a little slower than in the outside world. Besides, only at slow pace do you notice what is to be noticed, the little details that make a place special, and which are all the more gratifying to discover for oneself, rather than have them pointed out by guidebook or notice. In addition to the crosses, I had time to register that the church was cruciform in shape with a central tower and pyramid spire; that the crossing arch was dog-tooth Norman, its supporting pillars decorated with grotesque Adam and Eve caricatures. Outside I found a small, tranquil reed-fronded pond and beyond it the setting of an ancient holy well whose waters are dark, clear and still. The original church on the site seems to have been founded by a friend of Cybi, St Seiriol. A son of a king, like Cybi, he evidently found life at Penmon too public and retired, in the manner of Cuthbert of Lindisfarne, to a desert place. A quarter of a mile off the point lies a teardrop-shaped island that has variously been known as *Glannauc, Ynys Seiriol*, Priestholm, Ynys Lannog

and Puffin Island. In its third incarnation, some three generations after Seiriol, it became a place of sanctuary for a refugee
king, none other than Cadwallon, whose Northumbrian antagonist and former foster-brother King Edwin had hunted him down
as he himself had been hunted in exile. Fatally, Edwin supposed
that Cadwallon's exile here was permanent; that it would reduce
him sufficiently to be able to ignore him as a potential military
threat. In 633 Cadwallon allied with Penda of Mercia to exact his
revenge, slew Edwin at the battle of *Hæthfelth* and went on to rav-
age the Northumbrian heartlands before himself being killed by
the atheling Oswald of Bernicia.

It was late in the day; after a couple of brisk showers the skies
cleared and a magnificent sunset played its hand. I climbed to the
top of the hill to get a view of Priestholm, with the priory church
below and before me like a sentinel overlooking the strait. Among
emerald pastures soaked in golden yellow light lay the scattered
ruins of settlements, as there are everywhere on Anglesey. They

are conveniently labelled 'native'; few have been excavated properly, and it's hard to say if their very obviously Iron Age affinities (the remains of circular houses) confine them to the prehistoric period or if they may have continued as the vernacular architecture of the island right into the Early Medieval period. The tiny villages and hamlets that line the back lanes are composed of neat, low, whitewashed cottages with small square windows, slate roofs and painted doors. Many of these were once the cottages of fishermen, and you still see coils of rope and the odd lobster creel hung up on a gable end or next to a porch. Where they are exposed to westerlies, often there is a hardy hawthorn or crab-apple tree in a garden hedge, bent to the wind.

The reliability of those prevailing westerlies has always been a useful marker for the traveller; more constant in its footprint than a sun beneath cloud, a new moon or the northern star at midday. I had been pondering for some time how Dark Age travellers made their way through strange landscapes. I had already seen how the names of significant places might have offered clues. Climbing a prominent hill has always been a good way to gauge the lie of the land. In Dorset I had found that the hollow lanes of old route ways, like lines on the tube map, disorient and lead the traveller astray, giving the land a secretive, arcane and frustratingly distorted shape in the mind. It had been my plan on this journey that, at a suitable point, I would discard my maps and walk as it were *au naturel*, falling back on simple navigation methods, an innate sense of direction and knowing that, at times, I would get lost. But I hoped to work out how ancient travellers negotiated these lands, or at least to experience it second-hand. Sarah and I planned to climb Snowdon, and then part—she had a date with Loch Lomond and her wetsuit; I was aiming for the medieval pilgrimage site on Bardsey Island off the end of the Llŷn peninsula, a hundred odd miles away. After Snowdon, I told myself... after Snowdon. Meanwhile, I must decode the significant place names of north Wales: the Pens, Tys, Uchafs, Coeds, the Hlafod, the Llys and the Llan. I have a reasonable, if cautious, handle on English place names. Gaelic is beyond all ken; Welsh was enough to make the head spin. Nevertheless, the linguistic rules by which names change through time and warp from their original are well understood, if dangerous territory.

On the next day, during our progress south and west back towards the Menai Bridge, Sarah and I passed through an undistinguished village called Llandegfan (another early church site, foundation of St Tegfan, but no sign of him in suburban crescent or cul de sac). There was an air of what I can only call petit-bourgeois self-consciousness (pelargoniums and brutalised rose bushes against bare soil; trim lawns; block-paved drives; sensible cars). Out of the corner of my eye I caught sight of a sticker on a lamp post, which bore the imprimatur of *Cyngor Sir Ynys Mon* (Anglesey County Council) and the *Heddlu* (Welsh Police) and which said:

> *Nid oes*
> *croeso yma*
> *i fasnachwyr*
> *heb*
> *wahoddiad*

The convenient English translation on the opposite half said:

> Uninvited
> traders
> are not
> welcome
> here

Beneath was a bilingual note, in smaller print, of which the English vernacular version was: 'Please leave and do not return'. The warning to uninvited traders got me thinking about how the stranger or newcomer to a place negotiates an unfamiliar land, finds the inside track; I thought about it all the way to the foot of Snowdon, all the way to the top and down the other side, by which time I had figured out how Dark Age travellers managed to navigate through an unknown landscape.

We had breakfasted in Beaumaris, that Edwardian—Edward I, that is—stamp of the colonial boot. It looked very pretty but still, the historian in me felt uncomfortable: in Edward's new settlement only English and Norman-French residents had civic rights and the native Welsh of Beaumaris were largely disqualified from holding any civic office. I was disturbed to find a graffito on the wall of the loo in the café, to the effect that the Welsh are all illegitimate—and worse. I was angry. I tried to wash it off or wipe it away with a paper towel, but it had been scrawled with a permanent marker. Like Edward's castles. Onwards, in any case: to the bridge and a chance to walk across it, to look down on the whole length of the strait, to marvel at Telford's brilliance (he built it as early as 1826, before the Brunels started to dig their tunnels and plot their railways; before the Stephensons constructed *Rocket*, and only just after the opening of the Stockton–Darlington railway) and to ponder what a permanent link does to an island race. Hamish Haswell-Smith, the champion of Scottish islands, removed Skye from the new edition of his magisterial guide to Scotland's islands after the bridge was built across Kyle Akin from Kyle of Lochalsh. Some folk don't like their island status taken from them. The early monks would have sympathised.

On the south side of the bridge Sarah and I parted temporarily: she to fetch the car we had left in Bangor; me to walk on to a campsite rendezvous with her at the head of Llŷn Padarn, St Padarn's lake, half a dozen miles to the south of the Strait. Padarn was another contemporary of Maelgwyn, king of Gwynedd; a roving churchman and founder of monasteries, supposedly a

Breton from Armorica, to where a large number of British refugees are said to have fled from civil war and Anglo-Saxon invasion. It seemed impossible to avoid the saintly step of some early holy man in this land. The giants were there too: sky-high electricity pylons ferrying massive voltages from coastal power stations into and across the mountains, steel skeletons swaggering through glen and cwm, effortlessly fording river and straddling high pass, each pair looking like a monstrous tug of war between rivals for domination over the land. But this is a richly diverse landscape, too, full of small farms, hilltop forts and cairns, streams that drain glacial lakes and half-abandoned tiny cellular fields that must go back to a time when pioneer farmers enclosed what they could cultivate or cut in a year, expanding and contracting as the whim of fate and the ancestors dictated. This is a much quarried landscape: the scars are there for all time; and one curious by-product (for me) of the slate industry is its use for fencing: often I saw a field enclosed by long lines of vertical slates wired together. There are apparently impoverished villages and hamlets of small, ungenerous cottages, evidently affiliated to now defunct industries and looking as though they needed rescuing from whatever fate distant governments had invented for them. From poor villages, back lanes, power lines and scrapyards the land re-dressed itself in upland fatigues: narrow footbridges across waterfalls; ramshackle farmyards with geese and chickens and rusting machinery, bailer twine holding everything together; through long-abandoned fields thick with new rowan and field maple, bramble and bracken thicket, down rocky paths between exposed crags and into the shade of the mountains. All afternoon the air cooled.

Having successfully rendezvoused at the head of Llŷn Padarn, that evening Sarah and I walked beside the banks of the Afon Rhythallt along the line of an old industrial railway, to a small village pub where we ate well in a buzz of bilingual conversation.

MENAI BRIDGE

I remember, many years ago, harbouring the unworthy thought that the revived Welsh interest in their language was a convenient tool for making the English, the *Lloegr*, feel unwelcome and stupid, and therefore as discouraging of intercultural friendship as the English refusal to learn foreign languages. This time my encounter with *yr iaith Gymraeg* prompted overwhelmingly positive thoughts. In this part of Wales, at any rate, use of the indigenous language feels completely natural, everyone is effortlessly bilingual and equally happy to engage with linguistically impoverished monoglots like myself and Sarah. I have often thought that one should not be too hard on the English for their poor command of languages: after all, English is the second language of many nations, a global lingua franca. Which is the most natural second language for the English to learn: French? German? Spanish perhaps? Or—if our choice is governed by the size of linguistic populations or the future prospects of our graduates in a globalised economy—Mandarin, Russian or Hindi? After this trip I feel I know the answer. The English should all learn Welsh at school—it is, after all, the linguistic descendant of the native tongue of these islands, beautiful to listen to and rich in lore and poetic tradition. And the Scots should probably learn Gaelic. Wales has pulled off a remarkable feat in resurrecting its language, in giving it currency and absolute relevance.

Snowdon's peak was hard won. We took the long ridge route from our camping pitch at Cwm y Glo, where the view along the lake towards Llanberis—an egg-white and lapis sky poached in blue-black peaty water, the perfect sensuous U of the valley sides and Snowdon magnificently brooding on its alpine throne—made you want to put it in a jar and take it home. The marked path was invisible: it was all yellow gorse and purple heathery bog, with unsuspected ankle-breaking potholes; and the consoling prospect of cairn, burnt mound and hut circle that had lured us (or me) up there could not be seen beneath the blanket. As we reached our first viewpoint just below Cefn Du, a raw scar of abandoned quarry, and made a short descent to the trail above Llanberis (St Peris: sixth century), we saw our first trekkers. I had hardly seen any serious walkers all year and had begun to fear that we were a dying breed. But Snowdon is Britain's busiest mountain. Ahead and to our left the unmistakable chug of a steam train betrayed the line of the rack-and-pinion railway that takes reluctant climbers all the way to the summit in relative comfort. We kept to the long, round-about route of Maesgwyn and the Snowdon Ranger path, undemanding until the last section of zig-zags that drags you up the side of Clogwyn Du'r Arddu and onto the north ridge of Bwlch Glas. Here it was like being in the Lakes on a bank holiday, almost queuing to get to the top and surrounded by yapping or panting dogs. With a full rucksack, despite being in pretty good shape after a year of walking, I was glad to get to the top, even if the dizzying view came into focus only rarely from that clouded, misty height. *Yr Wyddfa*, the great tumulus, in ancient lore the tomb of a giant called Rhitta Gawr, is the mythical heart of the land of the Britons, the *Eryri* of the *Historia Brittonum* where the embattled tyrant Vortigern fled from his persecutors.

I have had few more surreal experiences than walking, glasses all steamed up and feeling somewhat overdressed and overequipped, into Hlafod Eryri, the modern café which sits just below the summit of the mountain at about three and a half thousand feet. It was standing room only, fuggy with the breath and sweat of walkers all hugger-mugger with trippers wearing T-shirts. We managed to get a sausage roll and a cup of hot chocolate and stood, semi-dazed, wondering at this overwhelming congregation of humanity in a wild and desolate island palace in the clouds. What the ancestors think is not clear. A small, fundamentalist part of me thinks that taking a railway up to the top of a mountain to a café is somehow disrespectful to the spirits of the place; but I also think it wonderful that the wheelchair-bound and the semi-ambulant can stand or sit on top of the world and share in the majesty of the view.

Here Sarah and I went our separate ways. She returned to the campsite and the car by the more straightforward route to Llanberis. I took the south-west ridge, Bwlch Main, a narrow, sometimes steep, rocky path that fell away dramatically on both sides and which in winter and dense fog must be deadly treacherous; but I was soon below the cloud, and the high country of the Snowdon range opened out ahead: tumbling streams and concave slopes, distant green valleys mottled by cloud and sun; sheepfolds, grey ridges and peaks, glacial lakes steeped in Arthurian legend (Excalibur lies at the bottom of one of them, supposedly). I still had a long walk ahead of me, so I kept up a good pace, easy enough with the big pack propelling me downwards into Cwm Llan. I stopped once or twice to take pictures, munch on an apple or oatcake with a mouthful of cheese. The descent had been exhilarating; now the quiet of the cwm, the jostling of soft waters in the burn and the occasional raking call of a raven lent the afternoon a timeless quality. Once, I followed the tempting line of an old mineral railway, hoping it would bring me out onto an easier path. It ended in a precipitous drop where an incline once transported slate down into the cwm below. I backtracked and came onto the marked path high above a sheepfold and small abandoned farm, below which a cataract tumbled towards the cwm of Glaslyn, the 'black pool'. Now I came into a land of veteran broadleaf woods, scrub birch and planted spruce. Instead of following the old mule trail down into the cwm direct, I tracked the contour round to the south-west, through bracken and sheep pen, splashy bog and craggy cleft, past another roofless old farmstead and shieling until, now level with the hills across the valley, I saw a densely wooded hump ahead of me which could only be Dinas Emrys, the fortress of Ambrosius Aurelianus. By now I had left all other walkers behind.

Fifteen hundred years ago Dinas Emrys would have paraded its power and wealth with banner, rampart and glittering spear; smoke would have curled lazily from the fires of a kingly hall; the sound of guards and lookouts would have barked, echoing across the valley; perhaps a bard might have been heard distantly, praising his lord in poetry and strumming his harp. Ambrosius and Vortigern are as ephemeral as Arthur, their names woven into countless legends of civil wars among the British chieftains of the fifth century, and of the defence against invading *Saes* or Saxons. While all three men appear in the semi-historical sections of the *Historia Brittonum*, Ambrosius is one of the very few 'real' people (the five tyrants aside) to be named by Gildas. Gildas says that he was the military leader who emerged among the Britons in the wake of the first wave of Germanic attacks, after the 'cruel plunderers' had gone home. He is described as a Roman gentleman, whose parents had 'worn the purple' (that is to say, they had held imperial rank) and who had been killed in the conflict. He won great victories against 'the enemy'. It is never entirely clear whether the most serious conflicts of the fifth century were internecine or as a result of federate armies under Germanic warlords turning against their British sponsors. They had, we are told in the Kentish Chronicle section of the *Historia Brittonum*, been brought to Britain to protect the island from Picts or Scots. But they were evidently first stationed to guard cross-Channel trade with Gaul. The Britons' 'proud tyrant'—often equated with the Vortigern of the *Historia Brittonum*, struck a fatal deal with the leaders, Hengest and Horsa, who first conned him into giving them Kent as their own and then, after internal disputes, ravaged the island and brought thousands more Saxon pirates from their homeland across the North Sea.

No one takes these stories at face value any more; but that is not to say they can't tell us anything useful. Legendary battles may be allegories of more nuanced conflict and tensions played out over generations. The reality is that Germanic immigration to these islands—now thought to have involved relatively small numbers (but see Postscript: Who are the British?—pages 423–6)—was a complex process, probably lasting as long as a whole century, and perhaps more. It may have been more evolution than revolution. There does seem to have been an overall reduction in the population of the British Isles in the fifth or sixth century, brought about by a combination of famine and plague, by the collapse of the imperial command economy and by the depredations of pirate slavers and small-scale but intense conflict among emerging polities trying to defend their territories. It is quite likely, however, that this reduction was not catastrophic in scale. Many of these territories may initially have been centred on the *civitates*, the ancient tribal regions recognised by the Romans; elsewhere they splintered into smaller units of power, less regional than local and more kin-based. The spheres of activity of characters remembered by legend as national heroes and villains might, in reality, have been local or regional, as was the case with many of the saints of the next century. Arthur may have been an exception—his recorded geography spans the west of Britain from Somerset to Dumfriesshire. Ambrosius belongs, if anywhere, to Eryri, to Snowdonia, whose southern approach Dinas Emrys watches.

The site of his fortress is now cloaked in sweating, lichen-encrusted jungle, the ramparts and walls almost impossible to make out. The modern approach from the north-east is an easy scramble; the original entrance to the south-west is steep. The topography, intimate and intimidating, is reminiscent of Dunadd and of Dumbarton. The narrative preserved in the *Historia Brittonum*[56] tells how Vortigern, whose people had turned against him, was advised by his magi, his druids, to construct a fort in this natural fastness. Three times his masons and carpenters built their ramparts, and three times they fell down in the night; then when he asked them the cause of this evil, the magi told Vortigern that he must find a child without a father (that is, he must be born of a virgin mother), kill the boy in the fort and sprinkle his blood there, so that the fort would be safe from attack (in a Christian context this has the sharp reek of pagan blood-sacrifice). The boy, according to the legend, was Ambrosius, but he turned out to be an unwilling sacrifice. He told Vortigern that the collapse of the ramparts was caused by a lake beneath the foundations whose existence neither magi nor masons were aware of. Ambrosius predicted that in this lake they would find two vessels; that the vessels contained a cloth in which two worms, one red, one white, were asleep. The magi duly found the vessels containing the cloth, and unfolded it; the worms woke, began to fight and after a long conflict the red worm was victorious. The boy revealed that it was a dragon representing the Britons and the white worm a dragon representing the invaders; but that the Britons could only achieve victory if he, Ambrosius, was given the fortress, representing the kingdom, and Vortigern departed to exile. So Ambrosius was recognised prophetically as overlord of the Britons. It's all good stuff, full of potent omen, divination and metaphysical storytelling. When Geoffrey of Monmouth borrowed this tale for his *Historia Regum Britanniae*, he gave the fatherless boy the name Merlin, whose early childhood he based on material from the *Historia Brittonum*.

The experience of the visitor is to wish that, somehow, one could be transported back in time to meet the protagonists and witness the dynamics of an Early Medieval royal fortress at first hand. Archaeological evidence suggests that the fortification here is of the right sort of date to fit Vortigern's and Ambrosius's fifth-century time frame: in excavations during the 1950s it produced sherds of Mediterranean pottery (table wares and amphorae) and a sherd from an oil lamp bearing the Christian chi-rho symbol, all of which must belong to a period before the middle of the sixth century. The absence of priests from the Vortigern/Ambrosius tale suggests that the story may originate in pagan tradition, although elsewhere in the *Historia* Vortigern is reproved by the British clergy and by St Germanus for marrying his own daughter.

The day after Snowdon and Dinas Emrys was one of discomfort and slog. I was as stiff as a board after the descent from the mountains; I still had another pass to cross as I headed due west against the glacial grain of the valleys; it rained most of the day; and to make matters worse a mistake on the Ordnance Survey map took me way off the trail and up to my waist in bog and bracken. I was not a happy walker. But the memory of Dinas Emrys and of that sticker on a lamp post on Anglesey kept me busy thinking about navigation, especially since my indispensable modern tool, the walking map, had got me lost. The 'Uninvited traders are not welcome' notice had set me on a train of thought which now, trudging soaked through wet lanes and across muddy fields, came to fruition.

There is a story, from the *Anglo-Saxon Chronicle*, of a Wessex king's reeve, who, on hearing of the arrival of three ships in the year 785, went to bring their captains to the *villa regia*, the royal manor, but was killed by raiders. The reeve had reasoned, fatally, that foreign ships must contain traders hoping for an introduction to the regional chief, which rather says something about the period between the arrival of the Anglo-Saxons and the late eighth century. In confirmation of that sense of order, these were times when royal palaces and local settlements were undefended. Great lords, who wished to control access to markets, to keep for themselves the perquisites of high-value exotic goods and to harvest news and information from travellers, kept a close eye on foreign trade. By the middle of the eighth century, kings such as Ine of Wessex and Offa of Mercia had begun to encourage the construction of coastal settlements like *Hamwic* (modern

Southampton), *Gipeswic* (Ipswich) and *Lundenwic* and *Eoforwic* (York)—well inland but on navigable rivers—where they could take a cut of the profits. This trend was accelerated by the transfer of royal land to the church, reducing the stream of goods supplied by renders. Now kings needed cash; and as early as the late seventh century they began to revive coinage as a means of solidifying the value of goods and converting organic, perishable renders to more portable and tradeable wealth. The Early Medieval core value of gift-giving, an unending cycle of obligation and response, was becoming systematised.

Key to the success of the trader was the introduction: uninvited traders—door-to-door salesmen, cold-callers and so on—were as unwelcome to the Dark Age lord as they were to the officious sticker-posters of Anglesey's twenty-first-century County Council. In the Early Medieval period, famously, groups of people travelling through the land were classified according to the size of the party. King Ine's Laws of the late seventh century accounted 'seven men thieves; from seven to thirty-five a "band", above that it is an army'. That is to say, men abroad, hence not under the protection of a lord, must consider themselves liable to be viewed with hostility unless they had legitimate business and carried bona fides. What guaranteed safe entry to, or passage through, the king's land was the right introduction. Business has always worked that way. When we need a builder or plumber, before we open the phone directory or search on the Internet, we ask our trusted friends if they know of a reliable one. Reputation matters. These days it is called 'networking'.

In order to gain entry to an exploitable market—a manor or the lord's hall, the villages that belonged to him—or to gain the confidence and hospitality of the abbot of a monastery, the Early Medieval traveller needed guarantees, and these came with either familiarity or an introduction from a trusted intermediary. The same rules applied to the intrepid explorers and missionaries of later centuries. If you wanted to travel to the fabled city of Gondar in Abyssinia or the court of Kublai Khan in Xanadu, you needed an introduction; and a guide. To avoid being hunted down and killed by the native warriors of indigenous tribes, the pioneering trappers and traders of colonial-era North America secured guides to lead them to their destination and introduce them to the chief who could guarantee them safe passage. That extraordinary, shocking scene in David Lean's *Lawrence of Arabia*, when Sherif Ali (the equivalent rank to the shire reeve of Anglo-Saxon England) of the Harith shoots Lawrence's guide because 'the Hasimi may not drink at our wells', shows what happens when the protocols are breached, inadvertently or by design (that film has been like an earworm on my recent journeys). For the medieval monk the risk might be obviated by a shared knowledge of Latin and the scriptures; by the humble clothing, lack of weaponry and bare feet of the pilgrim. The wrong brooch or accent, an inappropriate greeting, might prove fatal to the unwary. For the uninvited traveller in an antique land, there were many perils. Augustine had fatally misread the protocols when he met a convocation of British bishops in 601/2; he cannot have been the only foreigner to tread on native toes.

So I have become relaxed about journeying in the Dark Ages. I only ever once hired a guide, in northern Mali, on my way to see the fabled Dogon people of the Bandiagara escarpment. It didn't work out: I got sick, was laid up in a brothel in Mopti on the banks of the Niger, and had to pay him off. You sometimes hear awful stories of travellers trapped at airports without the right papers or sufficient money to buy them, caught in an endless cycle as outcasts. I imagine the same thing to have happened in the Dark Age court on occasion; a traveller without local language or sponsor, with insufficient status, credentials or wealth, suspected and detained indefinitely. Now I feel I could get around that world, through shire and manor, pagus[57] and civitas, without worrying about maps or trying to navigate by the stars or sun. I would hire a reliable guide—say, the oldest son of a *chæpman*[58] at an inn. I would pay him well to ensure he transported me to the royal manor on a good horse, that he instructed me in the correct protocols of the court (dress, greetings, arms and so on); that he provided me with access to the right people (the reeve; the lady of the court) and smoothed the path of my business (with the right gifts: marten furs, a garnet, a curious trinket like a shrunken head, an ivory plaque, an oil lamp carrying a chi-rho symbol or a small piece of the true cross). The value of dress and manner, of such niceties as the style and quality of a brooch on a cloak, could not be overestimated.

From the royal manor another guide, familiar with the orbit of this lord's influence and with his own local knowledge, might take me on the next stage in my journey. The account of the visit of Ohthere of Hålogaland—a Norwegian seafarer—to King Alfred's court shows that the best sort of guest came with lavish gifts, extraordinary stories and a few mates who looked like they could handle themselves. Ohthere provided the king with a detailed geography of the Northern seas, of its peoples and kings, with accounts of fabled trading centres like Hedeby in Denmark and of the goods that were traded throughout Scandinavia. In return for such fascinating and useful information—so useful that it was incorporated into the Anglo-Saxon edition of Orosius's history of the world—Alfred could give the trader invaluable access to new markets and royal contacts.

If I did not travel with a guide, if I stumbled blindly through the land and arrived unannounced at the gates of a fortress like Dinas Emrys, I could hardly be surprised if the gate closed in my face and someone shouted 'Gadewch a pheidiwch â dod yn ôl!' ('Please leave and do not return') or stuck a spear in my retreating back. The traveller needs a good guide.

I emerged from the misty, rain-lashed hills, and from my

contemplation, into a land of slate and woollen mills, of small walled pastures and broad, meandering streams. At Dolbenmaen I hoped for a hot plate and warm fireside for lunch, but the pub was shut and all I managed to find was a cold pasty and a bar of chocolate from the Post Office cum village store. But at least the rain had nearly stopped. The land here is still sufficiently marginal for the remains of cairns and hut circles—all of which could date from anywhere between the late Bronze Age and the Early Medieval period—to be dotted, like scabs, among rough pastures. On one green lane across a small plateau I passed the entrance to what must have been a Neolithic long barrow or chambered tomb, unmarked on the map and evidently never excavated. I found a circuitous route to a small farm called Llystyn Gwyn, just off the road between Porthmadog and Caernarvon and close to the site of a Roman camp. The farm seemed deserted. The roofs of the byres were holed, slates misplaced and doors swinging on squeaky hinges. I crept through its yards and gardens, feeling as though I were being watched. A white caravan was parked in a yard with half its aluminium side panel torn off; no curtains hung in the dark windows of the house; nettles grew uncontrolled in the garth. An old wrecked car stood there. It is one of the creepiest places I have ever been; and I am not easily spooked. It was as if the inhabitants had vanished minutes before, never to return. Beneath a slate lintel covered by turf and incorporated into a wall made of tumbled stone and old rubber car tyres, a slab of undistinguished sandstone must, I supposed, have been what I had come to see: Gwynedd's only *in situ* ogham stone. Had I been able to read anything in this flat, dingy light, the bilingual inscription, in the strange slashed alphabet of Irish ogham[59] and in Latin capitals, would have read ICORI FILIUS POTENTINI ('Icorix son of Potentinus'). The site is doubly special, for the element *Llys*—court, manor—in the name Llystyn Gwyn betrays the former presence of a noble hall there in the Dark Ages. Perhaps I should have waited for the sun to come out, as it eventually did that day; but I couldn't get out of there quick enough. Close to a small village just west of Criccieth I camped for the night and was sufficiently tired not to bother looking for a meal.

The next morning, still hellish tight in the muscles, hungry and longing for a hot bath, but at least well-showered and rested, I made my way north-west along switchback lanes and reflected that trying to navigate through a settled landscape with proprietorial rights on all sides would have been a mug's game. At the foot of Garn Bentyrch, one of those conical hills that dot the landscape of the Llŷn peninsula, I came to Llangybi, a church of that same St Cybi who founded the royal monastery at Holyhead. The present building, like almost all village churches in north Wales, is an unprepossessing Victorian thing with neo-Perpendicular windows. The entrance to the churchyard is a narrow covered gateway with a wrought-iron gate—the latter a ubiquitous feature of farms, fields and churches here. Just inside the gate an early simple cross-incised stone, the right shape and size to slot into what in Ireland would be called a *leacht* or table-tomb, suggested that Cybi's church had not lost all its early associations. In the cemetery I noticed that the gravestone inscriptions were about fifty-fifty English and Welsh.

A small stone stile in the farther wall of the churchyard led down a bank to the edge of a stream and a pair of low, ruined buildings: cottages, but not just any old cottages; that on the left housed *Ffynnon Gybi*, a dressed stone cistern from whose dark, clear depths a natural spring welled up. There are hundreds and perhaps thousands of wells and springs across Britain that have holy associations, often with a very local hermit or martyr, sometimes with some great patron-saint like Colmcille or Patrick. Generally, archaeologists assume that such springs must have been sacred in pre-Christian, animist cultures. The magic of pure water emerging from the rock, especially if it isn't contaminated by the pathogens associated with livestock and human habitation, is worthy of veneration. That such waters were believed to heal ailments and could sanctify the liturgy of a local priest or the baptism of an infant is not so hard to understand. At any rate, it was a rather lovely spot, green and quiet and perfect for a mid-morning break; and I drank the water.

I continued north-west, skirting Garn Bentyrch and now using as my mark the mottled heather-purple and scree-brown of Yr Eifl, at eighteen hundred feet a major landmark of the north coast of Llŷn. Before it stood the mammiform outline of another of the so-called Rivals (by an Anglicisation of Yr Eifl): Tre'r Ceiri, one of the great Iron Age hill forts of Britain. Iron Age it may be, but since the English translation of the name means 'Home of the Giants', how could I not climb it? Before the rise of the hills I was diverted by a loose pony adrift on a back lane. The owner didn't seem much concerned, but we ushered the beast back into its paddock all the same. At a smallholding I could not see the true path and chatted to the farmer before he showed me where the stile lay. On another path, diverted to circumvent a farmyard, the bramble was so thick that I tore my ear open and bled like a stuck pig for a couple of miles. In the late morning I came upon Llanaelhaearn, a village distinguished not just by well-known Latin inscription stones but, for the weary and hungry traveller, an excellent small café run by a Mancunian former Para' and Royal Engineer, Dave Watkinson. I was the only customer, but I don't think I did any injustice to his splendid breakfast. The news that day was dominated by the beheading by Islamic State militants of an American journalist, James Foley, so naturally talk revolved around the Middle East where Dave had served his time, mostly in the hellhole of Basra. He wasn't much impressed by my bramble-torn ear.

On, then, to the church, in whose graveyard I found the so-called Melitus stone, inscribed solely with that otherwise unknown Christian's name. I was more keen to see another stone

belonging here, inscribed in memory of *Aliortus Elmetiacos*—
Aliortus the Elmetian—that is to say, a native of West Yorkshire,
the British kingdom of Elmet. But find it I could not. I supposed
it to reside inside the church, which was locked with no trace of
a keyholder. Along the road from the church, on my way to the
foot of Tre'r Ceiri, was the site of another holy well, in this case
belonging to the seventh-century St Ælhaern who had given his
name to the village. These hills are steeped in early Christian tradition. If not all priests and holy men were literate, enough of
them were to keep Latin alive not, in the end, as a spoken language, but as a written form of intellectual expression, protocol,
faith and learning. But my suspicion, given the proliferation of
saintly names preserved in this landscape, is that sanctity may
have been applied to a significant proportion of the otherwise dis-
inherited aristocratic male population of the sixth century—perhaps the equivalent of the second sons of the manse who became
clergymen in the late eighteenth and nineteenth centuries. In
that time of plenty and of social upheaval, third sons could not
even expect a modest living in the church; many of them went
to London, or abroad, to seek their fortunes and became a generation of entrepreneurial innovators—Davy, Maudslay, Bramah,
Brunel, Faraday, themselves redrawing the landscape and becoming memorialised in buildings, bridges and the hardware of the
industrial revolution.

The tumbled drystone hut circles and curtain wall of the
Home of the Giants were memorable for their technical sophistication and architectural excellence, for the shelter they gave
from buffeting winds and for the huge view the hilltop offered:
back to Anglesey and to Snowdonia, south to the broad sweep
of Cardigan Bay and the heights of Cader Idris, west and south-
west to the long elephant's trunk of Llŷn with its dewdrop, Bardsey Island, far in the distance. Llŷn was and is part of Gwynedd,
the Venedotia of Latin memorials. The name was once supposed

to have derived from a legendary northern warrior, Cunedda, said to have brought his people here one hundred and forty-six years before the reign of King Maelgwyn and to have founded that dynasty. The attractive Cunedda story, preserved in the Northern genealogies in the Nennian compendium, relates that Cunedda and his eight sons were brought here to expel the Irish from the northern part of Wales and that, after their arrival, the Irish never returned to Britain. That there was Irish cultural and perhaps genetic influence on Wales in the Early Medieval period can hardly be doubted; there are stories of Irish raids—St Patrick was a victim of such slave-hunting pirates—in the fourth and fifth centuries. But they do not seem to have been expelled by Cunedda or any other Arthurian hero. To begin with, Welsh Llŷn shares its etymological root with Irish *Lein*, from the Irish tribal name *Lageni*, denoting those who lived in Leinster, the province lying to the south of Dublin on Ireland's east coast. And, although Cunedda fits neatly at the head of some genealogies, his name is more likely than not a back-formation from Venedotia and its Brythonic equivalent Gwynedd. A more plausible origin of the tribal name Venedotii is the Irish *Fein*, from another eastern Irish predatory kingdom.

The Irish, for their part, brought an energetic, vibrant Christian culture with them—hence the ogham on so many memorial stones. The Christianity of Gildas's day, which he may have liked to believe was thoroughly Roman, owed much of its character to an Irish church inspired not by Rome but by the desert fathers. If the Irish did settle Wales in large numbers, then they assimilated successfully—the Welsh, after all, speak Welsh and not Irish. Nor did they speak Latin: although the Romans subdued the whole of Wales, Wales was never Romanised. No Roman villas were ever built in these parts; it was a militarised zone with a headquarters at *Segontium* (Caernarvon). In the absence of a north-western Welsh *civitas* which might have formed a focus of local power in the wake of Rome's imperial decline, native elites seem to have exploited the political vacuum by reoccupying some of the ancient hill forts from which their ancestors had ruled and maintaining the native language. No Roman road penetrated the Llŷn peninsula.

From the natural vantage point offered by the Home of the Giants, watching *deus ex machina* spotlights piercing the cloud to illuminate a village here, a copse there, I moved on to the north coast: the weather was closing in and the air cooled. I camped for the night on a farm just east of Nefyn and there had my first hot dinner since before Snowdon. While I ate it rained, a biblical downpour that had tourists scurrying off the streets and into hotels and pubs or back into their cars. I sat complacently waiting it out, although I would have been less sanguine had I realised that I'd left the flap of the tent open. A schoolboy error. It was a damp night, the only small consolation a sunset over the Irish Sea of polar luminosity: vivid pink against grey, with an intense white halo around the sun.

My next day's target was to cross the peninsula again, this time north to south. I wanted to see as much of the landscape of Llŷn as possible, to take in as many of its evocative sites as I could. Walking is for me the best means of getting to grips with the broad brushstrokes of topography, political geography and scale of the distant past, as it is with the present. Even so, I felt an archaeologist's niggle at the back of my mind; a yearning to stick a spade in the ground at one—or all—of these sites and spend more considered time examining them.

For now, I found myself walking back through the streets and lanes of Nefyn, more or less empty at seven in the morning but for the postman and a few delivery vans. It was a Friday. Nefyn has managed to survive the fluctuating fortunes of tourism, fishing, farming and industry and reinvent itself as a quirky but functional hybrid with small businesses offering subsistence, if not wealth, to the local community. As well as hotels, it supports a variety of churches, from the originally sixth-century St Mary's to the non-conformist Sionist and Methodist chapels.

I walked up the slope behind the main street, followed a lane that took me through fields full of healthy-looking steers and found an overgrown path that led circuitously to the summit of Garn Boduan, a companion of Tre'r Ceiri: an Iron Age hill fort commanding the coastline and interior of the peninsula. A fortlet constructed later on its summit may date from the Early Medieval period. Here the stone roundhouses have been consumed by summer bracken and bramble (I ate half a pound of blackberries on the hoof, as I had on most days of this trip). From the air, the pattern of cellular houses looks like a nasty case of ringworm: there are nearly two hundred of them. At just under a thousand feet the summit gives more stunning views out to sea and along the peninsula, back to Tre'r Ceiri and beyond. These hill forts seem not to have been habitually occupied in their original incarnation, but used as summer gathering places where tribute was rendered, marriages and alliances brokered, chiefly justice meted out. The third of these massive enclosures stands on top of Carn Fadryn, just a few miles further to the south-west. Beyond it, I found myself looking directly towards my destination for the day, Abersoch, with Cardigan Bay beyond. Up here the wind was biting but there were signs that the afternoon might be kinder, so I did not stay to soak up the atmosphere, but retreated to the shelter of tree and lane.

There is no really direct route south from Garn Boduan. The topography is intimate and complicated and has to be negotiated via small valleys that thread their way through the volcanic, conical hills: progress was pretty, and slow. Llanfihangel, lying in the lee of Carn Fadryn's hill fort, offers no more than a modest chapel in what might once have been a circular graveyard. There are so many of these early *Llan* names that it's hard to believe they all reflect monastic foundations on the scale of Caer Gybi or Penmon. Many of them must have been tiny establishments, the result of patronage functioning at local level, perhaps competitively so: Jones has a holy man; I'm going to have a holy man. In any case, there never was a St Fihangel—the name is a local rendering of St Michael. The culture of these parts must have proved sympathetic to the idea of the hermit, the healer, the local wise woman. There is no sign in this land of a high cross (the nearest, I think, must be at Penmon), the stamp of missionary activity from Ireland to Scotland and Northumbria. It's also notable that the church dedications to saints do not seem to coincide with the names recovered from inscriptions in those churches or their graveyards, except in very rare cases (Llansadwrn in Anglesey offers an example in the form of a stone inscribed to Saturninus, the saint for whom the church—and the village itself—is named). These inscriptions, mostly dated to the fifth century on linguistic and epigraphic grounds, belong to a period when the indigenous diocesan rule of the Roman church fostered a network of priests, deacons and bishops, a hundred years and more before the arrival of multitudes of wandering saints.

Did these Roman clerics (the priests and deacons of Latin inscriptions) welcome Irish, Cornish, and Breton holy men and women among them; did those intrepid saints (St Ælhaern, St Cybi and their like) slip neatly into the vacuum left by a dying diocesan administration; or was the arrival of the foreign holy man and woman a subversive new element in the landscape? Either way, that their tradition has survived, even if only in name, for fifteen hundred years and more is a remarkable instance of continuity in the cultural landscape.

The dispersed nature of the settlements lends itself, perhaps, to such survival. Even so, cultures have to want to preserve the traditions of their forefathers. In Early Medieval Ireland those noble families who boasted descent from an érlam, or founding church patron, were always keen to demonstrate their rights over the land which they had given to found a church or monastery— that is why so many Irish genealogies survive. Maybe a culture that has always seen itself under siege from a powerful neighbour tends to reinforce those ties to the past, even if the seismic shift from native Catholicism to colonial Protestantism in the sixteenth century must have severed many cultural links to the past.

Because we find it so hard to identify distinct Early Medieval settlement features in the landscape—inherently hard to date and very often either indistinguishable from prehistoric remains or so ephemeral as to be invisible—the surviving evidence of the early church must stand witness to all the farmers, smiths, woodsmen, weavers, fishers, slaves and lords whose industry, patronage and productivity paid for the luxury of keeping men and women whose purpose was to pray for them.

The small village of Llangian proved more rewarding, later on in the day. Its setting is lovely: a couple of rows of neat but individual unpainted stone cottages at the bottom of a dingly dell where a stream tumbled into the Afon Soch, which gives its name to the little port of Abersoch.[60] Llangian has the church of St Cían, an otherwise unknown figure whose name is nevertheless suspiciously Irish. Here we have not just any old holy man finding a place to set up shop. Llangian, the historical evidence shows, was the centre of a substantial manorial holding in the Middle Ages: it supported a mill and tithe barn. The circular graveyard was surrounded by a vallum, a concentric ditch and bank which defined the sanctuary of an early monastery. In Welsh it was known as the *corflan*, literally 'corpse enclosure'; but it's an absolutely diagnostic trait of Irish-inspired monasteries, from Iona to Clonmacnois and Kingarth. Llangian, then, is the real deal: a monastery founded under the patronage of a powerful lord or local king during the great period of Western monasticism (the only partial excavation of the site has given up a radiocarbon date of *c.*AD 550). But the site was important even before Cían: in the churchyard stands a stone memorial belonging to perhaps a hundred years before his day: MELI MEDICI FILI MARTINI IACIT: 'Here lies Melus the doctor, son of Martinus.' It is unique in Britain, the only ancient memorial which survives to commemorate a doctor (unless we include the headless woman at Corbridge (see page 183). And by 'doctor' we might read something more, if we are inclined to a druidic interpretation of such things. For once the light was right so I could read the inscription for myself. I would have been delighted to see an image of the saint carved in relief, stirring potions in a barrel.

My last indulgence of the day was to pass through Llanengan on my way to a pitch overlooking St Tudwal's Island (you really cannot move for early saints here). The church of St Engan does not offer the tantalising realities of Llangian; it belongs to the fifteenth century and boasts neither monastic vallum nor Latin inscription. But the saint, properly *Einion Frenin,* is one about whom we know a little. He was a king of the Venedotian line claiming descent from Cunedda, and a brother and patron of that Seiriol who founded Penmon and the hermitage on Priestholm. He is said to have brought St Cadfan to Bardsey Island to found the important monastery there. Near by is a well, Ffynnon Einion, and his memory is preserved in the name of a cave, a hill and a distant farm. He counts, therefore, as much a royal patron as a holy man. Tudwal, another manifestation of the great flowering of the church in the middle of the sixth century, was a Breton holy man who, having been trained in Ireland, founded a hermitage on one of the two islands lying just off the point at Abersoch.[61] Later in his career he migrated to Brittany and was made Bishop of Tréguier by Childebert I of the Franks.

Saturday 23 August was my last full day of walking on the trail towards Bardsey. I wasn't sure if I would get there. Only a couple of boats make it regularly to the island, and given that the following day was a Bank Holiday, I figured I might be lucky to get a ticket. At least, for once, the weather smiled: I had a full day of skin-soaking, bone-warming sun as I walked the clifftops and coves, bays and promontories of the south coast, westwards towards Aberdaron. It was a day of sensory treats: a clutter of a farm, clusters of old drystone enclosures and sheep folds, a rotting barn, a small herd of very affable and characterful goats, a brilliant display of yellow and purple, the coconut whiff of gorse and buzzing carpet of heather—and all the time the rippling light of sun on the dark blue sea with the odd fishing boat laying a lobster pot or taking divers out.

I was glad to be ending this journey; it had been a long year and I felt all walked-out. I ate the last of my trail food early in the afternoon and came to rest at a campsite just shy of Aberdaron. I pitched the tent and strolled down into a busy village centre, crowded with Bank Holiday tourists and locals; the beach was a mass of bathers and picnickers. I drank a pint of beer in minor

ABERDARON

celebration and ate fish and chips sitting on a bench on the bank of the river that issues into the sea here. I stupidly neglected to explore the church which overlooks the bay, my Dark Age guidebook having failed to record two important early inscriptions.

Sunday: another jewel of a day, and I was up early with the sun. There was no point hanging around, so having stopped off at the excellent local bakery for a pastry and coffee I walked along the shore and then the clifftop path to Porthmeudwy, a tiny cove and slipway about a mile or so south-west of Aberdaron. I held out little hope of finding a passage to Bardsey, but I thought the early bird might catch a worm and before eight-thirty I was looking down on the cove from above. A woman emerged from the sea in a wetsuit. The man I subsequently knew as Colin Evans was leaning over the side of his small, powerful launch, talking to a man driving an old tractor. I had seen quite a few ancient-looking tractors along the coast, kept in good nick to take small boats down to the shore; here was a veritable museum of the things, all gaily painted and in tip-top condition. The launch was still on its trailer, twin outboards all shiny and fuelled up, ready to be lowered into the water by a dumper truck. I climbed down to the shingly beach and wandered over. Any chance of a ride out today, I said.

—Sorry, my friend, I'm fully booked.
—That's a pity; but no worries, I thought you would be busy on this weekend of all weekends.
—Are you here for a while?
—Just today and tomorrow. But I wasn't sure when I would get here, so I couldn't book.
—Yes, sorry about that.
—It's nice to see an old Fordson Major looking in such good trim...
—You know about tractors, do you?

—Used to have one [when I lived in my first wood: it was a cantankerous old thing and kept getting stuck in mud].

—Hard to get are they, up where you live?

—I know a man who has one or two. Matter of fact, I know where my old tractor is.

—I'd love to have another...

The conversation went on for a while. Trippers with tickets drifted down. I told Colin (we had by now introduced ourselves) about my trip on *Eda Frandsen* and how I'd walked all the way from Anglesey on a Dark Age pilgrimage. I laid it on, shamelessly, with a trowel until, eventually, he gave in.

The crossing took about twenty thrilling minutes at high speed with the launch bouncing like a powerboat on twin 135-horsepower engines. It fair blew the cobwebs away. Our party consisted of a few day-trippers and two families of farmers who raised sheep on the slopes of Cader Idris. For twenty years and more they had looked at Bardsey from across thirty miles of Cardigan Bay, through a telescope. They were finally fulfilling a promise to themselves to come to this magical place. At the little slipway on Ynys Enlli, the Island of Currents, Colin Evans disgorged his slightly dizzy passengers and stepped ashore to tell us all about the island community, of which he is a passionate member and advocate. He was among sympathetic listeners—my farming friends and me. We talked of traditional farming and landscapes, of early Christians and our shared feelings for community. They very kindly spoke mostly in English and I was suitably humble—and humbled. I later discovered that Colin is the son of poet Christine Evans.

For four hours, and with an admonition not to be late for the return leg, I wandered the mile-long island, from the flat, grassy plain on its exposed west side, to the five-hundred-foot-high ridge that gives sublime, soul-nourishing views back onto Llŷn; through the ruins of the abbey, past the old schoolhouse (now a small museum), the farmhouses that support the active agriculture and craft of the Bardsey community and provide accommodation for modern pilgrims—both Christian and, like myself, entirely secular—who come here every year. It reminded me of Iona, its sense of perching on the edge of the world. The island is owned by a trust and tenanted by the Royal Society for the Protection of Birds: Bardsey's habitat is maintained for wildlife through traditional farming methods. At the south end of the island there is a beautifully four-square, solid, red-and-white striped lighthouse standing, perhaps, in the enclosure of a prehistoric fort. Close to the roofless abbey church is a more recent chapel. Here are housed a cross and inscription stone: the setting simple, unaffected and absolutely genuine in its sentiment. Cows swished their tails in the shoreline fields; bracken, gorse and heather cloaked the hillside. Cadfan, the founder of the monastic community here in the sixth century, cannot have been the first to appreciate the island's beauty and its atmosphere of magic and tension.

In latter days (from perhaps the late eighteenth century) there was a King of Bardsey, the result of a local tradition that might have deep ceremonial roots. The last to wear the crown was an extraordinary man called Love Pritchard who, at the age of seventy-one, offered himself as a volunteer for service in the trenches of the First World War. He is said to have once rowed from Bardsey to Liverpool, an extraordinary feat. Bardsey was depopulated in the late 1920s when the community had shrunk so much that there were insufficient people to man the boats to row inhabitants on and off the island.

I could not believe that I had been lucky enough to finish this profoundly intense journey with such an uplifting and soul-invigorating send-off. Sitting on the slipway wall, admiring the texture and lines of a low-slung, time-battered barn overlooking the strand, watching a family of seals basking in the sun and enjoying doing nothing for the first time in ten days, the sense of journey's end, of fulfilment, came on strong. That day I learned much from Colin Evans and his deep-felt advocacy of the island way of life; from my farming acquaintances and from the island community who sustain it. Landscape archaeology is largely the study of what survives; and especially today the survival of that heritage takes special people of resilience and vision.

BARDSEY

Interlude   *The Tyne: Hexham to Ovingham*

St Wilfrid's crypt—reusing Rome—petrified—Corbridge—Bywell—
two Anglo-Saxon parish churches—toilet seats to towers—River
Tyne—shanty town—Ovingham and Ovington

ONLY TWO CRYPTS belonging to the first century of Anglo-
Saxon Christianity survive in Britain. Both were constructed
under the orders of St Wilfrid, an entrepreneurial, confrontational, love-him-or-hate-him, opinion-splitting Northumbrian
champion of Roman orthodoxy in the generation before Bede.
At Ripon, in the five or so years after 672, Wilfrid had a stone
church built on lands originally gifted to the Ionan community on Lindisfarne, and from which he had had them expelled.
Later, estates confiscated from schismatic[62] British churches
were added to his portfolio. The church and its magnificent crypt
were rededicated in a ceremony full of pomp, gold, purple and
triumphalism (and royal monikers signing over the freehold).
Wilfrid's other great foundation lay at Hexham, on lands which
a Bernician queen, Æthelthryth, had been persuaded to give to
the bishop on her abdication. The masons, glaziers and plaster-
ers whom he had brought from Francia to undertake the Ripon
project reassembled at Hexham (Old English *Hagustaldesham* –
perhaps 'Enclosure of the young warrior') in the latter half of the
670s for an even more magnificent project, as his hagiographer
Eddius Stephanus recalled:

> My poor mind is quite at a loss for words to describe it—
> the great depth of the foundations, the crypts of beautifully
> dressed stone, the vast structure supported by columns of
> various styles and with numerous side-aisles, the walls of
> remarkable height and length, the many winding passages
> and spiral staircases…[63]

The crypt survives, improbably, beneath the later abbey. It was
rediscovered in 1725 by workmen digging foundations, and later
incorporated into the new nave. Twice a day, visitors are allowed
to descend into its fuggy depths to test for themselves Eddius's contention. One weekend I persuaded Sarah to join me in
a short exploration. The steps are steep and narrow, the treads
worn concave from the passage of pilgrims' feet. It feels claus-
trophobic, like one of those old ghost rides at funfairs. It does
not pass for magnificent compared with the other great works
of giants that surround us: the gothic cathedrals of York or Canterbury that mark the medieval high point of Roman orthodoxy
and wealth; the engineering shrines of Telford or Brunel; the
football stadia, those mausolea of fortune and failure; the tunnels
and pylons that funnel and transmit the forces that power the
modern world. But to the Early Medieval pilgrim, whose limited
experience of churches was for the most part the hewn-oak and
thatched garden-shed variety of the Irish missionaries, here was
a work of giants re-emerged from their slumber.

Wilfrid's exercise in petrification—that is to say, his reintroduction of a solid, stone-built, permanent diocesan Roman
church and his very evident, deliberate demotion of the ascetic,
individual and schismatic (so far as he was concerned) Irish
church to the midden of history—achieved the desired effect. It
intimidated, awed, numbed the imagination of the visitor with its
overt imitation of the catacombs of Rome and the mausoleum of
St Peter. It also nested the experience of concentrated holiness:

like the monasteries at Nendrum and Clonmacnois in Ireland and St Blane's at Kingarth, it consisted of concentric rings leading from the external, profane world to the increasingly holy: *sanctus, sanctior, sanctissimus*.[64] The altar and subterranean shrine was the most holy place, preserve of the anointed priest, and the passages and anteroom that afforded ill-lit, mysterious glimpses or half-touches of treasures; the *sanctior* where the favoured pilgrims might be relieved of their offerings. The architecture of the Wilfridan church distanced the ordinary, the secular, the low-born from the masonic privacy of a priestly elite. Wilfrid, a veteran of the ultimate pilgrimage to Rome, brought back with him marvellous relics of the early saints and martyrs to add potency to his grand projects, and began to foster the cult of the martyred King Oswald.

In the barrel-vaulted bowels of the earth at Hexham, even if the complete scheme of stairways and entrances has been obscured and truncated by later building, one senses that something more subtle underpinned Wilfrid's desire to impose episcopal power on the Northumbrians. The stones used in the construction of the crypt were quarried from Roman sites across the river; and not just any sites. A recent survey by the archaeologist Paul Bidwell has shown that the apparently random distribution of odd fragments of wall-frieze or imperial inscription—a Roman altar, a Lewis-hole[65] or diamond hatching—are themselves relics binding the present to a mythical, imperial past and to the worship not just of a god, but of a pantheon of native deities, the lost race of giants confused and fused with the legionaries of a lost age. The main building blocks came from the bridge at Corbridge, which must have been defunct in Wilfrid's day. The fluted pilaster decorations can only have come from a very grand monument and this has been identified by excavation: a great tower mausoleum which stood just across the Cor Burn to the immediate west of the town at Shorden Brae. This may have commemorated an important victory by a Roman general in a war fought in the 180s. It must have ranked with the most magnificent monuments of the Empire. The absence of material in the crypt from the Roman town itself suggests that royal interests—that is to say, a royal township or *villa regia*—retained the rights to the town in Wilfrid's day: he was able to acquire the site of the abbey from the former queen's dower lands; but not materials from the king's own estate.

The crypt is all that survives of Wilfrid's church: the rest is a medieval and later compilation. But a truncated high cross commemorating Bishop Acca (*c.*660–740) can be seen in the south transept, and in the abbey chancel a souvenir of Wilfrid's pretensions survives in the Frith stool, a solid, carved sandstone episcopal throne decorated with interlace and skeuomorphic (see page 298) wooden moulding. It is not quite complete, and has been broken in half and cemented together—but its earthy solidity and fist-like presence, a bold statement of unashamed Anglian self-confidence, ring loud across the ages.

Sarah and I had miles to cover: we left the abbey in brilliant sunshine and made our way through Hexham's twisting medieval streets down to the river, looking occasionally back at its four-square tower punching through the skyline against the hills behind. The prominence on which it stands forms an unmistakeable triangle with Warden Hill, across the river to the north-west, and Corbridge to the north-east: three centres of power spanning the river and the centuries between the Iron Age and the age of the great Northern bishops. We crossed the Tyne and turned east towards Corbridge, past the dragon's-breath plume of steam exhaled twenty-four hours a day from the Eggers chipboard factory. Partly retracing the route that Colm and I had taken some months before, we passed below the Roman town and entered the village from the bridge, built a thousand years after Wilfrid scavenged its predecessor. St Andrew's church, at the centre of the

BYWELL

village, was constructed largely using materials from the Roman town—it belongs originally to the latter half of the seventh century, with a later Saxon tower. Given its location, it is tempting to think that this was a royal monastic church, a minster, set up to complement, or perhaps compete with, Wilfrid's basilica across the water.

If there was an eastward continuation of the Stanegate downstream from here, it has not yet been traced. We followed the main road as it rose away from the river onto higher ground above the flood plain and only by dodging down back lanes that zig-zagged to conform to post-medieval enclosures were we able to regain contact with the river where the valley narrows above Bywell. The 'spring in the bend', Bywell was once a thriving town known for its metalworking. Now there is a comfortable-looking estate ('Keep out' and 'Private' signs everywhere) with a castle, a couple of grand houses and little else barring two improbable parish churches standing within a hundred yards of each other. Both are pre-Conquest foundations. The reason for this apparent excess is that the boundary between two great baronies followed the line of the main street in the village which runs out at the bend in the river that gives Bywell part of its name. St Andrew's is no longer a consecrated church; but it has been sympathetically conserved and counts among the finest churches on the Tyne. Many of its stones came from Corbridge, and there is a persistent, if unprovable theory, that two circular stone piercings high up in the tower are Roman toilet seats recycled from the scatologically profane to the sacred. It's a nice thought. St Peter's, across the lane, became a much grander affair in the Medieval period, and little remains of its Anglo-Saxon origin. But in the south wall there is still a small DIY sundial, a hole into which one may poke a stick and read off the hours on its chiselled dial. Bywell was a serene and lovely place to pause for lunch: snowdrops lit up the graveyard on the riverbanks (it is said that in the great flood of 1771 corpses were washed from their graves here) and the air is alive with bird-song and the rush of water.

Just below Bywell is an important crossing of the Tyne, the first since Corbridge. The next is at Ovingham, a mile and a quarter along the river. Before that, we indulged in a stroll through one of the locally famous—or notorious—shanty towns that decorate (some might say deface) the north side on this stretch of the river. Some time in the 1920s farmers in these parts allowed city dwellers to escape the wheezing air of the docks and mines and build weekend shacks, scores of them, originally in wood with shingle roofs. Many survived the Second World War, used as evacuation accommodation while the wharves and docks downstream were being bombed. Some are semi-permanent residences. For two years I lived in one when times were pretty precarious and I had nowhere more secure to inhabit. They are a marvellous evocation of liminal existence, absolutely reminiscent of the creek-bound barges of the Essex coastal lands and archaeologically suggestive of many Early Medieval settlements. Organic and constantly evolving, they are more or less reluctantly tolerated by the local authorities, loved by their residents and jealously defended against planners and the odd thief or vandal. These are real communities. Their eccentric décor, gnome-rich handkerchief gardens and bespoke corrugated repairs are fascinating in a way that no corporate or ecclesiastical architecture can match. They are tangibly human and humane, a celebration of the vernacular.

The small village of Ovingham—'the farmstead of Ova's people'—on the banks of the Tyne is matched by Ovington (the 'tun' or village of Ova's people's farmstead) just up the road on the high ground; but of the two only Ovingham boasts another fine pre-Conquest church very like that at Bywell and complete with 'toilet-seat' piercings. With Corbridge, and another possibly early church at Warden, that makes four in a row along the north bank: there is something special about this side of the river.

CHAPTER SEVEN

Sense of place: *Donegal*

*Donegal and Northumbria—staying still—landscapes at speed—Bernician Studies Group—Lough Foyle ferry—Moville hostel—old friends—Cooley graveyard—shrines and crosses—skeuomorphs—finding monasteries—*shugh *and* bru—*stories and landscapes—Magh Tóchuir—Seamus O'Kane's bodhrán—brainstorming—*Joyful Pilgrimage—*insights—Malin Head—Kinnagoe Bay—back on the bike—Strangford Lough—Nendrum tide mill*

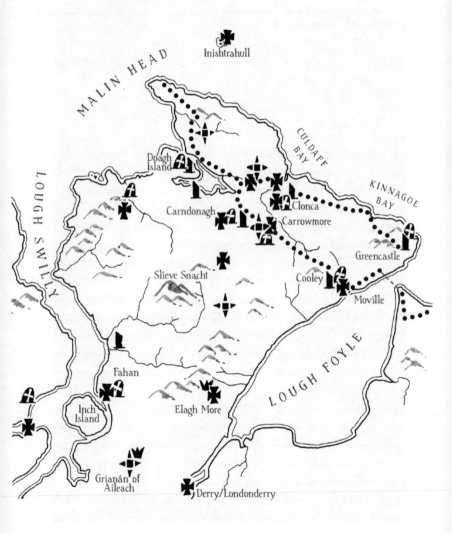

Two DAYS after returning from Bardsey Island (my son Jack, on his first solo adventure since passing his driving test, had driven down to Aberdaron from County Durham to pick me up), Sarah and I rode to Donegal on our motorbike. The timing could not have been better. I wanted a break from walking. I wanted to stay in one location long enough to immerse myself in the Dark Ages, to draw on its sense of place. Ireland, where the past lives as nowhere else in these Atlantic lands, was perfect.

Two Northumbrian kings of the seventh century, Oswiu and his son Aldfrith, had close ties to these lands; so did Colmcille, a native of Donegal. Several years ago the Bernician Studies Group (BSG) became interested in the landscape of Inishowen, the tooth-like peninsula that begins just west of Derry/London-derry and extends north to Malin Head. Armed with a couple of special items of equipment (the fluxgate gradiometer and a laser total station theodolite[66]), the enthusiastic support of colleagues and friends on Inishowen and the energies and expertise of group members, we have been able to recover the outlines of three early Irish monasteries. In 2013, by trial excavation, we proved that at least one of these, at Carrowmore, was founded in the late sixth century during the lifetime of Colmcille and many of the great saints of Wales and Scotland. With my colleague and fellow research director, Colm O'Brien (as bona fide an Irish name as you could wish for, though he is a Cheshire man by birth), we have scoured these lands, poring over maps, crawling through hedges, soaking up the extraordinary wealth of oral and documentary history stored and shared by its generous people. We have been able to build a model of how parts of the landscape worked in the Early Medieval period; and the more we delve into its riches, the more rewarding it becomes. Sometimes walking is not enough, even on the spot. Sometimes it is necessary to dwell. In early September 2014 we returned to Inishowen, this time to study an enigmatic cemetery which overlooks the small town of Moville on the west side of Lough Foyle.

Stranraer, the ferry port for the crossing to Larne in Northern Ireland, is a lot further from everywhere than you think until you try getting there by road. Even on the bike, which makes overtaking a lot easier, it is a good three hours from the Tyne Valley, across the North Pennines via the Tyne–Solway gap, then a little north past Gretna and its gaudy wedding anvils, and west for what seems like unending miles along the A75 through the old shires of Dumfries, Kirkcudbright and Wigtown. We rode it on a perfect late-summer's afternoon, warm and clear with no wind. On the bike, with nothing but your wits between you and eternity, the landscape behaves differently: senses go into overdrive; experiences and images stack up so quickly that you cannot assimilate them until night's rest. But you get a powerful sense of transition—from industry to arable, arable to pasture, pasture to forest, forest to shore, estuary to sea and of the smells that mark these shifts of environment; no wonder dogs get high when they stick their noses out of car windows. The soils change from yellow-grey Pennine sandstone to estuarine clays and then the vivid red sands of Dumfriesshire whose ruddy, soft stone supplies the building materials for its towns, villages, churches and farms. Signs passed at sixty miles an hour (I am being discreet in recording our speed) are dizzying snapshots of missed walking opportunities: the high cross at Ruthwell; Saint so-and-so's church; Ecclefechan and Eaglesfield (both of them suspected Roman church sites);[67] Mote of Mark, a mysterious coastal Dark Age fort and metalworking site; Dunragit, supposed royal fortress of the kings of Rheged; the Anglo-British monastery at Whithorn; inscription stones at Kirkmadrine. And everywhere we saw campaign slogans and banners for both sides of the Scottish Independence referendum (Dumfries looked to be a 'No').[68] The overall effect is to compress landscape, past and present, into a concentrate of a thousand and a thousand more years, and of journeys, lives and changes. It seems very like flying. It's an absolute blast.

On the ferry (kindly subsidised by P&O) we met up with the van-bound bulk of the party: Colm, whose career mine has paralleled in many ways, although he is a classicist who digs and I am a classically illiterate digger; Jack Pennie (who engineered bridges on the Irish side of the North Channel in his youth), our chief geophysicist; Joy Rutter, librarian, novelist and lover of all things Welsh; Deborah Haycock, part-time excavator and a veteran of our Heavenfield perambulations; and Sabrina Pietrobuono, a visiting Italian scholar who didn't know what was about to hit her. Sarah had met some of the group before and, being a nurse, whether she liked it or not she was the senior first-aider. Otherwise, she was under no obligation to play the amateur archaeologist for the next week. Others would join us in Moville.

The two-hour ferry crossing was a chance for a quick snooze and discussions about food shopping and other domestic matters. At some point we must have crossed the now-invisible wake of *Eda Frandsen*; memories of a long night on watch came to mind. An Ulster girl, Sarah was familiar with the voyage; her great grandfather was the harbour-master at Larne and she pointed out his house as we trundled down the ramp onto Irish soil. We left the van to make its own way from Larne, and rode off into the green rolling hills of Antrim.

There are two ways to get to Inishowen: one is the Derry road, which takes you through Antrim, past the north shore of Lough Neagh and across the easternmost hills of the Sperrin Mountains. Instead, we rode north-west to Coleraine, then beneath the massive cliffs of Binevenagh and out onto the sands of Magilligan Point, where the Lough Foyle ferry runs across its mouth to Greencastle. It's just another excuse to get on a boat; besides, the very kind people who own the ferry company give us a concession; and it's a fine way to arrive in the Republic. There are never any signs of customs points or security: the ferry leaves from a sloping concrete ramp and cars simply wait to board at the top of the incline.

Already a few vehicles had formed a queue when we got there at about four-thirty. In one of the cars was Sara Anderson, another group stalwart, on her second trip to Inishowen with one of her daughters. Ireland being such a small world of wondrous connections, it was no surprise to find that in another car was a good friend and colleague, Neil McGrory, with his wife Róisin and two daughters. They had just been shopping for school clothes in Coleraine. Neil and his family run a legendary pub and music venue in Culdaff; he is also a local historian and a man of universal knowledge of these parts, without whom we would never have been able to get our project off the ground. On the short crossing we chatted and caught up with news, promising to go over to the pub on Friday night.

The hostel at Moville, which we made our base, was welcoming, ramshackle and homely. Owned and run by Seamus Canavan, his daughter Cressida and her partner Chris, it lurks on the banks of a small trickling river at the inland edge of Moville, close to what purports to be Ireland's oldest bridge. The hostel might once have been an old mill: a clotted assortment of extensions, outbuildings and gardens overshadowed by gnarled, dripping trees that give the whole a thoroughly gothic air, like a Caspar David Friedrich painting. A peat stove burns in the kitchen-cum-dining-room; upstairs are a small library and reading room with internet connection and various bedrooms, showers and nooks and crannies that I never quite managed to explore. Very kindly Seamus had given Sarah and me the swanky room with double bed, loo and shower as well as a kitchen that became the equipment room for charging, drying and generally sorting our field gear. Catering was a group effort: we all mucked in until a rota was established. We ate, refined our plans for the week and were clearing up when our first visitor pitched up (news travels fast in these parts): Martin Hopkins, the man behind rescuing the nearby Early Medieval graveyard from oblivion and a fine friend of the project. We arranged to meet on site in the morning.

The graveyard called Cooley, which sits magnificently on a hill above Moville looking across Lough Foyle to Northern Ireland and out to the sea beyond, is a suitably enigmatic spot in a mystical land of folklore and heroic legend. Past this shore Colmcille is supposed to have sailed for Iona in the year 563. At the entrance to the walled cemetery is an ancient high cross, a pierced wheel on a tall shaft with narrow arms and an odd hole drilled off-centre through the stype—the shaft above the cross head. Otherwise unadorned, it bears no obvious clues to its date, although generally archaeologists suppose that the rougher and simpler the dressing and decoration, the older the cross. It's a dangerous assumption to make. All assumptions about Irish archaeology are dangerous.

The graveyard's cast-iron gates are held shut by means of a plastic canister filled with water tied to a rope on a pulley. By that expedient Martin's vegetation-management operatives (two sheep) are confined to their job of keeping down the weeds and grass which he and his group of volunteers laboured so long to clear some years ago. The cemetery wall encloses a rectangular area about fifty by twenty-five yards. The ruined walls of two buildings, supposedly churches, stand around ten or twelve feet tall. There is a scatter of gravestones and tombs belonging to the last couple of centuries, the names of their inhabitants still legible. Most of the cemetery is a higgledy-piggledy jumble: hundreds of unmarked head- and footstones, some of them bearing incised crosses—a mass of memorial anonymity spanning who knows how many decades and centuries. A sloping path more or less bisects the graveyard and ends at a small gabled building,

COOLEY GRAVEYARD

built almost entirely of rough-hewn stone slabs, about nine feet long by five feet wide and no more than seven feet high at the ridge. It has a small entrance low on the western gable end—only sufficient to poke one's head inside and squint up at the corbelled ceiling. A tiny slit in the east end admits just enough light to show a few scattered bones lying on the dusty, stony floor—whether of sheep or of a saint it is impossible to say without removing them.

It used to be thought that Moville was the site of a monastery founded by Finnian, teacher of Colmcille and in his own right a famous early Northern holy man; but we now know that was by misassociation with Movilla (whose abbey was founded by Finnian in the mid-sixth century) in County Down, near Strangford Lough. The Donegal Moville—the name means 'plain of the sacred tree'—does not feature either in the great hagiographies of the seventh century, nor in later martyrologies that record the geographic and genealogical associations of the saints. The cemetery's origins are, therefore, obscure. However, a Victorian survey of Donegal names the site as *Domnach Magh Bhile*; and the *Domnach* element is taken to refer to a tradition of foundations by St Patrick. At any rate it was a term not used for church foundations after the sixth century; and the small building, known locally as a 'skull house', looks very much like an early shrine. Thanks to the work of Martin Hopkins and his group, Cooley has in the last few years produced more evidence that it was a place of some ecclesiastical importance during the first millennium. The collection of incised stone cross-slabs known from the site now numbers more than a dozen, identified from careful observation in the right light. It is a very complex, concentrated miniature landscape. Nearly all the features we see could belong to almost any period before the Plantations.[69] The whole requires serious analysis; but there are clues to tease the archaeologist. Two years ago Martin noticed that one of these cross-incised slabs, which now leans against the inside wall of the cemetery, has a very special feature.

It is about three feet tall, broken at the top but clearly carved with a portrayal of a ring-headed cross. Martin saw that, at the bottom, the cross shaft had been finished to a tapered point, the way a wooden stake would be cut so that it could be driven into the ground. When he offered this inspired observation to Colm and me a couple of years ago, we did a double-take.

This is what we call a skeuomorph: the translation of a design feature from one medium (usually wood; but also metal) into another, often stone. The carver of this stone was used to making, or seeing, wooden memorial crosses driven into the ground and, in making the material transition to the more permanent stone, echoed what the builders of the hut circles at Din Lligwy had achieved: taken the original form and retained it as a decorative feature, in a sense a cultural fossil. Skeuomorphic representations of objects are a special class of artefact; they include wooden lathe-turned bowls from Iona which copied the everted[70] rim of E-ware pottery (jars, bowls and jugs in hard granular grey wares) imported from Francia in the seventh century, the finials of cruck-framed[71] wooden buildings copied in stone on shrines like our skull house, the Anglo-Saxon Runic script originally designed to be carved across the grain in wood, the mouldings on the Frith stool at Hexham and, in more modern times, the carrying through of carpentry joints into the cast-iron fittings of the Ironbridge at Coalbrookdale. Their significance is to mark a transition in technique and, surely, mental imagery. Thus St Wilfrid was scornful of those English and Irish monks who built their churches from hewn oak thatched with straw 'in the Irish manner'—it was unbecoming of the dignity of the pontiff and the mother church and more evidence of the schismatic, antiquated practices of the Irish—and of the community on Lindisfarne. Wood, and carved wooden images, carried overtones of paganism. Stone was permanent, orthodox. So a skeuomorphic cross makes us think we are dealing with a memorial tradition belonging to this transient phase. Does this, do all the crosses at Cooley, belong to the seventh century? In our minds was an idea that the skeuomorphism implied an already established tradition of wooden memorials at the same place, which would take the site back still earlier, perhaps into the sixth century like the monastic complex at Carrowmore, a few miles to the north-west.

We had six days, on this trip, to see if we could tease out the many complex elements of the site: how the rows of stones related to the skull house; whether the building remains were those of churches and, if so, whether we could say how old they were. Did the present outline of the cemetery, known to belong to the seventeenth century, reflect its original shape and extent? Would we find any more crosses and could we relate them to other phases? Could we confirm that a monastery had stood on this site? If we could, what could we say about its origins and its location?

Our hope of resolving some of these questions depended on deploying the gradiometer to peer beneath the pastures that surround the cemetery, on conducting a really detailed digital survey of all the features within it and, perhaps most important, staying put in the same place long enough to see patterns emerging from the chaos: patterns which archaeologists are trained to recognise but which are rarely obvious on first inspection. Even walking the landscape doesn't compete with sitting or working in it, day after day. It's like buying a house. On a first visit, big, bold things stand out: size, light, garden, décor. On a second visit, it might feel smaller; you look for other, more functional details, like where the stopcocks are; is there room for a washing machine? A professional surveyor will look at the roof structure; at the wiring. Only when you move in do you realise that the front door sticks, the shower leaks and the toilet flush is hopeless, that there's a damp patch beneath a window and that the curtains will simply have to go. That's what dwelling does for bringing out the detail.

On our first morning we set the kit up. Jack and his team laid out grids in the fields on either side of the cemetery, chaperoned by five huge Charolais bullocks whose attentive curiosity was amusing to those of us inside the wall and variously annoying or unnerving to those in the field. Our survey method was the same as that which we had deployed at Heavenfield (see page 231–2). At Cooley we already suspected that the fields might reveal features diagnostic of a monastic enclosure like that at Llangian which I had recently visited. An early map showed a kink in the field boundary to the north of the cemetery which hinted at a circular enclosure. And in the last days of our 2013 campaign we had quickly run the machinery over the fields at Cooley and produced what looked like a crude map of ditches and banks. Ideally, this year the gradiometer would not just confirm their existence, but also show the internal detail of any structures such as houses and churches although, inevitably, there would be a large gap in the middle where the cemetery, standing proud of the land around it, masks everything beneath—our machine cannot penetrate so many centuries of built-up grave deposits and disturbances and, besides, it's impossible to walk in a straight line in a cemetery full of stones, tombs and walls.

Four years ago, on a recce to see if it was realistic for the group to develop a project on Inishowen, Colm and I had come to the conclusion that, given Ireland's predominantly pastoral economy, aerial photography to detect crop marks and field walking to look for finds in ploughed fields were both closed to us as methods of locating early sites buried beneath the soil. Geophysics was the way forward, and we were incredibly lucky when Sunderland University gave us the funds to purchase our own gradiometer. We wasted no time in bringing it to Donegal and, in 2012, we succeeded in establishing the presence of a classic double-ditched circular monastic vallum at Carrowmore. In 2013 we repeated the experiment at Clonca, a mile north-east of Carrowmore across the peatlands, where a church and high cross still stand,

and produced even more spectacular results: a complex series of enclosures, trackways and a possible cemetery focused on the high cross. On the same trip we excavated trial trenches across the two ditches at Carrowmore, with a great deal of help from local volunteers, and proved the antiquity of that establishment. Our soil samples showed that we could retrieve crucial environmental data from the environs of the monastery; and we were fantastically lucky to find five tiny polished pebble gaming counters, of the sort that would have been played with on the merel boards of Inchmarnock (see page 35). We felt we had brought something to the party, that we could make a significant contribution to understanding the development of this landscape.

But nothing is straightforward here. To begin with, the complexity of local place names has us confused—we are mere novices at pronouncing written Gaelic; we find that most places have at least two, if not three alternative names, for whose derivation we rely completely on the local knowledge of our expert colleagues—and sometimes they can't agree among themselves. Even names for simple landscape features have caused all sorts of cross-cultural confusion. Locally, what we call a ditch is understood as a dyke, an upstanding boundary or field wall. The word for ditch locally is *shugh*, its bank a *bru*. Then there is the conflicting evidence of local oral tradition and opinion, often very firmly held, and the testimony of documents. There are numberless associations of all sorts of rocks, trees, crosses and standing stones with various families, holy men and legendary events. There are said to be ancient tunnels everywhere. Layers of continuity and discontinuity, like a much-kneaded geological pastry confection, tease and mislead. Vikings followed by Normans followed by Cromwell's genocidal rampage; plantations, rebellions, exploitation and colonial repression, all written into field boundary, parish, townland and *clachan*, place name and record. Pick the wrong straw from the pile and the whole thing collapses.

In England, where the historical evidence is generally a little simpler, there is much less relevant or useful oral tradition to assist or perplex the landscape archaeologist: in Ireland there is a whole universe of richly nuanced narrative which has to be interpreted as a textual source in its own right and woven into the broad tapestry we are trying to create, even if much useful material evidence has been lost or deliberately destroyed in acts of cultural barbarity. On top of that, the numinous quality of many early sites continues to endow them with spiritual meaning in the twenty-first century. At Carrowmore some visitors to our excavations admitted that they had only passed that way to visit the bullaun stone—a natural or hollowed-out depression in a stone that fills with rainwater, which thereby acquires healing powers—in the next field, in the hope of a cure for an ailment. The cutting down of trees such as the rowan is still widely regarded as taboo; roadside shrines and holy wells dressed with beads, photographs, coins and other offerings or mementoes are common sights. Here, past and present, real and supernatural, magic and rational are entwined in a way that wrong-foots the sometimes overrational critique of the hard-bitten professional fieldworker. The cultural texture and depth of Ireland's north-west, the lyricism and intellectual curiosity of its literary traditions, are part of the charm and fascination of these lands, even if they leave us scratching our heads from time to time.

We have been told an attractive story about the monasteries at Carrowmore and Clonca, which face each other across the River Culdaff and which are said to have been linked in some way—one the daughter house of the other, perhaps; there are rumours of a tunnel. The modern road crosses the river over a small stone bridge; to the north is an expanse of peat which once required a causeway to cross it. The late Mabel Colhoun, a distinguished local archaeologist, wrote that she had seen a section of the causeway—made, perhaps, from hazel hurdles staked into the peat.

According to the story, at the time when the two monasteries flourished, perhaps during the seventh or eighth century, monks used to process between the two. Since they were linked by a narrow causeway, the procession must have looked like a thin snake, as the monks crossed the bog in single file. The priest at the head of the column, setting out from Carrowmore, was said to have realised, as he reached the other side of the river, that he had forgotten his prayer book. So he called back along the line for one of the brothers to fetch it. By the time he stepped off the causeway and reached firm ground at Clonca, the prayer book had been passed back up along the line and handed to him. That such a tale has survived a thousand years in these parts does not surprise. Why such a simple, not very miraculous tale is still told is another matter. I think its importance lies in a missing preamble, which I suppose to have gone something like this: *There were at one time* so many *monks at Carrowmore, that it was said that when the priest* [perhaps St Comgall, the traditional founder] *was walking from Carrowmore to Clonca to celebrate Easter...*, etc. For the academic archaeologist, moulding such stories into the tentative narrative structures built on excavation and survey is as challenging as it is exciting.

Inishowen was the core territory of the kin group called Cenél nÉogain (pronounced as 'Kenneln Owen'); Éogain was a descendant of Niall of the Nine Hostages, the legendary fifth-century king who gave his name to the the Uí Néill family that dominated Early Medieval Ireland from the sixth to the tenth century. King Oswiu of Northumbria (r. 642–70), brother of the Oswald who raised his cross at Heavenfield, sired a child with a princess of Inishowen called Fina; that child was Flann Fina, or Aldfrith, scholar and later king of Northumbria (r. 685–704). The Inishowen peninsula looks both towards the sea and inland to Derry (supposedly a foundation of Colmcille) and early kingship sites at Grianán of Aileach and Elaghmore. Since the Cenél nÉogain became a dominant power in the north of Ireland in the Early Medieval period, the landscape of the peninsula may hold the keys to understanding how this early kingdom first established itself and then used the power structures and codes of kin, patronage and church to expand its influence.

The north part of Inishowen is dominated by the Magh Tóchuir (pronounced more softly than its spelling suggests to an English ear), a fertile plain which drains north-west into Trawbreaga Bay and the gaping mouth of Lough Swilly beyond. Around the edges of this plain are dotted prehistoric standing stones, early Christian centres and the ringforts and hilltop enclosures of a secular elite whose origins lie obscurely in the prehistoric past.[72] Just as on Llŷn, an understanding of the place and role of early churches and monasteries in their landscape sheds light on secular power structures, on the economy and culture of a period when the kingdoms of the Dark Ages emerge from the mists of prehistory. Add to that a traditional rivalry between Columban and Patrician churches for bragging rights over these parts and you have a heady mix of academic speculation and religious propriety which historically has seemed anything but trivial. Into this cauldron the English archaeologist treads with extreme caution in the knowledge that, apart from the superb field surveys carried out by Mabel Colhoun and Brian Lacey (the latter a kind supporter of our project), not a huge amount of practical archaeology has been conducted up here. With all these marvellous field monuments, and the chance to make a contribution to a key period in Ireland's past, we are like children in a sweet shop. But we are painfully aware that we might be perceived more as bulls in a china emporium.

In Ireland the social and professional are impossible to separate. We had a busy schedule and not much time to carry out our work; but during that first morning on site there was a more or less continuous, and welcome, stream of visitors: Sean Beattie,

△ *Morag*, Kyles
of Bute
'*Donald Clark, her owner
and skipper, plucked us off
the beach as cool as you
like*' (page 39).

ENCOUNTERS

▷ Inishowen—
Martin Hopkins,
Dessie McCallion,
Colm O'Brien
'*…during that first
morning on site there was
a more or less continuous,
and welcome, stream of
visitors*' (page 304).

◁ SOMERSET
'this layer cake of generations of farmers, drovers, artisans and cottagers' (page 220).

◁ ESSEX
'More back lanes; more rain… no one to meet by chance or talk to; no walkers of any kind' (page 118).

▽ HIGHLAND CATTLE, HALTWHISTLE BURN
'…peering curiously through their fringes at gawping passers-by' (page 92).

ENCOUNTERS

ENTREPRENEURS

△ Whitechapel
'tensions that hold this extraordinary urban orrery in perpetual, confounding, vibrant equipoise' (page 104).

◁ Moville, Inishowen
'We had been allowed the run of Rosato's bar... so we were guaranteed an audience' (page 315).

ENTREPRENEURS

△ WHITBY
'...*mecca for Dracula fans
mostly unaware of an
earlier, dramatic catharsis
between opposing moral
forces*' (page 421).

▷ TRACTOR AT
PORTHMEUDWY
'*It's nice to see an old
Fordson Major looking
in such good trim...*'
(page 277).

IDENTITIES

△ LONDON
'an emporium for many nations who came to it by land and by sea' (page 101).

▽ MERSEA ISLAND
'mile after mile of bright-painted beach huts' (page 125).

◁ TOBERMORY
*'all brightly coloured
houses, crowded jetties
and drunks'* (page 177).

IDENTITIES

◁ DORSET
*'This mannered human
landscape of field and
hedge, wall and fence, is a
very temporary borrowing
from nature'* (page 209).

▽ GLASTONBURY TOR
*'We were tolerant of one
another'* (page 223).

SPACES

△ SOUTH CADBURY
*'Let's get the Arthurian
record straight'*
(page 214).

▽ EPPING FOREST
*'one expects at any
time to come upon
a gingerbread cottage
inhabited by cast-off
children or lounging,
porridge-slurping bears'*
(page 110).

The Wall
*'three plough furrows racing eastwards across
the Northumbrian uplands'* (page 141).

highly respected historian, friend and editor of the *Donegal Annual*;
John Hegarty, an archaeologist who dug with us in 2013; Dessie
McCallion, an indefatigable rooter-around in Inishowen's past,
always ready to show you some odd treasure he has turned up;
and then another two group members arrived: Cowan and Catherine Duff are entirely responsible for the genesis of the whole
project. Catherine is a native of the west side of Lough Swilly;
and Cowan, a retired industrial metallurgist and old BSG hand,
persuaded us several years ago that we would not be able to resist
this landscape. He was right.

Meanwhile, I wanted to get the laser theodolite set up. I mastered these things many years ago when I ran the field unit at
Durham University; but I was rusty, and could perhaps have done
with shutting myself away for a morning with the manual. Until I
established a solid base station we could not start surveying, and
I hate to see people standing around waiting for me to tell them
what to do. Not that they were unhappy: Cooley Graveyard is a
lovely spot: green green hills, low stone walls, few trees, coloured
houses dotted about, very like the Isle of Man; those panoramic
views across the Lough and down onto the huddled townscape of
Moville; the shadow of Rathlin Island far, far to the north-east on
the very disc of the horizon; and an ancient graveyard to potter
around. It's a nice spot to be dead in.

Our visitors kept us pleasantly busy all morning, giving generously of their considerable store of local knowledge and understanding. The geophysics team got on with their grid-laying.
One or two more volunteers arrived to see if they could help
and Colm began a field class teaching Sabrina and local supporters Mary and Elizabeth how to draw to a proper archaeological
standard the dozen or so cross-marked stones that had been identified by Martin and others over the years. The plan was for me
to photograph them all later in the week. Almost immediately
this concentration of effort on a group of previously unrecorded

stone memorials yielded results; or at least significant questions. Some of them seemed to have been used as headstones; others to mark the foot of a grave in this crowded burial space. Some faced west, others east; some were evidently on their sides. Our conclusion was that all of the stones inscribed with crosses had been reused, that they had originally been in other positions. The more or less organised rows of graves did not, then, reflect the first phase of the cemetery. So how old were they? And how did such a modest community—Moville's growth into a small town is a nineteenth-century development, no earlier—produce such a large population to fill this cemetery to bursting?

By the end of the first day's play I had the theodolite working and had established my base points. The geophysics team had laid out their grids. We shared a convivial supper and as evening closed in on the town Sarah, Deb, Joy and I strolled down the road for a ritual and absolutely essential first pint of what Ireland is famous for.

Fieldwork is subject to fates out of our control. Much of the second day on site was a washout; we spent a couple of damp hours huddled behind sheltering walls or under trees; we retreated to the hostel, tried again and got a couple of hours' work done in the afternoon. Another friend of ours, Michael Hegarty, who besides living close to the site at Cooley and fixing it for us to get access to the fields, is also a Lough Foyle pilot and a highly entertaining companion, came up to us on his quad bike. He swore richly at us in at least two languages for our stupidity in staying out in the rain and persuaded some of us to retreat to his house to get warm and make tea. The day's work more or less ruined, we consoled ourselves with the thought of an evening outing to McGrory's where the food is divine—seafood chowder, bacon and cabbage with mash—and where, every Friday, musicians congregate to play traditional music. Róisin, Neil McGrory's wife, plays fiddle in the band and occasionally one or other of our number is co-opted. Neil and his brother John have their own band; and musicians come from across the peninsula and beyond to join in. I was delighted to introduce Sarah to the place, having told her many tales about it. We also had in the party an American student, come to work with Cressida and Chris on their perma-culture plot at the back of the hostel. She had never experienced Guinness before.

As the bar filled for the evening, musicians drifted in. Neil was the perfect unobtrusive front-of-house host, always attentive, never overly so; his sister Ann always in the background oiling wheels and making sure the place runs as though with no effort. There was a hum of noise: clinking glass, laughter, a fragment of song, friends met and stools scraped on the stone floor to squeeze another in. The bar is a great place for people-watching.

A grey-haired, slightly stooping man with bushy dark eyebrows entered the bar carrying a bodhrán case in his hand. His face looked somehow familiar. I got up and worked my way through the crowd to where Neil was standing at the bar, and asked him if it was Seamus O'Kane. Sure it is, he said. What, I said, *the* Seamus O'Kane? Yes, he said: you want to meet him? Seamus is not just one of the great bodhrán players but a renowned maker of these Irish frame drums. He is steeped in the tradition of the instru-ment and its music but is also a pioneer of modern construction methods, dragging the frame drum from its fringe status as the refuge of toneless skin thumpers towards being a tolerated and even respected component of the Irish folk ensemble. He has achieved this by using a much lighter frame, skin and stick than was common in the past; by designing a cunning tuning system to keep the skin at the right tension. The result is that in his hands the instrument sounds like a rather subtle bass guitar, full of tone and resonance, responsive and kinetic. Watching videos of him working, the amateur wonders how the hell he produces such a melodic and gentle beat. We chatted for a while about wood and trees, drums and music; he knew of my friend Stefan Sobell, the luthier, who has his own fascinating views on acoustics and musicality. I thought I might never get another chance, so I asked him if he would make me a drum. Sure he would: could I wait a month or two?

The buzz in the bar grew louder. In the background the musicians began playing, softly at first. Unconsciously, imperceptibly the buzz dropped and the punters began to listen with more than half an ear. There was Róisin on the fiddle with another, younger fiddler, an accordion player and a flautist; a guitarist strummed chords; Seamus caressed his drum, but concentrate as I might I couldn't see how he managed to forge his beautiful rhythm with such little apparent effort. Our chat died as a singer began a lament; the noise in the bar melted away and his voice rang out true and clear. The room filled to bursting. I went to the bar for a fresh round and Róisin nodded at me to ask if I had an instrument with me. I never leave home without a harmonica or two, so I sat in on a number, trading some little improvisation with the accordion player; the others joined in, in that unselfconscious way that good musicians can: first listening, then gauging the tune, then coming in for a chorus. Róisin had disappeared, so I stayed in her chair while the band started something else with the flute leading—a jig. Seamus leaned over and handed me his drum, so I had the double pleasure not only of meeting him but also trying one of his marvellous instruments before I acquired one. It was no kind of disappointment. Even so, it was only later on, when I was sitting at the back again and listening with concentration, that I began to see how his technique had become so popular with other musicians—the bass-style rhythm was neither loud nor penetrating but it underscored the melody and guitar chords, the bass notes perfectly clear and syncopating. We drifted away after one in the morning with the music still in full swing and wishing we could have stayed longer.

Saturday: a strong desire to linger in bed, but with the sun shining there was not a moment to lose. We were joined by John McNulty, who had flown into Belfast that morning; by Deb's husband, Dick, an experienced sailor who has given us useful insights into navigation in these waters; and by another friend from last year's excavation, Mervyn Watson. Halfway through the day the newcomer, Sabrina, announced that she had found a new, previously unobserved cross, obscured by grass and lying half on its side but immediately recognisable, as Colm and I walked across to see it, as another skeuomorphic wooden stake inscribed in stone. This was more than coincidence; it hinted at a local tradition of wood and stone cross-carving, and the striking similarity between the two representations very likely meant that they were contemporary, if not the product of the same sculptor.

Plotting the outlines of the cemetery, skull house and ruined walls with the laser theodolite, Sarah (co-opted more or less willingly as an assistant) and I began to see some order in the chaos. The entrance and slit in the skull house were perfectly aligned with the high cross outside the gate, which suggested that it (the cross) stands where it was first erected. We also spotted—a new observation—that two of the stones in the wall of the skull house were of dressed stone: they must have come from another building, though where and what that building was we cannot yet say. Patterns watched, patterns emerging.

We needed to understand the relationship between this apparently early shrine and the row-graves, the ruined walls and cross fragments; and while Jack's team of geophysicists started to produce meaningful results outside the cemetery, Colm and I sat down on a tomb in the afternoon and laid out in a notebook the fundamentals of what we could and couldn't say about the pure archaeology of the site. It was a thought-experiment conducted in the language of stratigraphy. The study of determining relative chronology by showing what event must come before or after another by virtue of superposition is the primary tool of the archaeologist. An object, building or layer which lies above another must have been placed, lost or deposited there later than whatever lies beneath. A disruption to the stratified sequence—a ditch cut across a boundary, a road running through the middle of a settlement—must also post-date it.

After half an hour of brainstorming we identified more than a dozen phases of activity: an original cemetery in which a small number of graves were marked by carved wooden crosses in various styles, over perhaps a few generations, and very likely focused on a single special grave of the nameless founder, buried in a small wooden shrine (examples have been excavated beneath several stone churches); a phase of transition from wooden buildings and memorials to more permanent, orthodox stone replacements (petrification); then the expansion and filling in of the cemetery by row upon row of—who? Monks? Too many of them, surely. There might be a thousand graves here, and those just the visible ones.

We had seen that the row-graves ran right up to the ruined walls on both sides, disrespecting (and so later than) any floors or interiors of whatever buildings had stood there. So the row-grave system as we saw it was later than the buildings, and by virtue of the fact that the rows bent slightly round it, they were also later than the skull house. At some point the cemetery wall had been constructed on its present alignment. Finally, early modern memorials showed that there had been a late, post-medieval phase of burial. But we could not absolutely date any of these phases except the last. The closer we looked, the more difficult it was to say what was going on where and when.

Sunday. Deb, Joy and I started to plot the positions of all the graves and their accompanying stones: it was the only way to determine if there were hidden patterns in the scheme of burials that might help tease out the cemetery's phases. We could see that many graves, if not all, had been covered either with a single slab or with several capping stones—these are called lintel graves. If we were able and allowed to remove the turf from the site we would gain a huge amount more detail and, no doubt, find more cross-inscribed stones. It was a tempting idea, but it would leave the site open to the depredations of erosion, vandalism and over-curious tourism, so for the moment we took it off the agenda. In the meantime, it was back to the business of looking for and recognising patterns. But it was a daunting task to map a thousand graves when, half the time, it was not clear where one started and another finished, half-buried as they were under thick turf. We could not complete the task in a week; but we could measure and plot enough of the graves to show that the game was worth the candle. And now, sure enough, Jack's survey began to show significant results: confirmation that there had been two enclosure ditches, or *shughs*, concentric like those at Carrowmore and Clonca; and a rectangular structure which might have been a timber building—a church or hall. It was now clear that the cemetery was located right at the centre of a double-ringed enclosure; and that the high cross stood inside that enclosure. And, emerging from the pattern of grey shades that reflect buried magnetic variations, we thought we could see circular structures, the right size for round houses... or for monks' cells.

On a clear late-summer's day like this the cemetery gave views as far as Rathlin Island, a key landmark and stopping-off point between Derry and the Western Isles of Scotland. We had passed it at night, from the other side, in *Eda Frandsen*; now we could see how intimately it was connected with points further west and with the monastic and kingly hinterland of Ireland. In June 1963, had we been standing on this spot, we might have watched the passage of a traditional lath and tarred-canvas curragh up the lough from Derry, carrying thirteen cloaked men in two watches pulling at six oars, with a square sail set amidships bearing the image of a cross. This was the *Joyful Pilgrimage*, sailed by Wallace Clark and his motley crew of companions, celebrating the fifteen hundredth anniversary of Colmcille's departure for Iona by re-enacting the saint's voyage from Derry to the Inner Hebridean island. Clark was an extraordinary man: consummate sailor, expert on the history of linen, commanding skipper and reviver of the traditions of the curragh. His boat was designed by Richard McCullough and built by Jim Boyd at a workshop in Bunbeg on the west coast of Donegal. Such vessels, though they survive in modern form, were a rarity in the 1960s; not many men knew how to go about constructing a traditional craft from scratch. This old style of boat-building, echoing an even older use of hide-covered curraghs mentioned in the *Life of St Brendan* and tested brilliantly by Tim Severin in *The Brendan Voyage*, was longer and narrower than the traditional fishing boats of the West coast. Designed for a large crew, with a high seagoing prow and a square transom, it must take on all weathers during an open sea voyage that might take a week, or two weeks. Such is the enduring potency of the name of Colmcille that Clark's expedition was part-funded by the then Bishop of Down and Dromore, as well as by many gifts of unasked-for help. For the safety of these twentieth-century avatars of Colmcille's original crew, and because many thought them mad, a naval fisheries protection vessel and a diesel-engined tender were on hand to fish them out of the sea at any time.

Canon John Barry, rector of Hillsborough, Co. Down, was the initiator of the project, crew member and chronicler of this latter-day peregrination in the book he called *Joyful Pilgrimage*. Remarkably, despite flaws in the design of the craft that became increasingly evident as the days went by, and despite having too few oars and too many passengers, the crew of the Iona curragh accomplished their journey in just eight days, via Port Ballintrae on the north coast, the south-west tip of Islay, the tidal island of Oronsay and the south coast of Mull. They were met on the strand below Iona Abbey by a large crowd, including the then Archbishop of Canterbury, Michael Ramsey.

Their first night's stop out from Derry had been on the shore at Castle Cary, less than a mile from Cooley cemetery. They had designed the boat, in the ancient way, both to be carried ashore and to be upturned to form their night's shelter; they could stop where they wanted so long as they had a strand to pull her up on. They were met everywhere with kindness, generosity, huge amounts of hot food and a shared pleasure in their achievement and their homage to Colmcille. They proved that even relatively untrained crews could pilot a craft across these seas at good speed; that the Early Medieval curragh was indeed capable of open-sea travel.

We were talking with some of our friends about this trip (I had some years ago met a member of the original crew by chance, in Greencastle museum, just up the coast from here, where there is a very similar craft). I think it was Sean or Martin who said, oral tradition has it that people came by sea from many parts to be buried at Cooley, partly because of its perceived holiness as a site (the Irish have long memories) and partly, perhaps, because of its special location close to the mouth of Lough Foyle and en route to the Western Isles where Iona lay. That might, at least, explain why the cemetery is so full. If only we knew who the founding saint was, could place them in time or in a genealogy of a known clan, it might tell us why this site had such resonance in the regional community.

As the week went on, doubts were, at least, assuaged on one count. The original monastic enclosure at Cooley was a busy place, full of internal structure and complexity. As we had shown at Carrowmore, high-density magnetic anomalies showing up in the *shugh* of the outer vallum appeared to provide evidence of metalworking. South of the graveyard another apparently rectangular building began to show, and there were signs of structural activity to the east, outside the outer enclosure ditch. This was a serious establishment. We now began to think of the following: we supposed that the founding saint had been interred close to the centre of the monastery or that the monastery had developed around the existing cemetery. Either way, the skeuomorphs suggested that the first phase had involved a wooden church and wooden memorials (as had the well-documented establishment at Lindisfarne). That phase had been followed by the erection of a stone shrine to house the relics of the saint (our skull house), possibly on a small mound, and around this a long-lived cemetery developed, with some of the graves marked by stone crosses of various styles. A high cross visibly marked the site for pilgrims and visitors. Perhaps a full monastery then developed around the cemetery, including a church and workshops, cells for the monks and perhaps guest houses. Sometime, we do not know when, the monastery fell into disuse (we might tentatively blame the Viking raids of the ninth century—this is, after all, a horribly exposed spot), the legends of its saint lost to record. After that it was still used for burial, perhaps by people from far distant places, at least until the fourteenth century (a date suggested by a decorative carving of that period on one of the slab covers to a grave). This phase was perhaps ended by the Black Death. What we know from our work at Carrowmore is that, given sufficient funds and permission, we could answer many of our questions by excavation.

On Sunday we carried on more or less uninterrupted: the rest of Moville had, it seemed, gone off to Croke Park in Dublin to watch County Donegal play in the semi-finals of the All-Ireland Gaelic football championship. It was a chance to take stock, for the unglamorous process of recording to take its course. Colm had undertaken not only to have all the known early crosses drawn—and we were finding a new one every day, it seemed—but also to write detailed notes on them. I doubt if there are any more crosses of this period to be found in mainland Britain, a landscape scoured by scholarly vicars, antiquarians and professional archaeologists for over two centuries. In Ireland it is still possible to make such discoveries, and there is a professional obligation to record and publish them which, for the archaeologist, goes hand in hand with the immense privilege of discovery. Our count was now nineteen crosses of various designs. Not only did we have our two wooden skeuomorphs, but a cross previously known had revealed, with a bit of cleaning, the incised shape of a square stone base—an even rarer example of the skeuomorphic translation of a free-standing carved cross into an incised 'drawing' of it.

One of our autumn jobs, apart from report writing, is to get group members making inked versions of the drawings, to go alongside the photographs, so that we have an archive made available for other students of the Irish cross tradition. Because we now have so many new examples from a single place, we can start to look at typologies and to compare them with traditions in other parts of Ireland, as well as the Atlantic coasts of Scotland and Wales. Detailed recording of the graves also yielded important insights into how the graveyard had been managed. It looked as though graves towards the west end of the cemetery were more widely spaced than those close to the skull house; and in the south-east corner, where several of the row graves have early modern inscriptions, we were able to show by their subtly different alignment that they had been inserted after the wall was built: they did not date the mass of graves, just a discrete later phase. I relished this week of being in a single place, watching, looking, recording, steeping myself in a landscape.

On Monday evening we gave a group presentation to the Moville community about our work. We had been allowed the run of Rosato's bar in Moville, our local when we were at the hostel, so we were guaranteed an audience; as it happened we had about thirty. That sort of event makes us feel we are not just taking from, but able to give something to the town, and perhaps to galvanise them into taking more interest in the amazing past on their doorstep.

On Tuesday, our last full day in Moville, we broke off in the early afternoon. I had promised to show Sarah a little more of the peninsula. So we got on the bike and headed west and north for Malin Head: first to the small town of Carndonagh, all brightly coloured houses and narrow, shop-crowded streets converging on a busy central square. A huge modern church sits on a hill so that the Almighty (or perhaps just the Pope) can look down on his congregation from a suitably lofty perch. The remains of a high cross depicting the crucifixion lie in the graveyard of an older, smaller church. Another, with classic interlace and the outline figures of holy men, sits beneath a thoughtlessly designed shelter that looks as if one ought to wait for a bus beneath it and which cuts out all the light. It is flanked by two smaller standing stones, like bollards: one showing the profile of a warrior with a sword on one face and a harpist and his instrument on another; on the other stone, a cat-like creature glares disconcertingly. These last two are decidedly Pictish in style, evidence perhaps that Colmcille's travels among the Caledonians were reciprocated.

From Carndonagh, sitting above the plain, we rode north and down into the Magh Tóchuir, the 'Plain of the causeway', the fertile fringe that gives onto lowland peat bogs and the tidal salt marshes of Trawbreaga Bay. We passed across the mouth of the bay on a long straight road raised above the marshes to Malin, a small, pretty village that calls itself a town and is set against peaty brown hills to the north.

On the bike, familiar scents, like the tang of a peat fire and silage, mixed with the sights of bright crimson fuchsia hedges and long rows of turf cuttings stretching out into the peatlands. Low whitewashed houses, now and then with a traditional thatched roof, echoed an older Ireland. Parts of this landscape as, sadly, is the case across most of the west of Ireland, have been blighted in recent years by the profusion of Celtic Tiger breeze block and concrete mansions, large, brash modern houses set in a half acre of land, many of which can't be and won't ever be paid for now that the recession has bitten so deep into Ireland's economy. Often these garishly decorated houses sit uncomfortably next to the earlier family home or farmstead that has been abandoned but never demolished. Often the new house lies unfinished because the cash has run out, and one hears tell that the government in Dublin will have to buy and demolish them; it's tempting for the tourist or archaeologist to bemoan the loss of vernacular architecture and the apparent littering of this lovely land by what seem ugly incongruences. But the people who live in the new houses like them, if they are not crushed by debt; their standard of living has risen dramatically in the last thirty years and there's no going back. Ireland moves on; but still, this part of Donegal seems a long way from the heart of government. Sitting out on a limb to the north of Northern Ireland, Inishowen seems more cut off than it should. To the west, on the other side of Lough Swilly, lies the ragged and beautiful coastline of the peninsula known as *Fánaid*, part of the Gaeltacht, or Irish-speaking area of the county. The county town, Letterkenny, is seen up here much less as a central place than nearby Derry now that the border is effectively down and geographic rationalism has returned.[73] One reason, we have been told, why our work here has been so well received, is that we are seen to be more interested in this part of Ireland than the authorities in Dublin; not many central government funds seem to come this way. Donegal does not have a single mile of public railway (the last of its narrow gauge lines closed in the 1960s) and the roads, so far as tourism goes, are poor.

The entrance to Trawbreaga Bay is narrow; on its south side sits Doagh Island, now connected to the main peninsula by a grassy spit but once only reachable by causeway. It is rich in memorial and rock art and may, in very ancient times, have been a preserve of the dead and the ancestors. I took the road slowly: you never know what piece of lumbering agricultural machinery will come round the next corner. The winding, twisty lanes that carry the intrepid out to Malin Head, the most northerly tip of Ireland, require caution. Despite the roads, there was a little huddle of parked cars and even a mobile coffee and refreshment van had set up shop in the grey car park beneath a grey Napoleonic-period watchtower on a grey afternoon. Concrete, car park and barbed wire together gave the place a tawdry feel; but you would only have to walk half a mile in any direction, or ponder on the weighted ropes that hold the old thatched roofs down on nearby cottages, to feel yourself in a place as wild and remote as Cape Horn. The wind does not let up. The pounding of salty white waves against the rocks, the dark, almost blue-black sea, the odd island set off in the distance can't fail to impress itself on any member of an island race. Just on the edge of the earth's disc, some six miles north-east of the point, lies the now uninhabited island of Inishtrahull, Ireland's most northerly land. It seems to have been the site of an early Christian cell, an extreme example of the hermit's preference for solitude and hardship.

Below the prominence where the old tower stands huddled close to a meteorological station and a navigation transmitter, there is a grassy plateau above the cliffs, an ancient raised beach. For years beyond recall visitors have taken pebbles and stones from the scree slopes around and arranged them into names that can be read from above. They reminded me forcibly of the Latin memorials of Wales, albeit with less exotic names: THERESA; JANA; DES; CAITLIN; the one that says EIRE is big enough to be seen even on satellite images.

Along the jutting line of the coast squat farmhouses sheltered in low folds of the land; in small inlets fishing boats had been pulled up onto the shore. Dark patches of undrained bog and dull saucers of light reflecting from small tarns pockmarked the green-brown mantle of autumn heather. Sheep and hardy cattle grazed in green fields that ran right down to the shore. One of the most remarkable features of this landscape is the absence of the barn—on the mainland they are a ubiquitous and unnoticed feature of British rural life. Here, hard winters are so rare—I mean hard as in months of lying snow; the winds can be searingly harsh and unremitting—that they graze their livestock the year round.

We took another road back towards the east coast, along the north edge of the Magh Tóchuir, and crossed the narrow River Culdaff (where McGrory's Bar was open, but much quieter than it had been on Friday night) that gives out onto the north-east coast of Inishowen. I had been meaning for a couple of years to locate Kinnagoe Bay, said to have a very fine beach and situated on the east coast of the peninsula. After some tutting and helmet-scratching when we couldn't make sense of map and road sign, we passed through a tiny hamlet—the local term is *clachan*—perched on top of a hill overlooking the sea—a much flatter sea than at Malin Head—and negotiated a couple of vertiginous hair-pins before coming down onto a sable-brown strand, absolutely deserted, where we parked the bike. The tide was halfway through its ebb. The beach, fringed by tall, scrubby machair grass and the odd blackthorn shrub, was set against cliffs draped in rampant, creeping vegetation. The sea was smoothly ironed, with only the long, menacing outline of a freight ship heading into the Foyle interrupting a perfectly flat horizon. I sat on a convenient, polished boulder in the middle of the beach. Sarah stripped off and swam. Apart from the almost silent lapping of wavelets on the shore, nothing stirred. It was a desert place suitable for a hermit to end his peregrination, build himself a modest cell, and set to contemplating his lord and master. It was either a metaphor for the gentle wind-down to a mad year, I decided, or the start of a horror film. Fortunately, no shark fin or siren from the deep appeared to spoil the moment and neither of us was mysteriously transported to some parallel reality. Sarah struggling, all wet, back into her bike gear provided the bathos to counterbalance the sublimity; and we rode back to Moville happily contemplative, to join in with a last-night meal in town.

We said our goodbyes that night, packed all the kit away into the van, looked at Jack's latest images from the highly gratifying survey of what we were now happy to call the monastery at Cooley. Sarah and I set off early in the morning. I wanted, before we sailed away from Ireland, to visit one of the great monasteries of the North. In the perfect, ethereal light of sunrise across the lough, we rode south along the west bank of the Foyle and crossed the border at Muff just before Derry, city of culture, religion and conflict now much revived and reinvented and a fascinating place to visit. It was from here that Wallace Clark's curragh departed in those seemingly more simple days before the civil-rights movement of the late 1960s inadvertently triggered thirty and more years of sectarian violence: an entire generation lived in fear. From Derry we rode east on the A6, through Dungiven, home to both the former Republican hunger striker Kevin Lynch, who died in the Maze Prison on 1 August 1981 after seventy-one days without food and whose face adorns placards mounted on telegraph poles along the main street, and to Seamus O'Kane, bodhrán-maker.

At the eastern edge of the Sperrin Mountains a spectacular escarpment gave onto the lowlands of Antrim and Lough Neagh, all sparkling in the sun. As a relative newcomer to these parts I am still struck by the overt affiliations of communities across Ulster: the odd tricolour here and there or a mural to a fallen warrior; kerbstones painted red, white and blue and defiant Union flags strung from lamp posts; the names of villages dimly remembered from atrocities reported in the news bulletins of my youth. Belfast, negotiated with the help of Sarah tapping me on the shoulder to point out the correct turn off a roundabout (and occasionally to a house where a relative lives, or lived), smelled of heavy industry, the air thick with smog. Giant yellow Harland and Wolff cranes, redolent of empire, hubris and the *Titanic*, passed to our left at the head of Belfast Lough. The Newtownards road heading east out of the city into a pastoral, gently folded countryside that might never have seen a gun or a bomb offered a sectarian fanfare of Unionist sympathy and passive-aggressive self-conscious identity. For those of my generation who grew up in the 1970s and 1980s, it speaks of fist-thumping rhetoric, sordid violence, establishment stupidity; or bravery and collusion, betrayal and stoicism. If, as a distant witness, I find it hard to credit how brutalised and psychopathic it all became, as a historian I can see the Dark Age parallels all too clearly. Bede, the great scholar and historian, was a monk who believed that all Britons were schismatic, and damned. St Wilfrid and Gildas were as uncompromising in their beliefs as any of the rabid sectarians of Ulster's twentieth-century Troubles. And one man's freedom fighter, the warrior hero of myth and legend, song and memorial, is another's terrorist, praised in poetry or cursed and damned, imprisoned or martyred.

We reached the seventh-century monastery of Nendrum, which sits on a small emerald island at the head of Strangford Lough, by a causeway that must be of equal antiquity, after a very slow, winding, beautiful approach that ate into precious time but led us gently by the hand away from the political strife of the twentieth century. It reminded us both, immediately, of St Blane's church at Kingarth on the southern tip of Bute; the same concentric, rising series of enclosures that give it a shape like a three-tiered wedding cake: *sanctus, sanctior, sanctissimus.* At the centre, on the summit of the hill, were a small church, a cemetery and tower, the latter a typical feature of Irish monasteries but probably not contemporary with the original foundation. On both sides the view was of narrow inlets and misty sun-graced

NENDRUM

islets with boats moored off them and flocks of geese gathering for their winter's passage south: all *Swallows and Amazons*. We were the only visitors and had the place to ourselves apart from a man with a strimmer: heritage sites here in Ulster are trimmed by the hand of the Ministry of Tidy Monuments—just as they are in England, where green lawns and well-pointed ruins give visitors the mistaken idea that this was what the past was really like. The small museum, discreetly tucked behind trees, was excellent. Otherwise, a ruin is much like any other ruin except that Nendrum's setting allows you to indulge the mind's eye in giving a flavour of its meaning in the landscape: its isolation intentionally half-complete, with one foot in a very real world of economy and authority, the other in a dreamworld of contemplation and divine love.

At Nendrum the real deal was waiting down on the shore. Here, where the tide laps just across the road from the foot of the outermost enclosure, almost as if the whole floats on the tidal mud of the lough, two low banks of stones, looking like unfinished breakwaters, betrayed a very special Dark Age marvel. These were the man-made lagoons of Nendrum's tide mills which, until 1999, had lain unrecognised for well over a thousand years. A brilliant series of technically challenging excavations by a team under Thomas McErlean (Colm and I met him on a visit to Coleraine University a couple of years ago: a splendid hands-on, old-school archaeologist whom we instantly took to) recovered the sequential remains of two mills of considerable sophistication. Much of the second mill survived intact, and because enough timber and structural details of the first were retrievable, it was possible to date the original construction to the year 619, just over twenty years after the death of Colmcille on Iona and the arrival of Augustine at Canterbury. Northumbria was the pre-eminent kingdom among the English and King Rædwald, the warrior buried in his ship beneath a mound on the banks of the River

Deben, still ruled the kingdom of the East Angles.

Like the latter-day example at Stratford on the River Lea east of London (see page 105), the Nendrum tide mill exploited differential levels of high and low tides. Incoming water was allowed through a sluice or sluices into the mill dam; at high tide the sluice was closed and, when the level of the outgoing tide fell below the penstock (a small, very carefully constructed stone chute through which water was funnelled), the penstock sluice was opened and water fell in a directed jet onto a horizontal turbine, several of whose paddles were retrieved during the excavation. Thomas McErlean and his colleague later produced a magnificent, beautifully produced volume[74] on the excavations that gives a vivid picture of their findings and of life at Nendrum. The engineering skills employed in its conception, construction and maintenance give the lie to any idea that the Dark Ages were inhabited by semi-savage primitives rooting around in old Roman rubbish heaps for a crust before retiring to their hovels. Hovels there were; but the elite of the Early Medieval world had lost nothing of human society's curiosity towards its universe, nor were their imaginations bound entirely by hand-to-mouth subsistence, a horrified superstitious fear of capricious spirits and a dread of the afterlife. They were intrepid and ambitious. The contract by which holy men and women were allowed freehold rights to land in perpetuity, fiercely protected by their descendants, allowed clever, industrious communities to invest sweated labour (their own and their serfs') in capital projects of increasing ambition. The products of these investments were, firstly, an agricultural surplus; secondly, a kingship with increasingly rational and legitimised ideas of statehood and governance; thirdly, the fruits of intellectual contemplation and craft specialisation: manuscripts, books, sculpture, stone churches, mills, a learned tradition preserved and transmitted by writing; and a knowledge network that linked the furthest ends of the earth on the North-west Atlantic coasts of the British Isles with the centres of the ancient world.

Rightly, archaeologists and Early Medieval historians do not use the term Dark Ages in academic journals and among themselves, even if it is a convenient and evocative tag for a period buried in obscurity and seen, for the most part, through a glass darkly. Out of the Dark Ages there came light.

Interlude *Ovingham to Newcastle*

Dark Age rules—shires and renders—navigable Tyne—Wylam and George Stephenson—tidal waters—Newburn and Ad Muram—Tyne bridges—Newcastle's origins—Rome's legacy

EARLY MEDIEVAL societies were not chaotic, but constrained by rules. Until they were codified in the first written laws—Anglo-Saxon in the early seventh century, Irish not much later; Viking during the late ninth and Welsh in the tenth century; Scottish in the twelfth century—these rules operated as custom. Kings, lords, reeves, *chæpmen*, traders, travellers, monks, drengs, ceorls and serfs knew what they owned and owed. Gift, exchange, obligation and reciprocity were bound tightly into an oral rubric. Much legislation written down during the Early Medieval period is concerned with compensation for crimes committed, rights encroached upon, responsibilities neglected. A lake of scribal ink was spilled in royal attempts to limit blood feud; that is why every member of each caste (slaves excepted) had a wergild, or blood-price, so that if they were murdered or wrong was done to them or their kin a price, under the king's writ, could be imposed rather than vengeance taken. Blood feuds, as the people of the Anglo-Scottish borders would know only too well in the Medieval period, meant anarchy.

Even at the time of the Norman Conquest many rules had not been written down; they did not need to be because their authority was unchallenged: they were customary, oath-bound. Those rules defined relationships between lord and patron, land and church, king and subjects, farmer and neighbour. Over the centuries their interpretation and implementation became increasingly complex, often bewilderingly so. Sometimes, even in their own time, administrators had trouble teasing out some of the inherited nuances that had accumulated since the Christian kingdoms emerged. And those that were not written down at all have to be reconstructed. For much of England, Domesday Book, compiled in the late eleventh century for William I so that he would know who owed whom what, is the first and most detailed comprehensive guide to those rights and obligations, particularly renders and services due from villeins to their lords. Boldon Book, a survey of the bishopric of Durham compiled a century later, partly supplements that survey in the north-east of England where, otherwise, there are large gaps in our picture of the region's economic geography.

It is only through the painstaking work of historical geographers and landscape archaeologists that we can begin to come to an idea of how rural society operated here. We now have a reasonable model of how Northumbria's shire system worked: based on townships, like those which developed, and which survive, along Hadrian's Wall, whose central place—the forts—attracted renders from surrounding farms, the system was hierarchical. Farm rendered to *vill*,[75] whose effective render territory would become the township; township rendered to the king. The royal township, or *villa regia*, sat at the centre of a shire from all of whose *vills* (the model was a group of twelve contiguous townships, honoured as much by the exception as in the observance) it collected renders and services. Over the centuries, and particularly after the reintroduction of coinage in the late seventh century, these renders in kind and service—a tax on agricultural produce, woodland rights, labour and military service—were increasingly commuted to rents; often landholdings were divided by inheritance, forfeit or alienation to the church.

The foregoing account oversimplifies reality, but it at least gives us a framework from which to work back towards the very late Roman period when an imperial monetary system failed and had to be replaced by local, then regional, renders. That Northumbria's shire system partially survived into the twentieth century is a remarkable testimony to the success and conservatism of that system inherited across fifteen hundred years.

In the fifth century, when the beginnings of this post-imperial model were felt in the countryside, there were no functioning towns as we would understand them. The evolution of their customs presents a more difficult problem. Resuming my eastwards pursuit of the River Tyne one day in February, I set out from Prudhoe station, over the river from Ovingham. The well-known rickety steel bridge here, barely wide enough for a small van, was undergoing major repairs, but pedestrians can still reach the other side via a footbridge. There has probably always been a crossing here. Just upriver is the site of an old ferry; there may have been a ford too, as there was below the old road crossing at Corbridge. The Tyne, now just ten miles shy of Newcastle, is here still a wild river, full of salmon and trout and supporting a healthy population of otters, and often bearing its teeth in white-water rapids. After two days of heavy rain it was in spate, and the idea of it ever having been navigable up as far as Corbridge seemed absurd. But rivers change. Lead mining higher up in the Pennines changed the topography of this valley for ever in the eighteenth and nineteenth centuries, scouring rivers out and releasing great quantities of rock and sediment. So we cannot say how it would have looked to the Romans; the thought that the bridge and fort at Newcastle and the supply depots near Tynemouth were not directly connected to the town at Corbridge seems equally hard to believe.

I kept to the south bank, with Prudhoe Castle high on its promontory behind me. It is such a strategic location that I have often wondered if the Norman motte here, constructed to tame a very hostile Borders population, had a Dark Age or prehistoric forebear. Below it, on the narrow floodplain, are industries heavily reliant on water: paper mills and chemical works. The wooded slopes opposite, at Horsley, formed part of the vast Percy estates of the Middle Ages: they have been continuously managed for as long as records go back, and are a reminder that the entire succession of human communities relied on a close relationship with trees, for fuel and materials, for hunting and grazing pigs. Early Medieval crafts were as dependent on wood as they were on water. Charcoal fuelled traditional industries like ironworking and gunpowder manufacture; wood ash was used in potteries and in glass-making. Later, the hard black coal that lay beneath these lands fuelled the belching engines that drove the Industrial Revolution.

A little further downstream, where the narrow upland course of the Tyne broadens out to reveal flood plains on either side, I crossed the river, over a now-disused industrial railway bridge to Wylam. This was the birthplace, in 1781, of George Stephenson, whose whitewashed cottage I passed on the line of an old waggonway. In 1812 or 1813 Wylam colliery acquired its first locomotive, *Puffing Billy*; nothing to do with George Stephenson, as it happens, but an indication of where he got some of his inspiration for later projects. The steam locomotive, brainchild of Richard Trevithick but largely developed in these coalfields, is an industrial equivalent of the stone church: the petrification of an ancient idea, that the secrets of nature can be bent to human endeavour. If at Ironbridge the new concept of iron construction was founded on the mindset of carpenters, then the locomotive was a product of blacksmiths, whose dark arts now unleashed unimaginable power on the imaginations of a new global empire.

At Wylam, a fashionably pretty village with a railway station that provides Newcastle with commuters, a weir runs under the present road bridge. A change in smell and muddy marks on the banks show that the highest tides reach here from the sea, although they did not always do so; dredging lower down the river caused it to scour a deeper course here. The present landscape on this north bank has been de-industrialised—country parks and long-distance cycle paths are the order of the day. Young trees, cinder tracks and picnic benches are its furniture. In the Early Medieval landscape archaeologists regard the regeneration of trees as a sign of sub-Roman decline, of rural depopulation and the abandonment of fields: the onset of a Dark Age. These days it is a sign of investment in landscape; but it is a heavily constructed landscape.

Almost no boats come up this far now; just the odd rower in a scull or a tourist cruise up from Newcastle. Before the eighteenth century, when the shipment of coal along rivers and waggonways became vitally important to the economy of the north-east, the tide rose only as far as Newburn, another three or four miles downriver, where I stopped for an indulgent pie and chips and sat in sunshine on the riverbank. Newburn was the site, in 1640, of a pre-Civil War battle between a Scottish Covenanter army and an English/Royalist force. There is a bridge here too, and anciently it was supposed to be the lowest fording point across the river. Early Medieval credentials are provided by those who identify Newburn with Bede's *Ad Muram*, a *villa regia* that hosted a politically important conversion and wedding ceremony in the 650s; and by its church, whose tower bears the same tell-tale signs of Romanesque architecture as those at Ovingham, Bywell and Corbridge: double round-arched windows piercing the tower. Its first, wooden church was burned down in 1067 during a Northumbrian rebellion against William I. The ford was marked earlier by a Roman fort; and the Wall passes less than a mile to the north. The presence of a fifth (or sixth) significant early church on the north bank of the river at an ancient crossing point increases, I think, the likelihood that a road ran alongside the river here in the Roman and Early Medieval periods. One wonders if it was used as a foundation for the industrial waggonways that followed this route during the age of the coal barons. No trace of it survives.

The identification of Bede's *Ad Muram* (literally 'at the Wall') bothers Early Medieval historians the way Corbridge bothers them. Bede says, unhelpfully, that the 'famous' royal estate lay close to the Wall, and that it was about twelve miles from the sea. It has been tentatively identified with either Newburn (with its early church and ford) or Wallbottle, whose name derives from something very like 'at the Wall'. But neither is, as Bede would have measured it (that is, by travelling the line of the river from its mouth downriver from his monastery at Jarrow) the right distance from the sea. From Tynemouth, twelve miles inland takes the traveller only as far as Newcastle. Newcastle did not exist in Bede's day; but a great bridge had crossed the river there. The Romans called it *Pons Aelius*, the 'bridge of the Aelian family' which included those two great wall-builders, Hadrian and Antoninus Pius; and the Wall again passes very close to the river. A major fort, the site of whose West Gate still lies on the main road heading out of Newcastle, stood here, perhaps providing a focus for a royal township. An important monastery was founded on the south bank at Gateshead (*ad capram*: the 'goat's head'); and by the later pre-Conquest period a settlement near where the Norman New Castle was constructed in 1080 was called Monkchester, indicating the one-time presence of a monastery there too. But archaeologists have as yet uncovered only fragmentary evidence of a substantial settlement here in the seventh century. It is the lot of our city archaeologists that their raw material is so hard to get at—brief pinhole glimpses of centuries of urban accumulation clutched at before a hole closes and another hotel or office block grows on deep-sunk piles. The big question is: was the Roman bridge, close perhaps to the line of the city's Victorian

Swing Bridge, still standing and passable in Bede's day? If so, it would have retained its value as a crossing place and been a suitable venue for a grand ceremony; if not, it may have remained obscure until William I's eldest son, Robert Curthose (an unflattering nickname: it means 'short-arse'), built his keep here in 1080. Newburn may still have a trump card to play. Two of the most important royal inauguration sites in Britain, at Scone and at Kingston in Surrey, were located at tidal reaches on, respectively, the Rivers Tay and Thames.[76] Did Newburn on Tyne boast a similarly significant site for Northumbria's Dark Age kings?

Newcastle's physical origins as a town are obscure. But a very rare surviving twelfth-century document, the Customs of Newcastle, appears to contain legal clauses of extreme antiquity that carry echoes not just of Anglo-Saxon burghal rights but of Roman and British laws on freehold, taxation, redress and conflict. The burgesses of the town in Henry II's day took great pains to defend rights and privileges that they regarded as customary and inalienable. These included the right to distrain (seize goods as compensation) upon foreigners without permission from the Borough Court; the right to first choice of goods unloaded at Tynemouth (surely a royal prerogative gifted to the town's freeholders); the acquisition of precious burghal status, including the inheritance of freehold land in the borough; and an exemption from the Norman mode of trial by battle. Burgesses were also exempt from *merchet* (a tax payable on a daughter's marriage), *heriot* (an inheritance tax); *bloodwite* (a fine for drawing blood) and *stengesdint* (a fine for striking someone with a stick). They claimed the right to own and operate an oven and a corn mill and a monopoly of cloth and wool trade in the town. Brewsters and baxters[77] were protected from arbitrary forfeits outwith the jurisdiction of the provost.

This is a powerful set of protections, whose origins have been very carefully analysed in a brilliant essay by Robert Fulton

Walker[78] and shown to derive from a range of Anglo-Saxon, Roman and Welsh (that is, native British) prototypes. We know that Roman legionary veterans settled in *colonia* (see note 84) enjoyed special rights of freehold and exemptions from certain taxes. Protectionist customs designed to encourage urban economies might have been introduced as variants of native law from the late seventh century onwards. It is striking that sets of customs defining the rights of Alfred's burgesses are dominated by church privileges; Newcastle's burghal customs are entirely secular. The Norman town's burgesses seem to have been successors to a very early set of customs; if so, the origins of the town lie deep in its obscure Early Medieval past.

I came to Newcastle's Quayside along the miles-long, smooth river promenade from where great battleships were once launched but where industry has been emasculated by the success of efficient foreign competitors. Across those muddy waters,

NEWCASTLE

Dunston's wooden coal staith—a rollercoaster with a fatal terminal drop—now lifeless apart from nesting gulls, is a monument to a lost race of subterranean delvers. It is flanked by desirable luxury properties for the north-east's aspirant office workers and a new generation of entrepreneurs. Car showrooms, swanky-looking hotels and science parks line the roads entering the city from the west. Soaring bridges carry road and railway a hundred feet above the Tyne while the incoming brown salty tide meets the fresh waters of the Pennines in a struggle as old as the hills. In the vacuum left by industry and mining, the powerhouse of the north-east attempts to reinvent itself as a shiny urban paradigm, and as a tourist destination.

I climbed away from the river along Forth Bank, the site of the world's first railway factory where George and Robert Stephenson's *Rocket* was built and whence the Stockton–Darlington and Liverpool–Manchester railways were plotted. A few hundred yards closer to the city centre, between the nineteenth-century railway station, which stands on top of Roman Newcastle's civilian settlement, and the massive Norman stone keep which sits above the fort, a fragment of the Wall line can still be seen poking through the pavement outside the city's Literary and Philosophical Society. The Lit & Phil, as it has been known since its founding in the Age of Enlightenment, houses one of the great libraries of Britain. The permanence of the Romans' civilising presence in Britain is recorded in a landscape of stone monuments—walls, roads, forts, inscriptions and early churches. It is also recorded in the institution which above all mapped the great Mediterranean project: the town. If the physical form of most of our towns now owes little to their Roman forbears, then at least their role as central places, where literate, thoughtful people might gather to debate the nature of the world, survives and thrives.

§ CHAPTER EIGHT

Speed: *Meigle to Canterbury*

*Picts and symbols—Roman roads—Inchtuthil fort—Gask Ridge
—Stirling Castle—Antonine Wall—Dere Street—Escomb church—*
Catraeth *and* Gododdin*—Aldborough Roman town—Goodmanham
—the Conversion—Humber bridge—Barton-on-Humber—Stow—
the kingdom of Lindsey—Lincoln and Paulinus—Ermine Street and
Icknield Way—St Albans—Stone chapel—Reculver—Isle of Thanet—
warriors and popes—Canterbury—Roman churches*

THE VILLAGE of Meigle straddles the A94 on the south side of Strathmore in the old Scottish county of Perthshire. Immediately to the north-west the Braes of Angus mark the Highland line, the edge of the Grampian mountains. Meigle seems once to have been the site of a Pictish monastery and royal estate; the small museum, housing more than thirty carved stones in a former Victorian school house, punches well above its weight. Some of the greatest indigenous art of the ancient British reposes here, where the Dark Ages are not merely illuminated but animated: dauntless warriors ride prancing horses into battle with hounds baying at their feet, bulls lower their horns and face off against one another; strange winged beasts process across friezes. A hybrid repertoire of Christian iconography—crosses, crucifixions and defeated serpents—is decorated, intertwined and psychologically melded with Z-rods,[79] mirrors, crescents and creatures of fabulous imagination, the encrypted semiotics of a proud and exuberant warrior culture. The Picts may be enigmatic, their language obscure and their symbols as yet defiant of the code-breakers' arts, but there is no denying their love of self-celebration, their pluralist relish in embracing the iconographies of Christianity and their animist prehistoric past.

The stone called Meigle 1, the earliest of the collection and belonging probably to the eighth century, was recycled from a prehistoric standing stone that bears traces of Bronze Age cup-and-ring marks. Its 'front' bears an elaborately interwoven, ornate cross of hybrid Irish form, a stylised wheel-head pierced by four circles, not a square inch left without interlace or knot work. The corners are filled with what look like wild boar and deer, and creatures of the imagination that seem impossible to describe. On the reverse is an apparent jumble of pictorial thoughts: a fish, a mirror and comb, warriors on horseback, a snake and Z-rod; an angel with spreading wings. Perhaps set up, or reused, as a gravestone to a great warrior—the explicitly Pictish symbols are believed to represent rank, status, maybe names and probably clan affiliation—and possibly later 'converted' to overtly Christian commemoration, these stones tease us with the promise of insight into the rich emotional and imaginative Early Medieval mind: it is a mind both grisly and glorious, fantastical and pragmatic, inhabiting parallel worlds of subsistence and warfare in a mindscape of magic and wonder, the dreamtime of the ancestors.

I am struck, though, by the contrast with those crosses and memorials with which we had spent time in Moville. There, sculpture lives on in its landscape; in a museum, divorced from horizon, setting, sunrise and sunset or archaeological context, these beautiful works of a lost race are diminished: shop-window mannequins, not people.

I had hoped to walk among the Picts; but I had another story to tell that began at Meigle and ended 705 miles away on the coast of Kent. Meigle marks the very end, so far as we can tell, of the Roman road system in the British Isles that began with the armies of Claudius crossing the Channel in AD 43. The legions built outpost forts north and east of here along the coast of Angus and Aberdeenshire, as far up as the Moray Firth: the furthest reach of a grand experiment to tame and enrol the British peoples into the Imperial project. But no metalled road has been proven beyond Perth and none can realistically be projected further than the line of the A94. What better place to begin a mad dash along the highways of the Empire?

Dark Age landscapes are best seen at walking pace when land and sea, river and sky behave as they did for our cultural ancestors. To understand them more minutely one must dwell for a while, steep oneself in a locality with a bounded horizon. But there was another dimension to the Early Medieval world. Stepping across the threshold of native settlement and trail, farm, field and woodland, onto the stone highways of the lost race of giants, was to experience the world at warp speed. If the Roman legions were like land-grabbing tanks, then the roads its armies laid were their tracks: an unstoppable grid of militarised policing that subdued by shock and awe. The speed at which cross-country travel became possible during the Roman centuries distorted and distended the map of Britain to a degree that is difficult to appreciate since the revival of road building in the eighteenth century. In the nineteenth century the electric telegraph had the same effect, joining Europe, America and the Indian sub-continent in an information web that shrunk communication from weeks to minutes. The internet video call has been a natural successor, but is merely incremental. The railways are the inheritors of the Roman idea of a Europe united by the speed at which horses and armoured troops might move. Our contemporary equivalent of that travel revolution on the human, physical scale has been the linking of Britain and Europe by an undersea railway, an idea that seemed fantastic to earlier generations but which is a logical successor to Watling Street and the Fosse Way.

What impact did that streamlining of landscape, the removal of the land's natural drag-effect, have on the Early Medieval world? How much of the Roman road network survived the fall of Empire? How many of those supposedly straight roads existed before Roman armies turned them into superhighways of suppression, co-option and commerce? In travelling from one end of the conveyor belt to the other, at speed, I hoped to experience something of that distortion of space and time; and to answer a few of my own questions along the way.

I travelled up from County Durham on the motorbike and spent a night in Perthshire with old friends, Malcolm and Fiona Lind. Malcolm was a fellow student in archaeology in the 1980s; both are teachers in schools around the town of Blairgowrie; both are gifted photographers. They look at the world from the edge of the Highlands, through a distinctly Northern lens. I was arriving in early autumn when the soft fruit harvest had been gathered and lorries full of tatties trundled along roads from farm to factory. It was a fortnight after the 'No' vote in the Scottish independence referendum and I found my friends in despondent mood: this is nationalist territory. We talked of democracy and of Scotland's cultural renaissance; of an idea of a North whose border lies somewhat south of Berwick, and of a long-nourished sense of estrangement from the centres of power, a conversation that might not, perhaps, have been unfamiliar to the clan chiefs of the second century; or the eighteenth. Plus ça change. We consoled ourselves with camera talk, with whisky, craic and music.

Beginning, the next morning, at Meigle, I followed the A94 back along the south side of the River Isla with autumnal orange and deep coniferous green Highland foothills of the Forest of Alyth away to my right. To the south the Sidlaw Hills separate fertile Strathmore from Dundee and the swift estuary of the silvery Tay. At Coupar, Angus I switched to General Wade's Military Road in my search for the most northerly of the great fortresses of the Empire. The general understood Roman roads and their military potential better than anyone—he knew that flat, all-weather hard-metalled surfaces gave him moral and tactical advantages over the enemies of the state. One road built in the right place supported by strategic forts allowed deep and lasting penetration of untamed landscapes. Commerce followed; and as the pragmatic British mercantile state of the eighteenth century knew very well, the best way to keep a subdued nation down was to trade with it, after which economics conducted their own diplomacy. Revolutions usually start with an unbridgeable gap between rich and poor.

Inchtuthil (*Pinnata castra*—the 'fort on the wing'), when I found it overlooking a broad meander of the Tay, looked like a gigantic abandoned football pitch whose touchlines were beyond vision: more than fifty acres in extent, with the odd inconvenient beech tree sticking up from a post-Roman burial mound along the touchlines slightly marring the appearance of rigid, square-bashing military order. It is a huge legionary fortress, ostensibly a memorial to the ultimately unfulfilled ambitions of Tacitus's father-in-law Agricola in the early 80s and the only legionary fortress anywhere in the Empire to survive completely intact, the site undeveloped by later entrepreneurs aside from a small native fort that lies just beyond its south-west corner. These were, Tacitus says, the headquarters of Agricola's XXth Legion during a triumphant three-year campaign to subdue the Caledonians; but it was a short existence: the legion withdrew, dismantled the fort, slighted the ditches and left behind nothing but a hoard of three-quarters of a million iron nails. Camp Bastion, a British airbase in Afghanistan's Helmand province, lasted twice as long. Tacitus's account of the XXth Legion's Caledonian campaign is a celebration of martial spirit, of the patriotic obligation to overwhelm a barbarian enemy. His stridently propagandist and triumphalist tone would have found favour with Joseph Goebbels. Archaeologists are much more sceptical now that they have excavated some of the sites associated with the Roman advance into Caledonia and found, to no one's surprise, evidence of a much more nuanced tale of success and failure, doubt, adaptation and response. Agricola has been demoted a few ranks from all-conquering hero to mixed-record C-in-C, Cal. Ops. The story of the Roman campaigns in Scotland appears to have been more complex, and to have lasted rather longer, than Tacitus wished his domestic audience to think.

Inchtuthil was full of melancholy; autumn seemed the perfect time to visit, with golden leaves falling in lazy arcs from trees, the skies leaden and portentous and my breath misty on the cooling air. There could, in a sense, be no more perfect memorial to the Giants than this unsullied, tangible imprint of their far-distant emperor and living god, re-absorbed by the earth like Fall's harvest.

Passing signs for Scone, where medieval kings of Scotland were inaugurated at the Hill of Belief—a probable prehistoric burial mound—I picked up the first clear traces of the Roman road network west of Perth along the line of the Gask Ridge above Strathearn. The road's straightness, its evenness, breadth and flanking drainage ditches were unmistakeable marks of legionary engineering. Constructed perhaps over a period of decades straddling the first and second centuries, it linked a series of intervisible signal stations and seems to have been intended not, perhaps, as a frontier like the Stanegate, but as a series of nodes from which basic military intelligence of native movements was gathered and transmitted up the chain of command: it is an early-warning system joined by a road that allowed the rapid movement of horses and infantry. On the bike, unless I stopped for a pee, to take a picture or refuel and consult the map, the dead-straight road was a worm hole, the landscape of forest and glen a blur, each crossroads passing too quickly to note the directions and distances of the places named on its finger posts. It was a sublime journey south, one of total concentration on the road and with no mental room for ambulatory musings on the Early Medieval landscape. Those were the indulgences of the walker. I was now travelling in the guise of a courier, not a moment to be lost, carrying news to distant parts in the hope that I might outpace their consequences.

There is evidence that Early Medieval couriers and their warrior lords relied heavily on the Roman road system. A remarkable story told by Bede, in his Life of St Cuthbert, relates how the holy man prophesied the destruction of the Northumbrian king Ecgfrith (r. 671–85). Succeeding his father, Oswiu, after a long and successful reign, Ecgfrith does not seem to have inherited the luck of the Idings. He married twice, but neither queen gave him a child. The first, Æthelthryth, retired to found Ely Cathedral, leaving her dower lands at Hexham to Wilfrid. The second, Iurminburh, who seems to have been a Frankish princess, but who took against Wilfrid, survived her husband, also took monastic vows and died childless. Such was the dynastic risk posed by a king without sons that Ecgfrith's sister, Ælfflaed, consulted her holy man Cuthbert, then Bishop of Lindisfarne and in his last years, about potential successors. Ecgfrith had unwisely invoked Cuthbert's anger, and that of Iona, by fighting a war in Ireland and taking Christian prisoners. In 685, the year in which he dedicated a church at Jarrow, the king alienated his bishop further when he took his armies on campaign in the land of the Christian Picts. Cuthbert saw that the moment of greatest danger was at hand.

> He set off therefore to Carlisle, to speak with the Queen, who had arranged to stay there in a convent to await the outcome of the war. The day after his arrival the citizens conducted him round the city walls to see a remarkable Roman fountain that was built into them. He was suddenly disturbed in spirit. He leaned heavily on his staff, turned his face dolefully to the wall, then straightening himself and looking up to the sky he sighed deeply and said almost in a whisper, 'Perhaps at this moment the battle is being decided.'[80]

Cuthbert immediately went to Queen Iurminburh and warned her to return to 'the royal city' (Bamburgh, probably; but perhaps York) in her chariot as soon as possible. Of many intriguing features in the story (not least of which are the survival of a Roman public fountain in seventh-century Carlisle and the queen's mode of transport), the most telling is the arrival, three days later, of a refugee from the battle bearing ill tidings. At a place called Nechtansmere the king had met his end at the hands of Bruide mac Beli's Pictish armies; his bodyguards slaughtered, his army routed. Never again would Northumbria so dominate the whole island of Britain. Even allowing for the narrator's exaggeration, it is nevertheless striking that a courier was able to reach the queen within three days of the battle (one can see how the story was retrospectively put together by marvelling companions of the far-seeing saint). There has been much speculation about the site of this battle. Traditionally it was associated with Dunnichen, close to Forfar in Angus, a day's march east of Meigle. It has often been suggested that a great Pictish stone at Aberlemno, which seems to depict a battle, commemorated the defeat of the Northumbrian armies. Alex Woolf, a pre-eminent Early Medieval scholar, has suggested another possible site: Dunachton in the Highlands, south-west of Aviemore. If one is to believe Bede's very precise account of the timing, a location close to the end of the Roman road system is, perhaps, more plausible, although the jury is still out. One hundred and eighty-odd road miles in three days, if true, represents a system of Bernician royal couriers every bit as competent as that of the Imperial legions: impressive; but not miraculous.

That Dark Age armies used the existing Roman road system is clear from the number of significant battles which took place on, or very close to, Roman roads, especially where they crossed significant rivers. Many of the monasteries donated by kings to their special holy men were sited in or near Roman forts at key points on the road network. In the late seventh and early eighth centuries, King Ine of Wessex retained a company of Welsh riders, apparently as couriers. The constructions of the Giants were real and were used as assets by Early Medieval kings, shrinking space and time and giving them significant advantages in controlling access to land and territory. Military campaigns often took place over long distances: Welsh kings in Northumbria; Mercians in Scotland and Essex; Northumbrians in Wessex, the Welsh Marches and East Anglia. Nor should we underestimate the Anglo-Saxons' awareness of what they had inherited. Bede knew that Roman engineers were responsible for roads, forts, walls and fountains, civic and military infrastructure. Inquisitive kings would have known from the learned men of the seventh century that the words of these ancients had also been preserved; that academic knowledge did not prevent them from constructing a mythological past in which Germanic and Roman dynastic progenitors conferred magical powers and inalienable rights on their line. Nor did deep-held pagan tribal traditions of ancestor-worship and the king-as-god prevent them from signing up to the new deal offered by an entrepreneurial, savvy and opportunistic church: that in return for land, a rational idea of kingship and a Christian state, kings should hold their office by divine right.

South of the Gask Ridge the Roman road passes, more or less untraceable, beneath modern routes and towns, past Stirling—Bede's *Urbs Iudeu*, where Ecgfrith's father, King Oswiu, was besieged by Penda in the early 650s. Here an ancient crossing at the head of the navigable River Forth underlines the strategic impact of Stirling's imposing natural citadel, as perfect a Dark Age fortress site as can be imagined. I caught up with the ancient road again before a slow cruise through the streets of Falkirk, where road meets Wall. In this case, it was the turf and clay dyke constructed during the reign of Antoninus Pius (138–161), Hadrian's overambitious successor, and abandoned within a generation.

Bede, misreading his sources, attributed it to the later emperor Septimius Severus (r. 193–211), although he got its geography right: cutting directly across the Forth–Clyde isthmus from sea to sea. Not much of the rampart remains, but I parked up next to the best-preserved section at Watling Lodge. Sure, it's impressive, like a tidal wave poised to crash onto the shores of some unknown country, seemingly toying with the antique beech trees which ride its crest and whose comparatively short lives of a hundred and fifty years are no more than flotsam on history's grand swell. With such models to work from it is easy to see how Dark Age potentates like Offa might decide to build one for himself. If holy men wished their achievements to be fossilised in the construction of stone churches, memorials and crosses, why would their temporal lords, addicted to all things glorious, impressive and *big*, not wish for such a monument to their earth-bound power. And these monuments, like the roads built by the Romans, still stand fifteen hundred years later; they were permanent.

From Edinburgh (*Din Eidyn*: the seat of the *Gododdin* of poetic legend), I was able to follow a familiar road home: the modern A68—Dere Street, which leads north from York in Deira (hence the name), defying topography and superficial logic. The modern motorist, driving at speeds somewhat in excess of the legionary standard of thirteen miles a day, is warned to beware of sharp bends and sudden crests. Any number of road accidents litter this route every year. The unwary motorcyclist is vulnerable to the sin of hubris; and in winter weather the upland sections are quickly made impassable by snow. It is a rollercoaster ride across Lammermuir and Cheviot, through Lauderdale and the border town of Jedburgh, skirting the immense Kielder forest and endless miles of bare sheep-dotted brae. Dere Street allowed Roman armies before, during and after the building of the Wall to penetrate deep into the territories of satellite tribes, the Votadini and Selgovae, whose relationship with the Empire was an ambivalent mix of envy and antipathy. Forts at *Trimontium*, in the Eildon Hills, where the road crosses the Tweed near Melrose, at *Bremenium* (High Rochester) and *Habitancum* (West Woodburn), each one securing a section of the route and monitoring its wild hinterland, passed me by in a blur. I have ridden this road many times; now I was looking at it through different eyes as I tried to take in both the scale of the ambition in attempting to tame these Debatable Lands, and its ultimate folly. No king's writ ran in these borderlands until there was a single monarch of both England and Scotland at the beginning of the seventeenth century. James VI of Scotland renamed them the Middle Shires, which shows, if nothing else, that he had a well-developed sense of humour.

Sometimes the modern road departs from its Roman predecessor, taking a more adaptive, empirical route across country, fording river and skirting steep slope. I have traced some of the abandoned route on walks through the Borders, where more human imperatives and practicalities allow the traveller on foot or horseback to respond to local realities. But in its essentials the Roman road survives; and that can only be because it has been in more or less continual use for nearly two millennia. Given the chance, nature eats roads for breakfast. Weeds appear within a year of traffic's cease; trees follow; landslide, flood and frost wreak havoc. We do not suppose that major repairs were carried out to roads in the Early Medieval period (bridges, perhaps, excepted); routes were maintained by traffic.

At Old Melrose a loop in the Tweed makes an almost enclosed peninsula where a famous abbey stood in Bede's day: here the youthful Cuthbert was trained by Eata (the abbot and later bishop so improbably commemorated in the church at Atcham on the banks of the River Severn (see page 71)). The monastery was supposedly a foundation of Aidan, the first abbot of Lindisfarne; but there has always been a suspicion among scholars that it had earlier been a British foundation; Bede knew it by its Brythonic name, *Mailros*. There are sufficient signs of Romano-British Christianity in the Borders—Latin memorial stones, aligned cemeteries and 'Eccles' place names—to suggest that a Roman episcopal church maintained itself here long enough to be absorbed into Oswald's Irish mission. That a native foundation like *Mailros* should survive close to Iron Age and Roman forts and a military road on a key crossing of the Tweed makes one appreciate the essential continuity of landscape foci. Roman roads and their crossings were centripetal. The three hills of Eildon in whose shadow Melrose lies dominate the horizon for many miles in all directions. They can be seen from the Border crossing at Carter Bar; from Cheviot and from the Lammermuirs. The logic of travelling through these magnificently open lands is ancient and compelling.

The village of Ebchester, which marks a crossing of the Derwent Valley and the boundary between Northumberland and County Durham, is the site of a former Roman fort, *Vindomora*. The modern place name suggests that it was appropriated by King Oswald's sister Æbbe (pronounced Abba, as in the pop group) to found a monastery. Its parish church, which sits within the outline of the old fort, was originally constructed using Roman masonry and is still dedicated to the saintly Iding princess. She also founded a house in less hospitable surroundings at St Abb's Head north of Berwick, on a rocky clifftop high above the sea. Appropriately, considering the martial history of her family, the church at Ebchester was later the burial place of celebrated sword-makers from the nearby village of Shotley Bridge. Joseph Oley, supposedly the last of a line of German craftsmen to settle in these parts with their armourers' skills, was laid to rest here in the nineteenth century. Shotley Bridge is my home too: a resting place before the onward journey south.

In many parts of County Durham the line of the old road must be reconstructed by joining the dots, one fort or town to another.

At Lanchester (*Longovicium*) on the River Browney not even a footpath survives. In odd stretches it coincides with a lane or B-road. The geography east of the Pennines is one of steep-sided wooded denes;[81] the grain of the land is unclear, like the confused swells of the sea after a storm. The Roman road tends to survive on higher, flatter sections useful as drove roads. Close to Bishop Auckland the Roman fort of Binchester (*Vinovia*), situated in a loop of the River Wear, appears unconnected to the road system. On the opposite, southern bank of the river I stopped, one morning some time after my Scottish ride,[82] at Escomb, where England's most complete early church survives somewhat against the odds. It is an austere, very northern sort of building: tall and narrow, its exterior walls smutty from the smoke of coal fires. The key hangs by the front door at one of the cluster of modern houses that rings the venerable church—there is no pretension here. The churchyard is circular, a clue, perhaps, to Irish or British influence. The precise date of its construction is unknown, although it must belong to the late seventh or eighth century; some say Wilfrid had it built, but it seemed to me to lack his grandiose orthodox stamp. It is simple in its magnificence: constructed in stone quarried from Binchester fort (a legionary inscription has been built into one internal wall; the chancel arch has been lifted wholesale from a military site). From the outside it looks more like a Borderer's defensible bastle house[83] than a church. The original entrance was a low door in the north wall. There is no tower, but a simple nave and smaller chancel or sanctuary with small windows high up: one's eyes are constantly drawn to the heavens. An incised cross, thick with layers of whitewash, survives in the wall behind the lectern; a larger cross, carved in relief and perhaps depicting a preaching high cross, now stands against the east wall behind the altar.

South of Bishop Auckland I picked up Dere Street again: unmistakably arrow-straight for several miles as far as Piercebridge,

where a Roman bridge across the Tees, its ruined footings stranded in a field by the meanderings of the river, forced a small diversion through the village and over a modern crossing. A few miles further south, at Scotch Corner, Dere Street is joined by both the trans-Pennine A66 (Roman-built, too) and its big brother, the A1; the Pennines of Swaledale closed in to the west; the Vale of York opened out to the east with the North York Moors distant and grey-hazy beyond. The dual carriageway takes a wide, sweeping arc around Catterick, site of a racecourse and Roman fort (*Cataractonum*) and, probably, of a legendary Dark Age battle. The town's prehistoric forebear may have lain upriver at Richmond, beneath the medieval castle below whose ramparts the Swale tumbles into a splendid cataract well worth the Latin name. *Cataractonum* survived into the fifth century and beyond. Inside the jaws of Swaledale a series of apparently defensive dykes is thought to belong to a period when Dere Street was a frontier between Deira and the British kingdom of Rheged, whose warrior lord, the fabled Urien, fought the kings of Northumbria as far north as Holy Island.

An epic battle lament that survives in much-evolved form as *Y Gododdin* (from the ancient British tribal name *Votadini*) seems to commemorate a siege here in the last decades of the sixth century, a tragic, failed pre-emptive attempt by a British confederacy of the Men of the Old North—the *Gwŷr y Gogledd*—to turn back Northumbrian territorial ambitions. Bede, and the *Gododdin* poet, called it *Catraeth* and in siting a mass-baptism by Bishop Paulinus in the River Swale here in about 627, Bede implies that it was a royal estate under King Edwin. My memories of excavating at Catterick are three unpleasant months confined within the stinky stalls of a cow barn on a farm whose foundations lay deep in the Roman and Dark Age past. Construction of a new slurry pit offered the chance for Catterick expert Pete Wilson and his team to get a sniff, so to speak, of the town's end. We peered through the keyhole, drew narrow conclusions and moved on. The nearby British infantry garrison is a reminder that useful places stay useful.

Now, thankfully, I passed Catterick at speed and rode on to the civitas capital of the Brigantes, the confederation of northern British tribes, at Aldborough. *Isurium Brigantium* was shut—English Heritage hibernates until April Fools' Day. The fifteenth-largest town in Roman Britain, nestling in a bend of the River Ure close to Boroughbridge and just above its confluence with the Swale, intrigues me because of its location. Like Wroxeter, it was intended to provide a less threatening replacement for the tribal headquarters, or *oppidum*, in this case at nearby Stanwick. It is the closest Roman presence to Wilfrid's seventh-century foundation at Ripon and the only substantial civilian settlement on the road between York and Corbridge. There are thoughts in the academic community that perhaps *Catraeth* succeeded to its tribal functions and status, lying at the core of a Dark Age kingdom of the Tees Valley. Bede may be referring to Aldborough, or to Catterick, when he describes a siege at an *oppidum* between a Deiran pretender, Osric, and King Cadwallon of Gwynedd during the campaign that led to Oswald's great victory at Heavenfield in 634. Aldborough is now just a pretty village off the main drag, deserted by legions, river and main road alike. But I stopped for a while anyway, peering over the fence to see what I could of its grassy-banked ramparts before taking a small, dead-straight road south-east towards York.

Eburacum, the greatest Roman fortress town of the North with its own *colonia*[84] and special place in imperial history, is worth its own journey. For now, I was able to spend a comfortable and cheery evening in the company of old friends, Bob Sydes and Sarah Austin. I first met Bob when I worked for him twenty-five years ago at an extraordinary lowland 'hill-fort' excavation in South Yorkshire called Sutton Common. It's the only site where I have had the privilege of excavating ramparts with their wooden palisade still intact and with the axe marks of the woodsmen who cut the stakes still perfectly visible. Their extraordinary preservation was caused by the anaerobic conditions that prevail in wetlands, now sadly drained by agriculture. Bob and I chewed over old times and current archaeo-gossip; Sarah and I over a fascinating exploration of visualising complex archaeological data that she has in mind for a doctoral thesis. Bob had just been to a conference in Derry, so we compared notes on Ireland, on that interesting city and on politics.

From York, Roman roads run south-west to Tadcaster (Roman *Calcaria*) to rejoin the Great North Road, and east towards the chalk Wolds of the East Riding and the River Humber. My first appointment was with Bede's most famous set-piece drama: the conversion of King Edwin. At Market Weighton, at the foot of the Wolds, I turned off the main road and wove my way through the back lanes of the town, up the gentle scarp behind it and into the village of Goodmanham. Here, Bede says, Edwin's chief priest Coifi, having been persuaded by the Deiran elite to renounce his paganism, rode out on a stallion wielding a spear, and cast it into the precincts of a temple that stood here. For Bede, drawing on oral traditions inherited from Edwin's descendants and preserved by his cult at Whitby Abbey, this was a decisive victory for Roman orthodoxy. Walking around the outside of the parish church (all locked up and no key to be had), perched on a raised rectangular graveyard in the centre of the village, perhaps on the exact spot of the earlier idolatrous temple, I contemplated what paganism and Christianity meant to the Northumbrians of the seventh century. So much of what we know about the church derives from medieval and later historical perspectives that it's hard to say. Bede's account is so coloured by both his distaste for paganism and his detestation of British schismatic practices that it's easy to be seduced into thinking that the conversion was intellectually and spiritually decisive, at least at the level of aristocratic elites if not among the populace.

Pagan and Christian alike revered bodily relics; both found spiritual solace and magic in natural springs and places with special atmospheres. The lives of all Britain's inhabitants revolved around the cycle of the seasons, the fertility of their crops and families, the celebration of quarterly festivals and the construction of places in which to contemplate, tender offerings and seek intervention from supernatural beings. Both pagan and Christian held deeply to animist sensibilities. It is easy to look at the monotheism of the Christian faith and see in it a rationalising, all-purpose, all-seeing god with the central redeeming figure of Christ unique in theological history. And it is similarly easy to miss the very evident parallels between the charismatic healers of the shamanic or druidic tradition and those of the New Testament. Jesus acts at the centre of a pantheon of disciples, martyrs, apostles and saints every bit as rich as the suite of ancestors and spirits that the Dark Age Germans, British or Irish employed as propitiatory agents. A host of local and celebrity saints fulfilled the same social and cultural functions as—and in some cases may have been identical with—animist deities residing at the bottom of wells, in sacred groves and caves, beneath rocks and still pools. Did not Pope Gregory, after first advising King Æthelberht to destroy pagan idols and their temples, then suggest to Augustine that he allow converts to raise huts of branches around his new churches and celebrate the Christian feast days as they had been accustomed to celebrate their former pagan feasts?[85] And do we not retain Œastra, Woden, Tiw, Saturn and the Moon in our calendrical vocabulary?

No fewer than four springs rise close by All Hallows Church in Goodmanham, each of which might have attracted offerings, seekers of healing powers and the wisdom of obscure oracles, both before and after the conversion. In a world ruled by capricious fates, divination was an arcane skill practised by wise men and women inheriting the gift from their forebears; a chance to turn the odds in one's favour or invoke sympathetic magic for the birth of a child or a calf, or for a bounteous crop. A similar impulse moves people to light a candle for a loved one or to pick 'lucky' numbers for the lottery. The animist spirit runs deep in the human soul. The Christian missionaries, at least the savvy ones, came bearing the promise of an upgrade, not a revolution.

In any case, on King Edwin's death the Northumbrian elite very quickly apostatised; a political vacuum immediately ensued, during which anarchy seems briefly to have reigned (proof, by the rule of exception, that the Dark Ages were generally anything but anarchic). Bede recalled that year (633–4) as one expunged from the annals of history by 'those who compute the dates of kings'. In the North, Christianity was very quickly revived in Irish form by a king who embodied the potency of royal saint and Christian martyr, tribal totem, virile battle chief and temporal overlord. Oswald's life and post-mortem career as inspirational relic factory straddles that divide like no other.

In the compelling throwaway detail of a miracle tale, Bede gives us incidental evidence that the Roman roads in these parts had a recreational as well as military value in the Early Medieval period. As a youth, Abbot Herebald of Tynemouth priory had served under John of Beverley. John, a former Bishop of Hexham, founded a monastery in the principal settlement on the Yorkshire Wolds around the year 700. We are told that one day Herebald, and the other young men travelling in a party with the bishop, came upon a level and dry section of road that seemed to them to be the perfect spot for a horse race. Reluctantly, the bishop allowed the youths to have their fun, but he refused Herebald's pleas to join them. Herebald eventually gave in to temptation, took his turn galloping up and down the course and was eventually thrown while leaping a great pothole, fracturing his skull on a rock. Needless to say, the powerful prayers and tender care of the bishop restored him to life.

I rode south, now, to the edge of Northumbria and the banks of the Humber, an immense arm of the North Sea that penetrates forty miles inland before it can be crossed by any conventional road, at Boothferry on the River Ouse. I ran out of road at Brough, formerly the Roman fort of *Petuaria* which both guarded seaborne traffic and acted as a ferry station for the crossing to Lindsey during and after the Empire. Snowy squalls blustered out of an uncompromising, flat north-west horizon. The wind-ripped river seemed impossibly wide, its currents impassable, the blue and white polka-dot sky overwhelmingly massive, bleach-cleaned and rough-shiny. Only a super-giant might conceive of a means of crossing this ocean of rivers dry-shod.

I sped over the Humber suspension bridge (free to motorcycles), fighting to keep the bike upright, freezing, hardly daring to contemplate the big blue eastwards view towards Hull, Spurn Head and the open sea. Landing in a strange country, a new world, I parked the bike on a nameless street in Barton-upon-Humber and took shelter in a café where I was restored by bacon, scrambled eggs and tea. Fortified, I set out to find Barton's famous church. St Peter's is a marvellous expression of Anglo-Saxon self-confidence. The first church on the site was not built until the tenth century; the tower and its unusual bolted-on baptistery are original, and stood on part of a mound or spur which might just have been an ancient burial place. Decorative stone pilaster arcades, one stacked above the other and pierced by later round and angular arched windows, give the tower an exaggerated sense of height and create an exterior illusion of interior, of lordly secular power. They are skeuomorphs, copied from wooden models which might be ecclesiastical or secular.

The history of the site is intriguing: the church stands close to what was a sub-circular manorial earthwork enclosure, with

a much earlier cemetery in the vicinity. The archaeologist Richard Morris raises the intriguing possibility that the church tower might have doubled as the fortified house of a thegn. St Peter's is a redundant church, the most completely excavated in Britain. It was also shut (English Heritage again), so I couldn't nose around inside and see its complexities for myself. Bob Sydes, who was part of the excavation team under Warwick Rodwell in the 1970s and who excavated many of the burials, had told me the previous night that several of the inhumations were accompanied by hazel wands (a distinctly pagan feature); one, in addition, by a ham bone which must thoughtfully have been provided as a meal for the occupant's onward journey.

I tracked west to pick up the Roman road opposite Brough at Winteringham on the Humber's southern shore. These are the flatlands of north-west Lindsey, a continuation of the Vale of York; so the road, now Ermine Street, aims like a slingshot due south for Lincoln, untroubled for the most part by cross-grained hills or rivers. A couple of miles off it, on either side, are settlements bearing recognisably pre-Conquest names: Brigg, Snitterby, Hibaldstow, Willoughton. But it is striking that so few existing villages lie along the route. The reason for this stand-offish relationship with the Roman road is that it lies on a chalk ridge; a little further west chalk joins clay, the land falls away and a line of life-giving springs shadows the road. To the east, villages, farms and hamlets line the edge of the lowland peat. I stopped at one of the few substantial villages on the route: Broughton, where a pre-Conquest church has a tower built in herringbone masonry with an external, cylindrical stair turret and a round-arched doorway. The scattering of names ending in −by was a reminder that I had entered the lands of the Danelaw, whose southern boundary ran roughly along the River Lea from the Thames at London and then north-west along Watling Street. These were lands ruled by Danish kings for two generations from the late ninth century following a treaty between Alfred of Wessex and Guthrum, leader of one of the Viking armies.

The uncompromising line of the Roman road now unrolled like a tape measure for mile after mesmeric mile until Scampton, where it has been forced to make way for the runway from which the Dambuster squadron (617) took off in May 1943. RAF Scampton is now the home of the Red Arrows. Here, too, a branch road leaves Ermine Street and heads north-west to join the Great North Road near Bawtry (site of King Æthelfrith's epic defeat by King Rædwald in 617 (see page 133) where it crosses the River Idle. I turned off and took a break at Stow, where the magnificent Saxon minster church, currently undergoing restoration, stood shorn of its windows and deeply shadowed behind flapping plastic tarpaulins. The chancel, incidentally, is decorated with a very rare carving of what appears to be a Viking longship; but in the terribly dim light I could hardly make it out.

I stopped close to the cathedral at Lincoln, visible for miles around on its hill at the end of the long Jurassic ridge on which Ermine Street runs, looking down on the River Witham and surrounded by a jumble of cobbled medieval streets full of shoppers and tourists. A number of very early churches stood in or close to the former Roman *colonia*. One of these churches, excavated at St Paul-in-the-Bail, adjacent to the castle, was built close to the forum. It may be the church constructed by Bishop Paulinus in about 630 after his conversion of the city's reeve, one Blæcca; if so, Paulinus seems to have been tapping consciously into the site's Roman heritage, just as he did at York; there is a suspicion, in fact, that St Paul-in-the-bail might have been built on the foundations of a Roman church.

There must have been independent kings of Lindsey, but their genealogies survive only in semi-historical form and by Bede's day the *Lindisfaran* had been absorbed into Northumbria, later to be transferred to Mercian overlordship. In the, perhaps, seventh-century Tribal Hidage, *Lindisfarona* was assessed at seven thousand hides, the same tributary value as the kingdoms of the East and South Saxons. Very little serious attention has been paid by historians to the extraordinary and obvious similarity of the name *Lindisfarona* and Lindisfarne; was the latter an Anglian bridgehead in northern British territory founded by a warrior band from Lindsey? At any rate, by the end of the ninth century Lincoln had become one of the Five Boroughs of the Danelaw.[86]

York already seemed a long way behind. Heavy early afternoon traffic slowed me almost to walking pace. South of Lincoln the survival of the original road, cluttered with later settlement, is patchy; sometimes it is no more than a muddy track; I still had miles to travel, so I took the modern A15 to Sleaford; then to Bourne, strong and gusty side winds making it difficult to control the bike at times. Passing through a coppiced wood gave me a short respite. I briefly rejoined the Roman road where it becomes King Street, then cut across fen country to Market Deeping, skirting the sprawl of Peterborough. In low golden sunlight, dazzled by the intermittent flashing shadows of pollard willows lining the banks of massive straight-cut drains, I stopped briefly at Crowland, a small island in the fens where St Guthlac built a hermitage in the late seventh century and where a later, famous chronicle was kept by the abbey's monks. Dusk was accompanied by glimpses of egrets, buzzards and a red kite.

I had no time for contemplation: a long day on the bike had chilled me and it was nearly dark when I made my destination: Bluntisham in Huntingdonshire, where my sister Sophie and her husband Roger made the weary traveller very welcome. Family chat; pointing out my route on a map; a bike check for brake oil, tyre pressures, lights and chain lube. Next morning, early, with the air still cool and breezy but in sunshine and with the promise of a warmer day, I edged back into the slipstream of the imperial road network on Ermine Street at Godmanchester (*Durovigutum*), just south of Huntingdon. Gradually the ruler-drawn road rose away from a flat land of fens, drains and sedges, over a distance of twenty miles, a day's travel for the pedestrian, towards the eastern rump of the Chiltern Hills at Royston. I stopped at a very friendly market café for coffee, got my bearings and, leaving the Roman road, edged up onto the scarp for a view back across Cambridgeshire and Bedfordshire. I parked next to a small woodland on the north-facing crest, as close as I could get to the point where Roman road meets prehistoric highway: the Icknield Way, which had travelled all the way from Wiltshire on its route to Norfolk; a road older than the Romans and cited as one of the great royal roads of medieval England. For a moment I had trouble discriminating between a cluster of Neolithic and Bronze Age burial mounds and the grassy-banked bunkers of a local golf course, until I got my eye in. Several historians have raised the possibility that Claudius's, Agricola's, Hadrian's and other Roman routes through Britain replaced existing originals, refining and rationalising them. In some cases that must be true; in others, the Romans drove entirely new lines through the landscape to connect arterial roads, adapting where they could but unafraid to float a new trail across bog, ascend steep hills and remove obstacles as they saw fit. There must, surely, have been many hundreds and thousands of customary trails—few of them, however, as substantial and long-running as Icknield—which underlie England's staggering profusion of public rights of way that still charm those who bother to walk them and which must bemuse the foreigner, as they occasionally do the more liberated nation of the Scots—who may roam where they please at home.

The Icknield Way continues north-east from Royston, from where it was used as the line for the Roman road towards Newmarket. A mile or so before it reaches the home of horse racing it is crossed by the imposing line of the Devil's Dyke, the most substantial of all Dark Age earthworks before the time of King

Offa. Current opinion is that it was built by the indigenous Britons of the fifth century to demarcate or defend their lands from encroaching raiders or settlers to the north-east. If so, it is an impressive monument to the organisational skills of a people derided by Gildas as incapable of resisting foreign invasion.

After a small contemplative break I cut south-west, not far from the line of the Icknield Way which weaves along the natural contours of the chalk ridge among farms, villages and towns. Past Baldock (my favourite English place name—it derives from the Old French *Baudac*, meaning Baghdad, and was named in commemoration of the Mesopotamian city by the crusading Knights Templars who founded it in the twelfth century), where Icknield Way and Great North Road cross; then for a while, almost lost among the leafy back lanes and sensuous folds of Hertfordshire's Chiltern hundreds,[87] I passed a pleasant, contemplative morning. I emerged about lunchtime in St Albans on Watling Street—the old A5 whose acquaintance I had made on foot in a seemingly earlier age at Telford and Shrewsbury.

In my late teens I dug with Roman archaeologist and mosaic expert David Neal at the site of a prosperous native settlement and Roman villa, Gorhambury, a couple of miles outside St Albans on the road out from *Verulamium*; this was an old hunting ground. *Verulamium*, whose sprawling ruins lie across the River Ver from the hill on which the abbey and town sit, was founded on an older settlement of the powerful *Catuvellauni* tribe. By the end of the fourth century it boasted a theatre to go with its basilica and forum. Alban was a British martyr of the third or fourth century, persecuted under one or other imperial clampdowns on Christianity. The Gaulish bishop Germanus visited his martyrium in about 429; Gildas confirmed *Verulamium* as its site in the sixth century. Bede recognised it in his day as an important place of pilgrimage.

The mostly Norman abbey, with its distinctly Continental

painted round arches and huge nave, almost a hundred yards long, sits in a fine place and may have been built over the site of Alban's martyrial church. Alban's cult was successful—he is one of only three named Christian martyrs in Roman Britain and the only one to have spawned a grand shrine and cathedral church. Intriguingly, lower down the hill in the old Roman town the parish church of St Michael's appears to have been built on top of an earlier basilica-type structure; Christian citizens of the fourth and fifth centuries lived in more tolerant times.

It was time to put some miles on the clock. The M25, palisading London in a mad four-lane fury of impatience, gives the provincial an idea of what the British peasant must have thought stepping onto the metalled roads of the Empire, caught up in the whirling white water of a canyon with no choice but to go for it pell mell and hope for the best. The biker needs to make his presence felt, look big and keep an eye like a hawk's on the stampeding migration to which he has inadvertently tied his fate. At some point I was aware of a narrow steel and concrete bridge with pedestrians dawdling across it whizzing above my head, an echo of my own earlier and saner route through Epping Forest; then we were through a chute, a short section of tunnel above which I had emerged from the forest into Epping itself. I crossed the Thames at Dartford, stopped at a petrol station for fuel and a short sanity break, then followed the unrecognisable route of Chaucer's pilgrims—what was once the A2, towards Rochester and the Medway and running parallel with Watling Street. Rochester, the former Roman town of *Durobrivae*, was the seat of England's second bishop, Justus, after Augustine at Canterbury. It marks the boundary between East and West Kent, ancient separate kingdoms.

I emerged from the conglomerations of Chatham and Gillingham, passed through Sittingbourne and found myself riding through a quiescent winter garden landscape of oast houses, orchards, hop fields and quaint roadside pubs. The land is densely occupied, fertile, giving of nature's fruits. It is striking that this route, rather than repelling settlement as I had found elsewhere, attracts it. Pilgrims, traders and diplomats travelling between London and the coast have always been good business; one imagines a string of roadside hostelries, shops, stalls and markets dipping in and out of existence, morphing between overtly secular, religious and mystical.

Just before the town of Faversham a small brown sign pointing to a field caught my speeding eye. At the next roundabout I doubled back, parked the bike and walked across a flint-strewn chalky brown ploughed field to where a ruined flint and brick building stood, a small copse of bare trees as backdrop. This at first unprepossessing structure is one of a handful of Early Medieval churches in Britain proven to be constructed on the ruins of a Roman mausoleum. St Albans abbey may have begun in this way. Was a notable Roman holy man or martyr buried here? Known as Stone-by-Faversham, it is a really remarkable survival. The word 'stone' may denote more than the very obvious fact of its construction. Elsewhere it seems to echo the knowledge that the Giants had built in stone in days long gone; that stone was a special, magical material (like ink and vellum) whose secrets were lost to Dark Age builders. The flint and red Roman brick walls of the earlier structure have been exposed and defined by excavation; now green ferns clinging to the mortar add a decorative garnish and in the low sunlight they glowed with earthy colours, silver grey flint glistening against terracotta brick.

From Faversham I took a line towards the north Kent coast. At Reculver (*Regulbium*), as at Bradwell-on-Sea in Essex, a former Roman coastal fort became the site of an important early church. In this case, erosion has left the massive twin towers at Reculver perching perilously on a cliff; no art of man could have contrived a more dramatic ruin, Gothic in nature's inspiration, Romanesque in execution. The sea was a perfect azure, sparkling in afternoon sunshine, the odd container ship or fishing boat floating on horizon's haze and the breeze swirling through skeletal arch and ruined nave. The church was a minster foundation, originally of 669. The immensely tall towers were spared destruction in later centuries by an edict of the Admiralty who declared it a navigation aid. Richard Morris has suggested that the original church may have played a role, perhaps with a beacon and smaller tower, as a lookout or lighthouse, watching trade pass up or down the estuary. But looking on the map I realised that its location is more special than that of any old coastal fort. It once sat at the mouth of the Wantsum Channel, which separated the Isle of Thanet from the rest of Kent. I rode across its much reduced, canalised channel, barely eight feet wide, without realising. When I got to the small village of Sarre, I stopped on a road still called Sarre Wall, once a causeway that joined the Roman road between here and Canterbury, to have a better look at both the Wantsum and the map. This was once shoreline; now it looks out onto flat fields bordered by drains cut through old peat. A bridge stood here before the channel silted up in the late Medieval period. In the nineteenth century an ancient burial ground was excavated close by. Grave goods included many exotic objects, and a number of sets of merchants' balances.

That got me thinking about St Augustine who, when his mission arrived in 597, was told by Æthelberht of Kent to wait on Thanet while he, the king, considered Pope Gregory's petition and the party's bona fides. Æthelberht had a Frankish Christian queen, Bertha, so he ought to have had some idea of what he was in for; even so, he was concerned to find out what these missionaries were up to. He was at first suspicious of some devilry. In the cast list of Early Medieval travellers they must qualify as either merchants or warriors come as an embassy from another great king. No uninvited traders.

These men had travelled all the way from the Bishop of Rome. They had impressive credentials, carried written documents which the king would not have been able to read, so Liudhard, his queen's personal priest, may have acted as go-between and translator. The key to the account we have from Bede is that the king made Augustine wait on Thanet, where prospective merchants set themselves up—one thinks again of Brian Roberts' idea of the caravanserai, camped on neutral territory on the edge of the king's lands. Here he could decide whether to admit them or not. The Wantsum, with Reculver guarding its northern seaward mouth, was his vallum, his physical and psychological border. Eventually Æthelberht let Augustine and his mission come to the court at Canterbury (*Durovernum*), where Roman buildings (not just a church, but parts of the theatre) still stood. Allowing Augustine to preach and convert, the king subsequently gave him lands 'suitable to his rank'. In other words, he accepted that the socially anomalous Augustine was of warrior rank, but not aiming to fight him for the kingdom (little did he know).

Sarre, then, and Thanet in general, had special significance in the Early Medieval landscape, as a frontier zone. I tried, as I stood on the sadly diminished banks of the Wantsum, to imagine a broad river with busy ferry boats crossing, the settlements on the island bustling with all sorts of travellers, hangers-on, traders, sailors, vendors and craftsmen, all living a liminal life and mostly hoping to be allowed to cross into the king's lands and make their petitions to him. Social and cultural tensions must have made this backwater a lively place. I thought of ports that I have visited: Boston, Mahon, Syracuse, Rotterdam: exciting, marginal places. The Wantsum Channel began to look like Hadrian's Wall in my mind's eye—a landscape of edges and edginess.

Close to Sarre, a mile or so east along the edge of Thanet where it looks south over flat, peaty reclaimed marshes, once open water, I came to Minster-in-Thanet, formerly the capital of the island when, perhaps, it was its own small tributary kingdom, like the Rodings in Essex; and where a large parish church stands not far from the site of a seventh-century monastery. A venerable yew tree grew in its churchyard; all was peaceful and quiet; all very English. The church was shut.

At the far south-east end of the old Wantsum channel, now the outflow of the River Stour, lies a twin of the fort at Reculver: Richborough (*Rutupiae*), the bridgehead for Claudius's invasion fleet in AD 43, subsequently a civilian settlement converted to use as a fort of the Saxon Shore in the late third century. It now lies inland, beached like a stranded whale, irrelevant. Across the marshes on the Thanet side lies Ebbsfleet, traditionally the site of Augustine's original landing in 597 and once the site of a tidal mill. I briefly worked at Richborough for Pete Wilson when his Central Excavation Unit team was doing the rounds of Kent in 1985. Central Unit, as it was known, was the provisional wing of what had begun as a department of the Ministry of Works, then became the Historic Buildings and Monuments Commission and is now known as English Heritage. It was a good way to keep one's hand in at some interesting sites, even if the trenches were small interventions in advance of drain-digging or new car parks. As it happens, before our arrival another team had been looking at a hexagonal stone structure elsewhere in the fort. It looked very much like an early font; and stone foundations excavated many years ago in the north-east quarter of the fort are now thought to represent the remains of a church with stone footings and a timber superstructure. So it seems that a late Roman church stood here. Richborough is also where the Roman road network begins and ends. I had run my Roman road race.

Except, that is, for a visit to Canterbury itself. I stayed overnight near Sandwich with my aunt Karen Crofts—strategically placed relatives are a boon for the traveller, to be sure—then, an early-morning's ride along the first Roman road in Britain: its exact route, oddly, is not known and the modern road that completes it is far from straight. I made the same mistake as I had at Faversham, missing a small sign to St Martin's church a quarter of a mile outside the city walls. At nine in the morning it was shut; a sign promised it would open at eleven. I parked the bike up nearer to the city, opposite the entrance to St Augustine's Abbey. My heart sank: English Heritage—closed until spring. Cutting my losses I walked through the old city gates and stood outside the fortress-like precinct of the great medieval cathedral. At £10.50 to get in, I thought better of a tour of Thomas Becket's shrine, which I have in any case seen before. What interested me about the setting was that, first, it lies along a line of churches that includes the abbey and St Martin's and second, that it is more like a castle than a cathedral, absolutely unapproachable except through either city walls or the mass of houses and shops that surround it. It is a religious citadel of spiritual princes; a Vatican.

The alignment echoes a frequent Roman pattern of roads and the cemeteries that grew up alongside them outside towns in the Empire. St Albans may be an analogous setting; there are many examples on the Continent. Where cemeteries and mausolea stood, some of them attracted the burials of martyrs or early Christian holy men. When, later, the shrines were marked by churches, the original cemeteries became Christian graveyards or were buried; only the churches survive above ground to mark that relict, funerary landscape.

I wandered outside the walls again. In a small garden, perhaps on the site of houses bombed during the war, stood bronze statues of King Æthelberht and his queen, original patrons of the Gregorian mission of 597. Tracking back to the car park I found, to my surprise and relief, that someone had opened the gates to the abbey; even if the museum and shop were shut, I could take a look at the ruins. At the west end stood the original church of Sts Peter and Paul, founded by Augustine and Æthelberht. The later abbey was built just to the east of it over the remains of a monastery founded by, and to house the relics of, Augustine and the members of his mission who became bishops or archbishops after him. Here too are the resting places of kings of Kent, including Wihtred (*c.*670–725) whose law code defined the relationship between king and church and the status of the traveller. The later

KING ÆTHELBERHT

structures: a crypt, now open to the sky; towering nave and choir walls; the abbey precincts, standing ruined among green lawns studded with plaques, telling the visitor what to look at. Towards the east end of the precinct are the stunted remains of a third church, St Pancras, which several scholars believe to be another late Roman foundation above a mausoleum or special grave, and still on the line of the road to Richborough.

At eleven o'clock sharp the doors of St Martin's opened. I was its first visitor that day, so I had the company of Ruth Matthews, the guide, to myself. I had already seen the outside: the walls are fashioned, as they are at Stone-by-Faversham, of flint and red Roman brick and tile, in sometimes decorative string courses, sometimes in apparently random patterns. They tell of a complicated structural history: one can make out blocked doorways and windows and the odd reused inscription. Inside, much later plaster has been removed to show various stages of refurbishment and redesign. The western chancel appears to be the oldest structure still standing, identified in part by a hard pink mortar that looks very Roman and whose mysteries were unknown in the Early Medieval period, unless Augustine brought specialists with him. St Martin's claims to be the oldest church in continuous use in the English-speaking world. But the shape and size, the feel and sensibility are those of a basilica; the inspiration is Roman. Bede says that Bertha (whose father was a ruler at Tours) and her priest Liudhard worshipped in a church dedicated to St Martin of Tours which had been built 'while the Romans were still in Britain'. This is the prime candidate to match that historical evidence; its claims are reinforced by the nineteenth-century excavation of a hoard of metalwork that included a gold medallion bearing the name, in reverse, of none other than Liudhard.[88] Whether, in fact, it was a Roman Christian church still standing and refurbished, or a new church built on an ancient mausoleum, like St Pancras or Stone-by-Faversham, is still debated. At any rate Ruth and I had a proper chinwag debating this and that point as she showed me the church's key features, glad, I hoped, to encounter a visitor who at least knew his Bede. For my part I had wanted to see this church in the flesh ever since Richard Morris introduced us to it in my undergraduate days. To be shown round arguably the oldest church in England by such an expert and passionate guide was a considerable privilege, a grand end point.

Interlude *Newcastle to Jarrow*

Heroes of the Revolution—*fences—industrial decline and revival—*
Segedunum *and Wallsend—last ferry—South Shields—Jarrow*
church—Bede—miner's lamp—Jarrow marchers

THE LAST LEG of my journey from Birdoswald, where the Dark
Ages began, to Jarrow, where Bede first lifted the veil on those
obscure centuries, started with a walk across Newcastle's Swing
Bridge in the company of an old friend, Dan Elliott. A decade ago
we made a film together called *Heroes of the Revolution*, for which
we travelled from one of Durham's oldest coalfields down to the
Tyne and then along it to the sea. Dan's cinematic, unsentimen-
tal directorial eye made me see the past as a new sort of narrative: situated in the present, constructed from images rather
than words, allowing the story to emerge as a dialogue with the
viewer. So I asked him to walk with me, from his flat in Gateshead, to Jarrow and to share his perspective on a much earlier
cast of heroes. Dan is a native of these parts, knows them better
than I do; and neither of us had walked this route before.

The Quayside, now thinly peopled but once crowded with
wharfs and shipping, carried us beneath the green steel arches
of the Tyne Bridge along a promenade that features Law Courts,
solicitors' offices and trendy eateries; on the south side the shiny
Sage concert hall, Baltic Art Gallery (converted from a flour
mill) and college flats reflected the sky back at us from their glass
walls; only the low, functional outline of a Royal Naval Reserve

establishment and its single grey patrol boat tied alongside are reminders of a maritime past.

The tilting Millennium footbridge, the last to cross the Tyne before it encounters the sea, and a paragon of engineering elegance, completes a set of seven bridges over the river. It is an overconstructed, superhuman landscape. But we found the quietness of the river, overlooked mostly by expensive flats with plantless, lifeless balconies, too eerie. Urban rivers need to be busy. With little to look at except an unchanging, endless set of railings, we fell to talking of our latest projects, travels and favourite places. Dan spends much of his time in Berlin, whose own Dark Age boasts a wall, or the fragmentary remains of a wall, that really was designed to keep people out. That discussion led to the Middle East and its tribal conflicts (more walls) and thence to the tribal kingdoms of our own Early Medieval world of warlords, fanatics and religious propaganda.

At some point we came to realise that the modern route along the river is all about fences: gated housing complexes, culs de sac leading to defunct factories with no way through for the traveller on foot; whole sections of the river blocked off by new developments stalled for lack of funds. The land is deserted; the riverside inaccessible, emasculated, the river abandoned. A marina seemed to offer visual excitement: particoloured boats shone bright in the sun; masts pricked the sky and the groan and creak of buoys and fenders made a change from the generic background drone of distant traffic; but there was nobody about and all the signs seemed to ward off the curious.

A little further along, on a northern reach of the river, we began to see signs of life after death: offshore oil-servicing industries; plant-hire compounds; small engineering firms; cable manufacturers with ships moored alongside. Then cranes; not the famous Walker cranes of the vast Swan Hunter shipyard (where we had filmed in its last, sad days) whence the *Ark Royal* was launched; those are gone, sold off or scrapped. Just off Wallsend High Street (whose name rather speaks for itself) we passed the tidy ruins of *Segedunum*, the Wall-supplying and terminating Roman fort, looking not quite so incongruous in a post-industrial land as it might. It could be a bomb site cleaned up. We had a beer and a sandwich in an encouragingly ordinary working pub at Willington Quay, then found ourselves forced to make a wide detour around the giant-swallowing entrances to the twin Tyne Tunnels that take the A19 beneath the river to emerge in Jarrow. We were channelled through a grassy business park with rigid, laid paths, token benches, easy-maintenance borders and cycle lanes. It's a creepy landscape, overdesigned, inorganic and inhuman, a stage set existing more in the imagination of town planners than in the lives of people. Close by is the entrance to a Victorian pedestrian tunnel that connects Wallsend with Jarrow, but it has been shut for maintenance these last couple of years and may never reopen; so we were forced to make another diversion, this time around the North Sea Ferry Terminal, before an improvised navigation brought us to North Shields and a more modest ferry, connecting the town with South Shields on the other side of the river. We passed a truncated row of terraces, all boarded up bar one or two recalcitrant residents. I look at such things as an archaeologist: abandonment and scavenging behaviour being the stuff of which the material past is made; Dan looked at them as a potential film set for one of his melancholic tales of real life. Either way, they fascinate: lives lived; families moved on; memories fading.

Tynemouth, site of a monastery in Bede's day and perhaps earlier, lay a mile further on towards the north-east. Even I remember the jumble of wharves and bonded warehouses that once lined the river here before they were levelled for housing projects that never materialised. There is something enriching to the eye and imagination about communities that develop organically; grand plans are often inhuman in scale; like Hadrian's project or Newcastle's 1960s T. Dan Smith-inspired concrete high-rises. We came back down to the river at North Shields, which boasts a working fish quay, is resilient enough to be a lively place still and is connected to the rest of Tyneside not just by its long-lived ferry boats but by the Metro rail system, an arterial route that nevertheless distances the river even further from people's lives. It seemed odd to cross the Tyne on a boat: this is the very last passenger ferry on the river but, I am glad to say, much used and cherished by workers, families and trippers; a pleasantly communal experience after so much walking through a land abandoned by people and governments.

The short distance from South Shields to Jarrow took us through an older landscape of small manufactories; smaller shops; Methodist chapels; terraces of houses, their front doors flush with the pavement; women with prams and elderly couples carrying small shopping bags; then around the vast complex of the Tyne Dock, a million-car car park waiting to take Nissan's polished beasts of burden across the world. Dan and I are fascinated by these human, often neglected landscapes of everyday survival, labour and unknowable relations. Past and present are constructed from unglamoured lives; their familiarity can blind us to their intrinsic narrative riches.

Immediately west of the Tyne Docks, squeezed between the filthy sewage-rich mud-flat channel of Jarrow Slake and an oil depot, lies Bede's church: St Paul's, Jarrow. Its survival—having perhaps been looted during a Viking raid in 794 (if the *Anglo-Saxon Chronicle's* 'Donemutha' is indeed Jarrow), abandoned after further attacks in 874 or 875, refounded two hundred and eighty years later, dissolved by Henry VIII and later cared for by Victorian antiquarians—is a small miracle. It contains the oldest surviving stained glass in Britain; small fragments, it is true, but they stand as an unmistakeable metaphor for a new light shining.

A recent ground-penetrating radar survey has shown that a crypt might yet survive intact below the floor of the existing chancel.

A Latin dedication stone records that a church was built here in the year 685 by Abbot Ceolfrith on land donated by the unlucky King Ecgfrith:

DEDICATIO BASILICAE SCI PAULI VIIII KLMAI

ANNO XV ECFRIDIREG

CEOLFRIDI ABBEIUS DEMQ

Q. ECCLES DO AUCTORE

CONDITORIS ANNO IIII

The dedication of the basilica of St. Paul
on the 9th day before the Kalends of May
In the 15th year of King Ecfrid;
and in the 4th [year] of abbot Ceolfrid, founder,
by the guidance of God, of the same church

The monastery, begun in 682 and supported by the king's grant of forty hides of land, was built by twenty-two brethren, half of them tonsured monks; the early Northumbrian monastic foundations emphasised the virtues of manual labour and strict poverty, the value of individual spirituality within a common enterprise. The church, one of that new generation of permanent stone structures paralleled at Ripon and Hexham, would have been furnished by gifts from its patrons, including the king who personally marked out the site of the altar. Windows aside, it would have been lit by torches and by lamps in hanging bowls; the altar, as Eddius's testimony says of Ripon, decorated with jewels, ornate psalm books and rich cloths. The monks, in contrast, lived in austere cells, poorly lit if at all and probably unheated. The monastery was carefully sited at the mouth of the River Don (now a shadow of its former self); on the east side, now subsumed by the unending Nissan car park, a royal township may have lain, later recorded as *Portus Ecgfridi*—Ecgfrith's harbour.

Jarrow is a twin of St Peter's in Wearmouth, built some five miles to the south and eleven years earlier by Benedict Biscop, scholar, mentor and intrepid traveller: they were 'one monastery in two places'. Between them, in the year 716, they supported six hundred monks. Bede (673–735) spent his entire life here, his outstanding scholarship one of the fruits of a mature intellectual church and of Biscop's libraries, which themselves were borne out of the new relationship between landholding rights and patronage. Jarrow's scriptorium, part of a substantial complex centred on two churches and their burial ground, and whose remains were excavated by Rosemary Cramp's team in the 1960s and 1970s, produced three of the great bibles of Early Medieval Europe—a stunning expression of hybrid Latin, Anglo-Irish and British cultures reflected in the art and literature of the Golden Age of Northumbria. That cultural hybridisation speaks for Britain's patchwork of linguistic, spiritual, material and genetic regions and localities, its exuberant mongrel races. Rosemary Cramp (now Dame Rosemary, Emeritus Professor of Archaeology at Durham University) makes the striking point that the dimensions of this structure are 'interestingly comparable with the large secular halls of the period'.[89] The whole resembles a township, a suitable residence for the highest level of nobility from whose ranks the abbots and abbesses of this Golden Age were recruited. Fragmentary hints of a monastic vallum were traced during the excavations, but have not yet been proven.

Close by, the open-air museum at Bede's World has recreated the sort of landscape that might have been familiar to Bede: the modest hall of a minor thegn; a sunken-floored building perhaps used to store grain; the stalls, sties and pens of a small farm complete with grunting pig-boar hybrids, native oxen and vegetable plot. A reconstruction of the enigmatic 'grandstand' which in Edwin's and Oswald's day stood at Yeavering at the northern

JARROW

edge of the Cheviots has recently been added, and a museum celebrates both the spiritual and cultural heritage of Bede's Northumbria in its transition from a self-doubting post-Roman world of fragile realities to one of self-confidence with an idea of a rational state looking to the future.

From Northumbria, Benedict Biscop made the pilgrimage to Rome, not just to honour the saints and martyrs but to gather fragments of knowledge that he might bring home to seed Northumbria's new age of learning. His second journey there was a book-buying expedition. On his third trip he accompanied Theodore of Tarsus, one of Canterbury's great archbishops and an impressive scholar, back to Britain. In later years Ceolfrith, resigning his abbacy at Jarrow, also travelled to Rome, taking with him one of three pandects, or complete bibles, as a gift for the Pope. He did not survive that last journey; but the *Codex Amiatinus*, now in Florence, did: it is a worthy monument to that half-forgotten cultural landscape. Bede himself hardly travelled at all; but his many important works, not least of them books on time and geography, were copied and distributed across Europe, seeding in their turn an age of scholarship which brought the light of intellectual reason—albeit ecclesiastically uncompromising—to Europe and was paralleled by a later great age of Arab scholarship in the south.

Dan and I filmed inside the church in 2004; but not because of Bede or the Early Middle Ages. We wanted to record Jarrow's small but significant part in a later enlightenment. On a window sill in the nave of the church sits a miner's safety lamp. In May 1812 a terrible explosion in a local pit killed ninety-two men and boys. The then vicar of Jarrow, the historian John Hodgson, was instrumental in the formation of a Society for the Prevention of Accidents in Coal Mines, which commissioned the Cornish chemist and inventor Humphry Davy to construct a lamp which would cast a safe light underground. The idea and technology of industrial safety was another Jarrow export, eleven hundred years after it enjoyed its first industrial revolution.

Tragically, Jarrow's most famous crusaders, the two hundred and seven marchers, accompanied by their local MP, Ellen Wilkinson, who set off from here to walk to London in 1936 to beg for help during the Depression, were discouraged by the Labour Party and the trades unions, ignored by government (Stanley Baldwin refused to meet them) and spurned by the nation's capital; their scant reward for a three-hundred-mile journey on foot a pound each for the train fare home. The last of those extraordinary ambulists, Con Shields, died in 2013 aged ninety-three.

Dan and I also took the train home: a modest two pounds seventy for the dozen or so stops to Gateshead that completed the circle of a short walk through two millennia.

Midwinter: *York to Whitby*

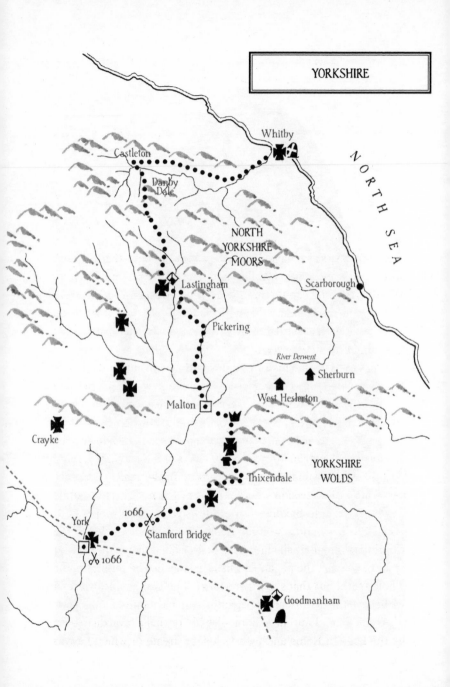

YORKSHIRE

NORTH SEA

Whitby

Castleton

Danby
Dale

NORTH
YORKSHIRE
MOORS

Scarborough

Lastingham

Pickering

River Derwent

Sherburn

West Heslerton

Malton

Crayke

Thixendale

YORKSHIRE
WOLDS

1066

York

Stamford Bridge

1066

Goodmanham

I N THE DARKEST days of winter I took a short trip through space and time: eighty miles and forty years, from York to Whitby; from 627 to 664: following the northern English from pagan wannabe Romans through the birth pangs of conversion to a Christian state integrated with Europe for the first time in two hundred and fifty years.

English narrative history begins with a convenient date: 597, the year when Pope Gregory sent his mission to the Angles and Saxons, led by St Augustine. That mission, derailed comprehensively by Augustine's faux pas with the indigenous British church (see pages 86–7) and stalled on its metropolitan launchpad by the apostasy of its patron kings in Kent, Essex and East Anglia, hung by a thread after its first quarter century. In the year 617, twenty years after the mission's arrival, there was no Christian state among the Anglo-Saxons. Canterbury's then archbishop all but packed his bags and set off for Rome; his two bishops fled to the Continent. The British church, as Bede tells us, made no attempt at all to convert the pagan English (he may not be telling us the whole truth, but that's another story). The two peoples were, if we believe the historical propaganda, sworn enemies.

Archbishop Laurence, admonished for his cowardice both by the Pope in Rome and by a visionary dream in which he was

scourged, changed his mind: he rallied, and succeeded in converting Eadbald, the apostate king of Kent whose father Æthelberht
had indulged, then sponsored, Augustine.

Enter stage-left Eadbald's sister, Æthelburh, and her priest,
Paulinus, a survivor of the original mission. Kentish princesses
were a valuable political commodity: savvy, educated, sophisticated; in marriage they bought kudos and the rewards of alliance
with the traditionally senior kingdom of the English. When
Edwin of Deira slew his brother-in-law Æthelfrith at the great
battle on the River Idle in 617 and became overlord of the northern Anglian kingdoms, Æthelburh was a natural choice as his
queen. Negotiations were opened with the convert Eadbald, who
insisted, however, that Edwin undergo baptism and a Christian
marriage ceremony (a form, if you like, of political submission).
Edwin demurred until such time as his own political position in
Northumbria was secure. For a few years he was busy expanding his realms through conquest and tribute, reconstructing
dormant networks of patronage and forging new ones. He subdued the Isles of Man and Anglesey and took tribute from them,
acquiring huge political capital in the process.

The time came when he had to decide his own and his people's
spiritual and political future. But one imagines a deeply conservative aristocracy, suspicious of what must have seemed the inflexi-
bility and fanaticism of the monotheistic Christian faith and concerned at how its adoption might affect their lines of patronage.
Pagan priests and churchmen were competitors for the attention
and generosity of their secular lord. Edwin's decision was delayed;
more years passed.

Bede constructs the story of Edwin's conversion as a series
of providential, semi-miraculous tales through which it is possible to glimpse complex political and personal motivations, even
angst; but the critical, precipitating event seems to have been a
double trauma. At Easter 626 an assassin came to Edwin's court

from the king of the West Saxons. He killed Edwin's bodyguard, a thegn named Lilla, with a murderous thrust from a sword tipped with poison; the same blow penetrated the king's flesh and he lay ill for some time before recovering. That same night his Kentish queen gave birth (perhaps prematurely) to a daughter. Edwin promised Paulinus and his queen, Æthelburh, that should he successfully wreak revenge on the West Saxons he would undergo conversion and offer his new daughter, Eanflæd, to the church. A year later, having slain five West Saxon warlords in the course of a punitive campaign, he was baptised in York: the first Christian king of the Northumbrians. Over the next year the warrior elites of Deira and Bernicia followed suit, enthusiastically or otherwise.

York is almost painfully familiar to me. I spent my undergraduate years here and know its streets and buildings, names and ways. Leaving the station on a morning that barely emerged from twilight, and crossing the river, I found myself walking almost thoughtlessly through streets thronged with Christmas shoppers and lined with associations from my own past. Here was the manhole through which, as students, we were allowed to enter the bizarre world of the Roman city's sewage system; there, I remember, I dug as a volunteer on an emergency excavation ahead of building works. On Parliament Street I looked in vain for a landmark that goes unnoticed by most tourists: two Regency buildings leaning away from one another because they sit astride the Roman city wall many feet beneath. Eventually I got my eye in; the gap has been filled and painted over.

In the gardens of the Yorkshire Museum I paid a visit to two upstanding monuments: the indomitable Multangular Tower, with its striking courses of red brick, built probably in the reign of Emperor Constantine (306–37) and perhaps under his personal supervision (he was practising for a larger project on the shores of the Bosphorus); then to a more secret, intimate, tragic structure, in an out-of-the-way shadow of the medieval stone ramparts: the Anglian tower. It is a much more modest, stunted affair made of scavenged, undressed stone with a low, round-arched doorway, now fenced off to deter drug-users from entering. Its original height is unknown. It may have been built in the reign of Edwin as he set about reconstructing the defunct Roman city for his new capital; if so, it is the only monumental structure to survive above ground from any Northumbrian secular power of the seventh century: evidence of Edwin's imperial Roman fantasies, perhaps. After about 900 it was buried beneath the earth ramparts of Viking *Yorvik*. It has a dark secret, darker even than the miserable cold, leaden day when I remade its acquaintance. Excavating it in July 1970, archaeologist Jeff Radley was killed when the earth walls of his trench collapsed and buried him. This was the archaeologist's nightmare in the days before steel shoring became mandatory in excavations below four feet deep. The plaque which once commemorated him has been removed. As a teenager I allowed myself to be persuaded to descend into a slit trench fifteen feet deep, unshored, in the shadow of another great church, the cathedral at Orléans. The thought makes me shudder. The only thing holding that trench together was the city's Roman wall, still standing, buried almost to the full depth of the hole.

Almost for the sake of it, I made a partial circuit of York's walls, themselves a patchwork construct of Roman and medieval pride and insecurity, and of Victorian nostalgia. The city's roofscape, beneath which it is in a constant flux of shifting businesses and populations, was unchanged: orange pantiles, jagged roof lines, soft red and brown brick, a Giant's Causeway of individual buildings and lives as it has been for a thousand years and more. I remembered the tropes that first-time visitors to York are treated to: that a Scotsman may be shot by a bow and arrow if caught within the city walls after dark; that here the streets are called gates, the gates are called bars and the bars are called pubs. York can sometimes seem too self-consciously like a theme park; but its roots are sunk very deep and from them grows a tree, a national sense of continuity.

I paid my respects to the Minster, which sits directly above the *principia* of the Roman legionary fortress built very nearly two thousand years ago. The vast church survives through a combination of luck and determination. In 1829 the ranting Methodist schizophrenic Jonathan Martin (brother of the apocalyptic painter John), attempted to burn it down and very nearly succeeded. In 1984, when I was living just up the road in Bootham, a lightning strike caused another conflagration, this time in the south transept. In its undercroft, excavated in emergency so that engineers could shore up the sagging piles of its colossal gothic superstructure in the 1970s, are Roman walls, now much tidied up; artefacts from two millennia of accumulating rubbish; and a story of engineering triumphs and disasters. On a small ceramic slab is scrawled a chi-rho, the early Christian symbol of sacrifice. It became fashionable during the fourth century after Constantine, declared Emperor here in 306, used it on his army's shields in battle. He proclaimed a policy of religious freedom, including toleration of Christianity, in 313 in the so-called Edict of Milan.

Edwin of Northumbria, under instruction from his priest, then bishop, Paulinus (incidentally the first man in our history to have a pen portrait written, so that we actually know what he looked like: dark, saturnine and with a pronounced hawk-like nose) is likely to have been coached in the story of Constantine's journey to enlightenment through victory in the Battle of the Milvian Bridge in 312. Even before his conversion, perhaps, Edwin began, self-consciously, to model his own kingship in imitation of an idea of empire provided by that legendary forebear and by his queen, bigging up the political and spiritual advantages of buying into Roman orthodoxy. Somewhere on the Minster green, just to the north of the medieval cathedral, Paulinus constructed a wooden church in which the king and his children were baptised among the ruined columns and paved streets of the former legionary headquarters, surrounded by the works of the Giants.

At the beginning of Edwin's reign there can have been no functioning civic society in this once grand, northernmost city of the Empire. A garrison without soldiers, fortress without a commander, *Eburacum* was conquered not by barbarians but by the forces of nature and the failure of its engineers to combat rising water levels—or perhaps just their apathy. It straddles the River Ouse at the centre of the Vale of York, a great flat, low-lying glacial plain that has always been prone to flooding and was particularly vulnerable during the cool, wet centuries of the mid-first millennium. The Ouse (a Brythonic name) drains the waters of the Pennine Rivers Nidd, Swale and Ure at the head of Humber's watershed. I well remember being cut off on its south side during the extraordinary winter of 1981/2, when the Ouse flooded to record heights (16 feet 7 inches above normal) and then froze. People walked across the ice; some fool rode a motorbike beneath one of the bridges. We huddled by a pathetic gas fire in our squalid student flat in Bishophill, not many yards above the chaos of the inundated riverbank.

After an afternoon's tramping around old haunts I reminisced about that time over dinner with archaeologist and friend Mark Whyman, with whom I'd shared that flat. Bishophill, somewhat swankier now than it was in our day, sits in what was once the Roman *colonia*: a plantation of retired legionary veterans designed to imprint the frontier zone with a small but significant outpost of the mother city; to remind the new citizens that their sponsors and overlords were the greatest military power in the world. In my mind's eye I pictured another walled colony, Derry/ Londonderry, in the seventeenth century, and conjured up a much vaguer idea of New Delhi or one of those enormous American overseas military bases (Diego Garcia; Bagram?) that are or were miniaturised states of the Union.

We fell to talking about York (by then called *Eoforwic*) in
Edwin's day. Mark is a veteran of excavations at Fishergate,
where a later seventh-century emporium sprang up in the decades after Edwin refounded it as a royal centre. At his death a
stone church, constructed under the supervision of Paulinus and

ANGLIAN TOWER

Æthelburh, remained unfinished, to be completed by his rival and successor Oswald. Bishop and queen fled south in fear of the new regime. One gets the feeling that life crept back to York, slowly, over decades. Its greatness as a city was not restored until it became capital of another kingdom, ruled over by Vikings in the ninth and tenth centuries when merchants and craftspeople, evidenced by the celebrated Coppergate excavations of the 1970s and 1980s, forged a critical mass of expertise and energy equal to anything engineered by their Anglo-Saxon antagonists.

After dinner and a beer I got my maps out and we pored over landscapes of our youth, when we lived our undergraduate summers digging: at Wharram Percy, high in the Wolds; at West Heslerton on the edge of the Vale of Pickering (when I wasn't in Dorset. . . or Hertfordshire). It seemed, looking back, that we must also have spent most of our term-time weekends on field trips in the back of our professor Philip Rahtz's Land Rover or in the company of other lecturers, steeping ourselves in a culture of fieldwork, of vernacular and church architecture, the rhyme and metre of road, lane, field, boundary and standing stone. We graduated, semi-fluent, in the language of landscape. I wonder, thinking of it, whether that itinerant excavators' lifestyle before, during and after university had not set me on the road to periodic nomadism, to a perpetual desire not to go back but always to look to the next horizon. Maybe that's why spending time in York makes me feel uneasy. Reminiscence is a record with a B-side.

On a morning of inexpressibly dismal murk, I set out from Colliergate clothed against rain and wind. Automatically, almost, I turned right into Goodramgate, noticing the presence or absence of pubs or cafés once frequented where I had met so-and-so that time, had said something stupid or laughed like a drain with mates. Out of the city, then, through Monk Bar, where a model shop has stood since well before my time. I passed a small development of houses and flats on Monkgate, new since my day; and I had to think for a moment to get my bearings, until I realised that this was where, in 1983, I worked through the winter on an excavation, supervising unemployed youths in work experience while attempting to salvage the medieval archaeology of the suburbs. Mud, ice and good craic are what I remember.

Across the River Foss I navigated the suburban roads of Layerthorpe (a Viking name, the *Thorp* element denoting a village or farm), Heworth and Tang Hall, with the school run, almost the last of the year, in full swing. This was new territory for me: no memories of this part of town where the houses are too comfortable for students to afford. I found the end of Bad Bargain Lane (which would have made a great address for rack-rent student flats) and, despite the discouraging name, followed it out into the flat, washed-out fields of Osbaldwick (Old English: Osbald's farm) and across the A64, the road to Scarborough and the North Sea.

I cut across country through back lanes whose right-angle turns were a dead giveaway to old country routes diverted by the process of enclosure; but the names—Holtby (a Danish village in a small wood), Warthill (a lookout point) and Gate Helmsley (the road at Hemele's island) speak of its Early Medieval past. The English live among Dark Age landscapes in Dark Age villages. The road in question, when I came upon it, was Roman, and it heads not for the sea but directly up onto the Yorkshire Wolds. Before that it must cross the River Derwent at Stamford Bridge, where I took shelter from squally, biting rain and treated myself to a warming coffee and a bun. Stamford Bridge is one of those evocative locations that summons images of Britain's violent, epic history. Here, in the late summer of 1066, King Harold Godwinson of England fought the Norwegian army of Harald Hardrada, one of the legendary warrior lords of the Viking Age.

Hardrada had invaded in early September with a large force, perhaps as many as fifteen thousand men in hundreds of longships. He had for an ally Earl Tostig, exiled brother of Harold and former Lord of Northumberland. At Fulford, just south-east of York, they defeated an English force under two earls, Edwin and Morcar. York surrendered. Harald's army marched from their base camp at Ricall, close to the Ouse, where they had left the bulk of their fleet, towards the strategic crossing of the Derwent at Stamford Bridge, to receive hostages and prepare an administration to rule the North. King Harold arrived with his army the same day, 20 September 1066, marching through an undefended York and determined to meet Harald for a decisive encounter.

The Icelandic historian Snorri Sturluson has left us with a dramatic account of the first sighting between the two armies:

> …as they approached the town they saw a large force riding to meet them. They could see the cloud of dust raised by the horses' hooves, and below it the gleam of handsome shields and white coats of mail. King Harald halted his troops and summoned Earl Tostig, and asked him what this army could be… the closer the army came, the greater it grew, and their glittering weapons sparkled like a field of broken ice.[90]

When it came to preliminary parleys, the English king is said to have offered his Norwegian counterpart seven feet of English soil—or as much more as he was taller than other men. Despite a heroic defence of the bridge by a single berserker warrior, and tremendous aggression on both sides, the English held the field; Hardrada was cut down and the last Scandinavian invasion of England ended in victory for Harold. If it had not been for the little matter of his defeat by Duke William of Normandy three weeks later, the action at Stamford Bridge might still be hailed among the English the way that Bannockburn resonates north of the border.

The wooden bridge is long gone; its stone replacement is a

busy choke-point for trucks and cars. Today's Stamford Bridge is not somewhere—just a small place on the way to somewhere. I took a back road heading south-east, rising gradually out of the Vale, and then cut east through the small village of Full Sutton, whose maximum-security prison houses an A-list of celebrity nasties. The filthy day suited its grim outlines. It was not a place to dwell for long and, besides, I only had about three hours of daylight left. I quickened my pace, tracing a muddy path out of the back of the village, crossed the Roman road again and headed up the less confrontational valley of the Skirpen Beck, a tributary of the Derwent whose otherworldly gentility was a world away from razor wire, floodlights and slamming cell doors. Skirpen and Beck are both Old Norse names; in this case they indicate a seasonal stream; not surprising, since the Wolds are chalk uplands whose valleys, with few exceptions, are dry during the summer. East Yorkshire abounds in Scandinavian place names whose northern limit, more or less, is the valley of the River Tees; there are virtually none in modern Northumberland; few in Durham. No one is sure whether the Vikings thought conquest of the lands to the north a game not worth the candle or whether there were only enough of them to fill Yorkshire.

The next village on my route towards the Wolds, now just a shade north of east, was the equally Norse-sounding Bugthorpe. It was an easy climb—in fact, barely perceptible; gradually the land falls away to the north and to the beck, while to the south narrow wooded denes cut into the soft edge of the Wold plateau and a much steeper route up Garrowby Hill is taken by the uncompromising Roman road (I had a sudden memory of my awful old motorbike stalling halfway up it on a winter's day much like this). I stopped at Bugthorpe, contemplating its empty rectangular green where a man sat in his car making a phone call and two women passed by on horses; otherwise it might as well have been deserted. I had a bite of lunch on a churchyard bench, checked the map and then moved on, keeping to the south side of the valley. The stream changed its name to Bugthorpe Beck and then to Salamanca Beck (it sounds as though it has been renamed after a Peninsular War battle; there is also a Waterloo Beck near by: perhaps the local squire came back with trophies of fallen Frenchmen and tales to tell of daring deeds on the Continent: a latter-day warrior thegn?). Where it emerges from the head of the valley the spring is called Chalybeate, a name indicating the presence of iron-rich minerals.

At Kirby (Old Norse: 'village with a church') Underdale, tucked into the side of the valley and nestling on the edge of its own beck, I stopped for a look inside the church, which boasts a decorated Romanesque doorway at the west end. This is matched by a taller, simpler and more imposing round arched doorway to the bell tower, and by a solemn chancel arch. Inserted into an interior wall was a much-weathered relief carving of a naked warrior, horned and wielding a spear. The plaque hanging next to it suggests that it is the Roman god Mercury; but the same figure adorns Anglo-Saxon brooches (this time playing the part of Woden) and earlier carvings of native British gods such as Mars Belatucadros: the symbol of vital, virile warrior manhood has a common root in the European pantheons. This version was found in the Rectory garden in 1916, evidence perhaps of a local temple. It's not exactly a comfortable orthodox Catholic image; but it is surprising just how many of our medieval churches contain distinctly pagan motifs.

I made a steep ascent from Kirby Underdale up along a ridge that led to the Wold top at about seven hundred feet. Here I crossed another Roman road that once patrolled the west edge of this unique upland landscape harbouring its own distinct accent, attitudes and sense of identity. If I was oppressed by York and the flat, wet Vale, my spirits were lifted now, just as they were the first time I ever came up here, by a feeling that I was floating on a

magnificent vessel in the clouds, riding a green, undulating swell
of grasslands which, even in their state of winter undress, seduce
the eye. I was happy to be back; even so, the light was failing and
a dark cloud that had trailed me up the valley was just about to
unleash its meteorological dogs of war. Looking back across the
grainy sweep of the Vale, I fancied I could see the faint silhouette
of the Minster's twin towers, seventeen or so miles away, burned
against the retina of the sun's weak, solstice eye as it snuck off-
stage having cast no warmth on winter's bleak fields. I did not
hang around, but took a small road north-east towards Thixendale, dipping down out of the wind and knowing that the Cross
Keys pub, my refuge for the night, lay just over the hill.

Even a cursory glance at the Ordnance Survey map shows
that the Wolds are crowded with the remains of ancient cultures.
Thousands of tumuli lie apparently scattered like broadcast seed,
just as they do on the downs of Wessex. Chalk and limestone
uplands were cleared of their trees very early by Neolithic and
Bronze Age livestock farmers exploiting the bounties of transhumant summer pastures: this has been an open landscape for
five thousand years. The seeming randomness of the burials does
not stand up to scrutiny. The natives interred their dead under
mounds of soil and stone, often on the skyline from where the
ancestors could look down on them and intercede with the fates,
reinforce their ties to a mythological dreamscape past and remind
others whose land it was. Joining the dots of these blips on the map
reveals that they also functioned as markers, for they often lie on
the edges of territories that later became our parishes. They took
the natural lie of the land, its watersheds and ridges, and drew
onto it an idea of belonging and owning: they are proprietorial.
Many parts of the Wolds are also delineated by linear earthworks
which seem to indicate the boundaries of what archaeologists
have sometimes called ranches (evoking cowboys). Sometimes
these earthworks enclose ridges and headlands, sometimes they

run right across valleys and often along the contours of valley sides. Some are very substantial; others may have been little more than hedge banks, keeping cattle on or off seasonal pastures. Beneath them all are the invisible remains of many more complex land divisions, burials, the traces of forgotten settlements and enclosures and the routes taken by ancient peoples onto and through this naturally bounteous geological citadel.

Very early on the second morning, before light, I hit the trail again after a stout breakfast. I had not been to the Cross Keys at Thixendale for many and many a year; but the landlord had been here since my undergraduate days and knew some of the colleagues and friends with whom I had dug near by. I was interested to know how the village and its few businesses were surviving an age of austerity. Just, was the answer. One of the locals sitting at the bar the previous night was about to leave: forced to give up his driving licence because of failing eyesight, he was having to leave the community that had been his home for more than half a century. Most of those who came to live in the village these days worked in Malton, Driffield or York; almost none of them ever came to the pub; and the Post Office was now closed, replaced by a mobile service whose social functions could not possibly match those of the local store. The village seemed no longer to function as a community. Families with children lived here; but not grandparents, the guardians of continuity and identity. The ancestors are nowhere to be seen; their voices silent.

It was cold; I was the only soul about, just me, the sheep and the crows. As I climbed out of the dale and back onto the Wold top I was bathed in the heatless glow of an orange sunrise. The land glistened and shivered with me; a maize crop, unharvested and brittle, rattled in the breeze and from it came a squawk as pheasants broke cover. Bare hawthorn hedges and gorse bushes in improbable yellow bloom might have offered a little shelter had I been in their lee. Seasoned walkers, once they have gained height, try to keep it; but I had a rendezvous with the past.

Over the next ridge from Thixendale lies the deserted medieval village of Wharram Percy, whose name alone is enough to suggest that it once formed part of the lands of the Dukes of Northumberland. Britain's longest-running excavations took place here, from 1950 until 1990. It was first identified by Maurice Beresford, a pioneer in the study of deserted villages, and excavated under his and John Hurst's direction. When Philip Rahtz arrived in York to become its first Professor of Archaeology, Wharram seemed a natural place to take his students for their excavation training; so we spent two summers here, tackling what became known as the North Manor. There was nothing quite like Wharram: more than a hundred and thirty people lived here during those summers, camping in the empty fields of the old village with the Victorian cottages down in the hollow acting as site offices and canteen. It was the sort of transient community, annually reassembled, that must have been familiar to the ancient pastoralists, bringing tribute to their lords at Beltane or Midsummer, reviving and forging relationships, feasting and coupling.

Oddly, I had never seen the place deserted: it now seemed creepy, with the roofless skeleton of the church poking up from the hollow of Deep Dale, the empty cottages beyond and bare flanks of the valley sides giving on to tidy grass humps and bumps that tell a story of double desertion: once by its medieval farmers and lords; and then, half a millennium later, by its archaeologists. My head buzzed with a score of half-remembered conversations and incidents (feasting; coupling). More nostalgia; more ancestors; more giants. Beresford, Hurst and Rahtz have all passed away. There is no dinner bell to sound, or scrape of trowel, only wind and birdcall. Villages need people, not ghosts. I hoped I was not looking at Thixendale's future. I had to orient myself for a few minutes before I was able to identify the site of 'our trench'. I could not stop here, but walked along the lane that is Wharram's only access to the outside world, and climbed back up onto the Wold top.

At North Grimston I went into the church to have a look at the font. Grimston is a place name for academics: formed by a Scandinavian personal name and an Anglo-Saxon suffix, it is the type-name for a large group of settlements called the Grimston hybrids (it sounds like an alien plant dreamed up by John Wyndham), which seem to tell of a Norse warrior elite buying or marrying or arrogating their way into the English squirearchy of the ninth century, perhaps by means of marriage to the lord's daughter (or widow). When people think of immigration they often think in genetic terms: a functioning, breeding family moving into new territory and producing offspring representing 100 per cent immigrant genes, perhaps diluted in the next generation. But a man or woman arriving and breeding with a native produces offspring carrying only 50 per cent immigrant genes to the next generation, genes likely to be diluted again and again. Our Grims will be represented by only half of their children's DNA and since we expect that warrior elite to be, by its very nature, small in numbers, the Norse genes would get swallowed up after only a few generations (although Grim might, admittedly, be sowing his oats more widely). (And see Postscript: Who are the British?—pages 423–6) More important for archaeologists and societies is whether the incomer assimilates or imposes their culture. One man's invasion and rapine is another's commercial and domestic opportunity in a new setting. But the Norse seem to have embraced the culture, including Christianity, of their adopted lands. The names that survive in the English landscape which seem to echo successive waves of immigration may exaggerate their genetic and cultural impact.

The font at North Grimston is a marvel of Early Medieval sculpture. Its date is not agreed by scholars; it could have been carved just after, or before, the Norman Conquest. It depicts

NORTH GRIMSTON FONT

Christ and his disciples at the Last Supper; a continuous frieze is completed by a crucifixion scene and a portrayal of an indulgent bishop. It is wonderfully affecting and a reminder, perhaps, of vernacular sensibilities underlying and reinforcing the Gospel message. The top of the font is a ropework cable twist; beneath that, the *Mona Lisa* smiling heads of the disciples line up in military rank, seated at the eponymous meal, behind a table which bears bowls, fish and round loaves with crosses incised into them. Most disciples hold a knife; several hands clasp what look like books to their breasts; their tiny feet poke out from beneath skirts like chair legs, seeming to prop up the massive stone cylinder. Seated slightly apart, Christ, a blazing solar halo behind him, holds his hands in an offertory gesture; his skirts look like the plumage of a giant raptor; his feet rest on the stretcher of a stool. Next to him is carved in a separate panel the figure of a bishop; perhaps St Nicholas, to whom the church is dedicated. In the crucifixion scene he is held up, like some tragic skeletal Punch, by Joseph of Arimathea and Nicodemus, head hanging lifeless on shoulder; again, the blaze of heavenly glory behind him. The apparent crudeness of the carving reinforces the starkness of the message and the boldness of the execution. I wanted to take it away with me. Pevsner called it 'mighty and barbaric'. Its rustic sensibility is enhanced by the presence of a Victorian single-furrow plough which sits behind it against the wall. Outside, the walls bear carvings—a pair of beasts cavorting; and a *Sheela na gig*, one of those crude, vulva-displaying depictions of female fertility and lust that adorn Norman churches in various parts of Britain but which do not seem to have iconographic roots any further back.

Tempting as it was to traverse the ocean of the high Wolds which lay to the east, my route could do no more than skirt them. Two miles north of Grimston I passed through Settrington, which marks more or less the north-west corner of the massif, and came down off the chalk. From here the view opens out onto

Malton and the Vale of Pickering, with Ryedale beyond and the Howardian Hills encroaching from the west. Somewhere near here, I believe, is the site of the Deiran kings' summer palace, their equivalent of Yeavering in Bernicia. Bede sites Edwin's hall, the location of the attempted assassination of Easter 626, standing by the River Derwent, whose line I could trace below me. The Derwent ought to flow towards the coast; but it actually rises at the far east end of the Vale of Pickering, close to the sea, and flows inland, fed by springs from the North York Moors and the Wolds, until it joins the Ouse south-east of Selby and flows thence into the Humber, Deira's and Northumbria's southern border. Deira is named from the Derwent: perhaps the 'land of the river of oak trees', or the 'land of the waters'; there is no agreement among experts. Either way, the Derwent, its vale and the Wolds form the core of the southern Northumbrian kingdom, the Deirans' ancestral homelands. Very early in the post-Roman period, the Wolds hosted a distinct culture reflected in large cremation cemeteries whose bespoke black decorated urns bear overtly Germanic cultural affiliations. The Anglians of Deira are also known to have reused ancient barrows to inter some of their elite, tapping into an idea of belonging and memorial that seems to appropriate, or reinvent, ties to the prehistoric ancestors, the Giants of the Early Medieval imagination.

Malton is a curiosity: to the south and east of the river it is called Norton; across the river it has two parts: Malton and Old Malton. Old-fashioned butchers and ironmongers, market pubs and rundown townhouses give it a sense of having been somehow left behind, although its position at the junction of Ryedale and the Vale of Pickering astride the A64, its status as a livestock market and its quaintness ought to ensure that it thrives. England has lost many villages over the centuries; it has lost few settlements as large as this. Malton will endure. I took my lunch sitting on the damp ramparts of *Derventio*, the Roman fort planted here in the late AD 60s to control this vital landscape pivot, to subdue the *Parisi* of the Wolds and the *Brigantes* of the Pennines. There is a strong temptation to suggest that, just as I had seen at Wroxeter and the Wrekin, there may be more than coincidental association between Roman fort and later ancestral seat. Was Edwin's palace, wherever it lay, a successor to the Roman fort as a seat of military power and patronage? Was the fort itself sited near some earlier, as yet undiscovered stronghold of the Iron Age tribes? There are no hill forts, as we traditionally recognise them, near by; but then, Yeavering only revealed itself by chance and aerial photography.

Edwin's Christian kingdom did not long survive his conversion and the grudging assent of Deiran and Bernician *gesiths*.[91] He was defeated and killed in battle in 632 or 633 by a combined army under Kings Penda of Mercia and Cadwallon of Gwynedd, whom Edwin had unwisely allowed to survive exile on the island of Priestholm off Anglesey (see page 249). Edwin's legacy was not, in the end, to bequeath a Christian state in the north: such were the Dark Age fates. But he had consolidated and reinforced Æthelfrith's power and maintained Northumbrian dominance as the most powerful warrior kingdom in the island; his ambition had briefly led to the revival of an idea of Roman imperium; and Bede cites as perhaps his greatest achievement the striking image that 'there was so great a peace in Britain, wherever the dominion of King Edwin reached, that, as the proverb still runs, a woman with a newborn child could walk throughout the island from sea to sea and take no harm'.[92] The king, we are told, even set up posts with bronze drinking vessels at springs along his highways (the Roman roads?) so that travellers might be refreshed; and no one had ever stolen one of these vessels. This was not just imperial hubris; it was an idea, apparently novel, of the king's peace. The modern traveller could do with some such conveniences: public drinking fountains, or at least a safe means of negotiating busy A-roads.

How far can we believe Bede's portrayal of Edwin as a force so powerful that he could impose domestic peace while at the same time conjuring an image of the horned, spear-wielding embodiment of tribal virility and martial brilliance? Eight miles east of Malton lies the tiny village of West Heslerton, where a paradoxically huge campaign of excavation has revealed the most complete example yet found of a settlement contemporary with the Golden Age of Northumbrian kings. Dominic Powlesland has been excavating and surveying this part of the Vale of Pickering since my time as an undergraduate. In those days Dominic was living an attractive, chaotic hippyish lifestyle in a house in the middle of the vale whose origins lay in a medieval abbey (there was a gothic arch in one of the bedrooms). His idea was that landscapes must be understood on the grand scale; when he excavated he had machines strip topsoil by the hectare; his geophysics team maps by the square mile. He was a pioneer of computerised on-site recording (I remember the night when he inherited his first computer from his father: an ancient Wang that he learned to programme from scratch). It was a colourful, exciting time; Dominic hardly ever seemed to sleep.

The Anglian village at West Heslerton is the most fully understood settlement of the period. Others of the same era—Mucking in Essex, West Stow in Suffolk, Sutton Courtenay in Oxfordshire—have only been partially recovered. Most Early Medieval settlements are inaccessible to archaeologists: they lie beneath contemporary towns and villages, a sign of the continuity our landscape has enjoyed for the last fifteen hundred years. Philip Rahtz used to say that nothing much has changed; the peasants pay their taxes and it doesn't much matter to whom they pay them.

If the traditional Bedan story of the coming of the English is to be believed, then West Heslerton ought to be a new settlement of the fifth century, contemporary with the pagan burials of incomers on the high Wolds. But that is not the case. The site was occupied in the late Roman period when a shrine was constructed around a spring that emerges from the north scarp of the Wolds along a stratum of clay. Earlier Roman and Iron Age habitation has been found by geophysicists in a strip of so-called ladder settlements that runs parallel with the north edge of the Wolds, but lower down in the Vale, closer to the rising water table. It was a densely settled landscape. The axes of many of the territorial boundaries here show that each community benefited from a strip of land extending from the river up through water meadows to arable fields to pasture, to the transhumant summer grasslands of the Wold top. As the water-table rose, settlements withdrew to slightly higher, drier ground. A string of villages like West Heslerton grew up on this line; the shrine perhaps reflects the preoccupations of a people whose water meadows had become too watery. The idea that the water of life flowed from the hills where the ancestors lived and died must have given many springs a sense of the sacred. From the Roman shrine, where there were bread ovens and scatters of food rubbish, including oysters—where there are pilgrims there is always trade—the settlement expanded into what we would recognise as a true village: houses, craft and industrial areas, pens for livestock; butcheries; perhaps even orchards, features that would be familiar if not to today's commuter villagers then to Thomas Hardy's *Woodlanders*.

Focus was maintained on the shrine; but despite the advent of Christianity West Heslerton survived until the ninth century—a half millennium of continuity. And it was never defended; there was no rampart or wall, no sign that the village was ever attacked or destroyed by fire. Micro-analysis of a staggering quantity of material retrieved from the excavations—still to be seen in final published form—has allowed specialists to look at very detailed levels of domestic life in an age which could not, here at any rate, be called dark. The complexities of animal husbandry are revealed in the species raised (sheep, pigs, cattle, goats) and in their management; wild food is found: fish and birds; there are beaver, deer and whale bones. It is tempting to match these finds with the evidence of contemporary food renders, of which the best source is the Laws of King Ine, which required a ten-hide estate to provide annually 10 cow hides, 10 vats of honey, 300 loaves, 12 ambers of ale and 30 of clear ale; 2 cows, 10 geese, 20 hens, 10 cheeses, an amber of butter, 5 salmon, 20 pounds of fodder and 100 eels.[93] Weaving was a principal activity; there were workshops where tools and devices were forged and maintained. Barley was malted for beer and, perhaps, winter fodder. A mill probably stood on the banks of the stream channel fed by the spring: a case of baking one's cake and eating it. Glass, pottery and lava querns from Europe are among the imported material found here. Most striking is the evidence of organisation, collective action and the hand of a planner—a lord who, living away from the village in a grand hall, exercised management of his dependent farmers and craftspeople. Here is a stable, organised social and economic landscape, successful by any standards, which shows that through political turmoil, famine and plague, ordinary indigenous people survived the Early Medieval period doing what people do: getting on with life.

Heslerton is the 'place of the hazel'; a reference, perhaps, to hurdle fences in the village which may have been its distinguishing characteristic for neighbours and visitors. A little to the east, the village of Sherburn has revealed evidence that suggests it was a major estate centre on this side of the Vale. The cemetery which belongs to West Heslerton has also been excavated— another unique feature of the project. Some at least of the individuals interred here seem to have come from outside the immediate locality—possibly Germanic or Scandinavian Europe, but not inconceivably western Britain—but if real cultural identity is defined by behaviour, they seem to have merged seamlessly into the native population. The proliferation of sunken-floored buildings—known as *grubenhäuser* or grub huts, they were once seen as a marker for Germanic peasant immigrants—is now thought to be an adaptation to a new sort of estate management. During the Roman period taxation seems to have been direct; but in the centuries of the Early Medieval period, of barn-conversions like those at Birdoswald and Wroxeter, renders such as ale, grain, dried meat and so on might have had to be stored on site before being taken to the *vill* or estate-centre at specified seasons. The so-called grub huts are larders or miniature barns; and so mature and effective was the economic and social model of the settlement that it was not forced to reinvent itself periodically. It worked and continued to work. That is a remarkable record of social and economic success and archaeologists are being forced to recognise that West Heslerton may be the norm for the Dark Ages, not the exception.

Old Heslerton is buried beneath hillwash and drifting wind-blown sand; today the village is a more modest affair. A church and pub, a small school and the grand house of the inheritors of its lordship survive. The former railway station house survives too; but trains pass it by at speed. The boundaries of the parish, formed as a territorial unit in the late Bronze Age and still partially traceable on the ground, are a legacy of the Giants and a continuous line of ancestors stretching back across the millennia.

My route lay to the west. From Malton I struck out through the Vale's bleak carrs,[94] crossing the River Rye before cutting across country along trackways that followed a co-axial mesh of drainage ditches and long lines of poplars. At Kirby Misperton ('church village by the medlar tree'), more or less at the dead centre of the Vale, I paused to check my map. The village is on a slight rise, a glacial moraine that protects it from inundation, and it may have been an Early Medieval estate centre or the site of a monastery, protected on all sides by marshes. The sense, in the fading afternoon light of a milky, flat day, that giants had been here before me was heightened when I looked south-west towards a dying sun and saw the outline of the Flamingoland theme park rides silhouetted against the purpling sky, skeletal and other-worldly. A last few kilometres of trudging along flat, straight, empty tarmac roads brought me to the edge of Pickering where I saw a second reverential depiction of St Nicholas in one day: a semi-detached house ablaze with Christmas lights, Santas, snow-men and reindeer.

An idea that the Vale of Pickering was the core of the Deiran homelands seems at first to be reinforced by its resemblance to the Magh Tóchuir of North Inishowen (see page 304). The remains of prehistoric land management look down on three sides. At its northern and western edges, just above the water margins, lay early Christian centres whose siting and deployment reveal the economic and social organisation of the landscape just as surely as West Heslerton does. Two years after Edwin was slain at Hat-field in what is now South Yorkshire, the Bernician exile Oswald reclaimed the Northumbrian kingdom in his father Æthelfrith's stead. Baptised and perhaps educated on Iona, he founded the monastery on Lindisfarne, completed Paulinus's church at York, and instituted an English Christian state which has survived ever since. His reign was short; his legacy lasting. After his death in 642 at Oswestry (see page 75) his brother Oswiu took up the reins of Christian kingship in imitation of the Irish church; but his poli-tics were blended with those of his wife, Edwin's prodigal daugh-ter Eanflæd, who had been brought up in exile at the Frankish court. A remarkable woman, her fingerprints are all over Oswiu's domestic policies, ensuring that they were informed by a more than parochial interest in missionary priests. Their combined strategy had a distinctly European flavour.

Oswiu maintained his family's patronage of the Lindisfarne community but, having married a Deiran, he recognised the need for a hearts-and-minds diplomatic initiative. Besides, his queen had her own lines of patronage. When a collateral member of her family, Oswine, sub-king of Deira, rebelled against the king and was then betrayed and murdered by one of Oswiu's thegns, Eanflæd persuaded her husband to found a monastery close to the site of the murder in expiation, and to appoint as its first abbot her kinsman Trumhere. Reading between the lines, we can see this as an attempt to avoid an otherwise inevitable blood-feud. There are two candidates for the site of the monastery, which Bede names as Gilling: Gilling West, near Scotch Corner, is a plausible option; but it might alternatively have lain on the very western edge of the Vale of Pickering at East Gilling, which lies on the line of a Roman road called the Street that runs up Ryedale from Old Malton.

In later years, when Oswiu was severely pressed by the predations of Penda of Mercia and was forced to give up an incalculable treasure to the Mercian king to ward off further invasions (the episode is a historical possibility for the origin of the Staffordshire hoard),[95] Oswiu promised his God that should he be victorious in battle he would give his daughter Ælfflæd and twelve estates to the church, six of which would be donated from lands in Bernicia, six in Deira; they were to be of ten hides (or family farms) each: modest in size, if one remembers the ten-hide render cited in Ine's Laws. After Oswiu's dramatic and decisive victory over Penda and his allies at the Battle of the Winwæd in 655, he duly delivered. The archaeologist Ian Wood has suggested that several of the Deiran monasteries can be identified around the Vale of Pickering: at Hovingham (which also lies along the Street) and Stonegrave, perhaps at Kirkdale, Coxwold and Crayke. In all of these places there is evidence for an early foundation.

The politics are suggestive: a Bernician king alienating core Deiran lands from potential rivals to his overlordship; the planting of a monastic colony to match those north of the Tyne and to give opportunities for non-martial careers among the Deiran royal family; the beginnings of a capital landholding system and an idea of a literate elite. This is not mere largesse: it is the politics of a rational attempt to construct a state. It must be read alongside the evidence from West Heslerton of a thriving rural population whose graft and economic success were capable of supporting the elite (warrior or monk) from their surplus. Above all, and taken with the Early Medieval penchant for interring aristocratic bodies in prehistoric burial mounds (and some of these overlook Ryedale and its Roman road), it suggests a collective sensibility to the ancestors and their landscape, an acknowledgement that they still felt the Giants watching them from the heights of the Moors and Wolds: sitting in judgement.

If the Dark Ages began at Birdoswald, their mutation into a new era can be traced here. But the Magh Tóchuir analogy cannot be taken too far. Oswiu was no fool: there is no evidence that he gave away, or allowed to be given away, any royal estates in the Wolds or along the southern edge of the Vale, the older territories of the Deiran homeland. That seems to have remained a secular, ancestrally potent landscape.

In any case, Oswiu's six new monastic estates were not the first footprints of this new venture. His nephew, Oswald's son Œthelwald, whom he had favoured with an appointment as Deiran sub-king and who repaid him with rebellion during the Penda campaigns, founded a monastery at Lastingham under the rule of Cedd, former bishop of East Anglia and one of four priestly brothers of Northumbrian stock. Lastingham lay:

> amid some steep and remote hills which seemed better
> suited for the haunts of robbers and the dens of wild beasts
> than for human habitation.[96]

When I walked into Lastingham village, on the southern edge of the North York Moors, during the morning of my third day, I

had already passed a party of tweed-clad hunters, with their Lab-
radors, out pheasant shooting. These are no longer the haunts
of robbers or very wild beasts: this is rich farming country. The
splendid, basilica-like church at Lastingham sits on a knoll overlooking a huddle of elegant houses at the centre of the village.
The springs that rise here, now regarded as holy wells, might
have been a focus for animist veneration and divination long
before Cedd, who is said to have had to cleanse the place from the
'stain of former crimes'. Cedd spent his last years there, dying
in an outbreak of the plague against whose virulence even Lastingham's celebrated remoteness was not proof. The first church
built here was wooden, in the Irish tradition. It was later replaced
by a stone church which may not have survived the depredations
of the ninth-century Viking invasions. It was not refounded until
the eleventh century, when the crypt that survives was constructed as a shrine to venerate its first abbot. I stood before the
altar and was tempted to ask the verger about the symbolic irony
of having a decorated Christmas tree in there (all very pagan),
but bit my lip and instead descended to the crypt. It is every
bit as evocative of the seventh century as if it had been built in
the years after Wilfrid, Cedd's successor, constructed his stone
crypts at Hexham and Ripon. It is part mausoleum, part chapel
with a foot in the pagan underworld and another in the church
of the Holy Sepulchre in Rome. The low lighting and ceiling, the
Romanesque sweep of the vaults and round-arched windows are
a world and more away from the Gothic elaborations upstairs.

In Œthelwald's donation one can trace the origins of a competitive element in monastic foundations, the starting gun for
several generations of entrepreneurial patrons. Monasteries
attracted wealth, particularly if they possessed saintly or royal
relics. Senior appointments tended to be kept within discrete
family lines. The community, in recognising the founding gift,
supported and legitimised that patron and his or her descendants

(if they continued to favour that church with gifts of land, relics and other treasure). Oswiu's founding of no fewer than six monasteries in one fell swoop might be seen as a competitive Bernician response to the patronage of sub-kings and other great lords of Deira.

The transition from a psychological landscape of animism, wooden idols, auguries, fragile temporal kingdoms and customary laws into the rational, state-based, stone-built book-keeping world of Bede's day could not be recorded more emphatically than here. A hundred years after Edwin's conversion, King Wihtred of Kent made it explicit, enshrining the basic guiding principles of medieval Europe in his first two decrees:

1. The church [is to be] free from taxation
1.1 And the king is to be prayed for[97]

From Lastingham a path led directly up onto the moors, a horizon-stretching, heather-bound, treeless plateau deeply incised by valleys. Its southern edge lies on limestone, but from here upwards the massif is sandstone. There is no shelter: cold as it was, I was lucky to be crossing on such a pure sparkling day of blue sky, green and purple moor and dry, sandy path. I was alone, an icy wind pressing me on. Cedd's monks must have grazed their sheep up here and taken their hives out into the flowering purple of its summer blossom. In winter they might have made this same crossing, on the way to Whitby, very much the senior house of the Deiran kingdom. With wolves, lynx and bears still roaming the wastes, it must have been a hazardous undertaking. Here and there lie the remains of more ancient burials and standing stones, reminders of earlier generations of pastoralists, and markers for travellers in an otherwise featureless upland plain.

At Rosedale Abbey (a Cistercian priory once stood here; virtually nothing remains of it) I came off the moor, hoping that the village store might sell me a pasty, or one of its cafés provide a life-giving cup of tea. But all was shut, even on a Saturday. I perched on a bench munching oatcakes and cheese and then, too cold to sit still, was on my way again, up the other side of the dale and onto Rosedale Moor at nearly fifteen hundred feet. Here, old iron workings, standing stones and weather-worn crosses jostle for attention at crossroads or the heads of valleys. As the sun crept towards the horizon I came down into Danby Dale and out of the wind.

Danby Dale is a curiosity. Bronze Age cairns look down on it like a frown. Not much more than three miles long, it runs directly north from the moors and opens onto the west–east-running Eskdale at Castleton. The village which gives the dale its name lies a couple of miles east of that. At the head of the dale a hamlet called Botton thrives improbably, cut off from the outside world. There is a sawmill here, an active school and a strong sense of communal pride in the place. It boasts a self-supporting community of vulnerable adults and their carers, a fragmentary survival of what seems like a lost sense of belonging.

What strikes the archaeologist, looking at a map, is the number of farms strung out on both sides, at identical heights, two thirds of the way up from the beck and lying just below a fringe of stone-walled meadows that have been carved out of the rough hillside where the valley sides become too steep to cultivate. The farms are linked, like a festoon of lights, by a single continuous track and they are spaced as regularly as if they had been planned. Each farm seems to own a strip of fields either side of the house, running up from the beck to the scarp so that each has a section of beck-side meadow, gently sloping arable fields and then pastures (a Vale of Pickering in miniature). Given the name of the place, which means 'valley of the village of the Danes', I am tempted to suggest that here is evidence of the *landnam* parcelling out of defeated territories by the Viking warrior King Halfdan among the veterans of his invasion army of the 860s. In 875, according to the *Anglo-Saxon Chronicle*, Halfdan 'shared out the lands of the Northumbrians and they were engaged in ploughing and making a living for themselves'. As if to add circumstance to my nice theory, at the back of the otherwise unprepossessing church that stands at the centre of the dale are two Anglo-Saxon stone columns, half-hidden behind later walls. It was now too dark for me to nose around the churchyard for Scandinavian surnames like Anderson or Larson; I must come back again, perhaps to get a closer look at the farmhouses and ask the locals if they know anything of its early history. For now I had my mind set on a hot shower and food in Castleton.

On midwinter's day I set off long before dawn on the last leg of my journey to Whitby. In a swallowing, hungry darkness I followed the edge of the high ground along the north side of Eskdale, looking across at the gaping mouths of valleys which bite, one after the other, deep into the high moors: Danby Dale; Fryup Dale; Glaisdale. Some time after nine it looked as though the sun might rise over the distant coast: the sky was a rippled purple, iridescent and supernatural. But that was the most I saw of it. The day never got much lighter.

Once I dipped down to cross a small beck by a footbridge, and the path led up through hazel coppice and oakwood before dodging around a farm. At Egton I hoped I would find somewhere open for breakfast; or at least a shop. But there was only a pub, and no signs of life. I took a small lane that climbed back to the edge of the moor, whose sheep must by now have been brought down onto lower, more sheltered ground for the winter. The odd burial mound caught my eye, a pimple against the purple-grey skyline. Far to the south-east, monstrously disproportioned, an immense concrete monument to Cold War paranoia, a scaled-up tumulus from the nuclear era, beat the landscape into submission on Fylingdales Moor. At Aislaby I came down to the banks of the

River Esk, and followed the main road that I knew must lead to Whitby, and the sea.

Whitby (Old Norse: 'White settlement'), Bede's *Sinus fari* ('Bay of the Lighthouse') and, most historians agree, the *Streanæshalch* of the famous synod of 664.[98] After his defeat of Penda, his only serious external rival, in 655, King Oswiu increasingly spent his political capital on extending the influence of the church and exploring its potential as an instrument of state. He sponsored alliances with Mercian royalty (a wedding and conversion ceremony at Newburn). He maintained Ionan influence at the community of Lindisfarne. At times he found himself outflanked by Deiran subkings, his cousin Oswine and his nephew Œthelwald both attempting rebellion. His son Alhfrith (by his first queen, Rheged-born Rieinmelth) set up a rival seat of ecclesiastical power at Ripon under the arch-entrepreneur Wilfrid. Wilfrid had been to Rome, was a zealous proselytiser on behalf of the orthodox and an enemy of both the British church and of Iona and its schismatic practices. It does not take the refined sensibilities of a political historian to appreciate that not only were these Deiran princes potential threats to Oswiu's idea of a unified Northumbria; they were threats to the future prospects of his son by Eanflæd: Ecgfrith. If Oswiu thought he could keep all the interested parties happy by allowing collateral members of the family to experience vice-regal power in Deira, he was being naïve; his queen was under no such illusion. Alhfrith was a problem requiring a solution.

The crisis came in 664 when the death of the Archbishop of Canterbury, Deusdedit (the first native-born holder of that office) forced Oswiu's hand. Bede tells us that the royal household had fallen out over their alternative celebrations of Easter. More prosaically, in order to have influence, as overlord of the English kingdoms, on the Pope's next metropolitan appointee, Oswiu must consider accepting papal and Roman authority. Wilfrid had

WHITBY ABBEY

succeeded in nurturing Romanist ideas in Alhfrith and might have played on the queen's orthodox upbringing to further pressurise the king. If Alhfrith were to make a military move, Deira and Bernicia must split, forcing a rift at the heart of Oswiu's new state project, not to mention in the royal bedchamber.

Oswiu called a synod to Whitby, whose abbess, Hild, is an outstanding figure of the age. This was a matter of state; and the state would decide in conference. A great-niece of Edwin and kinswoman of the queen, Hild hosted the synod. Her sympathies were Irish, like the king's and those of the abbot-bishops of Lindisfarne. On the Roman side, Wilfrid acted as spokesman (and agent provocateur) for the senior orthodox bishop, the Frankish Agilbert—and for his royal sponsor, Alhfrith. One of the most impressive aspects of the synod is its administration: if one thinks of the complexities of organising, hosting and feeding conference delegates today one's head spins. Whitby must have been planned ahead; extraordinary renders must have been forced on surrounding estates; envoys must have been sent by land and sea; temporary accommodation must have been constructed.

Oswiu's consummate outflanking of his opponents by agreeing that the English church must accept orthodoxy was a masterstroke of political subtlety that, perhaps more than any other contemporary development, shows the maturity and breadth of vision that the Oswiu/Eanflæd marriage had produced just a generation after the apostasies of the first quarter of the seventh century. Alhfrith was never heard of again (there is said to have been a fatal battle near Pickering, but Bede is silent). Eanflæd's son, the ill-fated Ecgfrith, who would come to grief in Pictland, eventually succeeded to the kingship. Wilfrid continued to be a thorn in the royal side for another forty years. But the English kingdoms were united in their orthodoxy and the Pope's eventual appointee to Canterbury, Theodore, proved to be a gifted reformer, administrator and educator who succeeded in resolving dangerous conflicts between the Christian English kingdoms. Only the Irish party lost out: many disillusioned monks returned to their native land. Even so the influence of Irish and Columban Christian culture did not end: it pervaded Northumbria's Golden Age and invigorated the conversion of northern Europe during the eighth century. In 670/1 King Oswiu was the first of his line to die in his own bed.

I had booked a room in a noisy town-centre pub, where Sarah was to join me for the evening. As the shortest day of the year merged imperceptibly with the longest night, I sat in the bar and witnessed a fight between two football fans infuriated by a goal they had just seen on the big screen TV from a local derby fifty miles away. That evening Sarah and I walked up through Whitby's narrow, Christmassy streets to the abbey on the headland, the sea a dark stain in the east and the lights of the town playing on the sheltered waters of its harbour; behind us the jagged ruinous outline of the successor to Hild's abbey, now a moody gothic ruin and mecca for Dracula fans mostly unaware of an earlier, dramatic catharsis between opposing moral forces played for the highest stakes.

Christmas 2014. Seamus O'Kane's bodhrán arrives and gets its first run-out at a gig. It is sensational. In the news is the most exotic delivery in history: a ratchet spanner is emailed from Earth to the International Space Station where it materialises in a 3D printer. Another import: the first Ebola case arrives in Britain from Sierra Leone. Some clever engineers are about to start work on a tidal barrage in Swansea Bay, reinventing seventh-century technology. Elsewhere, the winter mood is reflected in strife and disaster: tensions in eastern Ukraine and a plummeting oil price bring the prospect of civil war in that country and instability in Russia; millions of Syrian refugees face a winter in temporary camps; migrants trying to cross from Africa to Europe are abandoned at sea by their ship's crew; an Indonesian AirAsia flight from Surabaya crashes off Borneo, killing everyone on board; a ferry sinks—more deaths in the Adriatic Sea; soup kitchens and food banks ply their trade on the streets of Britain and hospitals overflow.

Ann. MMXIV Dies tenebrosa sicut nox.

A day as dark as night.

Postscript *Who are the British?*

As I was writing the last few pages of this story, my email inbox lit up with half a dozen messages: had I seen a new study, published in the science journal *Nature*, giving the results of the most comprehensive study yet of Britain's genetic geography? I hadn't, but I got hold of it the same day. And in an election year when immigration is a hot topic and there is much talk of 'native' and 'foreigner', it makes salutary reading.[99]

First, the method. More than two thousand people across Britain, all of whose grandparents were born within fifty miles of each other, contributed DNA to the study. The idea was to ensure that a genetic snapshot of the most stable elements of the population, taking us back to the late nineteenth century, was obtained. Two thousand samples make for a substantial genetic cross-section. They enabled the researchers to create a detailed map of genetic inheritance which could be compared with groups from similar studies across Europe. If Romans (that is to say natives of ancient Italy), Anglo-Saxons, Vikings or Normans invaded or immigrated in significant numbers, they would be spotted.

It has been known for some time that the vast bulk of the British population is ultimately descended from a relatively tiny number of Mesolithic hunter-gatherers who arrived some few thousand years after the end of the last Ice Age while Britain was still umbilically attached to Continental Europe. Migrations, particularly from north-west Europe, have periodically supplemented that genetic base. For the purposes of those interested in the first millennium, the new evidence complements rather than contradicts the view that a 'native' population of Celtic language-speaking Britons underwent significant but not wholesale change in the middle of the millennium. What is wholly new is an appreciation of just how stable and regionally discrete our genetic make-up is.

Let's take the potential genetic infiltrators one by one. Romans: none to speak of; they came, they saw, they made their money and went home, by and large. Not many soldiers spread their seed sufficiently broadly to affect the genes of the Britons. Not, that is, unless those soldiers came from the northern part of Germany which, as I have suggested, some may have done. Next: Angles and Saxons. The bulk of central and southern England is (or was in the late nineteenth century) made up of a single, homogenous, group. Somewhere between 10 and 40 per cent of their genes were contributed by natives of those areas traditionally associated with Anglo-Saxons: the base of the Jutland peninsula and northern Saxony; perhaps Frisia too. Now, somewhere between 10 and 40 per cent is a big difference, so it's worth thinking about those numbers. If the fifth-century population of the Anglo-Saxon kingdoms was in the region of a million, then a, say, 25 per cent genetic footprint from Anglo-Saxon immigrants or invaders would require there to have been something in the region of three hundred thousand of them. Wow! For the period that is a staggering number. The place-name specialists will nod their heads at that: look at England's names and her language—we talk English, not Welsh or Gaelic; but many archaeologists will find it hard to reconcile with the evidence they excavate.

There are ways through this scenario: a much smaller

pre-existing population in central and southern England; a smaller number of exceedingly randy and procreative males arriving; a much longer period of migration on a smaller scale; or an existing native population that already had lots of Germanic genes. Well, if we take the migration period to last a hundred years (most archaeologists would accept that as a likelihood), we are talking a thousand immigrants a year for a century. That still seems a lot. In context, it means that by about AD 600 every person in central and southern England had, on average, one grandparent of Germanic origin. There are are other possibilities, including the potential, reflected in some Continental accounts, of many 'Anglo-Saxons' migrating back to their supposed homelands: it's a complicated business, a genetic cat's cradle.

Leaving the problematic Anglo-Saxons for the moment, let's look at the pesky Vikings. Not guilty: there is very little Danish or Swedish influx at the right period for the Viking armies to have contributed much to our genes. Maybe Viking veterans were only into mature Anglo-Saxon women? In Orkney it was rather different: in the northern isles there is a very strong Norwegian component. Then there are the Normans. But no, we do not get any significant genetic influx from them either; they disdained large-scale coupling with the Anglo-Saxons whose aristocratic families had, in any case, largely been destroyed by civil war and conquest; that confirms what we already thought.

Perhaps the real highlight of this new study is the very striking regionality of the genetic groupings. The native British of Cornwall and Devon, for example, are distinct not just from the rest of Britain, but from each other. North and South Wales are also distinct from each other and from other Britons, as are the people of the Welsh Marches. The same goes for parts of Scotland; for Cumbria and Northumbria (where there are several distinct tightly clustered groups). There was no great Celtic tribe of Britain. The distinct regions that one experiences travelling through these landscapes are not just cultural; they go back to very ancient and very stable bloodlines.

So, what to make of those Germanic immigrants? Even if 25 per cent of English genes are Germanic, we would still like to know the historical detail. Are we talking two hundred families (two adults, three children) arriving every year for ten decades? That seems reasonable. Perhaps small tribal groups, like the *Hrothingas* of Essex, arrived in the three keels of Hengest and Horsa cited the Kentish Chronicle, only a hundred at a time. Or are we talking a thousand single male warriors a year, each of whom mated with three native women? Did these Saxon gene-bearers all arrive at the coast, working their way inland (via rivers like the Roding or the Ouse)? Did their genes then diffuse evenly or were there pockets, like East Yorkshire, Essex, Suffolk, where they turned up in much greater numbers and then slowly spread so that the whole of England is an eventual admixture? Does the archaeology of burials and buildings, language and art have anything more to say on the matter? Genetic identity is not the same thing as cultural affiliation or identity: these, as my travels through the past and present have shown, are much more subtly negotiated. Geneticists, archaeologists and historians will continue their arguments; we work our way slowly towards a truth that we can all live with. The past gets more interesting; never less complex.

Appendix One: Journey distances

Birdoswald–Jarrow	*November 2013–March 2015*	83 miles on foot; 0.5 miles by ferry
Rothesay–Kilmartin	*October 2013*	60 miles on foot; a short taxi ride; 5 miles on two ferries; 9 miles on a bus; 2 miles by car
Telford–Wrexham	*March 2014*	98 miles on foot
Falmouth–Mallaig	*April 2014*	555 nautical miles by boat
London–Sutton Hoo	*June 2014*	107 miles on foot; 2.5 miles on three ferries; 5 miles by bus
Wareham–Yatton	*July 2014*	96 miles on foot
Anglesey–Bardsey Island	*August 2014*	134 miles on foot; 4 miles by boat
Donegal	*August–September 2014*	612 miles by motorbike; 93 miles on three ferries
Meigle–Canterbury	*October 2014 and March 2015*	725 miles by motorbike
York–Whitby	*December 2014*	82 miles on foot

Appendix Two: Timeline

250s   Probable date of the martyrdom of St Alban near the Roman town of Verulamium

306   Constantine is declared Emperor at York

313   Constantine declares religious toleration in the Empire

367   A great 'barbarian conspiracy' is launched against Roman Britain by a coordinated attack from Picts, Irish, Saxons and rebellious frontier troops

383   Roman general Magnus Maximus proclaimed Emperor in Britain

407   The last emperor to visit Britain, Constantine III, leaves for the Continent

410   Imperial Roman administration dissolves in Britain

418   *Anglo-Saxon Chronicle* describes Romans in Britain hiding their treasure and fleeing overseas to Gaul

c.429   Germanus of Auxerre arrives in Britain to counter Pelagian heresy

431   Pope Celestine I sends Bishop Palladius to Ireland to preach Christianity

447   The *Annales Cambriae* describes 'days as dark as night'

449   Date, calculated by Bede, for the arrival of the Anglo-Saxons in Britain

457   *Annales Cambriae* records that 'St Patrick goes to the Lord'

486   Battle of Soissons: Clovis defeats Syagrius, last Roman prefect of northern Gaul, to become king of the Franks; subsequently converts to Christianity; dies *c.*511

516   *Annales Cambriae* records the battle of Badon Hill

537   *Annales Cambriae* records the death of Arthur, *Dux Brittonum*, in the 'Strife of Camlann'

547   *Annales Cambriae* records the death of Maelgwyn of Gwynedd in a great plague

565   Colmcille (St Columba) founds a monastery at Iona

590   Possible date for the Battle of Catræth: defeat of the British
            Gododdin army at the hands of ?Æthelfrith of Northumbria

*c.***592/3** Æthelfrith seizes control of Northumbria

597   Colmcille dies on Iona; the Augustinian mission from Pope Gregory
            arrives in Kent and he and his mission worship in a church built by
            the Romans

602/3   Augustine meets British bishops; he fails to prevent a schism
            between the British and Roman churches

615–16 Battle of Chester: Æthelfrith's armies massacre the monks of
            Bangor-is-y-coed; King Æthelberht of Kent dies and his son
            Eadbald apostatises

617   The battle on the River Idle: King Rædwald of East Anglia and
            Edwin of Deira defeat and kill King Æthelfrith of Northumbria;
            the Iding princes go into exile in Dál Riata

625   Probable date of the death of King Rædwald of East Anglia; his
            burial at Sutton Hoo

626   Assassination attempt on King Edwin by an emissary from Wessex;
            the birth of his daughter Eanflæd

627   King Edwin converts to Christianity and constructs a church at
            York

632   Battle of Hæthfelth: King Cadwallon of Gwynedd and Penda of
            Mercia defeat and kill Edwin of Deira; Cadwallon's army stays in
            Northumbria for a year; Northumbria apostatises

633/4   Battle of Denisesburn: Oswald Iding returns from exile in Dál Riata
            with a small army, defeats and kills Cadwallon and is recognised as
            king of Northumbria

635   Bishop Aidan is sent from Iona to found a monastery on Lindisfarne

642   Battle of Maserfelth: King Penda of Mercia defeats and kills King
            Oswald near Oswestry

643   Oswald's brother, King Oswiu, retrieves Oswald's remains and
            founds a cult of his bones

655   Battle on the River Winwæd: Oswiu of Northumbria defeats Penda
            of Mercia; founds six monasteries in Bernicia and six in Deira

664   The Synod of Whitby: King Oswiu of Northumbria declares in favour of Roman authority over Iona

669   Arrival in Britain of Archbishop Theodore of Tarsus—holds office until his death in 690

674   Wilfrid granted land to build a stone church at Hexham in Bernicia

685   King Ecgfrith of Northumbria dedicates a new monastery at Jarrow, and is killed in battle against the Picts at Dunnichen, predicted by St Cuthbert

687   Death of St Cuthbert on Inner Farne

688   King Ine succeeds to the throne of Wessex; rules until 729

691   King Wihtred succeeds to the throne of Kent; rules until 725

699   Guthlac of Repton becomes a hermit in the marshes at Crowland in East Anglia; dies 714

709   Death of St Wilfrid, aged seventy-five

716   Iona agrees to follow Roman orthodox rulings on Easter and other 'schismatic' practices

735   Death of the Venerable Bede at St Paul's, Jarrow, a year after completing his *Historia Ecclesiastica Gentis Anglorum*

757   Offa becomes king of Mercia; rules until 796

793   First Viking raid on a monastery: Lindisfarne on the Northumbrian coast

794   Iona attacked by Vikings

800   Charlemagne crowned Holy Roman Emperor

843   Cináed mac Ailpín succeeds to the throne of Pictland, until 858

865   The Great Heathen Army arrives in East Anglia and stays

876   'In this year Halfdan shared out the lands of Northumbria'—*Anglo-Saxon Chronicle*

871   The Battle of Ashdown; Alfred becomes king of Wessex after the death of his fourth brother, Æthelred

878   Battle of Edington: Alfred decisively defeats Great Heathen Army

?886   Alfred refounds London, building a burgh at Southwark; signs Treaty of Alfred and Guthrum, the Danish leader, who accepts baptism and a boundary north and east of the River Lea and Watling Street

899   The death of Alfred of Wessex, aged fifty; succeeded by his son Edward in Wessex

911   Æthelflæd, Alfred's daughter, succeeds her husband Æthelræd as ruler of the Mercians

918   Æthelflæd dies

924   Edward the Elder, king of Wessex, dies; succeeded by his son Æthelstan to 939

937   Battle of Brunanburh: Æthelstan defeats the combined armies of Scots, Norse and Britons

942   Hywel Dda – Hywel the Good—becomes effective king of all Wales; dies 950

954   Fall of the Viking Kingdom of York

978   Æthelred II 'the Unready' becomes king of England; deposed 1013 by Svein Forkbeard; he recovers the kingdom in 1014 and dies 1016

991   Battle of Maldon: an English army is defeated by Olaf Trygvasson; King Æthelred pays tribute of 10,000 pounds

995   The Community of St Cuthbert brings the saint's relics to Durham after an internal exile of over a hundred years

1013   Svein Forkbeard becomes the first Danish king of England; dies 1014

1042   Edward the Confessor accedes the throne of England

1066   Harold Godwinsson succeeds Edward the Confessor as King of England; battles at Stamford Bridge and Hastings bring to an end Viking invasions of England and the Anglo-Saxon age

1074   The arrival of three monks at Jarrow signals the revival of Northumbrian monasticism after nearly two hundred years

Notes

1   From 'The Ruin', translated by K. Crossley-Holland, *The Anglo-Saxon World: An Anthology*, Oxford World's Classics, 2009.

2   *vita*: the medieval hagiography, or 'life' of a saint. Famous examples include the *Vita Wilfridi* (Saint Wilfrid) and the *Vita Columbae* (Saint Colmcille). Plural *vitae*.

3   The so-called Kentish Chronicle forms part of a narrative sequence in the collection of early manuscripts known as the *Historia Brittonum* and popularly, if incorrectly, referred to as the work of Nennius. Vortigern is pre-eminent among those British leaders remembered by later historians for their ignominious dealings with the first Germanic warlords who won lands in Britain. The compilation belongs to the early ninth century.

4   From 'The Ruin', translated by K. Crossley-Holland, *The Anglo-Saxon World: An Anthology*, Oxford World's Classics, 2009.

5   shieling: a north-country word for a small hut and its associated enclosures, used by transhumant communities, later just shepherds, as upland summer settlements.

6   *crannog*: a circular wooden dwelling supported on piles driven into a lake bed close to the shore and connected to it by a raised causeway. There are superb reconstructions at the Crannog Centre on Loch Tay, Perth and Kinross and on Llangorse lake in the Brecon Beacons, Wales.

7   St Marnock: originally an Irish familiar name, from my (*mo*) Ernán. The name Marnock is associated with at least three church foundations, notably that of Kilmarnock; but there are several candidates for the historical figure, including an uncle and companion of Colmcille.

8   Bede, *Historia Ecclesiatica*, V.12. *Bede's Ecclesiastical History of the English People*, ed. and trans. B. Colgrave and R. A. B. Mynors, Oxford Medieval Texts, 1969; repr. 1994. The monk was Dryhthelm of Melrose who, when asked how he could bear the cold, replied, 'I have known it colder'.

9   There are other possible candidates for the principal royal fortress of the kingdom—Dunollie, near Oban, is cited as an alternative. But no site matches Dunadd for its wealth and its setting.

10   The exact source is unclear, perhaps somewhere in Francia. Colmcille's hagiographer Adomnán mentions a glass drinking vessel used by the Pictish king Bruide. Other glass objects from Dunadd include Byzantine tesserae and beads of Irish or Viking type.

11   Princes: those sons of great men deemed eligible for kingship. The Irish equivalent was *rígdomna*, literally 'material of a king'.

12   'Ozymandias' by Percy Bysshe Shelley, 1818.

13   The Romans may have introduced rabbits to Britain, but it was only after the Norman Conquest that they (the rabbits) and pheasants began to reproduce significantly in the wild.

14   The Laws of Wihtred, Decree 28, in *English Historical Documents Volume I:* c.*500–1042*. Edited by Dorothy Whitelock, Eyre Methuen, 1979, 2nd edition.

15   The *civitates* were the native tribes identified by Roman military strategists and administrators, through whose chiefs regional control was exercised. They were given undefended capital towns, connected to the road system and their kin given jobs to keep them sweet.

16   The list forms part of the British Historical Miscellany compiled in about 810 from a variety of sources and often published under the name of Nennius with the *Historia Brittonum* and *Annales Cambriae*. Many of the names on the list cannot ever have been cities or even towns— Lindisfarne, for example, was no more than a monastery, though it may once have had a fortress.

17   *Wealh*, the Old English name for the Britons, came also to mean 'foreigner'; but since those identifying themselves as Anglo-Saxons seem to have dispossessed many native Britons of their lands and rights, it may at times have carried implications of a lower caste, even a slave.

18   Reginald was a monk of Durham Cathedral, author of hagiographies on Sts Cuthbert and Godric. His otherwise unsatisfactory *Vita* of Oswald was written in 1165 and derives much of its material from Bede; the raven episode appears to originate in local tradition. John Leland, visiting the site in the sixteenth century, heard more or less the same story. By his day the raven had become a more impressive but less significant eagle.

19   Oswald's uncle, Edwin, also died a Christian martyr and later became the focus of a cult at Whitby.

20   Edward Lhuyd (1660–1709): a keeper of antiquities at the Ashmolean
      Museum in Oxford, linguist, antiquarian and naturalist of considerable
      talents. He is credited with first use of the term Celtic to refer to the
      ancient Brythonic and Goidelic languages of Britain and Ireland.

21   Augustine, the missionary sent by Gregory to bring the pagan English
      into the Universal church, arrived in Kent in 597, founded a church
      there and established sees at Rochester and London before turning
      his attention to what he believed were the archaic and unorthodox
      practices of the British church. See Chapter Nine.

22   *cantref*: more or less the Early Medieval British equivalent of the
      Northumbrian shire and the later Anglo-Saxon hundred, an estate
      made up of units from which food renders and services were demanded
      and brought to a central place, the *villa regia*; early Wales comprised
      around forty *cantrefi*; the 'trefs' of which *cantrefi* were composed has its
      equivalent in the 'tech' of Scottish Dál Riata and, perhaps, the generally
      larger *vill* of Anglo-Saxon England.

23   Celia Fiennes, *Through England on a Side Saddle in the Time of William
      and Mary*.

24   *De temporum ratione* ('On the reckoning of time'), written *c.*725 at
      Jarrow. Apart from calendrical calculations and instructions for
      determining the correct date for Easter, Bede also explains daylight
      length and the seasons and gives a historical account of the Julian and
      Anglo-Saxon calendars.

25   *Beowulf*, line 1359, from the translation by Michael Alexander,
      Penguin, 1973.

26   *wic*: Old English term for a farm or specialised settlement, often found
      as a suffix: for example, Keswick—'cheese farm'; Goswick—'goose
      farm'. When it occurs, especially with topographic variations, on
      coasts with gently sloping shores, it seems often to denote a periodic
      or opportunistic site for a beach market. The Gaelic and Brythonic
      equivalents may be 'port' and 'strand'—as in the Strand on the River
      Thames, which may have been the site of Anglo-Saxon *Lundenwic*.

27   pannage: the practice (and valuable right) of grazing pigs on beech and
      oak mast (nuts) in autumn; verderer: an official with legal powers to
      administer forest law and rights and practices on common lands.

28   Bede, *Historia Ecclesiatica*, I.30, ed. and trans. by Colgrave and Mynors.

29   Richard Morris, in *Churches in the Landscape* (see Recommended
     Reading, p. 443) cites two examples of the place name Stokenchurch, in
     Buckinghamshire and Middlesex, which seem to reflect the presence
     of a 'stockade' church of similar construction. Greensted is sometimes
     cited as the oldest surviving wooden church in the world.

30   The term 'heptarchy' belongs to the post-Medieval period; the idea that
     the Saxons 'established seven kings' can be traced as far back as Henry
     of Huntingdon's *Historia Anglorum* of the early twelfth century.

31   The Tribal Hidage is a list, drawn up perhaps as early as the seventh
     or eighth century, which records the tribute owed by subject tribes
     or smaller kingdoms to an unnamed king, possibly Edwin of North-
     umbria. Hide: generations of historians have argued over this very
     difficult term. If the *vill* is a place – a real piece of land with boundaries,
     fields, settlements—then the *hide* (Bede used the term *familiarum*) was a
     unit of render from the farms within a *vill*. But there is no arithmetical
     equivalent, no standard number of hides in a *vill*. The hide was a con-
     cept used to calculate how much such-and-such a settlement or king-
     dom owed in tribute or render; it was also used as a shorthand for value,
     but that value depended, naturally enough, on the productive surplus
     and wealth of that land.

32   Known as Æthelræd Unræd: an Anglo-Saxon pun. The whole name
     translates as 'Noble-counsel Ill-counsel'.

33   The Battle of Maldon. *English Historical Documents* Volume I: *c.*500–
     1042, edited by Dorothy Whitelock, 2nd edition, Eyre Methuen, 1979.

34   Their supreme commander was known, in the late fourth century, by
     the impressive title of *Comes Litoris Saxonici per Britanniam*: Count of
     the Saxon Shore.

35   Bretwalda; a term which first appears in the ninth-century *Anglo-Saxon
     Chronicle*, denoting a king able to wield imperium over all the other
     kings of Britain. In his *Historia Ecclesiatica* Bede makes claims for the
     overlordship of the same kings, but does not use the term.

36   *Beowulf,* lines 2649–56, translated by J. R. R. Tolkien, Harper Collins,
     2014.

37   From *The Wanderer*, translated by K. Crossley-Holland, *The Anglo-
     Saxon World: An Anthology*, Oxford World's Classics, 2009.

38   Rendered indefensible by the demolition of palisades and gates and the
     filling in of some ditches.

39　　Light + raDAR is a remote-sensing technology that measures distance by illuminating a target with a laser and analysing the reflected light.

40　　Adomnán's term – though by the late sixth century the name is archaic; Gaul has become Frankia.

41　　E-ware: a form of handmade pottery identified on many Early Medieval sites along both sides of the Atlantic coasts of Britain, often in association with royal or monastic settlements. It is believed to belong to the late sixth to seventh centuries and to have been made somewhere in south-west Frankia. The vessels are for domestic use, and may have been the property of merchants; some of the globular forms seem to have held valuable products such as dyes and spices.

42　　Pelagius, born probably in Britain in the late fourth century, was accused of preaching the doctrine of free will and rejecting the idea of original sin, anathema to later church orthodoxy. His teachings seem to have been especially popular in his native land; Gaulish orthodox bishops took it upon themselves to stamp his 'heresy' out.

43　　The whirlpool is caused by an underwater chasm nearly seven-hundred-feet deep which runs adjacent to a pinnacle just seventy feet below the surface, across which the yard-high tidal discrepancy must flow.

44　　St Michael the Archangel was a heavenly warrior rather than an earthly martyr, and early visions of him by Pope Gregory and others seem to have occurred on hills. The Benedictine monastery of Mont-Saint-Michel is the most famous of these elevated foundations.

45　　In spite of a great deal of speculation, no one has been able to con-vincingly demonstrate that it was anything other than an accident caused by reckless driving and sheer bad luck.

46　　Richard Morris is a distinguished polymath, Early Medievalist and church archaeologist, a veteran of the York Minster excavations of the 1970s and former Director of the Council for British Archaeology. He was one of my most inspirational teachers, and a generous patron and consultant in our later work at Christ Church, Spitalfields.

47　　*Nennius: British History and the Welsh Annals*, cited in John Morris, Phillimore, 1980.

48　　Ibid.

49 Gildas, *De Exidio et conquestu Brittaniae*, in Gildas: *The Ruin of Britain and Other Works*, ed. and trans. Michael Winterbottom, Phillimore, 1978.

50 Augustine's legacy was more complex; its long-term success can be attributed to the eighth Archbishop of Canterbury, Theodore (669–90), and his endorsement by Oswald's younger brother, King Oswiu, after the Synod of Whitby.

51 In tenths of nano-Teslas.

52 A Lifelong Learning community that actively researches Early Medieval Northumbria: www.bernicianstudies.eu.

53 Bede: *Historia Ecclesiastica*, III.5, translated by Bertram Colgrave, Oxford Medieval Texts, 1969.

54 Anglesey is an Old Norse name: 'the island of the Angles' (or English); first recorded in 1098. Môn and Man were collectively known in the Early Medieval period as the Mevanian isles.

55 *Hogan*: a circular, square or multi-sided wooden or stone dwelling roofed with bark or turf whose joints were and are packed with earth or mud for insulation.

56 Sections 40–2 which come part-way through the Kentish Chronicle, after Vortigern's granting of Kent to Hengest.

57 The smallest administrative division of a province in the Western Roman Empire from the later third century.

58 Keeper of a small trading post or hostelry where horses and accommodation might also be obtained. The term gave rise to the surname Chapman.

59 ogham: a twenty-letter alphabet of Old Irish inscriptions formed by carving vertical and diagonal strokes across the corners of memorial stones recording the name of a deceased person. It often accompanies a Latin inscription and may have derived from a direct transliteration of Latin. More than four hundred examples are known from Ireland, Wales, Cornwall and Scotland.

60 *Afon*: Welsh for river; so River Avon is a pleonasm. *Aber* in Brythonic means mouth or confluence, the equivalent of Gaelic *Inver*.

61 The other island, ironically, is owned by that latter-day hard man, Chief Scout and intrepid adventurer Bear Grylls.

62 Following King Oswiu's ruling at the Synod of Whitby in 664—see Chapter Nine. The Irish and British churches disputed Rome's means of calculating future Easter dates, the correct form of monks' tonsure and other matters of discipline and liturgy. Wilfrid denied the legitimacy of British or Irish bishops to ordain.

63 'Eddius Stephanus: Life of Wilfrid XXII', translated by J. F. Webb in *The Age of Bede*, Penguin Classics, 1983.

64 *Sanctus*: holy; *sanctior*: holier; *sanctissimus*: holiest.

65 Chiselled recesses on opposite faces of a stone block into which fit the points of a pair of levered calipers which grip as they lift.

66 total station theodolite (TST): measures distances and angles very accurately by bouncing a laser off a prism placed on the object or surface to be measured. The data are recorded digitally in three dimensions.

67 Eccles names: deriving from Latin *ecclesia* (and surviving in Welsh 'eglwys'), the name is believed to denote the presence of a late Roman British church; in each case, linguistic rules are applied to determine if the root of the name is indeed 'ecclesia' or something similar but unrelated.

68 Dumfries would return a 'No' vote of 66 per cent to 34 per cent, and the Scottish Borders a 'No' vote of 67 per cent to 33 per cent.

69 Confiscations of land by the English crown and its colonisation by English and Scottish settlers, almost all Protestant, during the sixteenth and seventeenth centuries.

70 'Everted': to turn inside out.

71 Crucks were formed from the long curved trunk of a tree split lengthways to make a matching pair. Two pairs formed the gable ends of a timber building.

72 Ireland boasts more than forty thousand of these sites called, depending on scholastic nomenclature, ringforts, raths or cashels. There are dozens on Inishowen; so many that to represent them on my map would be to give it a dose of the measles.

73 In the wake of the abolition of customs checks between European Community member states as part of the European single market, and the easing of the security situation following the 1998 Good Friday Agreement.

74   *Harnessing the Tides: the Early Medieval Tide Mills at Nendrum Monastery, Strangford Lough* (Northern Ireland Archaeological Monographs) by Thomas McErlean and Norman Crothers, Stationery Office Books, 2007.

75   *Vill;* shire: the *vill* was the fundamental territorial unit of the Anglo-Saxon rural economy. In the north of Britain these have survived as townships; in the south they equate roughly to, but predate, the old church parishes. The *vill* (*tref* in Wales; 'tech' on the West coast of Scotland) was the customary unit from which services might be rendered; in time, the term *vill* was applied to the settlement or central place at the heart of its territory, and the name of the *vill* was applied to the place. Early Medieval shires, unlike the counties with which they have been conflated in the modern period, were groups of *vills* with an important central place, belonging to a lord of at least the rank of *gesith*. The *villa regia*, or royal estate centre, is probably represented by the Anglo-Saxon palaces at Cheddar in Somerset, Rendlesham in Suffolk and Yeavering in Northumberland.

76   An insight offered by Alex Woolf in his great survey *From Pictland to Alba, 789–1070*, Edinburgh University Press, 2007.

77   A brewster is a female brewer, giving rise to a rare female surname; a baxter is a female baker. Other female surnames include Kempster (a wool-comber—as in 'unkempt hair') and Webster (a weaver).

78   *The Origins of Newcastle upon Tyne* by Robert Fulton Walker, Thorne's Students' Bookshop, 1976.

79   A Z-rod looks like a stylised lightning bolt often with decorated terminal; it is often found inscribed over a double disc (shaped like the link in a bicycle chain). V-rods, shaped as the name suggests, are often found inscribed over crescents.

80   'Bede: Life of Cuthbert XXVII', translated by J. F. Webb in *The Age of Bede*, Penguin Classics, 1983.

81   dene: a north-country word for a small valley, often wooded; the south-west equivalent is combe.

82   There was an unintentional break between my arrival home and the continuation of the journey—several months, in fact, during which I had to strip down and rebuild the bike's brakes, have a puncture fixed and then sit on my thumbs as winter's ice made a long bike journey too perilous.

83   bastle—a two-storey dwelling in which cattle were byred on the ground floor, with external steps leading to accommodation above. The Old English word *botl* and French *bastille* share a similar etymology.

84   A settlement constructed for retired legionary veterans, given special privileges. *Britannia* had five: besides York, at London, Lincoln, Colchester and Gloucester.

85   Via a letter sent to Bishop Mellitus a month after his first injunction to the king.

86   The other four were: Nottingham, Stamford, Leicester and Derby. They were retaken during the campaigns of Æthelflæd of Mercia and her brother Edward the Elder of Wessex during 916–17, reconquered by King Olaf of York in the 940s and finally recovered a year later by King Edmund.

87   hundreds: administrative units originating in Anglo-Saxon England and equating to the Welsh *cantrefi*.

88   Liudhard may have died shortly after the arrival of Augustine, whose fellow missionaries, according to Bede, first worshipped in the church before being allowed by the king to travel more freely and to restore or build their own churches.

89   R. J. Cramp, 'Monastic sites' in *The Archaeology of Anglo-Saxon England*, edited by D. M. Wilson, Cambridge University Press, 1976.

90   Snorri Sturluson, *King Harald's Saga*, translated by Magnus Magnusson and Hermann Pálsson, Penguin Books, 1976.

91   *gesiths*: the hereditary male warrior elite of Anglo-Saxon England, deriving from words that mean 'spear' and 'shield'. Once proven in battle, *gesiths* would expect to be rewarded by a gift of land on which to dwell and raise a family and from which to draw render as income.

92   Bede: *Historia Ecclesiastica*, II.16, ed. and trans. Colgrave and Mynors.

93   *English Historical Documents* Volume I: *c.*500–1042, edited by Dorothy Whitelock, Eyre Methuen, 1979, 2nd edition.

94   carr: wet, scrubby land characterised by stunted trees—dwarf birch and willow, etc.—bog, reeds and tussocky grasses; usually low in fertility.

95   Discovered in a field by a metal detectorist in 2009, it is a hoard of material scavenged from a battlefield, comprising more than seventeen hundred objects and fragments of gold and silver, precious stones,

millefiori and cloisonné, weighing a total of less than fifteen pounds. A suggested deposition date between the mid-seventh and eighth centuries may yet be refined by ongoing analysis.

96   Bede, *Historia Ecclesiatica*, III.23, ed. and trans. Colgrave and Mynors.

97   The Laws of Wihtred in *English Historical Documents Volume I: c.500–1042*, edited by Dorothy Whitelock, Eyre Methuen, 1979, 2nd edition.

98   Bede translates *Streanæshalch* as *sinus fari*; some historians doubt his ascription, since the name is better translated as 'a secluded spot used by lovers'. Strensall, near York, is a modern equivalent.

99   Stephen Leslie, Bruce Whinnet et al., *Nature*, volume 519, 19 March 2015, 309–33.

Recommended reading

This is a list of those books which I have found to be most useful on many travels, mental and physical, through the landscapes of the Dark Ages, and which might be of interest to readers wanting to continue their own journeys of discovery. Some are intrinsically readable; others I use for reference. Each one is a monument in its own right of scholarship and writing. Useful editions of some of the main historical sources are cited in the Notes, pages 433–442.

LESLIE ALCOCK: *Arthur's Britain*, Penguin (1971). There is a 2nd edition of 1989. Still the best overall guide to the archaeology of the Early Medieval period.

—— *Kings and warriors, craftsmen and priests*, Society of Antiquaries of Scotland (2003). The opposite end of the reductionist spectrum from *Arthur's Britain*: encyclopaedic coverage of Northern Britain in the Early Medieval period, but not a narrative read.

—— *'By South Cadbury is that Camelot…' Excavations at Cadbury Castle 1966–1970*, Thames and Hudson (1972). Riveting account of how excavation was done in the 1960s

STEVEN BASSETT (ed.): *The Origins of Anglo-Saxon Kingdoms*, Leicester University Press (1990). An impressive overview by experts in their own regions.

KEN DARK: *Britain and the End of the Roman Empire*, History Press (2002). I can't agree with some of Ken's conclusions, but it's a thought-provoking and valuable thesis.

NANCY EDWARDS: *The Archaeology of Early Medieval Ireland*, Routledge (1996). A very useful short summary of the complexities of the Irish material.

THOMAS CHARLES-EDWARDS: *Wales and the Britons 350–1064*, Oxford University Press (2014). A hugely impressive and comprehensive scholarly look at the fortunes of the British nations in the Early Medieval period. Fascinating; not bedtime reading.

JAMES FRASER: *From Caledonia to Pictland: Scotland to 795*, Edinburgh University Press (2009). Sometimes I don't recognise the North Britain portrayed by Fraser, but it's a serious account, and current.

W. G. HOSKINS: *The Making of the English Landscape*, Book Club Associates (1981). A classic.

LLOYD and JENNIFER LAING: *A Guide to the Dark Age Remains in Britain*, Constable (1979). It is now quite out of date and there are a few key omissions; but it's still the Dark Age traveller's Baedeker.

RICHARD MORRIS: *Churches in the Landscape*, Phoenix Giant (1989). The seminal work: beautifully written and indispensable.

HYWEL WYN OWEN and RICHARD MORGAN: *Dictionary of the Place-names of Wales*, Gomer Press (2007). Definitive.

OLIVER RACKHAM: *The History of the Countryside*, Weidenfeld & Nicolson (2000). The late woodland historian's splendid take on our landscapes: witty, quirky, intelligent.

PAULINE STAFFORD (ed.): *A Companion to the Early Middle Ages. Britain and Ireland c.500–c.1100*, Wiley Blackwell (2013). A collection of authoritative summary articles on all sorts of aspects of society and narrative history.

CHARLES THOMAS: *The Early Christian Archaeology of North Britain*, Oxford University Press (1971). Long out of date and in need of an upgrade; but I find myself going back to it time and time again. Compelling, passionate and insightful.

VICTOR WATTS, JOHN INSLEY and MARGARET GELLING (eds): *The Cambridge Dictionary of English Place-Names*, Cambridge University Press (2011). The latest edition of this comprehensive guide to place names in England. The standard work of reference if you can't get at or your area has no coverage by the individual county English Place Name Society volumes.

DOROTHY WHITELOCK: *English Historical Documents* Volume I: *c.500–1042*. 2nd Edition, Eyre Methuen (1979). The definitive collection in English of our earliest history.

Acknowledgements

My first thanks go to the trustees of the Roger Deakin Award, whose generous help contributed to both my travels and the provision of a camera. The Royal Literary Fund has been a continuing source of tangible and intangible support. Richard Milbank, Anthony Cheetham and the unflappable staff at Head of Zeus have been enthusiastic supporters of a project that carried all sorts of risks of failure. Sarah Annesley has been both a sometime indulgent companion on the trail and, at all times, a sympathetic and encouraging spirit.

Many, many hosts have put me up, helped me along the way and listened to my traveller's tales: the organisers of the Oswestry Litfest, Steve and Denise Lawson, Malcolm and Fiona Lind, Stephen and Christina Stead, Sophie and Roger Brown, Karen Crofts, June Kempster, Bob Sydes and Sarah Austin, Paul and Sarah McGowan and Mark Whyman. My thanks to all. Two other companions on the trail, Dan Elliott and Malcolm Pallister, made those walks memorable and inspiring. Pam Bowyer-Davis and Ruth Matthews were gracious and knowledgeable guides at Wareham and Canterbury.

I would like to thank Donald Clark and Colin Evans, both of whom plucked me off beaches when I might have been stranded, and several ferrymen whose names I neglected to write down. Special thanks go to skipper James Mackenzie, his crew and our shipmates on *Eda Frandsen*, for a special and unforgettable journey across the seas. The kind, generous and knowledgeable friendship of many colleagues in Donegal is much appreciated, as always; so too the support, interest and bloody awkward questions of my friends in the Bernician Studies Group, without whose insatiable curiosity and erudition this book would probably never have got off the ground. Colm O'Brien has, not for the first time, contributed more than he knows to shore up the holes in my knowledge. Lynne Bellew kindly read the manuscript and identified a number of errors.

Nameless and sadly unrecorded assistance and kind interest from various campsite owners, curators, passers-by, café proprietors, ferrymen, hoteliers and, in particular, the very kind man who gave us a lift from Achnamara, are acknowledged with gratitude.